I Was Britpopped

I Was Britpopped

The A-Z of Britpop: for anyone who grew up in
the nineties, and for some who didn't...

'From *Popscene* to *D'You Know What I Mean...*
and everything in-between(er).'

JENNY NATASHA &
TOM BONIFACE-WEBB

Valley Press

I WAS BRITPOPPED

was first published by the authors in 2016.

This second edition was first published in 2017 by
Valley Press, Woodend, The Crescent, Scarborough, YO11 2PW, UK.
www.valleypressuk.com

ISBN 978-1-908853-92-9   Cat. no. VP0109

Cover design by JP Cuison. Text design by Jamie McGarry.
Edited by Jo Haywood.

Contents

To Donna Boniface-Webb, who was there throughout the whole writing process, on both sides of the world.

&

To 'The Girls', Bron, Jen, Jenny, Laura, Marsha, Sara, Sez and Viki, who grew up together through the era.

Acknowledgements

UK chart data verified by the Official Charts Company

Proofreading and editorial advice by Robin Lewis

Legal advice provided by Tim Sissons

24 Hour Party People (2002), a film by Michael Winterbottom

Live Forever (2003), a film by John Dower

Bit of a Blur (2007), a book by Alex James

No Distance Left to Run (2010), a film by Will Lovelace & Dylan Southern

Supersonic (2016), a film by Mat Whitecross

Book cover designed by JP Cuison Graphic Designer/ Illustrator

Creative consultancy by Richard Clement

Infographics designed by Aaron Munday

Graphic Design by Jonas Sutkus

Ideas hero, Lisa Liu

NME, *Melody Maker*, *Select*, *Vox*, *Q*, HMV, Our Price, Virgin Records

CD and magazine collections of all our friends

Karina Howe, Jane Barr-Knight, Chris Webb, Scott Macrae, Reece Eaton & S.T. Kumaran

Preface

It was just a snapshot, a brief moment in musical history, but it took hold of Britain like the bittersweet antidote to an unknown drug, administered to a nation that had no idea it was so desperately needed. It was a design for living that owed a debt to Lennon & McCartney, Jagger & Richards, Strummer & Jones, Weller and Lydon.

Beginning with the release of Blur's single 'Popscene' in March '92, peaking with Oasis' triumphant outdoor live shows at Knebworth in August '96, and finally culminating in March '98 with Pulp's comedown album *This is Hardcore*, Britpop spawned icons: Liam Gallagher, Brett Anderson, Damon Albarn, Justine Frischmann, Jarvis Cocker; this was British culture exemplified to its extreme. This was Cool Britannia.

It was about *Top of the Pops* on a Friday evening, about tuning into the Top 40 on a Sunday, about the *NME*, *Melody Maker*, *Select* and *Q*; about learning the chords to 'Wonderwall' on a battered old acoustic guitar, desperate to form a band; it was about gigs in sweaty pubs, or huge open fields; it was about queuing up outside HMV on a Monday morning before school, knowing you'd be in trouble for being late, but not caring a jot. It was about all of this, and much, much more. But most importantly it was about us, about our 1990s, about our Britain. Britpop was ours and always will be.

Foreword One

The clue is in the title. This isn't Mersey-Beat or Madchester... this is Britpop. Unlike any other key British popular music movement, its origins lay not in one guarded corner of this sceptred isle, but across the entire nation that it swiftly cast its long shadow over. The focus may have fallen on London, but that was because the 'Big Smoke' was merely a metropolitan meeting point for those travelling from cities and towns all over the UK, everyone flocking to one mutually convenient spot to add their colloquial experiences of living in contemporary Britain to the great Britpop melting pot.

Liam sang of being sold songs in Mr Sifter's Burnage record store; Jarvis told us of an affair with a Greek student whilst studying at St Martin's College in London; and Damon took us right to the very edge of the British Isles in 'Clover Over Dover'. If the music was retrospective, then it was purposefully so to put Britain back at the centre of the argument. After all, the sixties bands they were quoting and emulating were from Britain.

For once there was no 'us and them', there was just 'us'. That's not to say there wasn't rivalry. Quite the contrary. It was the rivalry that gave Britpop its particular edge, and brought it to the attention of the Establishment. Britpop was just as much about music as it was about youth, rebellion and challenging the existing norm. Every movement needs its key rivals and Oasis and Blur sat at the centre, swirling together like oil and water. Their rivalry exemplified the perennial British problem: proactive Northern solidarity versus thoughtful Southern intellectualism.

At its worst, Britpop was a commercialised rehash of the 'Swinging Sixties'. At its best, it spoke for a freedom promised by Tony Blair but never fully delivered. Twenty years later, are we still remembering it fondly because, deep down, we know it was a beautiful but impossible dream? Was Blur's 'Country House' not a clear and concise precursor of the later extravagance of the bourgeoisie who systematically gambled, drank, snorted and ruined the country, leaving the current generation to pick up the pieces? How could it ever last, and as such, what did it ever mean?

Tom Boniface-Webb

Foreword Two

It's the summer of '95 and, during GCSE art, a friend plays me Oasis' 'Live Forever' on her CD Walkman. This pivotal moment led me to explore the musical era of my generation. Having previously listened almost exclusively to the Beatles, while wishing I'd been born decades earlier, Oasis opened the door to bands I could actually go and see rather than dream of seeing. There was no going back after this discovery. I chose to spend my time at indie clubs, Our Price and HMV, spending my pocket money on cassettes, CDs, gigantic posters, band T-shirts and, crucially, a ticket to Knebworth. Britpop became part of the incredible journey of growing up.

The term itself was being thrown around regularly in the music magazines I used to buy. The *NME*, *Melody Maker* and *Select* pushed both Suede and Blur to the forefront in '93 with the release of their respective albums *Suede* and *Modern Life is Rubbish*. A string of Britpop bands soon followed, most notably Oasis, Pulp, Elastica, Supergrass and Cast, and the movement crashed over into the mainstream in August '95 with the 'Battle of Britpop'.

The movement was, in part, a reaction to America's dominant grunge scene, led by Nirvana and Pearl Jam, which was itself a huge contrast to the concurrent Madchester scene led by the Happy Mondays and Stone Roses. Putting an end to grunge, the Britpop sound emerged, defined by its vocals sung in regional accents and references to British culture and everyday working-class life. The godfathers of Britpop took pride in their references to influential British rock bands, from the Beatles and the Stones to The Smiths and Joy Division.

A second wave of Britpop emerged in the noughties with the Arctic Monkeys, Kaiser Chiefs, The Libertines, Razorlight, The Maccabees and The Futureheads among many others; even American indie rock band The Killers – unashamedly influenced by Manchester bands The Smiths and New Order (who they took their name from) – had an identifiably English sound. But nothing could compare to the momentum of the '93-'97 Britpop period. It undeniably left its mark.

Jenny Natasha

Introduction

It's spring '97 and a 24-year-old man from Manchester has a haircut. Not huge news. Certainly not headline news. But still, it *was* headline news in *The Sun* – Britain's biggest selling newspaper – that a young man from Burnage had had his hair cut. Ridiculous, surely? Perhaps not when you learn that the young man was Liam Gallagher from indie-rock band Oasis, and the headline ran "Wonder-bald", an apt if somewhat crass pun on the band's most famous song 'Wonderwall'.

To understand why the press are paying so much attention to the length of Liam's hair, we must rewind to August '96: 125,000 people stand in a field singing every word of that famous song as he commands the centre of the stage in his trademark posture, hands behind his back, feet at right angles, chin jutting arrogantly upwards as he sings.

Rewind another year to the summer of '95 and that young man is on the BBC's *News at Ten*, a situation that someone of his age and stature would usually only find themselves in if they were dead or in court. But this was the 'Battle of Britpop', when Oasis fought arch-rivals Blur for the top spot in the charts. This was the 14th August '95, and what had begun as just another underground indie movement had just crossed over into the mainstream. This was Britpop.

But what do we actually mean when we say the word Britpop?

Most of us know what Britpop means to us, but to put it into words for the purpose of this book, we have decided it's: a collection of British bands who wrote songs specifically referencing British culture, with lyrics about everyday contemporary life lived by predominantly young people in the mid-nineties, more often than not sung in regional British accents. It marked a shift in musical direction, but built on Madchester and Baggy, combining their influences with sixties bands like the Beatles, the Rolling Stones, the Small Faces, Cream and the Kinks.

The music had a back-to-basics approach, with most of the bands comprising just four or five young guys and/or girls on vocals, guitar, bass and drums. In contrast to the dance music dominant in the early nineties, there were no drum loops and few synthesisers, returning instead to the simple rock 'n' roll spearheaded by those sixties bands. In '95, Liam Gallagher famously called for bands to "lock up your sequencers", and it was this approach – telling stories of modern-day living in a classical style – that gave Britpop its individual edge.

Britpop is perhaps the last great musical movement to come out of the United Kingdom, and one that, because of its name and specific lyrical references, could only ever be synonymous with the British Isles. Punk rock found its genesis in Iggy Pop's Seattle garage and its flashpoint, some six or seven years later, in Johnny Rotten's spit-stained 100 Club basement in London. It was a universal attitude with no borders. Britpop was more specific – it was about a time *and* a place – and if a band wanted to be part of the movement, but had the misfortune to form in another country, well, they just had to get on a plane and make sure that the linguistically-limited British folk could decipher their lyrics. It was an idea dreamed up by Damon Albarn in the summer of '92, put into practice by Brett Anderson and Justine Frischmann, cemented with candour by Jarvis Cocker and popularised by the Gallagher brothers.

It is hard to know where to begin writing about Britpop, so the A-Z format seems like the most appropriate choice. Our list includes nearly 500 entries on the key bands, albums, songs, music venues, clothing and other miscellany that made up this incredibly vibrant and crucial scene. However exclusive a musical movement is, the parameters are always going to be elastic, which is why we thought it was important to impose our own borders in terms of dates and what actually constitutes a Britpop band, song or album. Blur's debut album *Leisure*, for example, is not a Britpop album, while their second, *Modern Life is Rubbish*, most definitely is.

The book can be read consecutively or used as a reference book but, because of the A-Z format, it's not a chronological history. We have tried to put as much information into each entry as possible, without being pedantic or patronising, and have stuck with the order dictated by our A-Z format. This means our entry for Shed Seven's *A Maximum High*, for example, details the album and single releases but, if you want to know more about the band, you'll need to flick to the entry on Shed Seven themselves.

For us, Britpop began in March '92 when Blur released their stand-alone single 'Popscene' and ended after Pulp released their album *This is Hardcore* six years later in March '98. Within that period, we also decided that Britpop's peak years were '95 and '97, reaching its zenith when Oasis took to the stage at Knebworth Park in August '96. In our opinion, 'Popscene' was the first release that consciously acknowledged our definition of the Britpop sound. It could be argued that there were earlier releases, perhaps from the early nineties Manchester bands or from the Creation label, but we think they either belong to a preceding scene or just don't quite fit our criteria.

A notable example are Primal Scream. They signed to Creation in '84 and went on to release two Britpop-influenced albums in '95 and '97, but their later association with rock-fuelled electronica and previous association with the pre-Britpop indie-dance scene hangs too heavily for them to be included.

The same can be said for pioneering experimental-indie-rock giants Radiohead. Their second album, '95's *The Bends*, drew heavily on the Britpop sound and they could easily have continued along this path. But then they released *OK Computer*. Hitting record stores in the long hot summer of '97, this heavily melancholic album shot them into the megasphere and made them worldwide stars. They then seemed to distance themselves from Britpop, eventually returning with the indie-electronica album *Kid A* in '00. This, combined with the fact that Radiohead would need a whole book to themselves if we were to truly do them justice, means we decided not to include them here.

Plus, we had to draw the line somewhere and, because Blur played such an important role in the development of the movement, the release of 'Popscene' seemed an apt enough place to start.

As for Pulp's *This is Hardcore*? Well, what goes up must come down. What helped define Britpop was the exuberance of the heady days of the mid-nineties: the flamboyance, the hedonism and the feeling that, for a few years at least, life was an endless run of parties. On *This is Hardcore*, Jarvis Cocker lyricised his feelings that the hedonism had gone too far, summing up the sense in the country at large that the party was finally over.

To help us decide exactly what to include – and to keep the book concise – we have created further sub-sections. The bands are divided into the 'big five', the Britpop bands, and those on the periphery. The big five are Oasis, Blur, Pulp, Suede and Elastica, and we've included all their single and album releases for March '92 to March '98, as well as entries on each of their key members.

For the Britpop bands, like The Longpigs, The Bluetones and Shed Seven, we have covered all their top 20 singles and albums for the same period. And for the others, including The Cranberries and Catatonia, we have included only their top 20 singles and albums released in the peak years from January '95 to December '97.

As a bonus, we have also included entries on the myriad people, places, venues and things that made the scene so distinctive. Some people will undoubtedly disagree with our choices, but we feel our reasons are solid.

Why the focus on the UK singles and albums chart, and why only the top 20? Partly because we had to draw the line somewhere, but mostly because Britpop was not an underground movement. It was, as the name suggests, widely popularised, bringing previously unknown indie bands to the forefront of the charts. In those pre-internet days, physical sales of singles and albums made bands what they were.

The charts were where the money was made, but a number one single was also a status symbol. The mystique Led Zeppelin gained from never releasing singles in their seventies heyday would never have worked in the mid-nineties because it was a time when all the cards were laid on the table and everyone could see exactly what hand everyone else had. It was the era of lad mags, of ladettes and of *Men Behaving Badly*; of reputations made by the loudest voice and the biggest media splash. It was also a time before internet chat rooms, online forums, bloggers and camera phones, when you could get away with murder – or, at least, drug-taking – with only the newspapers to worry about.

There were few outlets to discover new music other than live gigs, record stores, magazine articles and radio play, so journalists and DJs held much of the power in breaking new bands. It was, after all, a journalist who coined the word 'Britpop'. Chart sales also meant money, and while bands in the noughties make most of what they earn from live gigs, Britpop bands could live quite comfortably on the proceeds of a high charting album.

If Britpop's finest were not exactly on a par with the heady royalties of the Rolling Stones or Guns N' Roses, they were still richer than their fans, and were, as such, inspirational. Unlike Mick Jagger and Axl Rose, they were also still part of the real world, providing an achievable target. Britpop's key figures made it clear that they were not the best musicians in the world; they just knew how to strum a few chords, formed a band with a bunch of mates and wrote some good songs. They were idols to school kids in mid-nineties Britain, who wanted to be just like them. Take it from us. We were two of them.

So, why now? Well, we think it takes 20 years of retrospect to truly appreciate a scene like this. The documentary *Live Forever* attempted it back in '03, but this was still years before Noel and Damon had made friends and performed together; long before Graham had been invited back into a newly reformed Blur; and before many of the key players had properly had time to reflect on their actions, inactions and reactions. It was certainly not enough time for any of them not to look back in anger.

Recent years have also seen a timely resurgence in Britpop-related activity, with albums turning twenty and re-released on vinyl, bands reforming, and the appearance of dedicated platforms such as Britpop News, a website reporting on the latest goings-on of all things Britpop; the Britpop Revival Show, a weekly radio show dedicated to playing the best in Britpop classics, as well as the forgotten ones; and the Star Shaped club night, which has become something close to a national phenomenon. Starting as a simple monthly club night in London that played exclusively Britpop tunes, Star Shaped (named after the Blur track from *Modern Life is Rubbish*) has grown to become the 'home of Britpop', hosting regular nights all over the UK. In the summer of '17, Star Shaped took their success to the next level, with a festival that spanned four UK cities attended by over 10,000, featuring a newly reformed Sleeper, Dodgy, The Bluetones, My Life Story and Salad Undressed. As a result, the Star Shaped gang can lay a claim to having been responsible for Sleeper reforming.

The whole idea of a musical scene is, of course, an arbitrary concept, and one often created and hyped by the press and society at large, rather than the creatives at its heart. If Damon Albarn invented Britpop, he certainly didn't do it to create a scene, but rather an ideal of what British music needed to be. Scenes are often reactionary constructs. With punk, it was about the dispossessed youth using the only tool they had at their disposal to shout down injustice from above. In a similar way, Britain was in a state of flux in early '92, having slipped into deep recession after the long Thatcherite years, and people were struggling to find their place. Kurt Cobain was the dominant figure in the music world and Britain needed to redefine its musical identity if it was to have any prominence. What better way to do this than to revert to form, to connect with our roots and to make honest music about ourselves and our lives?

Think of Albarn's lyrics to 'End of the Century': "We all say, we want to be alone, we wear the same clothes 'cause we feel the same". People inherently want to be part of the crowd, while simultaneously appearing individual. Intentionally or not, Albarn was positioning himself as a spokesman for a dispossessed generation, just as Johnny Rotten had done 15 years earlier. It wasn't as visceral and aggressive as punk, but this meant it could be more thoughtful, more whimsical and more philosophical. Few creative bands form with the intention of being part of a scene, and scenes are often created – ironically enough – as an abstract concept by the very people the bands are rallying against. This doesn't mean they don't exist. It just means they're harder to define, even by those who care the most.

We hope you understand our reasons for drawing the lines of the Britpop world where we have, and are able to relate our view of the scene to your own. It has been a joy to remember, to reminisce and to relive the days of our youth – and we hope you feel the same.

Jenny Natasha &
Tom Boniface-Webb
October 2017

A

Adidas (clothing brand)

The Britpop clothing brand. Oasis' appearance on MTV's *Most Wanted* in '94 with Liam sporting Adidas trainers and Noel a matching trackie top, encouraged the nation to go 'mad fer' it. The classic three-stripe firebird jacket, worn zipped right up to the chin, came in every colour and was often seen on both Liam and Blur's Damon Albarn, making it a key feature of the Britpop wardrobe. For punters, Adidas Gazelles were the footwear of choice for gigs, pubs and festivals, where they became a symbol of not just the music but of the cultural era.

In '11, Noel Gallagher proclaimed his love for the trainers by teaming up with Adidas Originals to release 200 pairs of limited edition 'NG-72' Originals trainers, featuring his face on the tongue to coincide with the release of the *Noel Gallagher's High Flying Birds* album. He teamed up with the brand again in '17 to release his version of the seventies-inspired Garwen trainers as part of Adidas' 'SPEZIAL' range. Both editions feature Gallagher's face on the tongue, and the latter includes his date of birth inside.

Ain't That Enough (single – Teenage Fanclub)

Charted: Jul '97; UK Chart Position: 17; Label: Creation; Album: *Songs from Northern Britain*

'Ain't That Enough' was the first of three singles to be released from Teenage Fanclub's sixth studio album, *Songs from Northern Britain*. Written by bassist Gerard Love, the single was the band's biggest hit and the only one to chart in the top 20, where it spent three weeks. Heralding a more commercially successful time for the predominantly independent band, the album reached number three in the UK Album Chart just a month later.

The single was released as two CDs; CD1 containing B-sides 'Kickabout' and 'Broken' and CD2 featuring a cover of Lou Reed's 'Femme Fatale' and the track 'Jesus Christ'.

Albarn, Damon (singer/songwriter – Blur/Gorillaz/The Good the Bad & the Queen/solo artist)

Perhaps the key iconic figure of the time, Blur's Damon Albarn could make a strong claim to having near single-handedly invented Britpop. It was, after all, his band's decision to move away from the indie-dance sound of debut album *Leisure* that led to a more back-to-basics approach, where layered sixties-style guitars were accompanied by lyrics about modern British culture; intricate poems that told tales of life as lived by him and his contemporaries.

Born on 23 March '68 in East London, his family moved to leafy suburban Essex, where Albarn stayed until leaving for London as an adult. At age 11, he attended Stanway Comprehensive School in Colchester, where he met future bandmate and Britpop icon Graham Coxon. The two youngsters considered themselves outsiders, but bonded over a shared passion for music while hiding from malevolent school-mates in the music labs, Albarn bashing away at a battered piano as Coxon accompanied him on his saxophone. Many years later, while Coxon was at art college and Albarn went to drama school, the pair formed what was to become Blur with Alex James and Dave Rowntree. The band were signed in '90 to Food Records, where they met with some success from the off. It wasn't until they set off on a long tour of America in the early nineties, however, that Albarn dreamed up the idea for a specifically British-tinged focus for the band and, putting pen to paper, began creating Britpop.

During the Britpop era, Albarn formed a heavily publicised relationship with Elastica's Justine Frischmann, which lasted eight years. The pair were very quickly dubbed the king and queen of the movement, and the end of the relationship in '99 inspired his songwriting on both the self-titled *Blur* and *13* albums, notably 'Beetlebum' (written whilst they were still together), 'Tender' and 'No Distance Left to Run' (the most visceral about the breakup).

Albarn has fronted many musical projects since Blur, including Gorillaz, *Monkey: Journey to the West*, The Good the Bad & the Queen, *Dr Dee*, his debut solo album *Everyday Robots*, wonder.land and the Orchestra of Syrian Musicians. Blur reformed in '09 for what was due to be a one-off gig at Glastonbury, but returned the following year and eventually released a new album, *The Magic Whip*, in '15. In '17, Albarn collaborated with Noel Gallagher on Gorillaz track 'We Got the Power'.

All Around the World (single – Oasis)

Charted: Jan '98; UK Chart Position: 1; Label: Creation; Album: *Be Here Now*

At nine minutes and 20 seconds long, the epic orchestral Beatles-esque 'All Around the World' is Oasis' longest single and, for some reason, 18 seconds longer than the version featured on third album *Be Here Now*. It was the last single Oasis released on Creation Records, and the band's fourth number one single.

Noel Gallagher wrote the song in the early days of Oasis, but wanted to save it until the band could afford the full orchestral backing he felt it deserved. The psychedelic animated video was as grand and Beatles-esque as the song itself, riffing on 'Yellow Submarine' and its imagery.

The CD single contained B-sides 'The Fame', 'Flashbax' and a version of the Rolling Stones' 'Street Fighting Man', and the cover featured the title track's letters written on a sandy beach.

All Change (album – Cast)

Charted: Oct '95; UK Chart Position: 7; Label: Parlophone; Singles: 'Finetime' (Jul '95, UKCP 17), 'Alright' (Sept '95, 13), 'Sandstorm' (Jan '96, 8), 'Walkaway' (Mar '96, 9)

All Change was the debut album by Liverpool band Cast. All the music and lyrics were written by frontman and guitarist John Power, formerly of The La's.

Recorded at Manor Studios, Oxfordshire, and Sawmill Studios, Fowey, and released in October '95 by Polydor, it became the fastest selling debut album in the history of the label, overtaking the debut albums of The Jam, Jimi Hendrix and John Power's biggest influence, The Who. Produced by John Leckie, the album put Cast among the ranks of Britpop legends Suede, Blur, Oasis, Elastica and Pulp, reaching number 7 in the UK Album Chart and spawning two top 20 and two top ten singles. It was the band's most commercially successful record.

The album cover featured the band on a plinth in London's Trafalgar Square. This clearly showed the pull of the capital on bands from the provinces, even if they were from a city with such a rich musical heritage as Liverpool. It also showed the universality of the Britpop sound – a sound so strong it did not end at city borders.

All I Want (single – Skunk Anansie)

Charted: Sept '96; UK Chart Position: 14; Label: One Little Indian; Album: *Stoosh*

'All I Want' was the first single from Skunk Anansie's second album *Stoosh* and the band's third top 20 single, peaking at number 14 and spending six weeks on the chart.

Though edging away from what is considered standard Britpop and much more in the hard rock genre, the track quickly cemented itself as one of the band's most-loved songs.

The single was released as two CDs, with CD1 containing B-sides 'Fragile', 'Punk by Numbers' and 'Your Fight' and CD2 featuring the tracks 'But the Sex Was Good', 'Every Bitch But Me' and 'Black Skinhead Coconut Dogfight'.

All You Good Good People (single – Embrace)

Charted: Nov '97; UK Chart Position: 8; Label: Hut; Album: *The Good Will Out*

Originally released through indie label Fierce Panda, 'All You Good Good People' was Embrace's first top ten single when re-released through Hut records, reaching number eight in November '97 and spending seven weeks on the chart.

Although momentum for the band was growing, building on their previous release 'One Big Family', an EP that reached number 21 in August of the same year, the single came out just as the main thrust of the Britpop scene was drawing to a close. It soon became an Embrace classic nonetheless.

The UK video for the single saw the band playing with a huge orchestra, which features heavily on the song, in Abbey Road Studios. Released as two CD singles, CD1 contained B-sides 'You Don't Amount to Anything – This Time', 'The Way I Do' and 'Free Ride', while CD2 featured a remix of previous single 'One Big Family' and two remixes of the leading track.

Alright (single – Cast)

Charted: Sept '95; UK Chart Position: 13, Label: Parlophone; Album: *All Change*

Not quite as famous as the single of the same name released by label mates Supergrass two months previously, Cast's second single was their second to enter the top 20 chart on its release in September '95. It reached number 13 and went on to spend five weeks on the chart, heralding the release of their debut album *All Change* a month later.

The single, performed on *Top of The Pops* and *TFI Friday*, appeared on CD and both 7" and 12" vinyl versions and included B-sides 'Follow Me Down' and 'Meet Me'. The video featured the band on a sofa watching themselves perform on TV.

Alright/Time (single – Supergrass)

Charted: Jul '95; UK Chart Position: 2; Label: Parlophone; Album: *I Should Coco*

Famed as much for its iconic video as for the band exclaiming "We are young, we run green, keep our teeth, nice and clean...", 'Alright' (along with double A-side 'Time') was the fifth single released by Oxford band Supergrass.

It peaked at number two on its release in July '95, spending ten weeks on the chart and quickly becoming the key Britpop teen anthem, with people both young and old wondering what exactly "running green" was. The song also featured in numerous films, most notably on the soundtrack to nineties teen flick *Clueless* and the Kellogg's Mini-Wheats advert.

The song's video – which featured the band in red, white and blue T-shirts bearing their names, cavorting on motor-powered beds – brought them to the attention of US film director Steven Spielberg, who wanted to create an irreverent Monkees-style TV show around them aimed at a young audience. The band, however, were fully aware of the limitations such a show imposed on The Monkees' career, and so astutely turned down the offer in a bid to stop the song becoming an albatross. They never dropped it from their live sets though, and still embraced it as a teen anthem.

As well as the less well-known double A-side 'Time', the single also included a cover of American songwriter Mickey Newbury's 'Condition' and 'Je Suis Votre Papa Sucre'.

Anderson, Brett (singer/songwriter – Suede/The Tears/solo artist)

Brett Anderson is best known as the androgynous, heroin-chic, lead vocalist and chief songwriter of Britpop co-founders Suede. A key emblem for Britpop, his early work with the band pushed what was initially an underground scene to the forefront of public consciousness.

Born on 29 September '67, Anderson grew up on a council estate in Lindfield, Sussex. As a teenager, influenced predominantly by David Bowie, he played guitar for various garage bands, during which he met Suede co-founder and bassist Mat Osman. In the late eighties, he moved to London to study architecture at University College London, where he met and started a relationship with Justine Frischmann and, shortly after, formed Suede. She initially played guitar for the band, but left when she got together with Blur's Damon Albarn.

Suede quickly began to make a name for themselves, with Anderson's vocals and extravagant stage presence, reminiscent of Morrissey and his hero Bowie, attracting much interest and soon making him synonymous with the bourgeoning Britpop movement. If Damon was the intellectual forerunner, Liam the symbol of brooding masculinity and Jarvis the wry social commentator, then Brett was the androgynous extrovert who came alive when performing. His persona was familiar enough not to be alienating, with just the right amount of individuality to carve out his own niche. A classic British rock 'n' roll star, who wasn't afraid to bare his soul through his songwriting, Anderson showed an emotional depth to match his stage performance.

His music courted just as much attention as his affected air of bisexuality; a sexual identity that, unlike Bowie, he later admitted did not actually interest him. Like Bowie, however, he used sexuality and the androgynous look he and the rest of Suede sported to promote the band, and it was his idea to have a couple kissing on the cover of their eponymous debut without revealing their gender (it's still a mystery today).

After Suede split in '03, Anderson reunited with former bandmate Bernard Butler to form The Tears. They released two singles and an album to much critical acclaim, but split in '06 so he could focus on his solo work. Between '07 and '11, he released four solo records, *Brett Anderson* ('07), *Wilderness* ('08), *Slow* Attack ('09) and *Black Rainbows* ('11). He then rejoined Suede, who re-formed in '10 for a string of live dates and, so far, two new albums. Anderson's memoir *Coal Black Mornings* is due for release in '18, in time for the 25th anniversary of Suede's debut album.

Angel Interceptor (single - Ash)

Charted: Oct '95; UK Chart Position: 14; Label: Infectious; Album: *1977*

'Angel Interceptor' was the third of five singles released from Ash's debut album *1977*, giving the band their second top 20 hit. It spent seven weeks on the chart and paved the way for the release of *1977* in May '96. The title was taken from an aircraft that featured in sixties science-fiction Supermarionation series *Captain Scarlet*.

The CD single B-sides included '5am Eternal' and a cover of John Lennon's 'Gimme Some Truth', taken from his first solo album *Imagine*. The cover artwork featured a blonde girl with yellow wings against a cloud-covered sky, while the back showed the same girl with devil horns.

Animal Nitrate (single - Suede)

Charted: Mar '93; UK Chart Position: 7; Label: Nude; Album: *Suede*

Suede's third single 'Animal Nitrate' was a game-changer for the band and for Britpop, sparking a chain of events in early '93 that popularised the new musical movement. When the *NME* realised Suede had been left off the '93 Brit Awards nominations list, the music magazine campaigned every week for the band to perform at the ceremony. This resulted in the song becoming their first top ten hit, spending a total of seven weeks on the chart.

The CD single contained two B-sides 'Painted People' and 'The Big Time'. The cover featured a man in a grey suit with a pig's head, who also appeared in the music video directed by Perdro Romhanyi and filmed on a council estate in London. The video was deemed controversial at the time for showing two men kissing.

Ash (band)

Taking their moniker from the first word they liked in the dictionary, Ash were formed in Downpatrick, Northern Ireland, in '92 by Tim Wheeler (vocalist and guitarist), Mark Hamilton (bassist) and Rick McMurray (drummer).

The band released a mini-album of seven songs called *Trailer* in

'94, which received airplay on Radio 1 from Steve Lamacq. This was followed by the hugely successful album *1977* in '96, which coincided with the band taking their A-levels. They were positioned at the rockier end of the Britpop spectrum, thanks to a bunch of distorted guitar-heavy single releases, including 'Kung Fu', 'Goldfinger', 'Girl from Mars' and 'Oh Yeah'.

Shortly after *1977*, the band recruited guitarist and vocalist Charlotte Hatherley and released second album *Nu-Clear Sounds* in October '98, post-Britpop. They then went on to release the number one album *Free All Angels* in '01, which included the hugely popular singles 'Shining Light' and 'Burn Baby Burn'. Hatherley left shortly afterwards. In the UK, the band have had five top 40 albums, and 18 top 40 singles to date. In '09 and '10, they released 26 singles, one for every letter of the alphabet. The band also toured their live album *Live on Mars: London Astoria 1997* in '16.

Ashcroft, Richard (singer/songwriter/solo artist – The Verve)

Best known as the frontman, chief songwriter, vocalist and occasional guitarist for Wigan band The Verve, Richard Paul Ashcroft was born in Wigan in September '71. As a lifelong fan of George Best, he spent his early days living and breathing football, playing as a junior for Wigan Athletic. He attended Upholland High School and Winstanley College, where he met all of his future bandmates. He lost his father to cancer at a young age, an early tragedy that overshadowed his formative years, influenced the direction his creativity took and pushed him toward a natural melancholia.

Ashcroft's extrovert stage performances earned him the early moniker of 'Space Cadet', and the band's releases were often accompanied by press articles about him dancing on mixing desks and, in an infamous episode, collapsing at the American music festival Lollapalooza. His near-skeletal figure and verbalisation about the importance of his band and their place in the music scene gave the music press their ideal whipping boy.

As Britpop developed in the early nineties, so did Ashcroft's songwriting style, and he soon began to take more control of the band's sound and output, moving them away from the space-rock of debut album *A Storm in Heaven* toward a more traditionally structured, often acoustic guitar-based sound. His lyrical talent later resulted in an Ivor Novello Award for 'Songwriter of the Year' in '98. Ashcroft's songwriting was influenced by what was happening around him, notably the work of friend and colleague Noel Gallagher, and his talents were publicly recognised when Gallagher wrote in the sleeve notes of album *(What's the Story) Morning Glory?*: *"Cast No Shadow* is dedicated to the genius of Richard Ashcroft".

Post-Britpop, Ashcroft has enjoyed solo success with albums *Alone with Everybody, Human Conditions* and *Keys to the World, United Nations of Sound* and, in '17, *These People.* In '10, he formed new band RPA & the United Nations of Sound, who have released one album. He is also known for his collaborative work with trip-hop electronica band UNKLE, his vocals appearing on the single 'Lonely Soul'. The Verve re-formed to headline Glastonbury and to release fourth album *Forth* in '08. Ashcroft met and married Kate Radley, former Spiritualized keyboard player, in '95. Together they have two children, Sonny and Cassius.

Astoria, The (venue)

The Astoria was an iconic music venue on Charing Cross Road in central London. It first opened as a cinema in '27 and became a concert venue in '76. Many Britpop performances and key cultural moments happened at this historic venue, which was controversially closed and demolished, to a much-publicised outcry, in favour of London's Crossrail in '09.

Hosting several legendary Britpop gigs, including shows from Blur's *Modern Life is Rubbish* tour in '93 and Oasis' *Definitely Maybe* tour in '94, the venue was seen as a key place for aspiring bands, and a key date on tours from bands at all levels. Oasis last played there in the year it was demolished, favouring it over much larger venues.

According to Creation Records' Alan McGee, the legendary gig on the eve of Oasis' *Definitely Maybe* debut album marked "the point at which you knew it was going to blow up" for the group. Other notable Britpop gigs include Pulp in January '94 and Elastica in October '94, supported by Ash, who later went on to headline themselves in March '97.

At the Club (album – Kenickie)

Charted: May '97; UK Chart Position: 9; Label: EMIdisc; Singles: 'Millionaire Sweeper' (Nov '96, UKCP 60), 'In Your Car' (Dec '96, 24), 'Nightlife' (May '97, 27), 'Punka' (Jul '97, 38)

Released on the last wave of the Britpop tide in May '97, *At the Club* was Kenickie's debut studio album, heading straight to the top ten in the album chart, where it spent three weeks.

It included singles 'Punka', 'Millionaire Sweeper', 'In Your Car' and 'Nightlife' and, in true nineties fashion, a hidden live track, 'Montrose Gimps It Up For Charity', which played after the end of final track 'Acetone'.

Produced by John Cornfield, Andy Carpenter and Kenickie's own Johnny X, the album was initially released by EMIdisc in the UK. The Japanese release included three bonus tracks: 'Kamikaze Annelids', 'Perfect Plan 9T6' and 'Girl's Best Friend'. The album cover, shot by photographer Warren Du Preez, featured the band lounging around on a leopard print sofa.

Attack of the Grey Lantern (album – Mansun)

Charted: Feb '97; UK Chart Position: 1; Label: Parlophone; Singles: 'Egg Shaped Fred' (Mar '96, UKCP 37), 'Stripper Vicar' (Sept '96, 19), 'Wide Open Space' (Nov '96, 15), 'She Makes My Nose Bleed' (Feb '96, 9), 'Taxloss' (Apr '96, 15)

Attack of the Grey Lantern was Chester band Mansun's debut album, peaking at the top spot in February '97. With its songs linked together via a string of progressively nuanced sound effects, it was probably the closest thing that Britpop had to a concept album, in the same vein as the Beatles' later work or Pink Floyd.

It was released by Parlophone, and produced by singer and songwriter Paul Draper, Mark Stent and Ian Capl. The album's number one position was preceded by Blur's self-titled album *Blur* and succeeded by the Spice Girls' debut album *Spice*.

The Beatles influence, particularly on final single 'Taxloss', is no coincidence, with similarities to both 'Taxman' and 'Tomorrow Never Knows', and the album is just as innovative as the music giants were in the sixties.

The album was critically heralded on release, with many noting

Draper's ingenuity in linking each track to the next with sound effects and background noises, leading to many new bands asking their producers for a Mansun-style approach to their own album.

Audioweb (band)

Manchester band Audioweb originally formed in '91 under the name the Sugar Merchants, after lead singer Martin Merchant. Fellow members included Sean McCann on bass, guitarist Robin File and Robert Maxfield on drums. They were signed to Mother Records.

They released just one self-titled album in '96 that spawned five singles: 'Sleeper', 'Yeah?', 'Into My World', 'Bankrobber', which made the UK singles chart top 20, and 'Faker'. A limited edition of the album was also released, which contained a bonus CD featuring live tracks taken from their Reading Festival gig in August '96.

The band split in '99, after releasing three more singles post-Britpop, 'Policeman Skank', which narrowly missed the top 20, 'Personal Feeling' and 'Test the Theory'. The individual band members went on to take part in other musical projects: Merchant formed the band Supa-Jamma, McCann and Maxfield played for Ian Brown and McCann also released new music under the name Fellow Traveller. The band re-formed in '16 to support the Stone Roses at the Etihad Stadium and to play a string of dates, culminating with a gig at London's 100 Club.

Australia (single – The Manic Street Preachers)

Charted: Dec '96; UK Chart Position: 7; Label: Epic; Album: *Everything Must Go*

'Australia' was the Manic Street Preacher's fourth consecutive top ten hit, and the fourth single released from their fourth album *Everything Must Go*. It spent nine weeks on the UK singles chart.

The song epitomised the shift in tone the band made between albums three and four, when they found influence in the Britpop sound and left behind the bleak imagery of *The Holy Bible* era. Rather than noting a direct desire to move to Australia, bassist Nicky Wire's lyric is more about a general wish to escape and experience new things, metaphorically manifested here in the vast open spaces of the Australian outback.

The CD single was released as two CDs; CD1 contained the B-sides 'Velocity Girl', 'Take the Skinheads Bowling' and a cover of Frankie Valli's 'Can't Take My Eyes Off You' and CD2 featured a remix of the lead track and two of 'Motorcycle Emptiness'.

Auteurs, The (band)

The Auteurs were: singer/guitarist Luke Haines, his then-girlfriend Alice Readman on bass, Glenn Collins on drums and James Banbury on cello. Formed in '91, the band established themselves on the Britpop scene when debut album *New Wave* was nominated for the Mercury Music Prize in '93, an award won that year by Suede. The two main singles released from the album, 'Lenny Valentino' and 'Chinese Bakery', both just missed charting in the top 40, peaking at numbers 41 and 42 respectively. Album-opener 'Showgirl' was also released as the band's debut single in December '92, although it failed to chart.

The band released two other albums during the Britpop era, *Now I'm a Cowb*oy in '95 and *After Murder Park* in '96, including two further singles to reach the UK chart, 'Back with the Killer EP' and 'Light Aircraft on Fire'. Post Britpop, the band released album *How I Learned to Love the Bootboys* in '99, which spawned the single 'The Rubettes'. Haines later went on to write his memoir, *Bad Vibes: Britpop and My Part in Its Downfall*, published in '09.

Avenging Angels (single – Space)

Charted: Jan '98; UK Chart Position: 6; Label: Gut; Album: *Tin Planet*

The lead single from Space's second album *Tin Planet* was their highest charting release to date when it reached number six in the UK chart in January '98, paving the way for the release of the album two months later. It spent a total of eight weeks on the chart, and signalled a return to form, easily making a case as the band's most catchy radio-friendly release to date ("calling all avenging angels, angels, kick-ass angels").

The single was released on two CD formats; CD1 featuring the B-sides 'I Am Unlike A Lifeform You've Ever Met', 'Bastard Me, Bastard You', and 'Theme From "Baretta Vendetta"', while CD2 included six alternative mixes of the title track. A limited edition blue vinyl was also available, with only 800 copies made. In '09, the single gave its name to the band's fourth compilation and best-of album, *Avenging Angels: The Best of Space.*

B

B-sides

The flipside of the 7" vinyl single took on a new meaning with the advent of CDs, when more than two tracks could be included. In the age of Spotify and iTunes, the B-side has somewhat lost its prominence, but during the Britpop years it was a key way for artists to offer more material to their fans.

For Oasis in particular B-sides became an important part of their release strategy. Noel Gallagher used the band's early singles as an opportunity to include acoustic songs, often sung by himself, such as 'Take Me Away' from their debut single 'Supersonic', acoustic versions of other songs, such as 'Up In The Sky' from the 'Live Forever' single, or live versions of popular songs, like 'Live Forever' live at Glastonbury '94 from the 'Roll With It' single.

By the time 'Some Might Say' hit the top of the charts in February '95, B-sides were vying for pole position with the A-sides. The band often opened with B-side 'Acquiesce' when playing live, and the B-sides to 'Wonderwall', 'Don't Look Back In Anger' and 'Whatever' featured prominently in their sets. 'The Masterplan', one of the band's strongest B-sides, featured as track four on the 'Wonderwall' single, and also gave its name to the band's B-sides collection album, which peaked at number two in November '98.

Ocean Colour Scene also released a B-sides collection called *B-sides Seasides and Freerides* to offer more material to fans before the release of their third album, *Marchin' Already*. It reached number four in March '97, signalling not just the popularity of the band, but also showcasing another side to their sound, different to their most popular radio-friendly tracks, something purely for the real fanatics.

B-sides also offered bands the opportunity to climb higher in the charts, with a CD released over two formats – CD1 and CD2 – meaning fans could buy both versions. This was a tactic often employed by

Blur. Space also did it, but their intention was to release music that represented another side of their musicality with remixes of their own material. Always interested in dance music, but knowing that it might well not sell as well as their indie-pop material, they would either remix tracks themselves or ask guest DJs to offer up a version. Their January '98 single, 'Avenging Angels', had six alternative versions of the title track, meaning there were seven songs on the CD single, as many as some albums.

By the late nineties, major labels began to complain that their mainstream pop acts suffered because they couldn't supply the same wealth of material, so it was decided that a single could have a maximum of three tracks to be eligible for the UK singles chart. This has carried over into the digital age and iTunes only classifies a release a single if it has three tracks or fewer, with each track a maximum of ten minutes in length.

The ease of access offered by the internet means there isn't much need for the traditional single/EP/album release strategy. Bands can now release material as and when they want on whatever format they choose – both streaming and downloading are now eligible for the charts – but their intentions remain largely the same.

Babybird (band)

Babybird were yet another indie band to find delayed but notable success in the mid-nineties. Formed by frontman Stephen Jones, other members included Luke Scott on guitar, Robert Gregory on drums, John Pedder on Bass and Huw Chadbourn on keyboards.

It was 'You're Gorgeous', the second single from the sixth album *Ugly Beautiful* that finally propelled the band into Britpop stardom. Peaking at number three, as well as achieving world chart success, it became one of the biggest selling singles of '96. Its lyrics were in a similar style to Jarvis Cocker's, with sexual references conveyed in a sarcastic manner, particularly mocking how photographers treat models.

Prior to the success of 'You're Gorgeous', Stephen Jones self-released five albums worth of demos, written and recorded at home and under the name Babybird. *I was Born a Man* was the first to be released in July '95, followed by *Bad Shave* in October and *Fatherhood* in December. In '96, *The Happiest Man Alive* was released in April, followed by *Dying Happy* in May. But it wasn't until the band were signed to Echo that chart positions were achieved and album *Ugly Beautiful*, released in October '96, peaked at number nine in the UK chart.

Bad Actress (single – Terrorvision)

Charted: Jul '96; UK Chart Position: 10; Label: Total Vegas; Album: Regular Urban Survivors

'Bad Actress' was the third single to be released from Terrorvision's third album *Regular Urban Survivors*, and gave the band their second top ten hit after 'Perseverance'. The track was regarded by some fans as a potential Bond theme.

CD1 included B-sides 'Oblivion', 'Middle Man' and 'Funny Feels Fine', while CD2 featured 'Fobbed Off', 'Too Stoned to Dance' and an alternative version of the lead track.

Ballad of Tom Jones, The (single – Space ft. Cerys Matthews)

Charted: Mar '98; UK Chart Position: 4; Label: Gut; Album: *Tin Planet*

The second single released from Space's second album, *Tin Planet*, was also their highest charting single, reaching number four in March '98. Featuring the lead singer of Catatonia, Cerys Matthews, on vocals, the song was a tribute to sixties crooner and fellow Welsh hero Tom Jones, with Matthews singing "I could never throw my knickers at you" and Scott replying "And I don't come from Wales".

CD1 featured B-sides 'Happy Endings', 'Now She's Gone' and 'Stress Transmissions' and, as was becoming a theme for the band, CD2 featured six remixes of the title track.

Bankrobber (single – Audioweb)

Charted: Feb '97; UK Chart Position: 19; Label: Mother; Album: Audioweb

'Bankrobber' was the fifth single to be released from Audioweb's self-titled debut album and the band's sole top 20 hit. It was a cover of The Clash's original released 17 years earlier, which itself peaked at number 12 in the chart.

The video shows the band on holiday on the Costa del Sol, surrounded by gangsters and women exercising. The band also performed the single live on nineties hit TV Show, *TFI Friday*.

CD1 included B-sides 'Theme from Tubba Relish', 'Who, Are They?' and 'Home', while CD2 featured a live version of the lead track, recorded at Radio 1 Sound City in Leeds, and two remixes. The cover artwork features the band with their palms held out, hiding their faces, with the letters for Audioweb written on them.

Battle of Britpop (14 August '95)

The Battle of Britpop was a defining moment as the biggest bands of the time, Blur and Oasis, released their singles 'Country House' and 'Roll With It' on the same momentous day. This chart battle not only cemented Britpop as a scene, but also went as far as defining the individual; you were either a Blur or Oasis fan, you could not be both. Sides were chosen and woe betide you if you answered incorrectly. This was a way of life.

Though both parties claimed the release date clash was a coincidence, Blur's Damon Albarn later admitted purposefully moving the date of their single release so that it clashed with Oasis'. The battle featured heavily in the national press, and even made it on to the *News at Ten*. Radio 1's Sunday evening chart show gained record listening figures, with everyone tuning in to see which band was victorious.

Blur won the chart battle, with 'Country House' making its way to the top spot, although they released the single on two CD formats, meaning die-hard fans could buy both copies and have their vote counted twice.

Oasis' 'Roll With It' peaked at number two, but many consider that, in the long run, the Northerners won the war. Almost exactly a year later, they played two record-breaking gigs at Knebworth to a whopping quarter of a million fans, and went on to achieve 23 UK top ten singles and an estimated 50 million in global record sales. This is compared to Blur's 13 top ten singles, and not even a third of the sales. Both bands failed to win a Mercury British Album of the Year prize, despite bagging two nominations each, but both did score heavily at the Brits, with Oasis earning five gongs in '96 and Blur four in '95. Both bands would later be awarded the Outstanding Contribution to Music Brit; Oasis in '07, Blur in '12.

Despite losing the war in terms of music sales, Blur are widely considered to be the band with more technically creative flair and greater longevity, churning out a string of hit albums. Oasis received much criticism for their *Be Here Now* album, which some saw as an attempt to cling to the rapidly decomposing Britpop corpse, while Blur moved on to pastures new, reinventing themselves yet again with their self-titled fifth studio album. It seemed so important at the time, but in retrospect perhaps it never really mattered who won the original battle after all.

Bawl (band)

Irish rockers Bawl were one of the few bands to contain a trio of brothers: lead singer, guitarist and pianist Mark Cullen, lead guitarist Darren and drummer Jason, who left their home in Finglas, Dublin, for a music career in London under A&M records. The line-up was completed by Stephen McBride on bass.

The band initially released several singles under their own label Dependent Records, including debut single 'Bathroom', plus 'Girl's Night Out' and 'Glen Campbell Nights'.

In '96 the band released their sole album *Year Zero* on A&M records, which was critically acclaimed and often compared to The Smiths. The album contained the track 'Beyond Safe Ways', which featured on indie compilation series *Shine 6*.

Post-Britpop, the band reinvented themselves as Fixed Stars and then, a few years later, as Pony Club (not to be confused with London band New Young Pony Club).

Be Here Now (album – Oasis)

Charted: Aug '97; UK Chart Position: 1; Label: Creation; Singles: 'D'You Know What I Mean' (Jul '97, UKCP 1), 'Stand by Me' (Sept '97, 2), 'All Around the World' (Jan '97, 1), 'Don't Go Away' (Japanese import only)

Be Here Now was the hugely anticipated third studio album from Oasis. It followed the number one albums *Definitely Maybe* and *(What's the Story) Morning Glory?*, was again produced by Welsh maverick Owen Morris and completed what Noel Gallagher would eventually refer to as the unofficial trilogy of albums from Britpop's biggest band.

Oasis fans were expecting great things from the band's third album and eagerly awaited any information regarding the new songs, but management company Ignition fought hard to control the media frenzy surrounding the album release and made sure marketing and promotion were kept to a minimum, only allowing those directly involved access to information, a feat that in pre-internet Britain merely fuelled fans' lust for new material.

When the day of its release finally came on 21 August '97, the album went straight in at number one, despite the fact that it was released, rather untraditionally, on a Thursday, in a move by the band to show just how successful they had become. At this point in the Britpop era, Oasis were huge. Having played to crowds of 250,000 across two nights at Knebworth the summer before, and featuring heavily in the media, with constant comparisons to The Beatles, there was an incredible frenzy surrounding the release of *Be Here Now*.

Initially, the response to the album was positive, but then people started to say it was the initial hype that drove sales and not the content, and that the album was not another *(What's the Story) Morning Glory?* Years later, the album continues to receive negative criticism despite selling so well. Noel himself felt the songs were too long, with too many guitar overdubs and not enough bass. It was nearly three years before they released another album, '00's *Standing on the Shoulder of Giants*, on which the much darker, more introspective tone marked a notable change in direction.

The cover image for *Be Here Now* featured Stocks House in Hertfordshire, former home of the head of the Playboy clubs in the UK, Victor Lownes. The band are standing around a swimming pool containing a floating Rolls-Royce, a nod to the heady extravagance of the time and a direct reference to one of the many misadventures of The Who's drummer Keith Moon, who once drove a Rolls into a swimming pool.

The album spawned four singles: 'D'You Know What I Mean?' in June '97, Oasis' first since '96's 'Don't Look Back in Anger', 'Stand by Me', which was kept from the number one spot by Elton John's Princess Diana tribute 'Candle in the Wind' in September '97 and 'All Around the World', which peaked at number one in February '98. Liam Gallagher's favourite 'Don't Go Away' was released on Japanese import only in late '98 for the real die-hard fans.

The album's title was taken from a quote by Beatle George Harrison who, on being asked what it meant to be around during the sixties, replied, "Be here, now". A feeling Noel attempted to recapture some 30 years later.

Beautiful Ones (single - Suede)

Charted: Oct '96; UK Chart Position: 8; Label: Nude; Album: *Coming Up*

'Beautiful Ones' became Suede's fourth single to reach the top ten, where it spent eight weeks in October '96. The second of five singles released from their third album, *Coming Up*, the song contained references to drugs, sex and early nineties youth culture. It opened with an immediately grabbing guitar line from Bernard Butler's replacement Richard Oakes, who co-wrote the song with lead singer Brett Anderson. The record was one of Suede's catchiest hits, with Anderson singing in perfect Bowie-esque falsetto, "Oh, here they come, the beautiful ones, the beautiful ones".

CD1 contained the tracks 'Young Men' and 'The Sound of The Streets' and CD2 featured B-sides 'Money' and 'Sam'.

The cover artwork was a direct reference to the song's lyrics about our celebrity-obsessed culture, and featured what appears to be a group of image-conscious celebrities, one wearing a T-shirt stating: "One Day I'll Be Free".

Beetlebum (single – Blur)

Charted: Feb '97; UK Chart Position: 1; Label: Food; Album: Blur

Blur's 'Beetlebum' was the opening track to their fifth and self-titled album and their second number one single after 'Country House'. It was the first of four singles to be released from the album and spent a total of ten weeks on the UK chart, with one week at number one. In the '10 documentary *No Distance Left to Run*, Damon Albarn said that the song is about his relationship with his then girlfriend Justine Frischmann and her addiction to heroin.

The song is also notable for being the first in which the band started to emerge from the Britpop bubble; out went the chirpy hand claps and 'oy guvnor!' references of *Parklife* and *The Great Escape*, and in came self-referential melancholic lyrics accompanied by Coxon's mournful distorted guitar lines. Just like 'Girls and Boys' had done three years before, 'Beetlebum' marked a notable change in direction for Blur.

Released as two CD versions in cardboard sleeves, the first contained B-sides 'All Your Life' and 'A Spell (For Money)', while the second featured a remix of the lead song and the tracks 'Woodpigeon Song' and 'Dancehall'.

Begging You (single – The Stone Roses)

Charted: Nov '95; UK Chart Position: 15; Label: Geffen; Album: The Second Coming

'Begging You' was the final single released by the Stone Roses, and was the third release from their second studio album *The Second Coming*. It was their eighth single to reach the top 20, where it spent three weeks.

The CD single featured four remixes of the lead track, and the Australian version also included the radio edit, which was a minute shorter than the album version. The video features the band playing a live gig, interspersed with scenes of strippers wearing the band's faces as masks. The cover artwork, featuring rows of the insides of floppy discs, was designed by lead guitarist John Squire.

Being Brave (single - Menswear)

Charted: Mar '96; UK Chart Position: 10; Label: Laurel; Album: Nuisance

Menswear's highest charting single, 'Being Brave', gave the band their only top ten hit. It was the last single released from their debut album *Nuisance*.

CD1 featured B-sides 'Sunlight on the Moon', with vocals by Rachel Norman, and covers of The Zombies' 'This Will Be Our Year' and Public Image Limited's 'Public Image'. CD2 included live tracks of 'I'll Manage Somehow', 'Daydreamer' and 'Stardust', taken from the band's Shepherd's Bush Empire gig in October '95.

Bell, Andy (guitarist/singer/songwriter - Ride, Hurricane #1, Oasis)

Andy Bell is the only Britpop musician to have played with five bands, three managed by Creation records. Born in Wales in '70, Bell grew up in Oxford and started playing guitar when he was nine. He met fellow musician Mark Gardener at Cheney School in Oxford, and together they formed Ride in '88, during the shoegazing era. Alan McGee signed them to Creation in '89.

Bell played guitar with the band from their formation until they split in '95 and, after a couple of years, made a comeback with another Creation signing, Hurricane #1. The band received mixed reviews and Bell, suffering from writer's block, ended up moving to Sweden with then wife Idha Övelius, a Swedish musician with whom he has two children, Leon and Leia. Övelius was also signed to Creation in the nineties, releasing two albums featuring Bell and Oasis drummer Alan White.

Shortly after the move, guitarist Bonehead and bassist Guigsy parted company with Oasis, leaving the band looking for replacements. It was then that Andy Bell got a call asking him to join his third Creation band. He remained with Oasis for ten years as bassist, contributing to songwriting as well as learning the bass lines for their entire catalogue of songs.

After Oasis split in '09, four of the members (minus chief songwriter Noel Gallagher) decided to continue under a new name, Beady Eye. Bell continued with them, playing guitar this time, until they split five years later. He married Polydor artists relations head Shiarra Juthan in '10 and, in '14, reunited with original band Ride for a worldwide tour. In '17, they released *Weather Diaries*, their first album in 21 years.

Belle & Sebastian (band)

Belle & Sebastian – named after the '65 children's book *Belle et Sebastien* by French writer Cécile Aubry – formed in Glasgow in January '96 and have released a total of nine albums to date. Though existing on the periphery of Britpop, the band have been included due, in part, to their formation at its peak, and because of their continuing legacy in the post-Britpop years.

The band has six members, led by Stuart Murdoch, who recorded demos with past member Stuart David and Stow College music professor Alan Rankine. The demos were released on the college's label Electric Honey and, due to the positive response, Belle & Sebastian went on to record their full-length debut album *Tigermilk*.

Following the success of the first album, Murdoch and David recruited fellow members Stevie Jackson on guitar and vocals, Isobel Campbell on cello and vocals, Chris Geddes on keys and Richard Colburn on drums, though the line-up did change a few times over the years. The band was signed to Jeepster Records and went on to release second album *If You're Feeling Sinister* in November '96. Sarah Martin joined the band on violin and vocals before the recording of the album. A series of EPs were released in '97, towards the end of Britpop era, including the band's first top 40 'single' *3...6...9 Seconds of Light*, which charted at number 32. Post-Britpop, the band have released six studio albums alongside various tours and festival appearances.

Bennett (band)

Reading band Bennett are best known for their '97 hit single 'Mum's gone to Iceland', their sole top 40 hit in the UK chart, where it spent two weeks. Often compared to Blur, the band formed in '93 as a four-piece, with vocalist Jonny Peer on guitar, Jason Aplin on vocals, guitar and piano, drummer Kevin Moorey and bassist Andy Bennett.

Signed to Roadrunner Records in '95, they released several singles including 'Someone Always Gets There First', which featured on indie compilation series Shine 8, and two albums, *Supernatural* in '97 and *Street vs Science* a year later, shortly after which they split.

Better Day (single – Ocean Colour Scene)

Charted: Nov '97; UK Chart Position: 9; Label: MCA; Album: Marchin' Already

'Better Day' was the third single released from Ocean Colour Scene's third studio album *Marchin' Already*, and their fifth consecutive single to reach the top ten. It peaked at number nine in November '97, spending a total of eight weeks on the chart.

It was the band's most personal and self-referential single, with lead singer and chief lyricist Simon Fowler singing about the difficult times the band went through before they finally found success and their 'better day'. The single was released on CD and vinyl, and featured B-sides 'The Best Bet on Chinaski' and 'On and On'.

Bis (band)

Scottish band Bis formed in Glasgow in '94 and consisted of members Steven Clark (Sci-Fi Steven), John Clark (Disco John) and Amanda Mckinnon (Manda Rin). The band's name was an acronym of 'Black Iron Skyline', a lyric from 'Twilight of a Champion' by The The.

Just a year after forming, Bis performed their song 'Kandy Pop' – taken from their EP *Secret Vampire Soundtrack* – on *Top of the Pops* before it had even been released, and before they had an official record deal (the only band to achieve this).

The band released their debut album *The New Transistor Heroes* in April '97. Follow-up albums *Social Dancing* and *Return to Central* were released post-Britpop before the band split in '03, playing their final show at Glasgow's King Tut's Wah Wah Hut. However, like many other Britpop bands, they re-formed in '10 to play a series of live gigs.

Bittersweet Symphony (single – The Verve)

Charted: Jun '97; UK Chart Position: 2; Label: Hut; Album: *Urban Hymns*

The opening track on the band's third studio album *Urban Hymns*, released on 16 June '97, 'Bittersweet Symphony' eventually became one of the biggest songs of the nineties, and a huge, if fittingly bittersweet, hit for The Verve. Prior to release, it became embroiled in a lengthy and arguably unjust legal dispute over the authorship of its iconic string-riff. Although it peaked at number two in the UK singles chart, the band never saw a penny of the money it made. Allen Klein, manager of the Rolling Stones, claimed that the song was based on a sample taken from Andrew Oldham's 'The Last Time', which was itself an orchestral version of the Rolling Stones' song of the same name.

Richard Ashcroft wrote the lyrics and, although the band claimed to have written the string-riff independently of Oldman's version, he negotiated a license to use a five-note sample from the recording. However, Klein claimed that the agreement was broken because a larger sample was used and, the day before the single's release, he renegotiated the agreement. In order to save money, the dispute was eventually settled out of court and 100 per cent of royalties went to Klein and the Stones.

Despite this, the song's legacy remains intact. It is a defining Britpop anthem, remaining in the UK charts for three months and achieving world chart success. It propelled the band, who had split after the release of their previous album *A Northern Soul*, back into the mainstream, and featured as the final song at many of the band's live concerts in subsequent years. Coldplay performed a live version of the track, with Ashcroft returning from semi-retirement to add vocals, at the Hyde Park concert 'Live 8' in '05.

The music video, directed by Walter Stern, also remains one of the most recognisable of the nineties, featuring Ashcroft walking down a busy street in Hoxton, London, completely oblivious to those around him, bumping into passersby without the slightest acknowledgement. It was later parodied by novelty act Fat Les for their '98 anthem, 'Vindaloo'.

In '99, the song played at the climax of the film *Cruel Intentions*; it has also featured in an episode of *The Simpsons* and was used by ITV as background music preceding some of England's FIFA and Euro football matches. Beyoncé and Madonna have each used a sample of the song in their world tours. The lasting legacy of the song changed the fortunes of one of Britpop's most iconic bands, finally pushing them to the dizzy heights of the upper echelons of the charts, receiving well-earned success.

The single was released on CD and featured B-sides 'Lord I Guess I'll Never Know', 'Country Song' and 'Bitter Sweet Symphony' (Radio Edit).

Black Grape (band)

Rising from the ashes of key Manchester Factory Records band the Happy Mondays, Black Grape were formed in '93 by former Mondays' members Shaun Ryder and Bez. It was a fresh start and a new chapter for Ryder after his well-documented drug addiction and the disagreements that surrounded the demise of Factory, the Hacienda and the Happy Mondays.

The rest of the line-up consisted of rappers Paul 'Kermit' Leveridge and Carl 'Pyscho' McCarthy, drummer Jed Lynch and guitarist Paul 'Wags' Wagstaff of Manchester band the Paris Angels. Leveridge and Lynch were former members of Ruthless Rap Assassins.

In '95 Radioactive Records signed the band, who went on to release debut album *It's Great When you're Straight... Yeah!*, which went straight to number one in the UK chart and achieved three top 20 singles. Follow-up album *Stupid Stupid Stupid*, released two years later, peaked at number two and spawned two singles 'Get Higher' and 'Marbles'. Post-Britpop, Ryder fired the band in '98 while touring. They reunited in '10, signed to Alan McGee's new Creation Management in '15 and released *Pop Voodoo* in '17, their first album in 20 years.

Blackwood, Sarah (singer/songwriter - Dubstar)

Sarah Blackwood is best known as the blonde-haired, smoky-eyed lead singer of Dubstar, replacing Steve Hillier on vocals in '93. Born in Halifax, West Yorkshire in May '71, Blackwood studied interior design at Newcastle University before moving to Manchester and joining the band. She enjoyed success with Dubstar throughout the nineties, reuniting with them in '10.

Post-Dubstar, Blackwood joined Creation Records' band Technique as the vocalist on their European tour supporting Depeche Mode. During that time, she began collaborating with fellow Technique member Kate Holmes, wife of Creation Records boss Alan McGee. Together they wrote material and formed electronic music group Client under the names Client A and Client B (Blackwood). The band collaborated with various musicians including Pete Doherty and Tim Burgess, and Blackwood remained with the band until '10.

Blair, Tony (politician, originator of New Labour and UK Prime Minister '97–'07)

Everyone acquainted with the Britpop era will remember when Noel Gallagher and Tony Blair chatted amiably at 10 Downing Street in July '97, just two months after New Labour had won an historic general election victory. Apparently, Noel asked him how he managed to stay awake on election night, to which Blair is reputed to have replied: "Probably not the same way as you."

Britain's longest-serving Labour Prime Minister had hosted the high-profile Downing Street media industry soirée, inviting various sports and music stars, to create an impression of a 'young' Britain. Noel was the last person anyone expected to show up but, unlike Britpop arch-rival Damon Albarn, who turned down the invitation, Gallagher was clearly a Blair fan. During the speech for the 'Best British Group' Brit Award in '96, he said the only people in the country giving hope to young people were his band, Alan McGee and Tony Blair.

Music-lover and guitar player Blair began pairing Britpop with New Labour pre-election, when he invited Damon Albarn to the Commons in '95, and it was this idea that politics could be for the young that helped give New Labour their landslide win in May '97, which was followed by a record-breaking three terms in government. Blair even used one-hit-wonder rock outfit D:ream's chart anthem 'Things Can Only Get Better' as the soundtrack for his campaign. Blair's keen understanding of the zeitgeist meant he could use the country's position at the centre of the musical world during the Britpop years to promote his electoral campaign.

Blinded by the Sun (single - The Seahorses)

Charted: Jul '97; UK Chart Position: 7; Label: Geffen; Album: *Do it Yourself*

'Blinded by the Sun' was The Seahorses' second single released from their album *Do It Yourself* and was also the band's second to reach the top ten in the UK chart, where it spent seven weeks in total. Written by frontman Chris Helme, the video featured the band in spacesuits, floating around in space.

Available on CD, cassette and LP, the single B-sides included 'Kill Pussycat Kill' written by John Squire, who also drew the cover artwork, and 'Moving On', written by Helme.

Bluetones, The (band)

Formed in Hounslow in '93 by Mark Morriss (vocals), Adam Devlin (guitar), Scott Morriss (bass) and Ed Chesters (drums), The Bluetones were a key part of Britpop with their classic hit singles 'Slight Return', 'Bluetonic' and 'Marblehead Johnson'. In '96 the band notoriously knocked Oasis' *(What's the story) Morning Glory?* off the top of the UK albums chart with their debut *Expecting to Fly*. The band also narrowly missed out on a number one single, with 'Slight Return' being pipped at the post by Babylon Zoo's mega hit 'Spaceman', which famously featured in a Levi's TV ad.

'Marblehead Johnson' was released as a stand-alone single in '96, peaking at number seven and bridging the gap between their debut and follow up album *Return To The Last Chance Saloon*. Released in May '98 at the tail-end of Britpop, the album peaked at number 10 in the UK chart.

Post-era, the band released third album *Science and Nature* in '00 with recently-joined fifth member Richard Payne's keyboards providing a focal point for The Bluetones' sound. The album peaked at number seven and was followed by a singles compilation album two years later. Alongside various tours, the band released three studio albums during the noughties, *Luxembourg* in '03, *The Bluetones* in '06 and *A New Athens* in '10. If Oasis, Blur and Pulp were the generals of Britpop, then The Bluetones were valiant lieutenants, maintaining the core values of the time and riding the wave as long as it lasted.

Bluetonic (single – The Bluetones)

Charted: Oct '95; UK Chart Position: 19; Label: Super Quality; Album: *Expecting to Fly*

'Bluetonic' was The Bluetones' debut single, released from their debut album *Expecting to Fly* and the band's first top 20 hit, spending three weeks on the UK chart. The video features the band wearing cat mask disguises to board a bus. The song is also on the band's compilation album *A Rough Outline*, released in '06.

One of the key lyrics was adapted from *Celia, Celia*, a poem by writer and British left-wing political figure Adrian Mitchell, the first stanza of which runs: "When I am sad and weary, when I think all hope is gone, when I walk around High Holborn, I think of you with nothing on".

The single was released on CD and featured B-sides 'Colorado Beetle' and 'Glad to See Y'Back Again?'.

Blur (band)

Key Britpop group Blur formed in London in '88, initially under the name Seymour. The line-up has only ever been: Damon Albarn on vocals, keyboards and acoustic guitar; Graham Coxon on guitar and vocals; Alex James on bass guitar and Dave Rowntree on drums. Albarn and Coxon formed a childhood friendship when they met at Stanway Comprehensive School in Colchester, Essex. They later met James at Goldsmith's College in London and Coxon introduced Rowntree to the band at around the same time.

After receiving a demo, Food Records' Andy Ross went to see Seymour play at the Powerhaus in Islington, London. Suitably impressive, the band were offered a record deal, signed in March '90 (in a pub), which required them to rename themselves 'Blur'. The first song the band wrote in the studio after their first practice became their first single, 'She's So High'. This made them realise what they could achieve – if they could produce a single after just one rehearsal, anything was possible.

Pre-Britpop, Blur released debut album *Leisure* in '91, with a sound heavily influenced by the Madchester and shoegazing eras. They scored their first hit with 'There's No Other Way' – an immediate indie-dance classic – that reached number eight in the UK singles chart in April '91.

After touring the US in '92, the band released single 'Popscene' in March that year. The song marked a notable change in their sound, with the emergence of horns and lyrics about nights out emphasising their unmistakable Englishness. Britpop was born. Albarn wanted more than ever to praise his British roots and turn against the tide of grunge. Although only gaining modest sales, *Modern Life is Rubbish* was the record to do this, capturing what would soon become known as the Britpop sound: sixties-style guitar riffs coupled with modern-day stories of English culture. The album began the band's trilogy of Britpop albums, which included '94's unit-shifting and award-grabbing *Parklife* and '95's *The Great Escape.*

The new direction worked. Albarn was soon on a songwriting roll and *Parklife* catapulted the band to huge commercial success, entering the chart at number one. It won four awards at the '95 Brits: Best Band, Best Single ('Parklife'), Best Video (*Parklife*) and Best Album (*Parklife*). With the release of fourth album *The Great Escape* in September '95, the band demonstrated that they were not only still capable of penning chart-topping songs, but also that they were getting better. 'Country House', Blur's first number one single, began the battle of Britpop when Oasis released 'Roll With It' in the same week. Blur won the battle, and Albarn even appeared on *News at Ten.*

While *Modern Life is Rubbish, Parklife* and *The Great Escape* capture the Britpop sound perfectly, Blur's musical direction shifted massively when Coxon's taste for American alternative rock bands influenced the production of fifth album, *Blur*, released in February '97. This stark change in direction kept the band commercially successful, with lead single 'Beetlebum' their second number one single and 'Song 2' an even bigger worldwide hit, but, when coupled with the anti-climax of Oasis' *Be Here Now*, its release marked the end of the Britpop era.

Blur were a versatile enough band to transcend Britpop, with '99's *13* taking the work they began with *Blur* and pushing it even further. Epic lead single 'Tender' was only kept from the top spot by Britney Spears' unstoppable global super-smash 'Hit Me Baby One More Time', and Coxon's 'Coffee and TV' made it onto the soundtrack of Hollywood indie hit *Cruel Intentions*. Unfortunately, Coxon's battle with alcohol caused his very public departure from the band while they were recording the underwhelming '02 album *Think Tank*. By this time Albarn had become more interested in his side project, the computer-generated outfit Gorillaz, and the band officially split after *Think Tank* had been toured in '03.

Six years later, they were back. What began as a few live performances at Glastonbury and Hyde Park in '09 eventually turned into a worldwide tour, a new single, 'Under the Westway', another two appearances in Hyde Park (the Olympics' closing ceremony in '12, and again in '15). They also recorded a new album, *The Magic Whip*, which was released in mid-'15 and went straight in at number one.

Blur (album – Blur)

Charted: Feb '97; UK Chart Position: 1; Label: Food; Singles: 'Beetlebum' (Jun '97, UKCP 1), 'Song 2' (Apr '97, 2), 'On Your Own' (Jun '97, 15), 'MOR' (Sept '97, 5)

Blur's self-titled album was the band's fifth studio album and the eagerly anticipated follow-up to '95's *The Great Escape*. The album signalled the end of the Britpop era, moving away from the sound they developed on *Modern Life is Rubbish* and *Parklife* and bringing them more in line with American indie bands such as Sonic Youth and Pavement. In the same way that grunge had pushed Albarn toward a more British sound, the over-saturation of Britpop propelled him back over the Atlantic to the burgeoning post-grunge scene. American indie bands were also a key influence on the developing taste of lead guitarist Graham Coxon, who took much more of a central role, including penning and singing the low-fi love song 'You're So Great'. His layers of distorted guitars spit and sizzle, nudging their way to the forefront of the record alongside Albarn's melodic vocal lines for the first time, and cementing the guitarist as a singular musician with his own signature sound within the band and the British indie and mainstream scenes at large.

Despite concerns at the band's label, EMI, about how the change in style would affect Blur's loyal fanbase, the album peaked at the top of the UK chart and achieved worldwide success. American-sounding single 'Song 2' also helped make the album the band's most successful in the US, where Britpop had previously failed to fully connect with audiences. 'Beetlebum', apparently written about Albarn's girlfriend Justine Frischmann, went to number one in Britain and many European countries.

Blur, however, remains an English album, with references to English and British culture, most notably on 'Death of Party', which was widely assumed to be Albarn's comment on the disappointments visited on society by 18 years of Tory rule before the optimism of the New Labour boom. Closing track 'Essex Dogs' conjures up a bleak view of life in mid-nineties Britain, while 'Chinese Bombs' returns the band to their pre-Britpop (and pre-Blur) Seymour roots and single 'MOR' sees Albarn worrying about how middle-of-the-road the band had become. Produced by Stephen Street, the album was recorded in Reykjavik, Iceland as well as London. It remains the band's most critically acclaimed album.

Bonehead (Paul Arthurs) (rhythm guitar/ piano – Oasis)

Paul Benjamin Arthurs was born on 23 June '65 in Burnage, Manchester. Famous worldwide for his nickname 'Bonehead', presumably due to his premature baldness, Arthurs was the rhythm guitarist and occasional pianist for Britpop legends Oasis. As one of the founders of the band, he played from their humble inception in '91 until '99, when he left during the recording of fourth album *Standing on the Shoulder of Giants*, claiming he wanted to spend more time with his family. Arthurs has two children, Lucy, born in '95, whose godfather is Noel Gallagher, and Jude, born in '97.

Before Noel joined the band, Bonehead and Liam wrote the songs, and their Stone Roses-inspired effort 'Take Me' even made it onto the band's early demos. After Liam and Noel, Bonehead was the band's most outspoken member and, at two years older than Noel, was for a long while the ranking old-timer. After leaving school in '81, Arthurs became a plasterer and started his first band, Please And Pain, in '84. In the late eighties he started a band called The Rain, which Liam Gallagher eventually joined, grabbing the attention of his brother Noel.

Arthurs' mother's front room, which Bonehead painted and plastered himself, is featured on the cover of Oasis' debut album *Definitely Maybe*. Noel wrote about Bonehead's BMW in the band's debut single 'Supersonic', and the man himself was later immortalised on the the track 'Bonehead's Bank Holiday'. Attempts made by Noel to get Arthurs to 'do a Ringo' were quickly aborted. Noel took the lead, but a somewhat inebriated Bonehead can be heard chatting away with drummer Alan White as the song fades out.

Boo Radleys, The (band)

The Boo Radleys were still relatively unknown at the peak of the Britpop era in '95. It was their sixth single, 'Wake Up Boo!', released from fourth album *Wake Up!*, that catapulted the band into the Britpop mainstream, peaking at number nine and remaining on the chart for two months, becoming a key summer anthem.

Though the band were signed by Alan McGee and counted Oasis and Teenage Fanclub as label mates, they had a particularly un-Britpop sound and focus. 'Wake Up Boo!', noted for its bright brass riff, layered backing vocals and chirpy melody, was a key Britpop anthem and featured on Britpop compilation *Shine Too*, but was totally at odds with the rest of the band's output and ambitions. And although the royalties bought songwriter Martin Carr his own studio, he later considered the song an albatross around his neck.

The band formed in Wallasey, Merseyside in '88 and included guitarist/songwriter Martin Carr, bassist Timothy Brown, singer/guitarist Sice Rowbottom and Rob Harrison on drums. The band's name is taken from the novel *To Kill a Mockingbird* by Harper Lee, which includes a character called Boo Radley. The drummer's stool changed hands three times over the years, with Steve Hewitt replacing Harrison and Rob Cieka replacing Hewitt. After the success of fourth album *Wake Up!*, which peaked at number one in the UK album chart, follow-up *C'mon Kids* was released in '96. It charted at number 20 and spawned three top 40 singles, taking them to end of the Britpop era.

Brazen (Weep) (single – Skunk Anansie)

Charted: Jun '97; UK Chart Position: 11; Label: One Little Indian; Album: *Stoosh*

'Brazen (Weep)' was the final single to be released from Skunk Anansie's second album, *Stoosh*. It finds singer and lyricist Skin at her most heart-felt and introspective. The track was the band's fifth top 20 hit and spent a total of five weeks on the chart. Skin told Select magazine that the song opens "with quite a demonic laugh, which fits in with the dark, violent mood of the song. Like 'Twisted', this is about the extremely sad situation I was in."

Three CD versions were released, with CD1 including B-sides 'Twisted', 'All I Want' and 'It Takes Blood And Guts To Be This Cool

But I'm Still Just A Cliché', all live recordings taken from a Radio 1 session, while CD2 and CD3 both featured four remixes.

Brit Awards, The

The Brit Awards, often referred to as 'the Brits', are the British Phonographic Industry's popular music awards and have been held annually since '82, though the first show was held in '77. The popularisation of the Britpop movement meant that the Brits were a key arena for the bands and their albums, and the '95 and '96 shows in particular were dominated by Britpop bands, with Blur and Oasis taking home key awards.

The '95 Brits, held at Alexandra Palace and hosted by Chris Evans, were fuelled by the Blur/Oasis rivalry, with both bands involved in public slanging matches prior to the show, in which they were up against each other for Best British Group. Moreover, it was a battle of the albums, with Blur's *Parklife* up against Oasis' *Definitely Maybe*. Blur took home three awards that night, while Oasis took away one for Best British Newcomer, for which Echobelly were also nominated. Despite Albarn's attempt to patch things up with Oasis by paying tribute to the band while collecting an award, saying "I think this should have been shared with Oasis", things were only just warming up ahead of the August '95 'Battle of Britpop' showdown.

The '96 Brits, held at Earl's Court and again hosted by Chris Evans, continued the Blur v Oasis rivalry, this time with Blur's *The Great Escape* up against Oasis' *(What's the Story) Morning Glory?*. The Gallagher brothers, keen to continue the rivalry, notoriously collected their Best British Group award while singing their own version of Blur's 'Parklife', with Liam changing the lyrics to "Shite-life". Oasis also took home awards for Best British Video and Best British Album, while Supergrass took Best British Newcomer. Blur left the show empty-handed.

Arguably the most controversial moment in Brit Awards history involved Pulp's Jarvis Cocker, who took to the stage during Michael Jackson's '96 performance of 'Earth Song' and waggled his bottom. Cocker was arrested following the incident, spending hours being interview in a police station before being released. He received a lot of support from those inside and outside the music industry after the event, with many claiming Jackson's performance was ridiculously over-the-top, painting the singer as some kind of Christ figure.

The '12 awards show saw Blur rewarded for their Outstanding Contribution to Music, presented by actor Ray Winstone. It was Blur's fifth Brit, adding to the four they collected in '95, and they marked the event with an incredible 11-minute set, kicking off with 'Girls and Boys' and 'Song 2', before inviting Phil Daniels on stage to perform 'Parklife'. The London Community Gospel Choir then joined them to perform 'Tender' and 'This is a Low'. Oasis had previously been presented with the Outstanding Contribution award at the '07 show.

Other significant shows include the '93 Brits, at which, to the surprise of many, Suede had been left off the nominations list. *NME* began a weekly campaign to get the band to perform on the night and it worked. Suede's performance of 'Animal Nitrate' prompted a new wave of British music to begin and, as the single reached the top ten, *Select* magazine released one of the most famous magazine covers of the Britpop era, titled 'Yanks go Home' with Brett Anderson splashed on the front. The '97 show saw Kula Shaker taking the award for Best Newcomer and classic nineties film *Trainspotting* taking Best Soundtrack.

Other highlights over the years at the live-streamed awards show have included Geri Halliwell from the Spice Girls almost popping out of her Union Jack dress live on stage, and a member of Chumbawamba pouring a bucket of water over Deputy Prime Minister John Prescott. Perhaps understandably, alcohol was banned from a subsequent awards ceremony, and later the decision was made not to stream it live.

Britpop Abroad

Cool Britannia and Britpop drew attention to Britain from all corners of the world and, in the same way that British bands attempted to imitate Nirvana and Pearl Jam post-grunge, bands from abroad were influenced by Britpop's biggest movers and shakers.

Bands in the English-speaking world have a long tradition of trading and sharing. British grunge-rock band Bush, for example, failed to find much success in the UK but, after moving to America and making more of lead singer Gavin Rossdale's Cobain-like voice, found notable and immediate success with their debut album, *Sixteen Stone*.

It worked both ways too, as Rossdale's future wife Gwen Stefani's American band No Doubt found success in the UK with third album *Tragic Kingdom*, which reached number three in the chart in January '97, bolstered by mega-hit 'Don't Speak', which reached number one in October '96. However, there are some bands that break all the rules, like Garbage who, despite having three quarters of their line-up hailing from the States, have consistently been classified as a British band due to the dominance of sole Brit Shirley Manson.

Eels are perhaps one of the best examples of a US import that found success in the UK. Having struggled to gain a following at home, their debut album *Beautiful Freak* went straight into the UK top five in August '96. Noted more for their post-grunge, dark, lo-fi sound, the band are not prime Britpop, but they made good use of the timing of their first record and its catchy pop-tinged lead single 'Novocaine for the Soul', slogging it out at the summer festivals to garner attention. Their success on the British side of the pond meant they could return to America triumphant.

In the non-English speaking world, Sweden has a long history of producing pop bands that find success abroad. From Abba in the seventies to The Hives in the noughties, you could be forgiven for assuming that English was their first language. The Cardigans and The Wannadies both found notable success during the Britpop period, featuring on the soundtrack to Baz Lurhmann's hit film adaptation of Shakespeare's *Romeo + Juliet* in '96, which bolstered record sales on both sides of the Atlantic.

The Wannadies toured extensively in their early days with other Britpop groups such as Sleeper and the Lightning Seeds (playing their first UK gig at the Dublin Castle in Camden), becoming a key part of the Britpop scene and signing to the same UK record label as Sleeper and the 60ft Dolls. The Cardigans on the other hand found success in their home country before coming to the UK in '95 to capitalise on single 'Lovefool' (the song that would eventually turn up in Luhrmann's film), which just missed out on a top 20 placing in September '96. Second album *First Band on the Moon* fared better, reaching number 18 in October '96, and the band became near constant fixtures in the UK charts for the next few years, during and post-Britpop.

Britpop Now (music TV show)

Britpop Now was a collection of 12 live performances from the BBC archive featuring some of the best Britpop bands of the time. The show, which aired on BBC2 in '95 and was presented by Damon Albarn, opened with Blur performing 'Country House'.

Other performances came from Elastica with 'Line Up'; The Boo Radley's 'It's Lulu'; PJ Harvey, 'Meet Ze Monster'; Menswear, 'Daydreamer'; Echobelly, 'Great Things'; Gene, 'London Can You Wait?'; Supergrass, 'Alright'; Sleeper, 'Inbetweener'; Marion, 'I Stopped Dancing'; Powder, 'Afrodisiac'; and Pulp, 'Common People'. Interestingly, Suede and Oasis were not invited to play on the show.

Broudie, Ian (singer/songwriter/guitarist/producer – The Lightning Seeds)

Born on 4 August '58, Ian Broudie found initial success playing guitar with various late seventies Liverpool punk bands, including Big in Japan, who also featured Frankie Goes to Hollywood's Holly Johnson and the KLF's Bill Drummond. Through much of the eighties, he laid down his guitar and retreated behind the mixing desk to produce some of Liverpool's key new wave bands, including Echo and the Bunnymen and the Icicle Works, as well as Manchester's post-punk outfit The Fall.

At the tail end of the eighties, Broudie picked up his guitar once more and formed key Britpop band the Lightning Seeds, with whom he had the most notable success of his career. This didn't stop him producing though, and he found the time to helm albums by key Britpop groups including Dodgy, Sleeper and Republica.

When the Lightning Seeds' hits dried up post-Britpop, Broudie returned to the mixing desk full-time, allying closely with Alan Wills' new Liverpool-based label Deltasonic and producing much of the early work of The Coral and, later, their close friends The Zutons. Both bands went on to enjoy much success in the charts; The Zutons are perhaps most famous for their single 'Valerie', which was turned into a mega-hit by Mark Ronson and Amy Winehouse in '07.

Broudie released a solo album in '04 and re-formed the Lightning Seeds for another album in '09. He produced Miles Kane's hit album *Don't Forget Who You Are* in '10.

Broken Stones (single – Paul Weller)

Charted: Sept '95; UK Chart Position: 20; Label: Go! Discs; Album: *Stanley Road*

The fourth single released from Weller's key Britpop album *Stanley Road* found him at his most mournful yet soulful. The single reached number 20 when it was released in September '95, spending four weeks on the UK chart.

The single was released on CD, vinyl and cassette with B-side 'Steam'. The video featured Weller on a pebbled beach, in line with the opening lyrics: "Like pebbles on a beach, kicked around displaced by feet, like broken stones all trying to get home".

Brown, Ian (singer/songwriter – The Stone Roses/solo artist)

Ian George Brown was born in Warrington near Manchester in February '63. He met future bandmate John Squire at primary school and, after hanging around the eighties mod-revival Manchester scooter scene, the pair formed what would eventually become the seminal 'Madchester' figurehead group the Stone Roses in '83. Heavily influencing, among others, The Charlatans and Oasis, the band were positioned as spiritual godfathers to the Britpop movement, and Brown, as the frontman and spokesman for the group, found himself an icon for a generation, including an adolescent Liam Gallagher, who modelled much of his early style on him.

Like many young musicians in the early eighties, Brown's formative musical influences included the Sex Pistols and The Clash, but he was also an avid attender of the infamous Northern Soul all-nighters, and it was at one of these gatherings that the American soul singer Geno Washington took something of a shine to the young Brown, telling him he should become a singer.

After the Stone Roses split in '96, most people expected lead guitarist and chief songwriter John Squire to find post-Roses success. However, when Brown finally released his debut solo album *Unfinished Monkey Business* (a sly reference to his moniker of 'King Monkey') in February '98, it proved to be critically and commercially successful, leading to a further six albums in the next ten years. While Squire pushed the Roses' sound towards guitar-led blues, typified by the multi-layered guitar lines of second album *The Second Coming*, Brown was more interested in electronic sounds, string riffs and keyboard-led samples.

During his first solo tour of Europe in October '98, Brown was arrested and subsequently convicted and sentenced to four months in prison for threatening behaviour against a stewardess on a flight back to Manchester from Paris. He claimed innocence but served his time in Strangeways prison in Manchester, where he wrote songs for his second solo album *Golden Greats*. In '11, the Stone Roses announced they would be re-forming after a 15-year hiatus, heading out on a worldwide tour in '12 with Brown once again at the helm.

Brushed (single – Paul Weller)

Charted: Aug '97; UK Chart Position: 14; Label: Go! Discs; Album: *Heavy Soul*

'Brushed' was the second of four singles to be released from Paul Weller's fourth album *Heavy Soul*. His 12th top 20 hit as a solo artist, the single spent four weeks on the UK chart and included B-sides 'Ain't No Love in the Heart of the City', 'Shoot the Dove' and an acoustic version of 'As You Lean into the Light'.

The single was released during a classic period of songwriting for the 'modfather' who, by this point, was positioned as a spiritual Britpop figurehead, most notably for Oasis and Ocean Colour Scene. The lyric "Looks like you're the next blessed in town", was a gentle nod to the next generation of bands.

Burgess, Tim (singer – The Charlatans/solo artist)

Timothy Allan Burgess is best known as the lead singer of The Charlatans, a band born out of Madchester and heavily influenced by the Stone Roses and the Happy Mondays. Born in Salford in May '67, he grew up in the nearby Cheshire town of Northwich where, as a young man, he worked in factory jobs and as a labourer.

Burgess started his music career as lead singer for the Electric Crayons, infamous for their Northwich Memorial Hall gig in '90, when the floor collapsed. Soon after, he joined The Charlatans, replacing their lead singer Baz Kelley and remaining with the band right up to the present day.

In '03, he released his first solo album, *I Believe*, which reached number 38 in the UK chart and spawned the singles 'I Believe in the Spirit' and 'Only a Boy'. Follow-up album *Oh No I Love You* was released nine years later, reaching 49 in the chart. Burgess spent 12 years living in Los Angeles, returning to the UK in '11 to start independent record label O Genesis, a year before his autobiography *Telling Stories* was released. He continues to work with The Charlatans.

Butler, Bernard (guitarist/singer/songwriter/producer – Suede/McAlmont & Butler/solo artist)

Bernard Butler has been a key presence on the British music scene for more than 20 years, taking on many roles as one of the key movers and shakers of the Britpop movement. Like so many other hopeful, talented teenagers, he began his musical career after answering an advert in the legendary 'Musicians Wanted' pages of the *Melody Maker*. Later, he teamed up with vocalist David McAlmont to produce the epic single *Yes* and, as a solo artist, his album *People Move On*, which paved the way for more producing work, most notably for early noughties *enfants terrible* The Libertines' debut single 'What a Waster'.

Born in north London on 1 May '70, the often shy and retiring young Butler found solace in music, particularly, like so many of his generation, The Smiths. Johnny Marr was not only the dominant influence on his guitar-playing skills, but also on his songwriting partnership with Suede singer Brett Anderson, which echoed the 'extrovert singer/genius guitarist' dynamic made famous by Morrissey and Marr. Anderson and Butler were the heart and soul of the group and it was their poles-apart chemistry that gave the band its early edge. Their personalities always clashed, but as they entered a period of new-found fame and fortune they began to move in starkly opposing directions.

It all came to an explosive head during the recording of Suede's second album *Dog Man Star*, when Butler – something of a workaholic – spent hours and hours layering guitar tracks and tweaking piano lines, while Anderson took on the role of show-off rock star, undermining his colleague's hard work with his forced extravagance. When Butler finally left the band, it was in the most acrimonious circumstances, and the pair did not speak until they finally made up when forming Suede spin-off group The Tears in '05.

Alongside other modern music legends like Radiohead's Johnny Greenwood, Blur's Graham Coxon and Muse's Matt Bellamy, Butler is considered to be one of the best guitarists of his generation. More recently, however, he has found himself on the other side of the mixing desk, producing singles and albums for a large and diverse range of British acts including The Libertines, The Cribs, Neneh Cherry, Sophie Ellis-Bextor, Tricky and Paloma Faith.

C

C'mon Kids (album – The Boo Radleys)

Charted: Sept '96; UK Chart Position: 20; Label: Creation; Singles: 'What's in the Box (See Whatcha Got)' (Aug '96, UKCP 25), 'C'mon Kids' (Oct '96, 18), 'Ride the Tiger' (Jan '97, 38)

C'mon Kids was the fifth album to be released by the Boo Radleys and, though far removed from their commercially successful previous offering *Wake Up!*, still achieved top 20 status in the UK chart, where it spent three weeks.

Recorded at Rockfield Studios in Wales, the album resulted in three singles: 'What's In the Box', 'C'mon Kids' and 'Ride the Tiger', all of which reached the top 40. The record was reissued in '10 and featured a bonus CD containing B-sides from the album's singles.

C'mon Kids (single – The Boo Radleys)

Charted: Oct '96; UK Chart Position: 18; Label: Creation; Album: *C'mon Kids*

'C'mon Kids' was the leading track from the Boo Radleys' fifth album of the same name. It was the band's second and final top 20 single in the UK chart (after 'Wake Up Boo!' released the year before), and spent two weeks on the chart.

The single was released on two CDs, with CD1 containing B-sides 'Spion Kop', 'To Beautiful' and a remix of 'Bullfrog Green' (taken from the album *C'mon Kids*), and CD2 'Nothing to Do But Scare Myself', a remix of 'From the Bench at Belvidere' and a remix of 'Fortunate Sons' from the *C'mon Kids* album.

The video features the band playing on a rooftop, reminiscent of the Beatles high above London's Savile Row, occasionally flitting to scenes of kids playing football.

Camden Town (home of Britpop)

Every movement needs a spiritual home and, for Britpop, it was the north London district known as Camden Town. Just a stone's throw north of Soho and easily accessible for London record companies, Camden's intricate array of markets, pubs, clubs and music venues – plus its notoriety for harbouring some of the capital's less salubrious citizens – meant the NW1 postcode was ideal for any aspiring Britpop star. *Melody Maker* came to refer to Camden's musical movement as "The Scene That Celebrates Itself", later adding "Camden is to 1995 what Seattle was to 1992, what Manchester was to 1989".

Oasis' label Creation Records was based in Regent's Park Road, Primrose Hill, which meant that the Pembroke Castle was the regular boozer for the band (Liam Gallagher was arrested outside the pub for breaking an insistent paparazzo's camera). The Sir Richard Steele pub in Haverstock Hill, Belsize Park – also known as 'The Steeles' – was also a Britpop haunt, and the Gallagher brothers were often spotted there, as was Chris Evans.

But it was the Good Mixer on Inverness Street, a two-roomed, not particularly special Irish boozer, that formed the social hub of Britpop. It was where Elastica shook hands on a deal with Deceptive Records; where Menswear were rumoured to have formed; and where Oasis were thrown out for harassing Graham Coxon, kicking off the Blur v Oasis rivalry. The Good Mixer was heavily publicised in the press as the place to spot a Britpop musician, attracting fans from around the country hoping to see one of their heroes. The Boo Radleys even mentioned the Good Mixer on their *Wake Up!* album in '95.

But it was not just the pubs that drew the Britpop faithful to Camden. It was also the music venues. It was often hard to differentiate between the two, the distinction being nothing more than an upstairs room with a PA system at the Monarch, the Dublin Castle, the Devonshire Arms, Underworld and the Royal Exchange, to name a few. Sometimes the distinction was that the pubs had more actual fans in them, looking out for their idols, rather than a sea of A&R men looking for the next big thing. Camden was also the actual home of Noel Gallagher and his then wife Meg Matthews, who moved from Arlington Road in '95 into a seven-bedroom house in Steele's Road, Belsize Park, which they named 'Supernova Heights'. Brother Liam and his then wife Patsy Kensit also formed part of the Primrose Hill scene, moving into nearby Elsworthy Road. Graham Coxon still lives in Camden today.

Candy Girl (single – Babybird)

Charted: Feb '97; UK Chart Position: 14; Label: Echo; Album: *Ugly Beautiful*

'Candy Girl' was the third of four singles released from Babybird's commercially successful debut album *Ugly Beautiful*. It was the band's second and final top 20 hit, spending five weeks on the UK chart.

The B-sides included 'Farmer', 'Oh What a Beautiful Day' and 'Amtrack'. The cover artwork featured a woman with chocolate dripping from her fingers and lips – a reference to Stephen Jones' lyrics asking the unknown subject to "lick my candy", itself a not-too-cryptic reference to something else entirely.

Candyskins (band)

Candyskins are considered one of the earliest of the Britpop bands. They began on the Oxford scene, often intermingled with the shoegazing scene and made famous by the success of Ride, Radiohead and Supergrass in '89.

All the members, apart from bassist Richard Brown, lived in the village of Islip and attended Gosford Hill School. The initial line-up consisted of Nick Cope on vocals, brother Mark on guitar, Brown on bass and drummer John Halliday.

The band released four albums and several singles throughout the nineties, but it was only the single 'Morning Morning' that made it into the top 40 of the UK chart, where it spent two weeks. The band officially split in '98, but have re-formed on several occasions since at Oxford's pinnacle live indie music venue, The Zodiac.

Cannon, Brian (artist)

Brian Cannon deserves a special mention as the British graphic designer who, with his Microdot graphic design company, was responsible for the design of the Oasis logo and all the band's UK promotional material in the nineties, including record sleeves for albums *Definitely Maybe*, *(What's the Story) Morning Glory?* and *Be Here Now*. What is remarkable – by modern-day standards– is that there is no Photoshopping involved; all the shots are real.

Cannon designed record sleeves for The Verve, including the covers for albums *A Northern Soul* and *Urban Hymns*. He was also responsible for the music packaging for Suede's *Dog Man Star* and did design work for other Britpop favourites Ash, Cast and the Super Furry Animals.

Cassettes (media format)

Though die-hard vinyl fans will undoubtedly disagree, CDs and cassette tapes were the most common formats during the nineties for pre-recorded music. Cassettes were also (and perhaps more importantly) commonly used for recording favourite songs off the radio and for creating mix-tapes that could be swapped with friends. When recording from the radio, the real test was to see if you could press the pause button before the DJ started talking. (Don't think for a moment that we're condoning this practice – we all know that infringement of copyright is a serious crime!)

Many fledgling relationships were cemented when teenagers let music speak for them when they couldn't find the words by creating a mix-tape for a new love interest. The skill was in using the song choices to reflect your feelings without seeming too obvious. Handing over a mix-tape was a key coming-of-age moment for virtually every child of the eighties and nineties, but it's not something that works in the same way in the days of Spotify and iTunes. "I've made you a Spotify playlist", just doesn't have the same ring to it.

As a matter of interest, the police still use cassettes to record interviews because the quality is apparently harder to forge than CDs.

Cast (band)

Cast were – alongside the Boo Radleys – the city of Liverpool's contribution to Britpop. The band was formed by lead singer and guitarist John Power in '92, shortly after he left Scouse legends The La's. It was during a tour with Oasis in '94 that an A&R rep from Polydor Records spotted Cast and subsequently signed them to the label in December of that year.

Debut single 'Finetime' was released in July '95, entering the UK chart at 17. The band then went on to have a string of successful releases that included debut album *All Change*, produced by John Leckie who had previously worked with The La's, the Stone Roses and The Verve. The record, which went platinum and became Polydor's bestselling debut LP, contained another three successful chart singles: 'Alright', 'Sandstorm' and 'Walkaway', all of which made the top 15. Cast's association with Britpop's key band Oasis saw them rewarded with a support slot at the era-defining Knebworth concert.

The band's follow-up album *Mother Nature Calls*, released in April '97 and also produced by Leckie, peaked at number three in the chart and remained in the top 40 for more than six months. The album produced three top-ten singles, 'Free Me', 'Guiding Star' and 'Live the Dream', and fourth single 'I'm so Lonely', which reached number 14. The album received mixed reviews, but paved the way for their next long-form release, '99's *Magic Hour*, which found its way to number six in the chart, spurred on by the hit single 'Beat Mama', which reached number nine three weeks earlier.

Post-Britpop, Cast have released studio albums *Beetroot* in '01, *Troubled Times* in '12 and *Kicking up the Dust* in '17. They have also signed with Alan McGee's newly-formed Creation Management.

Catatonia (band)

Although enjoying most success in the years following Britpop, Catatonia are considered one of Wales' key contributions to the scene, finding their own special place in British music largely via Cerys Matthews' distinctive Welsh vocals, brazenly projected across hit single 'Road Rage' (remember those rolling r's). Alongside Matthews were guitarists Mark Roberts and Owen Powell, bassist Paul Jones and Aled Richards on drums.

Fame came when hit single 'Mulder and Scully' peaked at number three in the UK chart in January '98, helping to push album *International Velvet* to the top of the charts. Single 'Road Rage' was released in May '98, also achieving top-ten chart success and making Catatonia one of the biggest post-Britpop bands. In the early years, Matthews and Roberts were said to be in a relationship, which apparently formed the basis for many of their lyrics.

For Catatonia, the Britpop years were about warming up for the success that would follow. Debut album *Way Beyond Blue* scraped into the top 40, reaching number 32 in October '96 and giving the band just enough recognition to propel them forward to more as Britpop waned. *International Velvet*'s follow-up, *Equally Cursed and Blessed*, appeared in April '99 and continued the band's run of chart success, peaking at number one, despite the guitar-led music scene not finding much success at the time.

Quarrels with their label meant the album's second single 'Londinium' – a song about the negative dominance the capital city has over Britain – was released against the band's wishes. Two years of silence followed as the band considered their future. They returned with 'Paper Scissors Stone' in August '01 which, despite peaking at number six in the chart, signalled the end for the band who split not long afterwards.

Away from Catatonia, Matthews collaborated with fellow Britpop band Space on the single 'The Ballad of Tom Jones', released in February '98, which led to her collaborating with Tom Jones himself on 'Baby It's Cold Outside', which featured on his hugely successful album of duet covers *Reload*.

Matthews joined BBC Radio 6 Music as a presenter in '08, and her dulcet Welsh tones can still be heard every Sunday morning as she spins music from a wide variety of genres, while throwing in the odd poem or recipe.

Celebrity Hit List (single – Terrorvision)

Charted: May '96; UK Chart Position: 20; Label: Total Vegas; Album: *Regular Urban Survivors*

'Celebrity Hit List' was the second of four singles from Terrorvision's third album, *Regular Urban Survivors*. Appearing in the charts just a few months after the album's first single, 'Perseverance', the track was the band's second top 20 hit, spending three weeks on the UK chart and regularly used to accompany *Match of the Day*'s Goal of the Week.

The CD single was released as a double bill known as Episode One and Two. Episode One contained a cover of Smokey Robinson's 'You Really Got A Hold On Me' and a remix of 'Tom Petty Loves Veruca Salt', which originally featured on '95's charity record *The Help Album*. Episode Two contained 'Don't Come Here' and 'Crossed Line On The Grapevine'. The cover artwork featured a helicopter flying through an explosion while a man wearing a black top hat and suit and holding a gun leaps out of the way.

Change (single – The Lightning Seeds)

Charted: Jan '95; UK Chart Position: 13; Label: Epic; Album: *Jollification*

The Lightning Seeds' first single to reach the top 20 of the UK chart since their debut 'Pure' five years previously, 'Change' really did change things for the band. It marked the start of their most fruitful period under new label Epic and was their biggest hit to date, reaching number 13 and spending a total of six weeks on the chart.

The single was released on two CD formats, with CD1 featuring B-sides 'The Life of Riley (Instrumental)', and 'Lucky You (Live)', and CD2 'Say You Will'.

Change Giver (album – Shed Seven)

Charted: Sept '94; UK Chart Position: 16; Label: Polydor; Singles: 'Mark/Casino Girl' (Mar '94, UKCP 77), 'Dolphin' (Jun '94, 28), 'Speakeasy' (Aug '94, 24), 'Ocean Pie' (Oct '94, 33)

Change Giver was the debut album from York's Shed Seven, produced by Jessica Corcoran and released on Polydor Records in September '94, just as the Britpop era was getting underway. It was a huge year for the band, with the debut album peaking at number 16 in the UK chart and spawning four singles, starting with the band's debut 'Mark', released in March, which peaked at 77, followed by top 40 singles 'Dolphin', 'Speakeasy' and 'Ocean Pie'.

Melody Maker, *NME* and *Select* all ranked it in their 'top albums of the year' and the band embarked on four UK tours to support the release, as well as featuring on the bill at Glastonbury, Reading and T in the Park. Other memorable performances in support of *Change Giver* and its singles include the band's debut on *Top of the Pops* in June '94 and on the *Mark Radcliffe Show* in September. The album re-entered the charts in '98, peaking at number 124.

Changing Man, The (single – Paul Weller)

Charted: May '95; UK Chart Position: 7; Label: Go! Discs; Album: *Stanley Road*

'The Changing Man' was the second single released from Paul Weller's third solo album, *Stanley Road*, on which it was the opening track. It was his most successful solo single to date, and his first top ten hit. It spent four weeks on the UK chart.

Moving away from his more acoustic previous album *Wild Wood*, the single's jangly semi-acoustic sixties guitar sound cemented the former Jam frontman as the godfather of Britpop.

The CD single contained a cover of Etta James' 'I'd Rather Go Blind', 'It's A New Day Baby' and a live Royal Albert Hall recording of 'I Didn't Mean To Hurt You'.

Charity (single – Skunk Anansie)

Charted: Apr '96; UK Chart Position: 20; Label: One Little Indian; Album: *Paranoid & Sunburnt*

Originally released in September '95 and hitting the number 40 mark in the UK chart, 'Charity' was the third single from Skunk Anansie. After the band's single 'Weak' reached number 20 in January '96, 'Charity' was re-released in April, this time climbing to number 20. It is the sixth track on debut album *Paranoid & Sunburnt*.

The single was released as two CDs. CD1 contained live recordings of 'I Can Dream' and 'Punk By Numbers' from a London Astoria gig in January '96. CD2 featured a further three live recordings: 'And Here I Stand', 'It Takes Blood & Guts To Be This Cool But I'm Still Just A Cliché' and 'Intellectualise My Blackness'.

Charlatans, The (band)

Influenced predominantly by the Stone Roses and other baggy bands, The Charlatans UK (not to be confused with their US counterparts) began life during the Madchester scene in the early nineties, finding considerable success and Britpop stardom in '95 with the release of their self-titled fourth album, and its follow up *Tellin' Stories* in '97.

There were several line-ups and record labels over the years, but the key personnel were Tim Burgess on vocals, guitarist Marc Collins, keyboardist Rob Collins, bassist Martin Blunt and drummer Jon Brookes. Sadly, Rob Collins died in a car accident halfway through the '96 studio recording of *Tellin' Stories* (released in April '97), the final act in a troubled life that had included a spell in prison for his part as the getaway driver for a robbery committed by a friend. Much of the band's original success can be attributed to his immediately recognisable Hammond organ sound (most notably on the band's second single, the number nine hit 'The Only One I Know'). Collins' death was a massive blow to the band, but they coped by carrying on, drafting in Martin Duffy on loan from Primal Scream.

In August '96, less than a month after Collins' death, the band supported Oasis at Knebworth. Two weeks after the gig, they released 'One to Another', which hit number three in the UK singles chart, prompting them to finally finish recording *Tellin' Stories*. Top-ten singles 'North Country Boy' and 'How High' were also released from the album, and the band ended their Britpop years with a hugely emotional tour. Tony Rogers eventually joined the band as their full-time keyboardist.

Tellin' Stories was noted for its heavier, more guitar-focused direction, which moved the band away from their trademark Hammond organ sound and found them a new audience during the Britpop years. It was this malleability that led to the band's longevity, outstripping most of their fellow Britpop acts and finishing the nineties with three of their first five albums hitting the top spot in the albums chart.

Sadly, the band's long-time drummer Jon Brookes succumbed to brain cancer in August '13 and the band held a tribute concert that featured Liam Gallagher's band Beady Eye and the Manic Street Preachers. The Verve's Pete Salisbury filled in on drums. The band continue to play and record together, releasing a string of albums during the noughties and, more recently, *Modern Nature* in '15 and *Different Days* in '17.

Charlatans, The (Album – The Charlatans)

Charted: Sept '95; UK Chart Position: 1; Label: Beggars Banquet; Singles: 'Crashin' In' (Dec '94, UKCP 31), 'Just Lookin'/Bullet Comes' (May '95, 32), 'Just When You're Thinkin' Things Over' (Aug '95, 12)

The Charlatans released their self-titled fourth album to huge success, achieving their first number one album since their debut *Some Friendly* five years earlier. It spent a total of 18 weeks on the chart (one in the top spot).

The album resulted in three top 40 singles, 'Crashin' In', 'Just Lookin'/Bullet Comes' and the top 20 single 'Just When You're Thinkin' Things Over', all released prior to the album, which was recorded at Monnow Valley Studio and Rockfield Studios. The album cover features a photograph of the band's faces against a black background, taken by Tom Sheehan. It was the last album to include keyboardist and founder member Rob Collins before his untimely death.

Commercially, the album marked a return to form for the band, who had been bothering the outer reaches of the top 40 since their debut, their success in part due to the burgeoning Britpop scene and their proximity to it. Stylistically, the album marked the end of an era for the band, whose sound developed for the next album, moving away from their trademark Hammond organ towards the indie guitar sound made popular by the scene, a change that would bring them even more success.

Charmless Man (single – Blur)

Charted: May '96; UK Chart Position: 5; Label: Food; Album: *The Great Escape*

'Charmless Man' continued the archetypal Britpop sound that Blur fans came to expect in mid-'96, but it would be the last Blur release to do so. Produced by long-time collaborator Stephen Street, it was the fourth single released from Blur's fourth album *The Great Escape*, following 'Country House', 'The Universal' and 'Stereotypes'. It was the band's seventh to reach the top ten, where it spent ten weeks.

The UK CD single contained 'The Horrors', 'A Song' and 'St Louis', while the European version featured B-sides 'The Man Who Left Himself', 'Tame' and 'Ludwig'. The video features a (charmless) man using an electric toothbrush and washing his mouth out with red wine. The song was track 11 on *Blur: The Best Of* album, released in '00.

Chasing Rainbows (single – Shed Seven)

Charted: Nov '96; UK Chart Position: 17; Label: Polydor; Album: *Let it Ride*

'Chasing Rainbows' was the first single to be released from Shed Seven's third album *Let It Ride*, and the band's fourth top 20 single, spending nine weeks on the chart and peaking at number 17. Released at what could be argued as the height of the band's prowess, this single found them at their most anthemic yet introspective, the lyric a simple but poignant ode to high expectations grounded by realism. The CD single included B-sides 'In Command' and 'The Skin I'm In', and the cover artwork featured a man waiting for his date outside a bingo hall holding a bunch of flowers.

With no releases in '97, this would be the last release from the band for more than a year. At first it seemed it might be a stand-alone single, in the vein of Cast's 'Flying' or The Bluetones' 'Marblehead Johnson', but its eventual addition to the band's third album negated this. By the time the band returned, the music scene had shifted and Britpop was over.

Chemical Brothers, The (dance duo)

This electronic music duo are not strictly Britpop, but the Chemical Brothers are associated with the era in many ways, most notably for collaborating with Noel Gallagher on number one single 'Setting Sun', and also for featuring on the bill at Britpop's biggest gig, supporting Oasis at Knebworth in August '96.

Ed Simons and Tom Rowlands were childhood classmates and both went to the University of Manchester. They started DJing under the name the Dust Brothers and remixing tracks for the likes of Leftfield and Republica, before eventually producing their own tracks, most notably, 'Chemical Beats', which was released on EP *Fourteenth Century Sky* in January '94.

Towards the end of '94, the Dust Brothers became resident DJs at the Albany pub on Great Portland Street, frequented by Noel Gallagher, Paul Weller and Tim Burgess. Before long they were remixing tracks for the Manic Street Preachers, The Charlatans and Primal Scream and, shortly after, Noel Gallagher is said to have asked them to remix a track he had written, but then changed his mind. The following year, as they embarked on an international tour with Orbital and Underworld, the original Dust Brothers – an American-based duo known for their heavy sampling – threatened legal action and Simons and Rowlands decided to change their name to the Chemical Brothers after their single 'Chemical Beats'.

After the release of debut album *Exit Planet Dust* the duo signed to Virgin Records and asked Tim Burgess to be guest vocalist on their next single 'Life is Sweet' – the first example of a Britpop-style vocal against a backdrop of big beats. It reached number 25 in September '95, paving the way for other dance groups such as the Prodigy. The release caught the attention of Noel Gallagher, who asked to feature on a future song in the same way as Burgess. Shortly after, the duo sent Gallagher a tape of a track they had been working on called 'Setting Sun'. The recording of Noel's vocals took him just fifteen minutes, and he is said to have kept the taxi running on the meter outside the studio. After recording his second collaboration with the band, 'Let Forever Be' in '99, Noel apparently said that his work with the Chemicals was some of the best he had done.

The band went on to become one of the most successful British dance groups of all time, with six of their seven studio albums reaching number one in the UK chart, and two of their singles also hitting the top spot.

Chemical World (single – Blur)

Charted: Jul '93; UK Chart Position: 28; Label: Food; Album: *Modern Life is Rubbish*

'Chemical World' was the second single to be released from Blur's second album *Modern Life is Rubbish* and features one of Graham Coxon's greatest guitar melodies. Sitting comfortably inside the top 40, where it peaked at number 28, the single spent four weeks on the UK chart.

It was released as two CDs. CD1 featured live tracks 'Never Clever', 'Pressure On Julian' and 'Come Together', taken from the band's Glastonbury Festival performance in '92. CD2 included B-sides 'Young and Lovely', 'Es Schmect' and 'My Ark'. The video features the band hanging out in a field surrounded by woodland, animals and snails.

The release, coupled with previous single 'For Tomorrow', confirmed the band's new direction, toward what would become known as the Britpop sound, and was most distinctive for songwriter Damon Albarn's storytelling lyric, voyeuristically peering at the world around him. Little did the band know that the stage was set for so much to come.

Cigarettes & Alcohol (single - Oasis)

Charted: Oct '94; UK Chart Position: 7; Label: Creation; Album: *Definitely Maybe*

'Cigarettes & Alcohol' was the fourth single to be released from Oasis' debut album *Definitely Maybe* and their most successful single to date, giving the band their second top-ten hit, and spending a total of 79 weeks on the UK singles chart.

The track exposed a rougher sound for the band, with the chugging guitar riff very similar to T-Rex's 'Get It On'. Songsmith Noel Gallagher later claimed that this song, along with 'Live Forever', summed up all he was trying to say through his songs. The main refrain of the lyric was: "Is it my imagination, or have I finally found something worth living for? It's a crazy situation, but all I need are cigarettes and alcohol."

The CD single featured a live cover of the Beatles' 'I am the Walrus', taken from their Glasgow Cathouse gig in June '94, a favourite set closer for the band that nailed their influences firmly to the mast. The B-sides 'Listen Up' and 'Fade Away' were also included, while the black and white video – oozing attitude – flits between the band playing on stage and them hanging out in a toilet smoking and drinking.

Anecdotally, the line in the song, "You might as well do the white line", a reference to drug-taking, was slipped past the censors when singer Liam Gallagher claimed he was actually singing, "You might as well do the white lime".

Circle, The (single - Ocean Colour Scene)

Charted: Sept '96; UK Chart Position: 6; Label: MCA; Album: *Moseley Shoals*

The fourth and final single released from breakthrough album *Moseley Shoals*, 'The Circle' is a gentle, lilting song that sings of endless Saturday afternoons where the "sunshine pours like wine", spearheaded by an immediately identifiable Steve Craddock guitar line. It peaked at number six at the end of a long hot summer in September '96, and spent a total of ten weeks on the chart.

The song also appeared in acoustic format on the band's *B-sides, Seasides and Freerides* album, released in March '97. The B-sides to the CD format release were 'Mrs Jones', 'Cool Cool Water' and 'Top of the World'.

Closed for Business (single – Mansun)

Charted: Oct '97; UK Chart Position: 10; Label: Parlophone; Album: n/a

'Closed for Business' was released as the lead song on the *Seven* EP, between Mansun's debut album *Attack of the Grey Lantern* and follow up *Six*. Entering the UK chart towards the end of '97, it was the band's second top-ten hit as well as their final Britpop-era single, spending three weeks on the chart.

The CD single was released as two versions: CD1 including B-sides 'K.I.Double.S.I.N.G', 'Everyone Must Win' and 'The World's Still Open'; and CD2 featuring two songs from debut album *Attack Of The Grey Lantern*, an acoustic version of 'Dark Mavis' and a live recording of 'Stripper Vicar'.

A multimedia section was also included, with four Mansun trailers and the video for previous single 'Taxloss'. The video, shot in black and white, features what appears to be an alien wandering through a small town, in which the shops are, fittingly, closed for business.

Cocker, Jarvis (singer/songwriter/guitarist – Pulp/solo artist)

Also known for the infamous 'mooning' moment, where he invaded the stage in protest at Michael Jackson's 'Earth Song' performance at the '96 Brit Awards, Jarvis Branson Cocker is more commonly known as the lead singer and frontman of key Britpop band Pulp.

Cocker's trademark 'geek-chic', complete with NHS-style glasses and tweed jackets, helped to define the term, and his presence helped to balance Britpop, counteracting the brooding masculinity embodied by Liam Gallagher with a quieter, more introspective intelligence. His bold and sincere lyrics told stories of working-class life in the north of England, of good times and bad times, of growing up in an environment he often felt trapped by and alienated from and, later, of the excesses of his much-yearned-for success and the dark, drink and drug-fuelled times so prevalent in the last days of Britpop.

He was as much at home writing anthems about collective experiences with universal themes, such as 'Miss-shapes' and 'Sorted for E's and Whizz', as he was penning thoughtful ballads about personal issues, such as the pained relationship he had with his father in 'A Little Soul', or meeting his future partner in 'Something Changed'. His songs, always written with distinctive wit, showcase his talent for writing for and about 'the people'.

Born in September '63 in Sheffield, Cocker founded the band Arabacus Pulp in '78. The name was inspired by a tradable commodity he discovered in economics class at the City School, aged just 15. Initially shy as a child, he thought forming a band might help him mix with people. His mother played an important part in his life, especially after his father left when he was just seven, and when his friends went off to university, she supported his decision to stay behind and focus on making music.

The band signed to Fire Records in '85, but suffered a major setback when Cocker fell out of a window trying to impress a girl with a Spiderman impression.

After several line-up changes and different record companies, the band finally found fame in the mid-nineties. By the time of the infamous Brit Awards incident, Pulp had released two successful albums and, despite a mixed response to the 'mooning', *Melody Maker* suggested Cocker should be knighted and Noel Gallagher said that he should receive an MBE.

In the late nineties, Cocker dated actress Chloe Sevigny before eventually marrying French fashion stylist Camille Bidault-Waddington. They lived with son Albert in Paris from '03 until their eventual split in '09.

Cocker's debut solo album *Jarvis* was released in '06, hitting the UK chart at number 37. His second solo album, *Further Complications*, followed in '09, performing better and reaching number 19. He was also involved in various musical and broadcasting side projects, most notably a brief appearance in *Harry Potter and the Goblet of Fire* as lead singer of the Weird Sisters, and taking over the Sunday afternoon slot on BBC Radio 6 Music in '10 with *Jarvis Cocker's Sunday Service*.

Collins, Edwyn (singer/songwriter/solo artist)

Edwyn Collins, Scottish musician, producer and Ivor Novello Award winner, is most commonly known for the hit single 'A Girl Like You' which, while not strictly Britpop, was played at many indie club nights across the country, due in part to its timely June '95 release. The single was a huge success for Collins, reaching number four, enjoying chart success worldwide and featuring on the soundtrack to the '95 film *Empire Records*.

Collins initially formed band Orange Juice in '79, and their single 'Rip it Up' made the top ten in the UK chart. In the mid-eighties, he began a solo career and signed with Creation Records' subsidiary Elevation. Later, he signed with Setanta, through which he released his biggest solo record *Gorgeous George*, which reached number eight in the UK album chart in July '95, after the success of 'A Girl Like You'. Its September '97 follow-up *I'm Not Following You* didn't fare as well, reaching number 55.

Collins parted ways with Setanta after '02's *Doctor Syntax*, signing with indie favourites Heavenly Records, through which he released two further solo records, '07's *Home Again* and '10's *Losing Sleep*, neither of which managed to live up to the success of his earlier work.

In '09, he received the Ivor Inspiration Award from the Ivor Novello Foundation after recovering from a devastating brain haemorrhage that struck in '05. In addition to his musical career, Collins has also produced and starred in his own Channel 4 TV series called *West Heath Yard* and released a book of illustrations in '09.

Come Back Brighter (single – Reef)

Charted: Jan '97; UK Chart Position: 8; Label: Song S2; Album: *Glow*

'Come Back Brighter' was the second single to be released from Reef's second studio album *Glow*, and gave the band their second top-ten single in the chart (after 'Place Your Hands'), where it spent eight weeks.

The single was released as two CDs, the first containing B-sides 'Resignation', 'It's Not What I Need' and 'Hawaiian Tooth', and the second featuring the tracks 'Back Into Line', a demo of 'Dom And Gary' and a version of 'Robot Part'. The video features the band playing on the moon, picking up the American flag and hurling it towards Earth.

Coming Up (album – Suede)

Charted: Sept '96; UK Chart Position: 1; Label: Nude; Singles: 'Trash' (Jul '96, UKCP 3), 'Beautiful Ones' (Oct '96, 8), 'Saturday Night' (Jan '97, 6), 'Lazy' (Apr '97, 9), 'Filmstar' (Aug '97, 9)

With visionary guitarist Bernard Butler gone, and his replacement a teenage former fan of the band, Richard Oakes, Suede's third studio album was never going to be an easy sell. When it finally appeared in September '96 though, the aptly named *Coming Up* became their most successful by far, propelling them to worldwide recognition. It contained some of Suede's most-loved songs, including the singles 'Beautiful Ones', 'Trash', 'Saturday Night', 'Lazy' and 'Filmstar', all of which reached the top ten. The album hit the top spot in its first week of release and spent a total of 49 weeks on the chart. It was also nominated for the '97 Mercury Music Prize.

Singer and chief songwriter Brett Anderson wanted to ensure this album was the complete opposite of previous record *Dog Man Star*, both in sound and commercial success and, since Anderson et al had been listening to a lot of sixties pop, the result was very Britpop and, unlike *Dog Man Star*, was actually recorded in the same studio at the same time, largely due to the additional songwriting contribution of new guitarist Richard Oakes.

Butler's ingenuity and experimentation made him a lead guitarist to admire, but his replacement's subtle arpeggios added an important accompaniment to the power of Anderson's developing songwriting. Most of the radio-friendly, pop-focused songs, led by album opener and key Suede anthem 'Trash', show a band not afraid to throw off the shackles of their former melancholia and let their audience know they are out to have a good time. The catchy choruses tell modern-day stories of sex, parties and drugs, and what it was like to be young in the nineties. There are still signs of what the band once were, however, particularly on third single 'Saturday Night', a quiet and tender love song that still manages to anchor the band to weekend parties with the line, "Oh whatever makes her happy, on a Saturday night".

Also accompanied by a keyboardist for the first time (Anderson's cousin Neil Codling), Suede 2.0 recorded *Coming Up* with Pulp producer Ed Buller in early '96, after nearly two years on the road. As well as being nominated for the '97 Mercury Prize, the album secured Suede's position as one of the most important British groups of the nineties and in the Britpop movement.

Common People (single – Pulp)

Charted: Jun '95; UK Chart Position: 2; Label: Island; Album: *Different Class*

The first single from career-defining fifth album *Different Class*, 'Common People' was Pulp's biggest release to date, and alongside 'Wonderwall' and 'Parklife' it quickly became one of the most important songs of the era.

Released in June '95 on Island Records, the single reached number two, where it was kept from the top spot – just like *Wonderwall* would be five months later – by Simon Cowell's novelty act Robson and Jerome. It went on to spend 14 weeks on the chart, making it Pulp's longest charting single.

Its story of working-class life in contemporary Britain was told from the point of view of Cocker as a young St Martin's College student, who attempts to educate a rich female Greek student in how to 'slum it'. Being a common person, it seems, is not all it's cracked up to be and Cocker rambles on about how difficult life is for the lower classes, the result being that she will never truly be able to understand because she can always run back to "daddy, who'll stop it".

It's a song about Britain's distinctive class divide, a divide between rich and poor that cannot be crossed.

The single was available to purchase on two CD formats, one 'daytime' version that featured B-side 'Underwear', and a 'nighttime' style with acoustic versions of 'Razzmatazz', 'Dogs are Everywhere' and 'Joyriders'.

Connection (single – Elastica)

Charted: Oct '94; UK Chart Position: 17; Label: Deceptive; Album: *Elastica*

Elastica's hook-driven single 'Connection' quickly became their most well known. Released in October '94 on Deceptive Records, it peaked at number 17 in the chart, where it spent five weeks in total. The album version was released on their debut *Elastica* the following year and also featured as the theme tune to *Trigger Happy TV*, a practical joke reality TV series on Channel 4.

Elastica's third single was their second to make the top 20, and very quickly marked its territory as a key anthem of the Britpop movement, remembered for its signature riff and running time of just 2 minutes and 21 seconds. It cemented the band's reputation as one to watch and paved the way for their eponymous number one album in '95. The single was accused of sounding too similar to The Wire's 'Three Girl Rhumba' and the matter was settled out of court.

The CD single included B-sides 'See That Animal', co-written by Suede's Brett Anderson, 'Blue', written by Elastica's lead guitarist Donna Matthews, who is featured alone on the single's cover, and 'Spastica'.

Consideration (single – Reef)

Charted: Apr '97; UK Chart Position: 13; Label: Sony S2; Album: *Glow*

'Consideration' was the third single to be released from Reef's second studio album *Glow*, and the band's fifth top-20 single in the UK chart, where it spent eight weeks. Totally at odds with the rest of the band's output, and as such nearly unrecognisable as Reef, 'Consideration' was a tender and tuneful ballad that saw lead singer Gary Stringer's typically gruff voice firmly in its falsetto.

The CD single was released as two versions. The first featured 'Allotment', 'New Thinking' and a radio edit of the lead track. The second contained B-sides 'Claypits' and live recordings of 'Higher Vibration' and 'Come Back Brighter', both taken from Dave Mason's Liverpool radio show.

The video features the lead singer hanging from a rope net, which he lets go of at the very end after the band's instruments have fallen all around him.

Cool Britannia

It was Liam and Patsy in a bed on the front cover of *Vanity Fair*; Geri Halliwell's iconic Union Jack dress at the Brit awards in '97; Ewan McGregor hurtling down Princes Street; Liz Hurley in 'that dress!'; Damien Hirst, Alexander McQueen, Tony Blair and *Loaded* magazine. For a brief time between '95 and '97, Britain was a cool place to be. Some thirty years after Carnaby Street had been swung by the Stones, the Beatles and the 'Summer of Love', Britain was back.

It was fuelled by the music, but that was only part of it. Britain was booming and the attention was well earned. Tony Blair knew how to play the game, and in this pre-9/11 era, it became very easy to believe the hype. Noel Gallagher went for tea at number 10, Danny Boyle urged us to "choose life" and even the English football team found themselves in the semi-finals of Euro '96.

The fact that they lost to Germany on penalties reminded us that this wasn't '66 all over again, and that the good times could only last for so long. Within ten years, Tony Blair would divide the people of Britain by sending the country to war in Iraq, the destruction of the twin towers would show the West that it wasn't invincible, Gazza would have an alcohol-fuelled nervous breakdown and, once again, Britannia would no longer be considered cool. Here's to the next thirty years!

Coombes, Gaz (singer/guitarist/songwriter – Supergrass/solo artist)

Massive sideburns aside, Gareth Michael "Gaz" Coombes is best known as the lead guitarist and vocalist of Oxford band Supergrass. Born in March '76 in England's most studious of cities to mother Eileen, an English teacher, and father John, a food scientist, Coombes initially played classical piano before moving on to guitar.

He met future bandmate Danny Goffey in the school playground, where the more senior Goffey accused the infant Coombes of stealing his best Top Trumps. They formed their first band, The Jennifers, not long after, while both were still in their teens, along with Nic, Danny's brother and guitarist, and bassist Andy Davies. They landed a contract with Nude Records (who also signed Suede) in '93, but quickly disbanded after releasing their only single, 'Just Got Back Today'.

Coombes and Goffey went on to form Supergrass with bassist Mike Quinn, who Gaz met when the pair both worked in the local Harvester steakhouse. Their debut album *I Should Coco* was released during the peak of Britpop, the summer of '95, giving them a sharp rise to fame. Coombes continued with Supergrass until '10, when the band acrimoniously split.

Having learnt from the mistakes of previous rock/pop icons such as The Monkees' Mike Nesmith, who was plagued by his bubble-gum-pop alter-ego ever after, Coombes was keen to be taken seriously and, in '96, not long before the release of Supergrass' second album *In it for the Money*, he shaved off his famous indie-locks and sported a crew-cut instead. The concurrent change in sound between albums one and two for the band was notable.

Shortly after Supergrass split, Coombes and Goffey released album *Turn Ons* in '10, under their side-project cover band The Hotrats (initially the Diamond Hoo Ha Men). The album includes covers of tracks by The Kinks, the Sex Pistols and the Beatles (their version of 'Drive My Car' featured on an advert for the mobile phone company Orange).

Finally, Coombes got down to business with his solo career, releasing his debut album *Here Come the Bombs* in '12, followed by *Matador* in early '15.

Cornershop (band)

Britpop and Indian music came together when brothers Tjinder and Avtar Singh formed Cornershop. The former was singer, guitarist and songwriter, the latter bassist, alongside drummer David Chambers and Ben Ayres on guitar, keyboards and tamboura.

Though serious about their art, the band were tongue-in-cheek when it came to their subject matter and much was made of their humorous choice of stereotypical Asian references, including their name and their debut album *In the Days of Ford Cortina*, released in '93, which was pressed on curry-coloured vinyl.

Several releases later, the band finally found some short-lived commercial success after Norman Cook, aka Fatboy Slim, remixed their '97 single 'Brimful of Asha'. The single, which had failed to dent the top 40 in its original incarnation, made its way to number one. The band's '02 album, *Handcream for a Generation*, featured sometime mentor Noel Gallagher on guitar.

Country House (single – Blur)

Charted: Aug '95; UK Chart Position: 1; Label: Food; Album: *The Great Escape*

"So, the story begins..."

Blur's 'Country House' was the lead single from the band's fourth album *The Great Escape*, and one of the biggest songs of the era. It was the band's first of two number one singles, and spent 14 weeks on the chart.

The band's label, Food Records, changed the single's release date to coincide with Oasis' 'Roll with it', and its success is partly due to the two bands battling it out for the number one position. Behind the boisterous pomp and vigour, however, there actually sits an intelligent musing on class, money and taste by chief songwriter Damon Albarn. The video, directed by Cool Britannia figurehead Damien Hirst, included actors Keith Allen and (future *Little Britain* star) Matt Lucas, as well as page three girl and model Jo Guest and the band playing a board game called "Escape from the rat race".

With its big brass section and 'Alright guvnor' Cockney style, the song is unmistakably Britpop and can usually be quoted word for word by anyone who grew up in the era. The lyric follows the story of an unnamed 'city dweller' (later revealed to be Food Records cofounder David Balfe), who decides to leave behind the rat race to live in his "very big house in the country".

There were two versions of the CD single. CD1 featured B-sides 'One Born Every Minute' and 'To the End', while CD2 included live recordings of the lead single, 'Girls & Boys', 'Parklife' and 'For Tomorrow' taken from their Mile End Stadium gig in June '95.

Coxon, Graham (guitarist/singer/songwriter – Blur/solo artist)

Graham Coxon is best known as the spectacled lead guitarist in one of Britpop's biggest bands, Blur. His defining riffs and solos are arguably the most creative melodies not just in Britpop, but in British pop history. From the shoegazing days of 'There's no Other Way' to the early Britpop sounds of 'Chemical World', post-Britpop's 'Tender', solo effort 'Freakin' Out', the luscious 'You're So Great' and beyond, there is little doubt that Coxon is one of British music's most important guitarists.

Born in March '69 in Rinteln, Germany, where his father was stationed as an army band leader, Coxon and his family eventually moved to Derby then Colchester, Essex, where he met future Blur bandmate Damon Albarn at the Stanway School. Coxon enrolled at Goldsmiths to study art while Albarn went to drama college, but their musical connection remained. Eventually, Coxon left his degree half way through to pursue a career in music, but his artistic roots didn't leave him and he designed the artwork for all his solo albums as well as Blur's *13*.

His shy, quirky demeanour and reluctant popstar image seemed to work well alongside Albarn's cocky exterior until a dispute in '02 culminated in Coxon being fired from the band. During the recording of the band's seventh album *Think Tank*, he checked himself into the Priory to tackle his alcohol addiction. The timing clashed with Albarn's sabbatical from side-project Gorillaz and the pair fell out.

Having already recorded three solo albums while still with Blur, Coxon went on to record another three and release a single with Paul Weller called 'This Old Town'. At the end of '08, Coxon and Albarn rekindled their brotherly relationship and the reunion culminated in a series of live dates with Blur.

Coxon continued to record solo albums and was also involved in the creation of Pete Doherty's '09 solo album *Grace / Wastelands*, producing and playing guitar on every track. Coxon has two daughters, Dorelia, with current partner Essy Syed, and Pepper, from a previous relationship, and lives in a London town house in Camden.

Cranberries, The (band)

Ireland's The Cranberries are often left out of British musical history due to their phenomenal success on the other side of the pond, but their distinctive Gaelic rock sound means a special place is reserved for them in the Britpop pantheon.

Formed in Limerick in '89 by brothers Mike and Noel Hogan (bass and guitar respectively) with drummer Fergal Lawler, it was not until original singer Niall Quinn was replaced by Dolores O'Riordan in the early nineties that the band found their distinctive sound. It is O'Riordan's folky Irish twang that makes the band so memorable, and it was not long after her arrival that they found huge commercial success with debut album *Everyone Else Is Doing It, So Why Can't We?*, released in '93, and peaking at number one in the UK chart.

Subsequent albums *No Need To Argue* (which spent a whopping 124 weeks on the chart) and *To The Faithful Departed* found their way into the top ten on both sides of the Atlantic during the Britpop years, and were a mix of heavy rock guitars and tender acoustic ballads. As the band's sound developed, so did O'Riordan's lyrical skill and, on *No Need To Argue* in particular, she began to include the political as well as the personal.

Many of the band's most famous singles, such as 'Zombie', 'Linger' and 'Salvation' made their way into the UK top 40, and featured on numerous Britpop compilations. Like Nirvana and Oasis, the band were also one of the few acts asked to do a famous *MTV Unplugged* session. After releasing a further two albums after the Britpop period was over, the band split in the early noughties, only to re-form in '09 and release a sixth studio album in '12.

Creation Records (record label)

Creation Records was probably the most famous label of the Britpop era, and the one most synonymous with the movement. It was founded by Scot Alan McGee, Dick Green and Joe Foster in '83. The label's earliest signings included the Jesus and Mary Chain, Primal Scream, My Bloody Valentine and Ride, though it was McGee's discovery of Oasis at King Tut's Wah Wah Hut in Glasgow in '93 that gave Creation unprecedented success for an independent label.

In '83, the newly-founded label released its first single, by The Legend, after McGee took out a £1,000 loan and, a year later, had its first commercial success with the Jesus and Mary Chain's 'Upside Down'. However, it wasn't until '90 that things really heated up for the label, when both Primal Scream and Ride produced top 40 singles, and Ride's debut album *Nowhere* made the top 20. After this, the label went from strength to strength and, in '91, Primal Scream released the indie-dance crossover hit *Screamadelica*, Teenage Fanclub put out *Bandwagonesque* and My Bloody Valentine released the classic *Loveless*. In '92 Ride's single 'Leave Them All Behind', made the top ten and Primal Scream headlined Glastonbury Festival, as well as winning the Mercury Music Prize for *Screamadelica*. That same year McGee sold Sony almost half the shares in the label to gain access to worldwide distribution.

Creation, and in particular McGee, were the only label able to manage the notoriously difficult Kevin Shields from My Bloody Valentine, who nearly bankrupted them several times over with huge studio costs that yielded no releasable results. Years later, Rough Trade called on McGee to help control the new wild children of British indie-rock, The Libertines. In '93, Creation signed Oasis and, over the next few years, the band brought the label much success, firstly when their debut album *Definitely Maybe* went straight to number one in the UK chart, and then when its follow up *(What's the Story) Morning Glory?* became the third biggest-selling UK album ever.

As well as Oasis' success, the Boo Radleys secured a top-ten hit with 'Wake Up Boo!', and McGee signed Welsh band Super Furry Animals, who released five albums and numerous singles, all to much critical and commercial acclaim. McGee would refer to the Super Furries as the last great Creation band, anchoring the label to the Britpop period even further. In '99, Alan McGee left Creation Records. A year later, Primal Scream were the last band to release a single and album on the label.

Cut Some Rug/Castle Rock (single – The Bluetones)

Charted: May '96; UK Chart Position: 7; Label: Superior Quality; Album: *Expecting to Fly*

'Cut Some Rug' was the third and final single to be released from The Bluetones' debut album, *Expecting to Fly*, and also included the track 'Castle Rock', which didn't feature on the album. Reaching number seven in May '96, it became the band's second top-ten hit, following 'Slight Return', and spent nine weeks on the chart. Like so many of their contemporaries, the band found themselves going through the Britpop rite of passage that was playing live on Chris Evans' nineties magazine show *TFI Friday*.

The CD single featured B-side 'The Devil Behind My Smile', while the Japanese version included a bonus track, 'No. 11'. The video showed the band playing in the cramped back room of a laundrette, watching a man get into a washing machine with his clothes (and the inevitable chaos that follows).

D

D'You Know What I Mean (single – Oasis)

Charted: Jul '97; UK Chart Position: 1; Label: Creation; Album: *Be Here Now*

By the time Oasis' eagerly anticipated 10th single was released, it had been 15 months since fans had heard any new music. In that time, the band had played Loch Lomond and Knebworth, ended their biggest tour of America prematurely after a much-publicised Gallagher brothers' falling-out, and had more headlines written about them than anyone else.

There was little surprise then that the first single from third album *Be Here Now* went straight to number one on its release in July '97, spending 25 weeks on the chart.

As was becoming a classic Oasis trademark by this time, the B-sides were just as strong as the A-side, with track two 'Stay Young' (an ode to not growing older) vying for position as the A-side. The ballad 'Angel Child' saw Noel take the lead vocal, as he did on a cover of David Bowie's 'Heroes'. The video saw the band stepping off a helicopter to perform in what appears to be a post-apocalyptic world.

Dark Clouds (single – Space)

Charted: Feb '97; UK Chart Position: 14; Label: Gut; Album: *Spiders*

'Dark Clouds' was the fifth and final single released from Space's debut album *Spiders*. It was the band's fourth consecutive top-20 hit, spending eight weeks on the UK chart. The video features the band playing their instruments on a green platform floating through the sky.

There were two CD versions of the single; CD1 featuring an alternative version of the lead track, plus B-sides 'Storm Clouds' and 'Darker Clouds', and CD2 B-sides 'Children of the Night', 'Influenza' and 'Had Enough'.

Dark Therapy (single - Echobelly)

Charted: Sept '95; UK Chart Position: 20; Label: Fauve; Album: *On*

'Dark Therapy' was Echobelly's sole chart entry in '96, and the third and final single to be released from second album *On*. The song was completely different in style to the previous two uplifting singles, being much darker and more thought-provoking. It was the band's second and final top-20 release, and spent a total of three weeks on the chart.

The video was extremely poignant, featuring a close-up of lead singer Sonya Madan singing and occasionally crying against a black background.

The CD format, which had a frightening looking puppet on the cover, featured B-sides 'We Know Better', 'Atom' and 'Aloha Lolita'.

Day We Caught The Train, The (single - Ocean Colour Scene)

Charted: Jun '96; UK Chart Position: 4; Label: MCA; Album: *Moseley Shoals*

Britpop classic 'The Day We Caught The Train', the third single from Ocean Colour Scene's second album *Moseley Shoals*, was their biggest hit and quickly became their most well-known song. After extensive airplay, the summer anthem peaked in June '96 at number four in the UK chart, where it spent a total of 11 weeks, launching the group into a string of top-ten singles and beginning an extensive commercially successful period for the band.

The CD single included B-sides 'The Clock Struck 15 Hours Ago', 'I Need a Love Song' and 'Chicken Bones and Stones'.

Daydreamer (single - Menswear)

Charted: Jul '95; UK Chart Position: 14; Label: Laurel; Album: *Nuisance*

'Daydreamer' was Menswear's second single and still remains one of the era's most identifiable songs, launching the band into the top 20 of the UK singles chart, where it spent four weeks. Sounding like a cross between Blur and Elastica, the single was criticised for being too similar to Elastica's single 'Line Up', which itself was said to be too close for comfort to seventies English rock band Wire's 'I am the Fly'. Despite this, it was the band's first big hit and the one they are ultimately remembered for.

Taken from their sole album *Nuisance*, the single was the second of five singles. The CD format included B-sides 'Gentleman Jim' and a live version of album track 'Around You Again'. The limited edition EP version included extra tracks 'I'll Manage Somehow', 'Second Hand' and a remix of the lead track.

Definitely Maybe (album - Oasis)

Charted: Aug '94; UK Chart Position: 1; Label: Creation; Singles: 'Supersonic' (Apr '94, UKCP 31), 'Shakermaker' (Jun '94, 11), 'Live Forever' (Aug '94, 10), 'Cigarettes & Alcohol' (Oct '94, 7)

The debut LP by Oasis, *Definitely Maybe* was Britpop's first huge album. It is still thought of not only as one of the best debut albums of all time, but also one of the best albums of all time.

Liam Gallagher's raw, untarnished vocals slice through each song with belief and unrivalled passion, melding perfectly with older brother Noel's wall-of-sound layered guitars and classic songwriting that marries the measured skill of John Lennon with the nihilism of Johnny Rotten. Whether it's the guttural, in-your-face chant of album opener 'Rock 'n Roll Star', the anthemic melancholia of 'Slide Away' or the acoustic irony-laden 'Married with Children', this album has it all. It's hard to believe, even with 20 years' hindsight, that this was a debut LP.

It was no surprise that the album, released in August '94, found immediate success, heading straight to number one and becoming the fastest selling debut of all time.

The recording of the album, in contrast, was initially unsuccessful. Oasis worked with producer Dave Batchelor at Monnow Valley Studio near Monmouth, but the sessions were not up to scratch and the band were disappointed when they heard them back. The album was re-recorded at Sawmills Studio in Cornwall with a new producer, Mark Coyle, but the results were still unsatisfactory, leaving the band incredibly frustrated, knowing they had racked up a pile of studio expenses and still had to stick to the recordings they had. Luckily, Creation's Marcus Russell reached out to Owen Morris, a Welsh producer with an engineering background, who miraculously managed to turn the existing recordings into something positive. Basically, he saved the album.

Years later, Morris, who also co-helmed the mixing desk for Oasis' second and third albums, claimed to have done very little actual producing on the record, instead simply guiding the band's creative lead Noel Gallagher, who provided the key vision and decided on the trademark moments, like the layers of guitars, reminiscent of sixties producer Phil Spector's wall-of-sound approach to recording.

To follow up such an incredible debut should have been the toughest case of 'second album syndrome' ever. Difficult for most bands, but not for Oasis.

Denim (band)

Birmingham band Denim were formed from the ashes of Lawrence Hayward's eighties post-punk band Felt in '92.

While debut album *Back in Denim* captured a post-glam rock sound, it was follow-up album *Denim on Ice*, released in '96, that got caught in the Britpop net, largely due to key tracks 'Council Houses', 'Job Centre' and 'The Great Pub Rock Revival', each packed with lyrics detailing British working-class culture.

Similar in style lyrically to Jarvis Cocker, the band supported Pulp on tour, though they did not achieve any UK chart success. Their final release was compilation album *Novelty Rock* in '97, featuring a string of B-sides and new material.

Design for Life, A (single – Manic Street Preachers)

Charted: Apr '96; UK Chart Position: 2; Label: Epic; Album: *Everything Must Go*

'A Design for Life' is Welsh band the Manic Street Preachers' most famous song, and the one that marked a notable change in fortune for the band. It was the first single taken from the band's fourth studio album *Everything Must Go* and was released in April '96, peaking at number two and spending a total of seven weeks on the UK singles chart.

The first song the band released after the disappearance of guitarist Richey Edwards, the single signalled a key turning point for a band that were previously renowned for their bleak, anti-establishment outlook. Influenced by the changing times, Oasis were also partly responsible both for the marked change in direction and for their burgeoning success. Noel Gallagher was a fan and gave them a support slot on his band's '95 tour, which brought them to a whole new audience.

The lyrics, the first to be written exclusively by bassist Nicky Wire, explored themes of working-class pride and class conflict. At the '09 opening of Cardiff Central Library in Wales, the band unveiled a plaque inscribed with the first line of the song, "Libraries gave us power".

Two CD versions of the single were released. CD1 included B-sides 'Mr Carbohydrate', 'Dead Passive' and 'Dead Trees and Traffic Islands'. CD2 contained two orchestral versions of the lead track and a vocal mix of the song 'Faster'.

Different Class (album – Pulp)

Charted: Oct '95; UK Chart Position: 1; Label: Island; Singles: 'Common People' (May '95, UKCP 2), 'Sorted for E's and Whizz/Misshapes' (Sept '95, 2), 'Disco 2000' (Nov '95, 7), 'Something Changed' (Mar '96, 10)

Pulp's fifth studio album was a gigantic success partly because it was released at the height of Britpop in October '95, but mostly because it contained a string of the band's best and most memorable signature singles: 'Disco 2000', 'Something Changed', Sorted for E's and Whizz', 'Mis-Shapes' and, of course, 'Common People'. The album went to number one in the UK chart, won the '96 Mercury Music Prize and announced Pulp as one of the most important bands of the Britpop era.

Released through Island Records, it was the band's second major label release after their breakthrough *His 'n' Hers* the previous year, marking a change in fortunes that aligned with the confidence of chief songwriter Jarvis Cocker's more commercially-focused output.

The album title not only refers to the British class system, but also to the band being in a class of their own – a statement that could be perceived as arrogant had it not come from the mind of Cocker, whose songwriting always managed to remain objective. The key message, "We don't want no trouble, we just want the right to be different. That's all", is emblazoned on the back of the album. This clearly struck a chord with many youngsters the length and breadth of the British Isles and gave the awkward alternative scenester a new cult hero.

The cover artwork is a photograph of a real wedding, with added lifesize cut-outs of the band. It came about when a photographer working on the Pulp album was asked by a friend to photograph his brother's wedding. Pulp wanted real people, preferably at a wedding, on their cover. It was almost like it was fate.

Despite his growing reputation for the quality of his lyrics, Cocker cheekily begs on the album sleeve that listeners not read along with the printed song lyrics while listening to the music, causing consternation among many teenage fans torn between wallowing in his words and slavishly following his instructions.

Disco 2000 (single – Pulp)

Charted: Dec '95; UK Chart Position: 7; Label: Island; Album: *Different Class*

After 'Common People', Pulp's most memorable song is 'Disco 2000', the third single to be released from career-defining album *Different Class* in December '95. It was the band's third single to reach the top ten, and spent 14 weeks on the chart. The two versions of the CD single both featured various mixes of the lead track. Version one also featured 'Ansaphone' and 'Live Bed Show'.

It tells the (presumably) imagined story of the song's protagonist and his lifelong friend Deborah ("it never suited yer"). The pair were born on the same day and their mothers joked that one day they would grow up and get married. But they didn't. Instead the 'I' of the story was forced to watch from the sidelines as Deborah became the popular girl at school, fancied by all the boys. The song is, therefore, the confession of a typical adolescent, struggling to come of age in mid-nineties Britain, where the millennium still felt like science-fiction.

Here's a bit of Britpop trivia for you: the lyric about the couple meeting when they're older "by the Fountain down the road", is not referring to a water fountain, but a Mile End pub frequented by Jarvis and co.

Divine Comedy, The (band)

Irish band the Divine Comedy have undergone several line-up changes since forming in '89, with frontman Neil Hannon remaining the one consistent member. It was the album *Casanova*, released in '96, and more specifically hit single 'Something for the Weekend', that propelled them into the Britpop furore. The band released a total of six albums on label Setanta between '90 and '98, before moving to Parlophone/EMI in '01.

Hannon named the band after the epic narrative poem (that he found on his father's bookshelf) written by 14th-century Italian writer Dante about a journey through hell, purgatory and heaven. This literary alignment became one of the band's early trademarks, reflected in the fact that 'Something for the Weekend' is a retelling of Stella Gibbons' novel *Cold Comfort Farm*.

As the band's success grew, so did their reputation for producing catchy three-minute pop singles rather than albums and, as a result, Hannon's songwriting developed too. He soon became known for his tongue-in-cheek ironic slant on life, and key singles 'The National Express', 'The Pop Singer's Fear of the Pollen Count', 'Frog Princess' and 'Becoming More Like Alfie' all looked at aspects of modern life from a position of humour and irreverence uncommon among other pop bands at the time. This allowed the Divine Comedy to carve out their own special place at a time when money could still be made from selling singles.

Hannon also showed his versatility with the fittingly poignant ballad 'Songs of Love', which went on to become the theme song (minus the lyrics) for nineties cult hit Irish sitcom *Father Ted*.

Dizzy Heights (album – The Lightning Seeds)

Charted: Nov '96; UK Chart Position: 11; Label: Epic; Singles: 'Ready or Not' (Mar '96, UKCP 20), 'What If...' (Oct '96, 14), 'Sugar Coated Iceberg' (Apr '97, 12), 'You Showed Me' (Apr '97, 8)

Dizzy Heights was the Lightning Seeds' fourth album and the band's second to reach the top 20 in the UK, after *Jollification*, and spent 31 weeks on the chart. It was recorded on a barge rented from The Who's Pete Townshend at Eel Pie Island on the River Thames near Twickenham.

The band's sole number one hit 'Three Lions' was released during work on the album, inevitably slowing down the release, but didn't feature on the album itself. The album spawned four singles: 'Ready or Not' and 'What If', which both charted in the top 20, and 'Sugar Coated Iceberg' and 'You Showed Me', which made the top ten.

The cover featured a series of coloured paper planes, with each single below a paper plane on the back.

Do It Yourself (album – The Seahorses)

Charted: Jun '97; UK Chart Position: 2; Label: Geffen; Singles: 'Love is the Law' (Apr '97, UKCP 3), 'Blinded by the Sun' (Jul '97, 7), 'Love Me and Leave Me' (Sept '97, 16)

Do It Yourself was The Seahorses' sole UK album. Released in June '97 and peaking at number two, it spent a total of 49 weeks on the chart. The album went on to achieve platinum success, mainly due to former Stone Roses prodigy John Squire, who formed the band as his next project after the spectacular implosion of the Roses.

The album resulted in two top-ten singles, 'Love is the Law' and 'Blinded by the Sun', and one top-20 single, 'Love Me and Leave Me', which Squire co-wrote with Oasis' Liam Gallagher. Recorded at Hollywood's Royaltone Studios and produced by the legendary Tony Visconti, the album's promo tour included support slots with Oasis, the Rolling Stones and U2. The cover artwork, created by John Squire, was a photograph of a globe made of jigsaw pieces.

Do You Remember the First Time? (single – Pulp)

Charted: Apr '94; UK Chart Position: 33; Label: Island; Album: *His 'n' Hers*

The third single released from breakthrough album *His 'n' Hers*, Pulp's 'Do You Remember the First Time?' marked a change in fortune for the band. It was their first single to enter the UK top 40, where it peaked at number 33 in April '94 and spent a total of eight weeks on the chart.

The single was released on CD, 7" and 12" vinyl. B-sides included 'Street Lites' and 'The Babysitter'. The song went on to find considerable success when played live by the band and remained a staple part of their sets for the rest of their career.

Dodgy (band)

Famous for their hit single 'Good Enough', Dodgy began in '88 when drummer Matthew Priest and guitarist Andy Miller moved from Worcestershire to London, where they were joined by bassist and vocalist Nigel Clarke. They made it clear early on that they were against the shoegazing and grunge movements, focussing instead on the melodic themes of the sixties, which brought them into the Britpop fold.

Debut *The Dodgy Album*, released in '93, was produced by Ian Broudie of the Lightning Seeds, but it wasn't until second album *Homegrown*, released the following year, that the band achieved any real recognition. During the recording, they shared a studio with the Stones Roses, who were recording *The Second Coming*, and it was here that Nigel Clarke famously dubbed Ian Brown 'King Monkey'.

The album peaked at number 28, but the band finally cracked the top 20 with the re-release of remixed single 'Staying out for the Summer', which gathered momentum on the radio, and the top ten with their third studio album, the more commercially driven *Free Peace Sweet*, which peaked at number seven in the spring of '96. The album was propelled by popular singles 'In a Room' and 'If You're Thinking of Me', but it was the number three hit single and summer anthem 'Good Enough' that confirmed the band's upward trajectory.

The original line-up split in the early noughties and, though a few comeback attempts were made, it wasn't until '12 that the original trio began playing together again. They have since released a further two studio albums *Stand Upright in a Cool Place* in '12 and *What Are We Fighting For* in '16.

Dog Man Star (album – Suede)

Charted: Oct '94; UK Chart Position: 3; Label: Nude; Singles: 'We are the Pigs' (Sept '94, UKCP 18), 'The Wild Ones' (Nov '94, 18), 'New Generation' (Jan '95, 21)

The follow-up to their classic eponymous debut album could have been tough for Britpop frontrunners Suede, but their rather cryptically named second album, *Dog Man Star*, reached number three in the chart, despite its much darker tones and distance from the album that made them stars. Released on Nude Records in October '94 and produced by Ed Buller, the lyrics were mostly inspired by lead singer Brett Anderson's introduction to the world of psychedelic drugs, which was reflected in the tone of the whole record.

Three singles were released: 'We are the Pigs', 'The Wild Ones' and 'New Generation'; the first coming just a month before the album, clearly stating that an album far removed from Britpop's often cheery headiness was on its way.

The darker content of the album also reflected the personal lows the band were experiencing, with guitarist Bernard Butler's father recently having passed away, and his growing alienation from Anderson and the rest of the band evident. By the time the album came out he was no longer in the line-up.

Legend has it that relations broke down to such an extent that the band finished recording the album in separate studios, sending tapes back and forth with insulting messages tagged on the end. Tensions grew from the taut relationship between the two creative leads, Anderson and Butler, a relationship which had initially given the band its individual sound.

Butler was an introspective musician, obsessed with mastering his instrument and sitting alone in hotel rooms writing songs while his bandmates partied into the night. Extrovert Anderson was the antithesis of this, with the two clashing to such an extent that Butler finally walked out. In retaliation, Anderson named Butler's favourite song and lead single for the album 'We are the Pigs'.

There's no doubt though that the fruits of this incendiary relationship were often incredible. 'We are the Pigs' is a sneery, guttural anthem for doomed youth, perfectly juxtaposing – not unlike the two creatives' relationship – the other key single, the delicate and tender love song 'The Wild Ones'. Both are now considered two of the best songs written by the band (or by either of the individual songwriters) and helped to place *Dog Man Star* as a key addition to the Britpop canon.

Don't Look Back in Anger (single – Oasis)

Charted: Mar '96; UK Chart Position: 1; Label: Creation; Album: *(What's the Story) Morning Glory?*

'Don't Look Back in Anger' was the fourth and final single released from Oasis' second album *(What's the Story) Morning Glory?* and the last new release for more than a year from Britain's biggest band. It was the first single to see songwriter Noel Gallagher take the lead vocal, with brother Liam sidelined to miming the piano chord intro (nabbed from John Lennon's 'Imagine') on the band's performance on *Top of the Pops.*

It was the band's second UK number one single after 'Some Might Say' and spent a total of 39 weeks on the chart. It also quickly became a live favourite, with Noel often leaving the audience to sing the key chorus lyric "So, Sally can wait". Who the mysterious Sally was has never been revealed, although the song was later dedicated to the Gallaghers' mother, Peggy. The pre-chorus lyric "Stand up beside the fireplace, take that look from off your face" was apparently a reference to her attempts to get her sons to stand still for a photograph.

The B-sides were every bit as strong as the A-side. 'Step Out', another Noel lead vocal, was originally intended for inclusion on *Morning Glory*, until Stevie Wonder's agents allegedly demanded 100 per cent of the royalties due to the song's resemblance to his hit single 'Uptight'; 'Underneath the Sky' was a decidedly introspective musing featuring a four-part piano solo; and Slade's 'Cum on Feel the Noize' was the band's first cover released since their version of the Beatles' 'I am the Walrus'.

The single's impressive cover artwork by Brian Cannon features the band's instruments surrounded by thousands of carnations, which were said to have been imported from Holland and almost a third of them dyed blue. The idea came from a story about Ringo Starr returning to a recording session with the Beatles after a period of illness to find his drum kit covered in flowers.

More recently, 'Don't Look Back in Anger' has been given extra poignancy after being adopted as the undisputed anthem of the day by crowds at the One Love Manchester concert in aid of victims of the Manchester Arena terrorist attack in the early summer of '17 and, later, as a response to the attacks in London and the Grenfell Tower fire. It began with a spontaneous rendition of the song in St Ann's Square in Manchester after a countrywide minute's silence.

Coldplay then played it at the One Love Manchester concert, Liam Gallagher performed an acapella version at Glastonbury in June '17 and Noel Gallagher sang it at the We Are Manchester benefit gig in September '17.

Dots and Loops (album - Stereolab)

Charted: Oct '97; UK Chart Position: 19; Label: Duophonic UHF; Singles: 'Miss Modular' (Sept '97, UKCP 60)

Dots and Loops was Stereolab's fifth album and their second to achieve top-20 status, after *Mars Audiac Quintet*, spending two weeks on the chart. Produced by Andi Toma of electronic music duo Mouse on Mars, who also contributed to several of the album's tracks, it was recorded in Chicago and Dusseldorf, embracing a complex layered sound that stands apart from the band's previous albums, which feature a motorik drone.

The album produced one single, 'Miss Modular', which reached number 60 and spent two weeks in the chart. The track 'Parsec' was used in the '98 Volkswagen Beetle launch advert, known as 'flower'. The Japanese version of the album featured bonus track 'Off-On'.

Drawn to the Deep End (album - Gene)

Charted: Mar '97; UK Chart Position: 8; Label: Polydor; Singles: 'Fighting Fit' (Nov '96, UKCP 22), 'We Could be Kings' (Feb '97, 17), 'Where are They Now?' (May '97, 22), 'Speak to me Someone' (Aug '97, 30)

Drawn to the Deep End was the second studio album from London band Gene, and the second to go straight into the top ten, spending a total of five weeks on the chart. It was also the first to be released on new label Polydor.

Containing two of the band's most popular singles, favoured live set opener 'Fighting Fit' and one of their biggest hits 'We Could Be Kings', the album formed the basis of their sell-out Royal Albert Hall concert, which featured a full orchestra. Snippets of the gig can be heard on the deluxe version of the album released in '14, which includes a bonus CD full of rarities and live performances.

The album showcased a certain musical maturity, with more prominent keyboard lines mixed in among The Smiths-style guitars, and lyrical development from frontman Martin Rossiter, who was depressed at the time, despite the band's marked success.

The album, combined with a rigorous touring schedule throughout much of '97, cemented Gene as favoured sons of the Britpop scene. However, while they found much chart success during the Britpop years, it didn't last once the scene waned. It would be almost exactly two years before follow-up album *Revelations* found its way into record stores, peaking at number 25.

Drink Me (album – Salad)

Charted: May '95; UK Chart Position: 16; Label: Island Red; Singles: 'Your Ma/Plank' (Jul '94, UKCP 82), 'Drink the Elixir' (Feb '95, 66), 'Motorbike to Heaven' (May '95, 42), 'Granite Statue' (Aug '95, 50)

Drink Me was the debut top-20 album by Salad and spent three weeks on the UK chart. It produced four singles, the first two, 'Your Ma/Plank' and 'Drink The Elixir', charting in the top ten, and containing the tracks 'Open', 'Kiss My Love', 'Julius' and a live version of 'Diminished Clothes'.

Third single 'Motorbike to Heaven' contained B-sides 'Diary Hell' and 'I Am December', and the fourth, 'Granite Statue', featured 'It's For You' and 'Ici Les Amigos'. Both reached the top 50.

Drop Dead Gorgeous (single – Republica)

Charted: May '97; UK Chart Position: 7; Label: Deconstruction; Album: *Republica*

'Drop Dead Gorgeous' was the third single from Republica's debut self-titled album, after 'Bloke' and 'Ready to Go' and was the band's sole top-ten hit in the UK chart, where it spent seven weeks. The single proved to be one of their most popular hits after 'Ready to Go'.

There were two CD versions of the single, both featuring the track 'Out Of This World', remixed by the Chemical Brothers. CD1 also contained remixes of the lead track and 'Bitch', the original taken from the album, while CD2 featured B-sides 'Mutha' and 'Holly', the latter taken from the album.

The video featured lead singer Saffron in a silver metallic dress.

Drowners, The/To the Birds (single – Suede)

Charted: May '92; UK Chart Position: 49; Label: Nude; Album: *Suede*

Suede's debut single, released while Britain was still in the thrall of grunge and Madchester and not quite ready for Britpop, was also their lowest charting single, sitting just inside the top 50 and spending just two weeks on the chart. But it didn't matter, because with the release of this brash, confident tune, Suede not only picked up where T-Rex had left off, but also played a major part in setting in motion what would eventually become known as Britpop.

Bernard Butler's trademark distorted semi-acoustic Epiphone guitar gelled perfectly with Brett Anderson's sensual, androgynous vocal to announce the arrival of a major new act. The song has gained popularity over time, becoming one of the band's signature singles and epitomising the Britpop sound.

The single was released as a double A-side with 'To the Birds', which did not feature on the album, and the B-side 'My Insatiable One'.

Drugs Don't Work, The (single – The Verve)

Charted: Sept '97; UK Chart Position: 1; Label: Hut; Album: *Urban Hymns*

The second single released before the highly anticipated appearance of landmark album *Urban Hymns*, 'The Drugs Don't Work' could not have been more different in tone and style from its predecessor 'Bittersweet Symphony'.

It showcased the band's more introspective acoustic sound, spearheaded by singer and songwriter Richard Ashcroft, a long-time admirer of close friend Noel Gallagher. The song surprised most when it reached the number one slot in the UK chart, where it went on to spend 20 weeks, cementing the popularity of the band and filling the gap left by the disappointment of Oasis' third album, *Be Here Now*.

The lyric is reportedly about a time Ashcroft took acid and saw a vision of his dead father. He tried many times after that to repeat the experience, but never managed to see the same apparition, hence the drugs not working. The song is also remembered for the lyric "like a cat in a bag, waiting to drown", signalling Ashcroft's ideas about the futility of life, and how we're all just "waiting to drown".

Two CD versions of the single were released, the first featuring B-sides 'Three Steps' and the original demo of the lead track, and the second a remix of 'Bittersweet Symphony' plus 'The Crab' and 'Stamp'.

Dublin Castle, The (music venue)

Famous mainly for its association with eighties two-tone bands such as Madness and the Specials (whose pictures adorn the walls to this day), Camden's the Dublin Castle also became a popular live music venue for Britpop acts in the nineties. Some say it helped launch the movement by providing four walls, a roof and a rather oddly shaped stage on which the bands of the time could showcase their talents to a sea of A&R men who, at the height of Britpop, often out-numbered the regular punters.

Like its contemporaries the Good Mixer and the Monarch, the Dublin Castle was a mutual meeting place at the heart of the scene, in a similar way to the 100 Club for the Sex Pistols and The Clash in the late seventies. Positioned at the top of Camden's Parkway – on the way to London Zoo – there is nothing very remarkable about this small Victorian boozer, other than its reputation, which continues to feed its cultural legacy to this day.

Dubstar (band)

Dubstar, most commonly known for their hit singles 'Stars' and 'Not so Manic Now' are Sarah Blackwood on vocals, and Steve Hillier and Chris Wilkie on everything else.

Initially a two-piece band called The Joans, they formed in '92 in Newcastle-upon-Tyne, where they were spotted by record producer and talent manager Graeme Robinson in a club in '94. Robinson became their manager, overseeing their signing to Food Records, which was experiencing a somewhat fruitful time courtesy of the success of Blur's *Parklife* album. American producer Stephen Hague, known for his synth pop influence, worked with the band on debut album *Disgraceful*, which was released in July '95 and contained top-20 singles 'Not So Manic Now' and 'Stars'.

The album was extremely well received and Hague went on to produce the band's second album *Goodbye*, released in September '97. Despite having no hit singles, it charted better than its predecessor, reaching number 18. But the show was finally over when the band found themselves outside the bubble of Britpop, and '00's *Make It Better* failed to even enter the top ten. The band reformed in '10, but are yet to release a new album.

E

Earl's Court (music venue)

Earl's Court was a 20,000-seater live music and exhibition centre in south-west London that was hugely significant to the Britpop movement as the venue for the infamous '96 and '97 Brit Awards, as well as two gigantic Oasis gigs. The first, in November '95, came straight after the release of *(What's the Story) Morning Glory?* The footage also featured on the *There And Then* live Oasis video, interspersed with the band's other career-defining gig at Manchester City's football ground, Maine Road. The first Earl's Court gig was also the first time that Oasis invited the Bootleg Beatles on stage for their version of 'I am the Walrus'.

The Brit Awards came to Earl's Court for the first time in '96, famous for Jarvis Cocker's bottom-waggling incident during Michael Jackson's performance of 'Earth Song'. The second time Oasis played Earl's Court was after the release of their hotly anticipated third album, *Be Here Now*, and featured The Verve as special guests, not long after they had released their *Urban Hymns* album. The venue finally closed its doors for good in summer '14 to be transformed into luxury apartments (just what London needs more of).

Easy (single – Terrorvision)

Charted: Jan '97; UK Chart Position: 12; Label: Total Vegas; Album: *Regular Urban Survivors*

'Easy' was the fourth and final single released from Terrorvision's third studio album *Regular Urban Survivors*. It followed the previous single releases into the UK top 20, where it spent four weeks.

The video, directed by Paul Morgans, featured giant "Rock God" versions of the band in London, doing everything from lying on hammocks and bridges to playing guitar in the middle of the road.

There were two versions of the CD single. The first featured live tracks 'Discotheque Wreck', 'Pretend Best Friend' and 'Enteralterego', all recorded at Leeds Metropolitan University for Sound City in April '96. The second included a further three live tracks from the same performance: 'Middleman', 'My House' and 'Bad Actress'.

Echobelly (band)

Echobelly, best known for hit single 'King of the Kerb', were one of the few female-fronted Britpop bands. They were led by Delhi-born vocalist Sonya Aurora Madan, who formed the international line-up with Swedish guitarist Glenn Johansson in '93, along with bassist Alex Keyser and PJ Harvey's former drummer Andy Henderson. Madan's vocals were often compared to Morrissey, embracing the British accent and the angry but melodic songs harnessed by the Britpop sound.

Debut EP 'Bellyache', released in November '93, secured the band a contract with Rhythm King, part of Epic Records, and, just as the Britpop movement was gathering momentum, debut album *Everyone's Got One* was released in July '94. It hit the UK top ten with ease, thanks to singles 'Insomniac', 'Bellyache', 'Close... But' and 'I Can't Imagine The World Without Me'. The band went from strength to strength, with R.E.M inviting them to open for them on their *Monster* tour and Madonna expressing interest in signing them to her Maverick record label. Follow-up album *On*, released in September '95, out-performed its predecessor and reached number four in the UK chart. It was propelled by three top-20 singles: 'Great Things', 'Dark Therapy' and the band's most well-known single 'King of the Kerb'.

Next came a third album, *Lustra*, released at the end of '97, with a further three released since the Britpop era ended, *People Are Expensive* in '01 and *Gravity Pulls* in '04, *Anarchy and Alchemy* in '17, plus two greatest hits albums, *I Can't Imagine The World Without Me* in '01 and *The Best of Echobelly* in '08.

Eggman (band)

Singer and guitarist Simon Rowbottom, aka "Sice" from the Boo Radleys, formed a side project known as Eggman in '96 and released one album *First Fruits* for Creation Records.

The album contained ten short tracks including the band's sole single 'Not Bad Enough', which also featured on indie compilation album *Shine 5* and contained the B-side 'Identikit'.

The band, whose name perhaps paid homage to the Beatles 'I Am The Walrus' lyrics ("I am the eggman, they are the eggmen"), were slightly overlooked due to the popularity of the Boo Radleys. While similar in sound to the mother band, the album moved on from '95's *Wake Up Boo!* with more uplifting and psychedelic sounds.

Elastica (band)

Elastica were Britpop's first female-fronted band and one of the few, alongside Blur and Suede, to emerge right at the start. Ex-Suede member Justine Frischmann (guitar/vocals) and Justin Welch (drums) formed Elastica in '92 with guitarist Donna Matthews, who answered an advert placed in the now famous 'musicians wanted' pages of *Melody Maker*, and bassist Annie Holland. The band's punk rock sound stemmed from late-seventies bands, notably Wire and the Stranglers, unlike most other Britpop bands who were largely influenced by English groups from the sixties. The timing of their releases and intimate association with Suede and Blur, via Frischmann's personal relationships, propelled them into the movement, with Frischmann quickly becoming Britpop royalty.

Elastica wore their influences on their sleeve, a tactic that unfortunately resulted in accusations of plagiarism and two out-of-court settlements. Second single and first top-20 hit 'Line Up' bears a striking resemblance to Wire's 'I Am The Fly', and third single, iconic Elastica and Britpop anthem 'Connection', contains a riff very similar to 'Three Girl Rhumba'.

The birth of Elastica came when Frischmann left Suede, taking with her many industry contacts, including Mike Smith of EMI Publishing, who financed a demo tape, which soon found its way around the industry in early '93. This led to a "no lawyers, no contracts" handshake deal with Deceptive Records at the Good Mixer in Camden.

In the following months, Elastica supported the likes of Blur and

Pulp on tour and released the limited edition 7" single 'Stutter', which resulted in a Best New Band gong at the *NME* BRAT awards in early '94. Follow-up singles 'Line Up' and 'Connection' both achieved top-20 chart success and *Top of the Pops* performances. Frischmann's relationship with Blur's Damon Albarn made the tabloid headlines (Welch and Matthews were also in a relationship). The hype surrounding the band at this time was huge and a defining moment came when Frischmann starred alongside Thom Yorke and Brett Anderson on an *NME* cover in '94, before Elastica had even released an album.

With the anticipation surrounding the band, it was no surprise when debut album *Elastica* went straight in at the top spot in the UK chart, leaving the band with only one thing to do – conquer America.

Blur, Oasis and Suede initially failed to make much of an impact stateside and, while Elastica were more successful in America and enjoyed several tours, they didn't fare much better in the long-run. Hardships soon began to take hold, marking the start of a turbulent five years. The biggest strain was the band's heroin abuse. Bassist Annie Holland struggled with touring and left at the height of the band's success, which led to several line-up changes in an effort to keep the band going. This proved difficult, and when Frischmann's relationship with Albarn broke down in spectacular fashion, she disappeared from the public eye. Welch's relationship with Matthews also broke down, and she – by now suffering deeply from her heroin addiction – also left the band. She would later clean up and attempt a comeback of sorts in Todd Haynes' '99 glam-rock film *Velvet Goldmine*, performing a version of the New York Dolls' 'Personality Crisis'.

With no new material and no more live gigs, the record company soon deserted what was left of Elastica, a feat made somewhat easier by the fact that no contract had ever been signed.

Several years of hiatus ensued before Frischmann eventually reassessed, pulled herself together and gathered up the remnants of the original line-up (bar Matthews) plus a few new members in April '00 to release second album *The Menace*. She even managed to tempt Holland off the dole and back into the band. However, things had changed in their time away, and the album failed to achieve anywhere near the success of its predecessor, despite a lengthy tour. After releasing non-album single 'The Bitch Don't Work' in '01, the band announced they were splitting, this time for good. In '17, the band reissued their debut album to coincide with Record Store Day and were pictured together, minus Frischmann, at Abbey Road Studios.

Elastica (album – Elastica)

Charted: Mar '95; UK Chart Position: 1; Label: Deceptive; Singles: 'Stutter' (limited edition, Nov '94, UKCP n/a), 'Line Up' (Feb '94, 20), 'Connection' (Oct '94, 17), 'Waking Up' (Feb '95, 13)

The eponymous debut from Elastica is one of Britpop's defining albums, and one that still resonates in UK music history some twenty years after its initial release.

The album became the fastest-selling debut in UK chart history, overtaking Oasis' *Definitely Maybe* when released by Deceptive Records in March '95. It entered the charts at number one and was nominated for the '95 Mercury Music Prize. The album was also received well stateside, an achievement considered all the more important as many fellow Britpop legends failed to equal it.

Containing 15 fast-paced, hectic punk songs crammed into less than 40 minutes, the formula was simple: catchy guitar hooks, shouty choruses and lyrics about sexual inadequacy, drinking too much and a general apathetic attitude to modern life. Five were released as singles. Debut limited release 'Stutter', which came out in November '93, is kept to just two verses and two choruses, as short and sweet as the sexual intimacy Frischmann refers to when she sings "You've had too much wine to stumble up my street".

'Line Up' was the second single, released in February '94, and the first to break the top 20, peaking at exactly number 20 in the UK chart despite receiving a lot of criticism and even legal action for sounding almost identical to Wire's 'I Am The Fly'. The criticism continued with next single 'Connection', released in October '94, which lifted the guitar riff from Wire's 'Three Girl Rhumba'. Even so, the single made it to number 17 and was later used as the theme tune to Channel 4's *Trigger Happy TV*. 'Waking Up', released in February '95, was the band's biggest hit, reaching number 13, and featured the popular lyric, "Make a cup of tea, put a record on". However, the band's habit of provoking legal action continued, with the Stranglers this time claiming Elastica stole their riff from 'No More Heroes' (the case was settled out of court). 'Car Song' was the final single off the album, released in January '96, and, like 'Stutter', only made the US and Canadian charts.

Blur's Damon Albarn, Justine Frischmann's then boyfriend, plays keyboards under the name 'Dan Abnormal'. His presence can be felt throughout the album, particularly as subject matter on the introspective track 'Never Here', where Frischmann sings of "too much

TV and curry" with a guy who's "far too busy writing rhymes that didn't scan".

Elcka (band)

Formed in '93, Elcka were Simon Harrold on vocals, guitarist Marcus-Sanford Casey, bassist Rhodes, keyboardist Matt Barker and Darren Berry on drums. The band released a few EPs on indie label Nectah, including 'Leather Lips', 'Boho Bird' and 'Games We Play'.

Eventually signed to Island records, the band released one album, *Rubbernecking,* in '97, which they promoted while supporting Morrissey on his *Maladjusted* tour.

The album contained singles 'Supercharged', the only single to make the top ten, where it spent one week, 'Look at You Now', which featured on indie compilation album *Shine 6*, and 'Nothing to Lose'. The band amicably split in '98.

Electronic (band)

The first of Manchester's supergroups, Electronic (the emphasis is on the 'Eee') were Bernard Sumner from Joy Division and New Order, and Johnny Marr from The Smiths. The band released three success-ful albums in the nineties: *Electronic* in '91, *Raise the Pressure* in '96 and *Twisted Tenderness* in '99, all charting in the top ten. A 'best of' album was released in '06 entitled *Get the Message* and the band also featured on indie compilations series *Shine* volumes 1, 6 and 7. Elec-tronic collaborated with the Pet Shop Boys' Neil Tennant and Chris Lowe on 'The Patience of a Saint' and debut single 'Getting Away With It' and several tracks on their second album, *Raise the Pressure*, were co-written with Kraftwerk's Karl Bartos.

The original concept of the band when they (unofficially) formed in the late eighties was to release synth-pop or electronic records anony-mously with no links to either of their famous groups or to the acid-house scene that Manchester was becoming famous for at the time. However, after the success of 'Getting Away With It', they decided on a more commercial route and ditched the anonymity in favour of a more traditional band-led approach, with Sumner taking centre stage on vocals, while Marr backed him up on guitar. The result was a clear side-runner to the Britpop scene, pushing the Manchester sound to a wider audience.

Embrace (band)

A key part of the second wave of Britpop, West Yorkshire band Embrace are songwriting brothers Danny and Richard McNamara on vocals and guitars respectively, drummer Mike Heaton and bassist Steve Firth. Touring keyboardist Mickey Dale officially joined the band in the mid-noughties.

Formed in '90, it wasn't until debut single 'All You Good, Good People' was released in February '97 on Fierce Panda Records that they began to make waves. After the success of the limited edition release, they signed to Hut Records (home of The Verve) and put out the 'Fireworks' EP in May '97, which went straight into the top 40 at number 34. 'One Big Family' narrowly missed out on the top 20, but the re-release of 'All You Good, Good People' threw the band into the top ten, just as the Britpop scene was coming to an end.

The band's debut album *The Good Will Out* was released in March '98 to much critical and commercial acclaim and, although their rise came at the tail-end of Britpop, it clearly owed a debt to the scene, filled as it was with Oasis-style anthems alongside delicate ballads.

The band inevitably drew comparisons to Oasis because of their northern roots and the fact that they were fronted by two brothers. Coldplay would later pick up where Embrace left off. To date the band have released seven albums, including one B-sides album and a new album, *Love Is A Basic Need*, due to be released in '18.

End of a Century (single – Blur)

Charted: Nov '94; UK Chart Position: 19; Label: Food; Album: *Parklife*

'End of a Century' was the fourth and final single released from Blur's third studio album *Parklife*. It was the band's fourth single to reach the top 20 of the UK chart, where it spent a total of six weeks. The video is of the band's live performance at Alexandra Palace and features the actual live audio of the track. The CD version featured B-sides 'Red Necks', written by guitarist Graham Coxon, and 'Alex's Song' written, perhaps not surprisingly, by bassist Alex James.

Lyrically, the song managed to sum up the feelings of many young people in mid-nineties Britain, as so many on the *Parklife* album did. The looming end of the 20th century brought with it a feeling of impending and perhaps unwanted change, of a future unknown and untested, but in reality, as Albarn sings, it was "nothing special", and what we're doing and who we're doing it with today is a much more pressing issue.

England's Irie (single – Black Grape)

Charted: Jun '96; UK Chart Position: 6; Label: Radioactive; Album: n/a

'England's Irie' was a non-album single from Black Grape and a collaboration with The Clash's Joe Strummer and actor Keith Allen. The single was a musical contribution to the Euro '96 Football Championship and was recorded at Real World Studios in Bath.

It was the band's fourth top-ten hit in the UK chart, where it spent seven weeks, and also featured on the official Euro '96 album *The Beautiful Game*.

The CD single included three six-minute remixes of the lead track, 'Pass The Durazac Mix' and 'Suedehead Dub', both mixed by Richard Norris who also worked with Debbie Harry, Dubstar and the Pet Shop Boys, and 'Mel's LA Irie Mix', mixed by Hein Hoven.

Euro '96 (football tournament)

The '96 UEFA European Football Championship, hosted in England, helped catapult the feelgood vibe of the Britpop era to a whole new audience, even though England lost to overall winners Germany in a classic penalty shootout in the semi-finals (echoing their loss six years earlier at the '90 World Cup in Italy).

England's own Alan Shearer was awarded the 'Golden Boot' for scoring the most goals, and it was the first Euro championship to feature 16 teams instead of eight. The whole country got into the football spirit and the British Royal Mint commemorated the occasion with a special £2 coin displaying 16 rings, one for each team.

Like Italia '90, music played an important role in proceedings, with "football's coming home" chanted across the country. Liverpool band the Lightning Seeds collaborated with comedians Frank Skinner and David Baddiel on one of the tournament's most popular songs, and England's official theme tune, 'Three Lions'. Even Tony Blair quoted the song at the Labour Party conference saying, "Seventeen years of hurt, never stopped us dreaming, Labour's coming home".

Evans, Chris (TV/radio presenter)

Chris Evans, one of the UK's most successful and well-known TV and radio presenters, played a significant role in the rise of Britpop thanks to his Channel 4 show *TFI Friday*, which regularly featured live music and was a must-play for any mid-late nineties band releasing a record that week, virtually guaranteeing a chart position the following Sunday.

From September '92–'94 Evans was known to all schoolchildren, or anyone up early enough, as the co-host with Gaby Roslin of Channel 4's flagship morning show *The Big Breakfast*, famous for extraterrestrial puppets Zig and Zag, the family of the week, 'don't phone, it's just for fun!', and Paula Yates' 'on the bed' interviews.

Evans later set up Ginger Productions to host and produce his first 'own brand' programme, *Don't Forget Your Toothbrush*, which aired on Channel 4 on Saturday nights between '94 and '95. The irreverent show followed in the tradition of light-hearted family entertainment like *The Generation Game*, *Blind Date* and *Noel's House Party*, and paved the way for *TFI Friday* to follow. He finished each show singing with that week's guest, including performances with legends like Barry White and Andy Williams, and live music from Jools Holland and his band.

In '95, Evans returned to early mornings to host Radio 1's *Breakfast Show*, well known for features such as 'Honk Your Horn' and 'In Bed With Your Girlfriend'. The slot was incredibly successful, with Evans attracting a much wider audience than previous host Steve Wright. While still on the show in '96, Evans began producing *TFI Friday* via Ginger Productions. At this point, he was regularly in the public eye with a string of celebrity relationships and the media taking a keen interest, especially in his drinking antics.

Following numerous complaints about his Radio 1 show and fallouts with BBC management, Evans finally left one breakfast slot for another, boosting audience numbers on Virgin Radio. Unlike previous bosses, the new management allowed him to take Friday off to concentrate on *TFI Friday*.

Post-Britpop, Evans sold Ginger Productions to Scottish Television, *TFI Friday* got cancelled, he married teen pop sensation Billie Piper and was dismissed from Virgin Radio for repeatedly failing to show up for work. A string of TV and radio shows followed – notably his slot on Radio 2 – and in '15, after a 20th anniversary special of *TFI Friday*, the show returned for another series. Evans then had a short stint as the host of *Top Gear*, but the less said about that the better.

Everybody Knows (Except You) (single – The Divine Comedy)

Charted: Mar '97; UK Chart Position: 14; Label: Setanta; Album: *A Short Album about Love*

'Everybody Knows (Except You)' appeared as the second track and sole single on the Divine Comedy's fifth album, *A Short Album about Love*. The single became the band's third top-20 hit in the UK chart, where it spent four weeks, after 'Something for the Weekend' and 'The Frog Princess'.

There were three versions of the CD single, each featuring live tracks from the band's Shepherd's Bush Empire gig in '96. CD1 featured Burt Bacharach's 'Make It Easy On Yourself', 'A Drinking Song' and debut single 'Something For The Weekend'; CD2 contained 'Johnny Mathis' Feet', 'Your Daddy's Car' and 'Europe By Train'; and CD3 the B-sides 'Bath, Tonight We Fly' and 'Middle Class Heroes'.

Everyone's Got One (album – Echobelly)

Charted: Sept '94; UK Chart Position: 8; Label: Rhythm King; Singles: 'Bellyache' (Nov '93, UKCP n/a), 'Insomniac' (Apr '94, 47), 'I Can't Imagine the World Without Me' (Jul '94, 39), 'Close... But' (Nov '94, 59)

Everyone's Got One was the debut album from Echobelly, released in September '94 on Rhythm King. It was the record that got them invited to open for R.E.M on their *Monster* tour and got them noticed by Madonna, who wanted to sign them to her label and get them a major label record deal. The album spent four weeks on the UK chart and was the band's first of two top-ten albums, preceding *On*, released the following year. It contained the singles 'Bellyache', 'Insomniac', 'Close... But' and 'I Can't Imagine the World Without Me'. The Japanese release of the album featured two bonus tracks, 'Centipede' and 'Sober'. In '14, an expanded version of the album was released, featuring B-sides and live material on two CDs.

Lead singer Sonya Madan's strict Asian upbringing was reflected in some of the album's lyrics, such as "I was brought up, I've been told, that a husband is the goal" on 'Father, Ruler, King, Computer', and, "A woman's group is still a second-class convention. Look around who has the power" on 'Give Her a Gun'.

Everything Must Go (album – Manic Street Preachers)

Charted: May '96; UK Chart Position: 2; Label: Epic; Singles: 'A Design for Life' (Apr '96, UKCP 2), 'Everything Must Go' (Aug '96, 5), 'Kevin Carter' (Sept '96, 9), 'Australia' (Dec '96, 7)

Everything Must Go was the Manic Street Preacher's fourth studio album, released at the height of Britpop in May '96 and the first record without chief lyricist and rhythm guitarist Richey Edwards (though his lyrics did feature in several songs). Under scrutiny from fans worried about how the band would fare without Edwards, the album entered the UK chart at number two, immediately becoming their most successful to date. The album contained four top-ten singles: 'A Design for Life', 'Everything Must Go', 'Kevin Carter' and 'Australia'.

Many of the songs embrace the use of horns, synths and strings to create a more anthemic sound. This was in stark contrast to their previous albums, all of which were brash and nihilistic, embracing different aspects of rock history.

Influenced in part by Oasis, chief musical arranger and lead guitarist James Dean Bradfield managed to tap into the anthemic and brighter sound of Britpop while still remaining faithful to the band's integrity by mixing a more commercial sound with typically deep and intense lyrics. Edwards provided snatches of lyrics – and even played on the album closer 'No Surface, All Feeling' – but much of the album was recorded after his disappearance. Lead single 'A Design for Life' drew the band back together after many months away, and with its focus on working-class pride rather than their missing friend, it meant they could enter a new phase in their musical development.

The new direction paid off, and the rest of the album took shape very quickly, with Bradfield linking anthemic melodies to bassist Nicky Wire's often dark lyrics. 'The Girl Who Wanted to be God' is about American poet Sylvia Plath, 'Kevin Carter' is about a Pulitzer Prize-winning photographer who killed himself because he couldn't deal with the horrors he had seen photographing victims of famine in the Sudan, and 'Interiors' is about the ill-fated artist William de Kooning.

These songs sat alongside the beautiful and tender 'Small Black Flowers that Grow in the Sky', the only song from the album that Edwards heard before his disappearance, and the Manics' first and only love song, 'Further Away', penned by Wire for his wife. This album was the sound of a band growing up, leaving behind the lipstick and the nihilism and getting to grips with themselves and their abilities as a group. The increased authenticity paid off, attracting newcomers by the score while retaining their notoriously loyal fan base.

In August '96, the band played songs from the album at Knebworth while supporting Oasis and, at the '97 Brit Awards, they received three awards for 'Best Album', 'Best Group' and 'Best Live Act'. In '06, a deluxe, expanded edition of the album was released to mark its 10th anniversary.

Everything Must Go (single - Manic Street Preachers)

Charted: Aug '96; UK chart Position: 5; Label: Epic; Album: *Everything Must Go*

'Everything Must Go' was the second single released from the Manic Street Preachers' fourth studio album of the same name. It was the band's third single to reach the top ten and their eighth to reach the top 20 in the UK chart, where it spent a total of ten weeks. The song continued the band's change in musical direction following the disappearance of Richey Edwards.

The single was released as two separate CDs, the first including B-sides 'Black Garden', 'Hanging On' and 'No-One Knows What It's Like to Be Me', and the second a remix by the Chemical Brothers and two by the Stealth Sonic Orchestra. It was also available on cassette, featuring a live acoustic version of Burt Bacharach's 'Raindrops Keep Fallin' on My Head'.

Expecting to Fly (album - The Bluetones)

Charted: Feb '96; UK Chart Position: 1; Label: Superior Quality; Singles: 'Bluetonic' (Oct '95, UKCP 19), 'Slight Return' (Feb '96, 2), 'Cut Some Rug/Castle Rock' (May '96, 7)

The Bluetones debut album *Expecting to Fly* was the record responsible for knocking Oasis' *(What's the Story) Morning Glory?* off the number one spot of the UK chart in February '96. However, it spent just one week in the top spot before Oasis took it back again.

Recorded at Ridge Farm Studios and produced by Hugh Jones, who also worked with The Charlatans, Dodgy and Echo & the Bunnymen, the album, which spent 31 weeks on the chart, featured a peacock on the cover and resulted in the top-20 single 'Bluetonic' and top-ten singles 'Slight Return' and 'Cut Some Rug', which together totalled 23 weeks on the chart.

An expanded two CD edition was released in '09, 13 years after its initial release, reaffirming its original success.

F

Fantasy (single – The Levellers)

Charted: Oct '95; UK Chart Position: 16; Label: China; Album: *Zeitgeist*

'Fantasy' was the second and final single to be released from the Levellers' fourth album, *Zeitgeist*. Released during a fruitful time of shortlived commercial success for the band, the track became their sixth single to reach the top 20, spending six weeks on the UK chart. It was available on CD, cassette and vinyl and contained B-sides 'Sara's Beach' and 'Searchlights'.

Written by lead singer Mark Chadwick, the song tells the story of a young wannabe musician and DJ whose passion to succeed is not quite matched by his abilities and who, eventually, ends up as a scornful Parliamentarian. It typifies the band's tendency to pen songs about a dispossessed class, eager to matter but often struggling to find their place, and chimed well with Britpop's leaning towards lyrics about contemporary life in Britain. Its anti-establishment ethos makes it a live favourite even now.

Fashion

From a Blur-esque Fred Perry polo shirt to an Oasis-style oversized parka, Britpop fashion was so distinct that Liam Gallagher eventually opened his own shop on the corner of London's ultra-cool Carnaby Street, named Pretty Green after a track by The Jam. The Fred Perry polo proved popular for either sex, usually paired with jeans and

Adidas Gazelles or Sambas. Unless, of course, you preferred Vans or Converse. The question: "Are you Adidas or Vans?" was almost as important as "Are you Blur or Oasis?".

From England's Three Lions to the Gallagher brothers' Man City shirts, football kit was everywhere, as were checks, paisley and the Union Jack, which appeared on T-shirts, dresses, parkas, bags, blazers, band patches and badges.

Levi jeans were popular – who could forget the late '95 advert featuring Babylon Zoo's debut single 'Spaceman', which in turn became the fastest-selling UK single since the Beatles' 'Can't Buy Me Love'. Suits, usually reserved for slick Britpop supergroups, also became a thing. And let's not forget your standard Kappa joggers and Fila sports shirt.

Men favoured scruffy hair – that just got out of bed look – or, if they were really 'mad fer it', 'a Liam' (long fringe and long over the ears and sides). Gals on an indie night out went for glittery eyeliner, a mini rucksack to hold all their makeup and maybe a yin yang necklace or choker.

Fat Neck (single - Black Grape)

Charted: May '96; UK Chart Position: 10; Label: Radioactive; Album: n/a

'Fat Neck' was a non-album single released by Black Grape six months after the release of their debut album *It's Great When You're Straight, Yeah!* It was the band's third top-ten single in the UK chart, where it spent seven weeks, and, for better or worse, featured Johnny Marr from The Smiths on guitar.

The CD single B-sides included a mix of 'Yeah Yeah Brother' taken from their debut album and a live cover of the Sex Pistols' 'Pretty Vacant' from TV show *TFI Friday*. A vinyl edition was also available with the lead track remixed by Goldie. The video featured footage of the band both on and off stage, capturing the essence of their everyday life.

Female of the Species (single – Space)

Charted: Jun '96; UK Chart Position: 14; Label: Gut; Album: *Spiders*

The breakthrough single for Liverpool's Space, 'Female of the Species' impressed not only with its quirky lyric, capturing singer Tommy Scott's somewhat jaded romantic experiences and subsequent musings on the world's women (and how they are deadlier than the males), but also because it took Britpop outside the realm of electric guitars and drums. Keyboardist Franny Griffiths used samples and a multitude of layered keyboard sounds that would never have been found on an Oasis record.

After debut single 'Neighbourhood' reached only 56 in the UK chart, 'Female of the Species' impressed when it was picked up by radio and went straight into the top 20, where it spent ten weeks, setting the tone for debut album *Spiders*, released three months later. The CD single featured B-sides 'Looney Tune', 'Give Me Something' and an instrumental version of the lead track.

Filmstar (single – Suede)

Charted: Aug '97; UK Chart Position: 9; Label: Nude; Album: *Coming Up*

'Filmstar' was the final single to be released from Suede's third album, *Coming Up*, and the band's seventh single to reach the top ten of the chart, where it spent four weeks. There were two CD versions of the single, with CD1 containing B-sides 'Graffiti Women' and 'Duchess', and CD2 featuring live performances of 'Rent' and 'Saturday Night'. The track was also available as a 7" vinyl, which included a demo of the single.

Stylistically the song summed up Suede at this point in their career and the outlandish opulence that went along with the *Coming Up* album. Gone was the thoughtful yet dark cynicism of *Dog Man Star*, and in came the life of the filmstar, "propping up the bar, driving in a car, it looks so easy" (well, it did when Suede did it). The song featured as the live set closer for much of this period in their career.

Finetime (single - Cast)

Charted: Jul '95; UK Chart Position: 17; Label: Polydor; Album: *All Change*

'Finetime' was the debut single from Liverpool band Cast, taken from their debut album *All Change*. It was the first of several releases to feature in the top 20 of the UK chart, where it spent four weeks. It showcased frontman John Power's flair for writing punchy, immediately catchy, pop-rock songs.

The single was released on CD and cassette, with the band in an old-fashioned lift behind cage-like doors on the cover, and featured B-sides 'Better Man' and 'Satellites'. The band performed the single on, among others, *Top of the Pops* and *MTV's Most Wanted*.

Flying (single - Cast)

Charted: Oct '96; UK Chart Position: 4; Label: Polydor; Album: n/a

Cast's 'Flying' followed in the tradition of Blur's 'Popscene', Oasis' 'Whatever', and The Bluetones' 'Marblehead Johnson', all of which were released after the singles from the first album were exhausted and the second album was yet to be recorded. The intention, in those pre-internet days, was to encourage people to buy a 'bridging-single' that rode on the waves created by the band's first album and kept them in the public eye.

It clearly worked as 'Flying' became the band's biggest single to date, peaking at number four in the UK chart, where it spent seven weeks in total. The CD singles featured B-sides 'Between the Eyes', 'For So Long' and a live version of previous single 'Walkaway' recorded at the Feile Festival.

Food Records (record label)

Food Records is the label responsible for signing Blur, and for releasing 'Trouble' by female teen pop duo Shampoo, who coined the phrase 'Girl Power' long before the Spice Girls even existed.

The label was initially set up as an independent in the mid-eighties by David Balfe (later the subject of Blur's 'Country House'). A musician himself, Balfe grew up in Merseyside, playing with and managing bands including Echo & the Bunnymen with fellow musician Bill Drummond (of the KLF). Together they founded Zoo Records in the late seventies and, between them, managed, played in and published music by several acts including The Proclaimers, the KLF and the Teardrop Explodes.

After moving to London in the mid-eighties, Balfe founded Food Records, where he was joined by partner Andy Ross. Things progressed quickly and, shortly after signing a distribution deal with EMI, Food signed their first multi-million selling international band Jesus Jones, known for hit single 'Right Here, Right Now'. A year later, in '89, they signed Seymour, a fledgling London-based punk band, insisting that they change their name to Blur. In the same year, the label released 'The Food Christmas EP', which charted at 63 and featured Food artists covering each other's songs.

A multi-talented man, Balfe directed Blur's first two music videos, 'She's So High' and 'There's No Other Way', the latter of which became the band's breakthrough hit single, charting at number eight in April '91. In '94, when Blur were beginning to wrestle the Britpop crown from Oasis, Balfe, the "professional cynic" who was "paying the price of living life at the limit", sold Food to EMI and escaped to "a house, a very big house in the country", inspiring the lyrics for Blur's first number-one single 'Country House'. Andy Ross continued to run Food records under EMI, signing bands including Dubstar, The Supernaturals and Idlewild, until it was finally folded into Parlophone in '01.

For the Dead (single – Gene)

Charted: Jan '96; UK Chart Position: 15; Label: Costermonger; Album: *Olympian*

'For the Dead' has an opening melodic guitar riff that is signature Gene. It was the band's debut single, initially released as a double A-side with 'Child's Body' in May '94.

The single's initial limited edition copies sold out in a couple of days and the track was named *NME*'s single of the week. It was re-released in January '96, becoming the band's second top 20 hit, after 'Olympian', in the UK chart, where it spent three weeks.

The CD single B-sides included 'Child's Body' and live tracks 'Sick, Sober & Sorry' and 'Truth, Rest Your Head', recorded for the BBC1 *Evening Session* from their Helter Shelter performance in July '95.

For Tomorrow (single – Blur)

Charted: May '93; UK Chart Position: 28; Label: Food; Album: *Modern Life is Rubbish*

'For Tomorrow' was the first single released from Blur's second album *Modern Life is Rubbish*, and thus an early forerunner to the Britpop movement. The opening acoustic chords announced an immediate shift in tone from the indie dance, shoegaze vibe of debut album *Leisure*.

In the opening line, songwriter Damon Albarn brings the band crashing into the modern world by announcing "He's a 20th century boy", presumably singing about himself and his kind, and turning his gaze onto contemporary life, a key trait of the Britpop movement.

Released on two CDs, the first included a six-minute version of lead track 'For Tomorrow (Visit to Primrose Hill Extended)', and B-sides 'Peach' and 'Bone Bag'. The second included tracks 'When the Cows Come Home', 'Beachcoma' and an acoustic version of the lead track.

Single-buyers were clearly not quite ready for this new sound, and the song only just reached the top 30 of the UK chart, where it spent four weeks. It remains, however, a live favourite to this day.

For You (single – Electronic)

Charted: Sept '96; UK Chart Position: 16; Label: Parlophone; Album: *Raise the Pressure*

'For You' was the second single released from Electronic's second album *Raise the Pressure*. Co-written by Kraftwerk's Karl Bartos, it was the band's fifth top-20 single, spending two weeks on the UK chart.

Released as two CDs, CD1 contained B-sides 'All That I Need' and 'I Feel Alright', while CD2 featured mixes of 'Free Will', 'Disappointed' and 'Get the Message', the last track taken from debut album *Electronic*. The video shows the band performing in a graffiti-sprayed caravan that eventually gets destroyed by a tank.

Forbidden City (single – Electronic)

Charted: Jul '96; UK Chart Position: 14; Label: Parlophone; Album: *Raise the Pressure*

'Forbidden City', the first track released in four years by Electronic, was taken from their second album *Raise the Pressure*. It was the band's fourth top-20 single, spending nine weeks on the UK chart and featuring as the opening track on the 'best of' album, *Get the Message*, released in '06. Backing vocals were provided by Denise Johnson, known for her incredible work on Primal Scream's *Screamadelica*.

The single was also released in the US, Australia and Germany, with B-sides 'Imitation of Life', 'A New Religion' and 'Getting Away With It'.

Found You (single – Dodgy)

Charted: Mar '97; UK Chart Position: 19; Label: A&M; Album: *Free Peace Sweet*

'Found You' was the fourth and final single from Dodgy's third album *Free Peace Sweet* and the band's fifth top 20 hit, spending three weeks on the UK chart. B-sides included 'I Can't Make It', with the cassette and vinyl versions also featuring a cover of the Beatles' 'Revolution'.

The cover featured the band standing in the snow looking up into the camera. It was likely taken from the video, which features them playing their instruments against a snow-clad mountainous back-drop, reminiscent of the Beatles' 'Ticket to Ride'.

Free Me (single – Cast)

Charted: Apr '97; UK Chart Position: 7; Label: Polydor; Album: *Mother Nature Calls*

The first single from second album *Mother Nature Calls* saw Cast pick up where they had left off, continuing their four-to-the-floor in-die rabble-rouser sound. The song breached the lower half of the top ten in spring '97 and, at ten weeks, was the band's longest-running single on the chart.

Released as two CDs, CD1 included B-sides 'Come on Everybody', 'Canter' and an acoustic version of the lead track, while CD2 featured 'Release My Soul' and 'Dancing on the Flames'. The cover artwork, by Brian Cannon, showed a butterfly in a cage suspended above the clouds.

Free Peace Sweet (album – Dodgy)

Charted: Jun '96; UK Chart Position: 7; Label: A&M; Singles: 'In a Room' (Jun '96, UKCP 12), 'Good Enough' (Aug '96, 4), 'If You're Thinking of Me' (Nov '96, 11), 'Found You' (Mar '97, 19)

Dodgy's third album *Free Peace Sweet*, a pun on three-piece suite, was by far their most commercially successful. It was their only album to make the top ten in the UK chart, where it spent 44 weeks. It contained top-20 singles 'In a Room', 'Good Enough', 'If You're Thinking of Me' and 'Found You', and was released to positive reviews.

The album was produced by Hugh Jones, who also worked on their previous album *Homegrown* as well as with bands including The Bluetones, The Charlatans and Gene. The cover artwork shows the title carved into a tree trunk.

Frischmann, Justine (singer/guitarist/songwriter – Elastica)

Justine Frischmann was a key player in the formation of Britpop. Best known as the lead singer of Elastica, she started out as the guitarist in Suede, dating frontman Brett Anderson before splitting with him and leaving to form her own group and a much-publicised relationship with Blur's Damon Albarn.

Born on 16 September '69 in Kensington to Jewish parents, her mother Russian and her father a Hungarian holocaust survivor, Frischmann studied architecture at University College London, where she met Anderson. Although he was initially on a town planning course, Frischmann persuaded him to switch to the same course as her so they could juggle studying with the beginnings of what would eventually become Suede.

While she was still in the band, Frischmann and Anderson broke up and she started dating Albarn, who she met when Suede supported

Blur at Brighton's Zap Club in '90. Inevitably, this caused too much friction and, as they were both also failing the third year of their courses, Anderson left university to focus on Suede while Frischmann left the band and re-sat her papers. That year, Suede became huge. Their success actually boosted Frischmann too, making her see it was possible to get a deal and to make a greater contribution – something she'd found frustrating in Suede.

Frischmann formed Elastica in '92. There were ups, but there were also dramatic downs, most notably the heroin addiction that spread through the band and her rocky relationship with Albarn, which came to an end in '98.

When Elastica broke up in '01, Frischmann moved in with English/ Sri Lankan recording artist Mathangi Arulpragasam (stage name M.I.A), collaborating on a few songs for her debut *Arula*. While the nineties had been about music, the noughties were more about art. In '03 she co-presented a BBC series about modern architecture called *Dreamspaces* and the following year presented arts programme *The Southbank Show*. Frischmann now works as an abstract painter and lives with her husband, a professor of atmospheric science, in Boulder, Colorado.

Frog Princess, The (single – The Divine Comedy)

Charted: Nov '96; UK Chart Position: 15; Label: Setanta; Album: *Casanova*

'The Frog Princess' was the third and final single from the Divine Comedy's fourth album, *Casanova*. It was the second top 20 single for the band and spent two weeks on the chart.

Two CDs were released. 'A Casanova Companion No.3' contained B-sides 'Motorway to Damascus', 'A Woman of the World' and a demo version of 'Lucy'. 'A Casanova Companion No.4' featured a demo version of 'Something for the Weekend', as well as 'Neptune's Daughter' and 'Tonight We Fly'.

From a Window/This Morning (single – Northern Uproar)

Charted: Feb '96; UK Chart Position: 17; Label: Polydor; Album: *Northern Uproar*

'From A Window/This Morning' was the second single from Northern Uproar's self-titled debut album. It came out as a limited edition double A-side 7" single and as a CD with 'From a Window' as the lead track and featuring B-sides 'Credibility', 'My Mind's Eye' and 'This Morning'. It was the band's sole top 20 hit in the UK chart, where it spent three weeks.

Further (album – Geneva)

Charted: Jun '97; UK Chart Position: 20; Label: Nude; Singles: 'No One Speaks' (Oct '96, UKCP 32), 'Into the Blue' (Feb '97, 26), 'Tranquilizer' (May '97, 24), 'Best Regrets' (Aug '97, 38)

Further was the debut album by Aberdeen band Geneva. It achieved a top-20 spot in the UK chart, where it spent three weeks.

The record contained the singles 'No One Speaks', 'Into the Blue', 'Tranquilizer' and 'Best Regrets', all of which claimed top-40 spots in the UK chart. Production was led by Mike Hedges, known for his work with The Cure, The La's and the Manic Street Preachers. The album, packed with Geneva's signature guitar melodies and lead singer Andrew Montgomery's haunting vocals spanning an impressive vocal range, received positive reviews.

G

Gallagher, Liam (singer/songwriter – Oasis/Beady Eye)

Self-styled cock of the walk William John Paul 'Liam' Gallagher was the undisputed (at least in his own mind) crown prince of Britpop and Cool Britannia. Born to Irish parents Peggy and Thomas in Burnage, Manchester, in '72, Gallagher didn't discover his passion for music and confidence in his singing ability until his late teens. Growing up, stealing, breakdancing, avoiding his abusive father and annoying older brothers Noel and Paul occupied much of his time. At the age of 18, he joined The Rain, changing the band's name to Oasis after seeing the word on a poster on his bedroom wall. As the group rapidly rose to fame, he became known for his classic rock star charisma, positioning himself as one of the leading frontmen of Britpop. His lairy, mouthy attitude often resulted in disputes with journalists and photographers and, as Britpop took hold of the nation, he became a constant fixture in the news headlines, becoming the poster-boy for Cool Britannia.

While best-known as the lead singer of Oasis, he also founded Beady Eye in '09 and and started fashion brand Pretty Green (named after a song by The Jam), which basically sells everything Gallagher would wear himself. Like his brothers, he's a huge Manchester City FC fan, regularly attending games with his sons and getting involved in the launch of their new kit in '11.

Competing with older brother Noel for songwriting credentials was always going to be hard, but on Oasis' fourth studio album *Standing on the Shoulder of Giants*, Gallagher junior sang his own self-penned ode to stepson James (son of wife Patsy Kensit and Simple Minds singer Jim Kerr), 'Little James'. On Oasis' next album, his contribution went even further with the inclusion of key track 'Songbird' – this time a ballad penned for second wife Nicole Appleton – which reached number three in the UK chart.

In recent years, Noel has been heard to say that Beady Eye are just one tune short of being a good band. Despite this, Liam remains one of British music's most important and popular frontmen. In '15, he returned to the stage to perform The Who's 'My Generation' alongside Roger Daltrey, the Lightning Seeds' Ian Broudie and Ringo Starr's son Zak Starkey on *TFI Friday*. He also put in a barnstorming performance at One Love Manchester in '17 to raise money for families affected by the terrorist attack at Manchester Arena, has performed at a string of festivals since, including Glastonbury, released his first solo album, *As You Were*, in October '17 and was awarded Rock 'n' Roll Star of the Year at the GQ Awards.

Gallagher, Noel (guitarist/singer/song-writer – Oasis/solo artist)

Without the boyish good looks of his younger brother ('our kid'), Noel was never going to be the frontman or the face of a movement, but there was never any doubt exactly whose band Oasis were. He was the power behind the throne.

Born in Manchester in '67, the middle child of Irish parents Peggy and Thomas, Noel Thomas David Gallagher shared a bedroom with younger brother Liam, while older brother Paul had a room to himself. Perhaps as a result of trying to deal with his violent father, Gallagher was often in trouble, including expulsion from school when he was 15 for throwing a bag of flour over a teacher. He found comfort in music during his early teens, playing his father's guitar until his mother bought him his own. When Peggy and the boys finally left Tommy, Noel maintained limited contact with his father to secure the odd construction job. Once he found his own work, all contact ceased.

It was an accident on a construction job that set in motion a chain of events that eventually led to the creation of Oasis' debut album *Definitely Maybe*. Noel sustained an injury when the end of a gas main fell on his foot, resulting in his relocation to the company's storehouse. Noel began bringing his acoustic guitar to work, and it was there that he wrote future Oasis classics, notably 'Live Forever'. Legend has it that even as he was writing it, Gallagher knew it was an important song and that his future was secured, as long as he could find the right band to play it.

In the late eighties, Gallagher blagged himself a job as a roadie and, later, guitar-tech with the Inspiral Carpets after meeting the guitarist at a Stone Roses gig. In '91, returning from an American tour with the band, he found his brother Liam had joined a local band called The Rain. Gallagher senior initially offered his services as lead guitarist and, before long, insisted on taking over the role of chief songwriter too.

Liam and band member Bonehead were only too happy to give up the songwriting; the latter is rumoured to have cried after hearing Noel play 'Live Forever' for the first time. Noel insisted that the band rehearsed every day and, pretty soon, they began playing at the Manchester Boardwalk (where their heroes the Stone Roses had often played). Just two years later, they were famously spotted by Alan McGee at King Tut's Wah Wah Hut.

From playing an Epiphone Sheraton guitar emblazoned with the Union Jack, which he debuted at Oasis' Maine Road gig in April '96, to drinking champagne with the Prime Minister in Downing Street, you'd be hard-pressed to find someone more identifiably British than Noel Gallagher in the nineties. The Epiphone was a gift from first wife Meg Matthews, who he married in June '97 in a Las Vegas ceremony. The pair were married for three years, with Matthews giving birth to daughter Anais in '00. In '11, he married Scottish-born Sara McDonald, and they have two sons, Donovan and Sonny.

Aside from music, Noel has only one other thing in common with Liam – his undying love for Manchester City Football Club. In '12, he helped with the launch of their new Umbro kits.

Though Noel has not branched out into the world of fashion like Liam, he has launched and maintained a successful solo career (as everyone knew he would). It was two years after Oasis split in '09 that he finally announced his first solo album under the name Noel Gallagher's High Flying Birds. The self-titled album was released in October of the same year and was followed up by *Chasing Yesterday* in March '15. Both achieved number one spots in the UK chart.

His third album is due for release at the end of '17. This follows a busy few years of touring, including a headline performance at the We Are Manchester benefit gig to officially reopen Manchester Arena following the terrorist attack, and a collaboration with Damon Albarn on Gorillaz track 'We Got the Power'.

There is no denying that Noel Gallagher is one of Britain's greatest ever songwriters, sitting alongside many of his own heroes, including Lennon & McCartney, Jagger & Richards and Paul Weller. His taste is notably diverse though, and when asked which of his heroes he wanted on the cover of *Definitely Maybe* he opted for the fifties/sixties songsmith Burt Bacharach.

Game On (TV sitcom)

Appearing on BBC Two in February '95, and set almost exclusively in a small three-bedroomed flat in Battersea, south London, this cult sitcom followed the misadventures of twenty-somethings Matt, Martin and Mandy, as they piled their way through endless cups of tea, chicken biryanis, bottles of Jack Daniel's, and copies of *Zitt* magazine (clearly based on *Loaded*), each of them disdainful of the others while struggling to find their own sense of identity in nineties Britain.

Martin was the desexualised nerd whose ginger hair, schoolboy naivety, terrible dress-sense and glasses made him totally repellent to women. Mandy struggled to be taken seriously in her male-dominated workplace because of her blonde hair, curvaceous figure and easy nature. This served to feed her insecurity and resulted in a mounting debt as she lavished money she didn't have on clothes she didn't need to attract men she didn't like, who then didn't take her seriously in the workplace. Matt saw himself as one of those men: overly-macho, testosterone-fuelled and unapologetic in his pursuit of fast cars and bimbo girls. He was, however, heavily in denial after the death of his parents and had developed such severe agoraphobia that he never left the house.

They were incredibly different but inextricably bound to one another by their own shortcomings and social failures. Mandy couldn't leave the flat because she owed Matt several month's rent; Martin couldn't leave because he didn't know anyone (except Willy Busoom at the bank); and Matt couldn't leave because of his agoraphobia.

As in much great comedy, *Game On* found its strength in tragedy. It laid bare earnest insecurities prevalent in lower middle-class twenty-somethings; insecurities about their physical appearance, sexual virility and professional success, exacerbated by lad-mags, TV lifestyle programmes and whatever else the zeitgeist had to offer that could be experienced from behind closed doors. Matt's situation proved that, if necessary, you could live your life without ever leaving the house and, as such, coolly predicted the movement away from personal interaction that the internet age would bring.

The first season was genre-defining, with Ben Chaplin capturing the housebound, bully-boy, macho-tastic Matthew Malone much more effectively than his replacement Neil Stuke in the unnecessary following two seasons.

Garbage (band)

They might be a Britpop band, but Garbage are just a quarter British. Frontwoman Shirley Manson is Scottish, but the rest of the band – Duke Erikson, Steve Marker and Butch Vig – are American. Garbage formed in '93 as a trio, with Manson joining a year later after leaving her previous band, Angelfish.

Butch Vig might have been responsible for producing Nirvana's '91 classic studio album *Nevermind*, but Garbage are considered synonymous with the Britpop era, making every effort to avoid association with America's grunge scene by producing pop songs mixed with a variety of genres, from trip-hop to rock. In light of this, their sound could be considered on the hard side for a Britpop band, but Manson's attitude and personality, combined with the timings of their releases and continued inclusion on Britpop 'best of' compilation albums, makes them a key group in the canon.

The band became Mushroom UK's first worldwide signing and their debut album, *Garbage*, was released the day after the 'Battle of Britpop' in August '95. It was a huge success in the UK, reaching number six in the chart and containing singles 'Vow', 'Only Happy When it Rains', 'Queer', 'Stupid Girl' and 'Milk', all released in the Britpop period.

Post-Britpop, follow-up album *Version 2.0* was also a huge success, debuting at number one in the UK chart and spawning singles 'Push It', 'I Think I'm Paranoid', 'Special', 'When I Grow Up', 'The Trick is to Keep Breathing' and 'You Look So Fine'. Since then, a further four albums, *Beautiful Garbage*, *Bleed Like Me*, *Not Your Kind of People* and *Strange Little Birds*, have been released alongside numerous tours. The band's autobiography, *This Is The Noise That Keeps Me Awake*, was published in '17, the title taken from the lyrics of their '98 single 'Push It'.

Garbage (album – Garbage)

Charted: Oct '95; UK Chart Position: 6; Label: Mushroom; Singles: 'Vow' (Mar '95, UKCP 138), 'Only Happy When It Rains' (Sept '95, 29), 'Queer' (Dec '95, 13), 'Stupid Girl' (Mar '96, 4), 'Milk' (Nov '96, 10)

Perhaps the most American-sounding Britpop band, Garbage's eponymous debut album was still Britpop nonetheless. Although three

Americans were the core of the group, it was Scottish singer Shirley Manson who provided the vocals, much of the songwriting (predominantly the lyrics) and the outward facing representation of the band.

Perhaps not as assured as their later work, their debut still contained many of the band's most well-known and well-loved songs, including 'Only Happy When It Rains' and breakthrough hit 'Stupid Girl', which found its way into the top five in March '96, some five months after the album's release, ensuring it remained in the chart well into '96 and in the top ten for 131 weeks.

Like all their subsequent albums, it was recorded at drummer Butch Vig's Smart Studios in Madison, Wisconsin, and enjoyed chart success on both sides of the Atlantic, garnering the band nominations and wins at both the Grammys and the Brits; a feat not matched by many of their Britpop contemporaries.

The album was a surprisingly dark and welcome contrast to the string of upbeat Britpop albums released that year and, as a result, remains one of the era's most memorable moments.

Gene (band)

Gene were a four-piece indie band comprising Welsh vocalist and keyboardist Martin Rossiter, Steve Mason on guitar, Kevin Miles on bass and Matt 'the Hat' James on drums. Previously called Sp!n, and with Stephen Street as producer, the band went through many line-up changes in their early days. Mason's bassist brother John left after being involved in a road accident, and original lead singer Lee Clark moved on as he was disgruntled with the early direction the band was taking. After recruiting Miles on bass, Mason spotted Rossiter in an indie club and Gene was finally born.

The band signed in '94 to Costermonger records, a label set up by *NME* journalists Keith Cameron and Roy Wilkinson specifically to push Gene into the music (and Britpop) limelight. The band's debut single, double A-side 'For the Dead' and 'Child's Body', was released in May '94 and received glowing reviews with *Select* and *NME* making it their single of the month and week respectively. The band were often compared to The Smiths, and Rossiter made no secret of the fact that he was a longtime Morrissey fan, echoing his hero with similarly deep, emotive lyrics concerned with the human condition and vibrato vocals sung in an English accent.

In '95, the band played their first UK headline tour, resulting in an

NME Brat Award for 'Best New Act'. Two months later, debut album *Olympian* was released to predominantly positive reviews. It charted at number eight in the UK and is frequently referred to as one of Britpop's defining albums. It contained many of the band's most-loved songs, including singles 'Sleep Well Tonight', 'Haunted By You', 'Be My Light, Be My Guide' and the epic title track 'Olympian'.

Standalone LP *To See the Lights*, featuring live tracks, rarities and covers, was released the following year, and peaked at number 11. Then their highly anticipated second album *Drawn to the Deep End* was finally released in early '97. Similar to the debut album, it peaked at number eight, though it spent just five weeks in the chart. The album contained classic single and live favourite 'Fighting Fit', as well as 'We Could Be Kings', one of many devastating love songs featured on the album.

Post-Britpop, a further two albums have been released: *Revelations* in '99 and *Libertine* in '01. The band split amicably in '04 and debut album *Olympian* was re-issued in July '15 to commemorate its 20th anniversary.

Geneva (band)

Aberdeen-based band Geneva, who initially performed under the name Sunfish, formed in '92 with Andrew Montgomery on vocals, Steven Dora and Stuart Evans on guitars, bassist Keith Graham and, after ditching their drum machine, Douglas Caskie on drums and percussion.

Strongly influenced by The Byrds, The Smiths and Suede, the band created a more sophisticated, darker Britpop sound compared to the laddish, raw sounds of, say, Oasis. Consequently, a demo made its way to Nude Records, home to Suede, and the label signed the band after seeing just one rehearsal.

Debut single 'No One Speaks' was released in '96, full of Britpop glory with synth strings tearing through Montgomery's Brett Anderson-esque vocals. This was followed up with 'Into the Blue' in early '97, another single released from debut album *Further*. Two more singles were released from their top-20 debut, 'Tranquilizer' and 'Best Regrets', with all four singles hitting the UK top 40. Three years post-Britpop, follow-up album *Weather Underground* was released but failed to chart well.

The inception of this band is a rather fine example of the absurdity of the Britpop scene at its height. It has been said that bands were being signed before they had properly formed, let alone played any real gigs. And if they did make it all the way to the Monarch, the Hope and Anchor or the Dublin Castle, there were likely to be more A&R men in the audience than actual paying punters.

At no time in Britain's musical history was it so easy for bands to get signed – and to lose their own sense of themselves in the process. It should be hard for bands to get signed; they should have to struggle and not be cosseted in the comfortable bubble that a scene like Britpop creates, otherwise it doesn't mean as much if they make it, and any money they make can feel unearned and meaningless.

Getting Better (single – Shed Seven)

Charted: Jan '96; UK Chart Position: 14; Label: Polydor; Album: *A Maximum High*

'Getting Better' was the second of five singles to be released from Shed Seven's second album *A Maximum High*. It spent three weeks on the UK chart and was the band's first top-20 single. It featured B-sides 'Only Dreaming' and 'Song Seven'.

The single is also on the band's two compilation albums *Going for Gold* and *The Singles Collection*. The video features the band dressed like kings at a large feast being fed by pretty women and entertained by a jester.

Girl from Mars (single – Ash)

Charted: August '95; UK Chart Position: 11; Label: Infectious; Album: *1977*

'Girl from Mars' was the second single released from Ash's debut album *1977*, and the band's first to reach the top 20, narrowly missing out on the top ten. It spent a total of six weeks on the UK chart, and the cover artwork featured a winking girl with green skin and short black hair.

The CD B-sides included six-minute track 'Astral Conversations with Toulouse Lautrec' and 'Cantina Band', which reflected the band's love of *Star Wars* and its famous 'space tavern' known as the Cantina. The CD sleeve even says "Cantina Band was originally performed in

the most wretched hive of scum & villainy in a galaxy far, far away".
It also refers to the girl from Mars as "Sarah from Islington".

In keeping with the *Star Wars* theme, the Australian version of the CD featured live versions of 'Darkside, Lightside' and 'Goldfinger', both taken from the *1977* album, plus 'T-Rex' and 'What Deaner Was Talking About', recorded live at Studio 227 in Sydney.

Girlie Show, The (TV series)

Channel 4's *The Girlie Show* ran for two series from '96–'97, replacing *The Word* in the key "stumble in from the pub" slot of 11pm on Friday night. Its aim was to promote 'Girl Power' and all things 'ladette', and future Radio 1 (and 2) DJ Sara Cox popped her presenting cherry as the show's host.

She was joined on screen by Claire Gorham, Rachel Williams and Sarah Cawood. Highlights included the Spice Girls' 'Spice Advice', which gave live advice to members of the audience, and 'Wanker of the Week', in which the show's presenters would pick on a male celebrity who had upset the status quo that week.

The latter typified what the creators of the show were attempting to achieve: a show for the ladette, echoing the success of lifestyle magazines like *Sky* and *Loaded*, which encouraged the rise of the 'lad' in nineties Britain. He was loud, brash and full of lager, and so was she. She challenged the stereotypical role of women but, while the suffragettes and women's lib aimed for equality on their own terms, ladettes arm-wrestled lads across the battlefield bar, matching them drink for drink.

The show received mixed reviews. It was often criticised for its tacky, occasionally amateurish presentation and was ultimately canned after two runs. Despite this, its lingering popularity among a small but dedicated band of followers has given it retrospective legendary status.

Girl Like You, A (single – Edwyn Collins)
Charted: Jun '95; UK Chart Position: 4; Label: Setanta; Album: *Gorgeous George*

'A Girl Like You' was the key release from Edwyn Collins' third solo album *Gorgeous George* and his only single to reach the top ten. It spent a total of 17 weeks on the UK chart, and went on to chart worldwide.

The CD single B-sides included an acoustic version of 'If You Could Love Me', a demo of 'Don't Shilly Shally' and 'You're On Your Own'.

The single is not typical of the Britpop sound, but is still generally associated with the scene because of its release date, which coincided with the peak of the era, and its channelling of sixties' sounds. The distinctive drum sample was lifted from American singer-songwriter Len Barry's single '1-2-3', released in '65.

As well as feeling like it was superglued to the radio playlists for an eternity, 'A Girl Like You' also made it on to the soundtrack of Allan Moyle's '95 coming-of-age film *Empire Records*, McG's '03 film *Charlie's Angels: Full Throttle* and various TV programmes and adverts.

Girls and Boys (single – Blur)

Charted: Mar '94; UK Chart Position: 5; Label: Food; Album: *Parklife*

'Girls and Boys' was the first of four singles to be released from Blur's third album *Parklife*, and the band's first top ten hit since '91's 'There's No Other Way'. It spent eight weeks on the UK chart.

After the disappointing performance of second album *Modern Life is Rubbish*, things initially looked bleak for the forward-thinking Blur. Then word got out that they had some good songs and the tide turned. With its funk-inspired bass line and chirpy disco beat, 'Girls and Boys' wouldn't have sounded out of place on the stereo of a late-opening Greek island tourist bar. It also managed to marry several genre styles, while remaining decidedly 'Blur', once Graham Coxon's assuredly distorted guitar joins the song halfway through the first verse.

The lyric is about the then burgeoning trend of cheap package deals and Club 18–30 holidays, frequented by a young white-collar workforce with time and money to spend on Mediterranean holidays, in search of sun, sea, sex, drugs and alcohol... lots of alcohol.

The locals welcomed the moneyed many, actively encouraging the loosening of morals and promiscuity not usually practised by uptight Brits. Years later, the town councils of Magaluf, Ibiza and Crete would come to regret embracing British youth so warmly, while Britain resented its deplorable reputation amongst its European cousins. But, in '94, the party was just getting started.

The single was released on two CDs. CD1 included B-sides 'Magpie' and 'Anniversary Waltz'; CD2 'People in Europe' and 'Peter Panic'. The Pet Shop Boys also put out a remixed version of the song on both 7" and 12" vinyl.

Glastonbury (music festival)

Glastonbury was where it all started for Britain's numerous music festivals, and the world's greatest musical event continues today on a more or less annual basis.

Founded in '70 by farmer and land-owner Michael Eavis, for many years it was the UK's only outdoor festival, eventually joined by Reading, which now signals the start of the summer-long festival season.

It was home to many key sets from Britpop bands in the nineties but, crucially, Glastonbury has always been about much more than just music; a fact confirmed by the event selling out six months before the line-up is even announced. Its legendary status offers a rite-of-passage for many audience members, and for the bands, who know that a good reaction can make their fortune.

There are several stages scattered around Worthy Farm, and plenty of places to experience, explore and enjoy non-musical happenings, from the Stone Circle to Shangri La. For five nights, the farm is home to approximately 175,000 people, an enormous increase from the initial 1,500 who made up the audience of Glastonbury year zero (and were each handed a free pint of milk on entry).

During the Britpop years, the line-up grew and grew, largely thanks to what was known then as the *NME* Stage, later renamed the Other Stage. In '93, Suede headlined, preceded by The Verve and The Auteurs; while in '94 the stage hosted Blur, the Manic Street Preachers, the Boo Radleys, Pulp, Echobelly and Oasis.

One year later, as Britpop's momentum increased, Oasis took to the Main Stage and the *NME* Stage line-up was even bigger with Elastica, The Charlatans, Dodgy, Gene, Sleeper, Supergrass, Ash, Marion, Menswear and The Verve all playing over the weekend. Glastonbury took a year off in '96 and many festival-goers headed to Knebworth instead, where Oasis played to an even bigger audience of 250,000 over two days. In '97, Glastonbury was home to Britpop's finale as Supergrass, Cast, Ocean Colour Scene, Dodgy, Echo & the Bunnymen, Republica and the Longpigs all took to the Main Stage and the newly named Other Stage hosted Kula Shaker, Ash, Mansun, The Bluetones, Echobelly, The Seahorses, Kenickie, the Super Furry Animals, Dubstar, Geneva, Catatonia and Embrace.

Glow (album – Reef)

Charted: Feb '97; UK Chart Position: 1; Label: Sony S2; Singles: 'Place Your Hands' (Nov '96, UKCP 6), 'Come Back Brighter' (Jan '97, 8), 'Consideration' (Apr '97, 13), 'Yer Old' (Aug '97, 21)

Tenuously linked to the Britpop scene by proximity, Reef were more of a classic rock band. It was the lead single from second album *Glow* that launched them into the charts and the music scene proper. 'Place Your Hands', a slow-burning but inevitable hit whose long-lasting legacy competes with Republica's 'Ready to Go', is still featured on TV shows and adverts 20 years after its initial release.

The key singles, 'Place Your Hands' and follow-up 'Come Back Brighter', perfectly represent the no-frills, riff-heavy sound that pervades *Glow*. Each track is a slightly altered version of the two hit singles, while lead singer Gary Stringer's rough baritone voice, combined with guitarist Jesse Wood's use of the Les Paul Standard, puts the album's sound much more in line with American artists like Lenny Kravitz and Pearl Jam. Only on the single 'Consideration' did they alter their hard rock formula, with Stringer in a rare moment of tender falsetto alongside the band's only use of strings. The momentum of lead single 'Place Your Hands' meant the album entered straight in at number one in the chart when it was released in February '97.

Going for Gold (single – Shed Seven)

Charted: Mar '96; UK Chart Position: 8; Label: Polydor; Album: *A Maximum High*

Perhaps Shed Seven's most well-known song, 'Going for Gold' was the third of five singles released from second album *A Maximum High*. It was the band's biggest hit, peaking at number eight in the UK chart, where it spent five weeks. The single was performed live on *TFI Friday* and the title also gave its name to the band's first 'best of' album, released in May '99.

The CD single featured B-sides 'Making Waves' and 'Barracuda', while the cover artwork featured a naked woman with golden skin and, on the back, her silhouette (perhaps a reference to the James Bond film, *Goldfinger*). The woman also appears in the video wearing a bikini and dancing behind flames, interspersed with the band playing against a red background.

Going Out (single - Supergrass)

Charted: Mar '96; UK Chart Position: 5; Label: Parlophone; Album: *In it for the Money*

Supergrass' previous single, 'Alright', was a difficult act to follow, but 'Going Out' also made the top five of the UK chart, where it spent seven weeks. It was the first of five singles released from second album *In It For The Money*, paving the way for follow-up album success.

The video's opening credits, "A Dom & Nic film", referred to directors Nic Goffey (drummer Danny's brother) and Dominic Hawley, who also directed the video for Oasis' 'D'You Know What I Mean' and the Chemical Brothers' 'Block Rockin' Beats' among others. It featured the band playing on a bandstand in Battersea Park, London, from daylight until dark, wearing long coats and scarves.

Visually alluded to throughout the video, the song's lyric was about the invasion of privacy suffered by pop stars, particularly when hitting the town. The chief lyric ran "If you want to go out, read it in the papers, tell me what it's all about".

The CD B-sides included 'Melanie Davis' and a live version of 'Strange Ones', taken from their first album and recorded at the Plaza Ballroom in Glasgow.

Goldfinger (single - Ash)

Charted: Apr '96; UK Chart Position: 5; Label: Infectious; Album: *1977*

'Goldfinger' was Ash's highest charting single, reaching number five in the UK chart, where it spent nine weeks. It was the fourth of five singles released from the band's first official album *1977*, and arguably their most anthemic song. It also featured on the classic indie collection *Shine 5* as the opening track.

For such a grand song, the video was mediocre, featuring the band simply playing "down in the basement" as per the lyrics. The CD single contained B-sides 'I Need Somebody', written by bassist Mark Hamilton, 'Sneaker', written by Hamilton and Barry Peak of band Backwater, and a cover of Smokey Robinson's 'Get Ready'.

Good Enough (single – Dodgy)

Charted: Aug '96; UK Chart Position: 4; Label: A&M; Album: *Free Peace Sweet*

The summer anthem of '96, 'Good Enough' was Dodgy's biggest hit single, finally peaking at number four after several months of continued radio airplay, just like their single 'Staying Out For The Summer' had done the previous year. It spent eight weeks in the UK chart and was the band's only top-ten single, featuring B-sides 'Speaking In Tongues' and 'Lovebirds on Katovit'.

The band's usual jangly guitars and layered vocal lines were joined this time by an electric piano that gives the song its distinctive sound. The positive spin – "If it's good enough for you, it's good enough for me" – also acted as a strong message that caught the public imagination that summer. The song propelled album *Free Peace Sweet* to further success, and kept it in the top ten for 44 weeks.

Good Feeling (album – Travis)

Charted: Sept '97; UK Chart Position: 9; Label: Independiente; Singles: 'U16 Girls' (Apr '97, UKCP 40), 'All I Want to Do is Rock' (Jun '97, 39), 'Tied to the 90's' (Aug '97, 30), 'Happy' (Oct '97, 38), 'More Than Us' (Apr '98, 16)

Travis were notably late to the game when it came to Britpop, but their debut album found its way into this book because of its September '97 release. In many ways, this is more of a Britpop legacy record, with the band influenced by the scene rather than part of it.

It's the sound of a band with some great ideas, but who are just starting out and won't really come into their own until the release of second album *The Man Who* in June '99. 'Good Feeling' sees them finding their feet in a changing musical environment. The influence of Oasis hangs heavily over this album. Noel Gallagher was, in fact, a fan, asking the band to support Oasis and appearing on stage to play guitar on key single and album opener 'All I Want to Do is Rock'.

The album is less successful in its overall sound, but has a few stand-out tracks, such as the quirky single 'U16 Girls', a warning to all male listeners to check the age of the girls they go out with; the upbeat live set closer 'Happy'; and the beautifully restrained ballad 'More Than Us'. The album managed to sneak into the top ten, peaking at number nine in September '97 and setting the band on an upward trajectory that would outlive Britpop.

Good Mixer, The (pub)

Renowned as *the* Britpop pub, Camden's the Good Mixer on Inverness Street seems like much ado about nothing when you first walk in. It looks like a regular boozer with two rooms, a couple of pool tables, heavily tattooed staff and dated furniture, yet some of Britpop's most historic moments took place within its four walls. A regular haunt for Blur, Oasis, Elastica, Menswear and the Boo Radleys, among others, it was where Elastica made a no-fuss, no-lawyers, no-talk-of-money handshake deal with Deceptive Records over a packet of peanuts.

According to legend, it's also where Blur and Oasis had their first minor scuffle, possibly setting in motion their infamous feud. Oh, and apparently Menswear formed there.

Goodbye (album – Dubstar)

Charted: Oct '97; UK Chart Position: 18; Label: Food; Singles: 'No More Talk' (Jul '97, UKCP 20), 'Cathedral Park' (Sept '97, 41), 'I Will Be Your Girlfriend' (Jan '98, 28)

Goodbye was the second album by Dubstar and their highest charting, reaching the top 20 of the UK chart, where it spent two weeks. The album resulted in three singles: 'No More Talk', which was released as two CD versions, 'Cathedral Park' and 'I Will Be Your Girlfriend'. The Japanese version of the album included bonus tracks 'Unchained Monologue', 'La Bohème' and 'Goodbye'.

The cover artwork for the UK release – the last album to be released during the Britpop period – featured what appears to be an electric armchair. The band went on to release their final album *Make It Better* three years later, though this did not chart in the top ten.

Gorgeous George (album – Edwyn Collins)

Charted: Jul '95; UK Chart Position: 8; Label: Setanta; Singles: 'If You Could Love Me' (Mar '95, UKCP 98), 'A Girl Like You' (Jun '95, 4), 'Keep On Burning' (Mar '96, 45)

Gorgeous George was the third long-format release by Edwyn Collins and his only album to find its way into the top ten of the UK chart, where it spent nine weeks.

The album resulted in three singles: 'If You Could Love Me', which sat just inside the top ten; the mega-hit 'A Girl Like You', Collins' only top-ten hit; and 'Keep On Burning', which made the top 50 and was included on the '96 re-issue.

The album was released worldwide, with the Japanese version adding a bonus five tracks to the existing 12, including St Etienne's remix of album track 'Out Of This World'. The Australian version was released with a bonus CD as the 'Australian tour edition' and featured a track with Suede's Bernard Butler, 'If Ever You're Ready'.

Gorky's Zygotic Mynci (band)

Welsh band Gorky's Zygotic Mynci (pronounced: Gorky's Zigotic Monkey) were formed in '91 by Euros Childs, John Lawrence and Richard James, who all met at comprehensive school in Carmarthen, Wales. Childs' sister Megan joined the group soon after on violin and the line-up changed several times along the way.

The band, like the Super Furry Animals, sang in English and Welsh. They released several albums throughout the nineties and noughties, including *Barafundle*, which was released towards the end of the Britpop era in April '97. It contained the band's biggest single 'Patio Song' and was produced by Gorwel Owen, who also worked with the Super Furries. The band initially signed to record label Ankst, who released the first three albums, before moving to Fontana and eventually Mantra. The band split in '06, a few years after the release of their final album *Sleep/Holiday*. They also released compilation album *20: Singles & EPs '94-'96*.

The band's name came from a combination of "Gork", school slang for someone stupid, "Zygotic", picked up from a biology class about "zygotes" (fertilized egg cells), and "Mynci", using the Welsh spelling rules for "Monkey", although it's not a direct translation.

Govinda (single – Kula Shaker)

Charted: Nov '96; UK Chart Position: 7; Label: Columbia; Album: *K*

Kula Shaker found their individual edge by marrying traditional Indian music with British rock music, and nowhere is this better represented than on their fourth single from debut album *K*, 'Govinda', released in November '96. The fact that the song was sung entirely in Sanskrit did not put off its predominately English-speaking audience, and the song reached number seven, spending a total of ten weeks on the chart.

The song, which quickly became a live favourite, was released as two CDs, both containing B-side 'Gokula'. The first also included 'Hey Dude', recorded live at London's Astoria, and 'The Leek', while the second featured two remixes of the lead track.

Although singer and chief songwriter Crispian Mills claimed the song was an original composition completed with a vocal line created from a prayer to the Hindu god Krishna, George Harrison had previously produced a similar sounding song featuring singers from the Radha Krishna Temple in '70.

Grand Prix (album – Teenage Fanclub)

Charted: Jun '95; UK Chart Position: 7; Label: Creation; Singles: 'Mellow Doubt' (Mar '95, UKCP 34), 'Sparky's Dream' (May '95, 40), 'Neil Jung' (Aug '95, 62)

Grand Prix was the fifth studio album by Scottish band Teenage Fanclub and their first of two to reach the top ten of the UK chart, where it spent a total of five weeks. The album resulted in the top-40 singles 'Mellow Doubt' and 'Sparky's Dream', and 'Neil Jung', which sat just outside the top 60.

The album, released at the height of Britpop, received generally positive reviews. Opening track 'About You' sets the tone for the album, complete as it is with the band's signature sixties vibe and jangly music alongside lyrics about being hopelessly in love. The album cover featured a car provided by one of the Formula One racing teams, with the band's name emblazoned on the front. The Australian version of the album contained a bonus CD featuring previously unreleased B-sides and an acoustic version of 'About You'.

Great Escape, The (album – Blur)

Charted: Sept '95; UK Chart Position: 1; Label: Food; Singles: 'Country House' (Aug '95, UKCP 1), 'The Universal' (Nov '95, 5), 'Stereotypes' (Feb '96, 7), 'Charmless Man' (May '96, 5)

Blur's fourth studio album *The Great Escape* was released one month after its first single 'Country House' won the Battle of Britpop, trumping Oasis' 'Roll With It'. Much like its lead single, the album became known predominantly for its association with this key battle, but *The Great Escape* was much more than that.

Achieving enormous commercial success in the UK, it also went on to chart worldwide, becoming the band's first to crack the US. It also completed what chief songwriter Damon Albarn later described as 'the British trilogy of albums', which also included *Modern Life Is Rubbish* and *Parklife*. This line-drawing, combined with the album's critically lacklustre reception (despite its commercial success), meant that a change in direction was signalled. Two years later, *Blur* was released.

The album resulted in a further three singles, including 'The Universal', which was released in November '95 and peaked at number five in the UK chart. Now the band's typical live set closer, it was known for its beautiful orchestration by London-based horn section the Kick Horns, and the *Clockwork Orange* video, which featured Albarn wearing heavy eyeliner. The fact that the video was based on Stanley Kubrick's classic film was lost on many of those who saw it because the film was banned until the death of the director in '99.

'Stereotypes', which was released in February '96 and charted at number seven, features Albarn's infamous lyric "Wife-swapping is the future". And 'Charmless Man' was yet another single to make the top ten, charting at number five in April '96. Other notable inclusions on the album are the voice of future London Mayor Ken Livingstone, who narrates on the track 'Ernold Same'. Like nearly all the band's albums, Stephen Street produced and Food Records released.

Great Things (single – Echobelly)

Charted: Sept '95; UK Chart Position: 13; Label: Fauve; Album: *On*

'Great Things' was the first of three singles to be released from Echobelly's second album *On*. It was the band's first of two top-20 hits, followed by 'Dark Therapy' the following year, and spent three weeks on the UK chart.

The single was performed on nineties music show *The White Room* and on *Top of the Pops*, for which the band wore school uniforms.

The single was available to buy on two CDs. The first included B-sides 'Here Comes the Scene', 'God's Guest List' and 'On Turn Off'. The second featured 'On Turn On', 'Bunty' and 'One After 5am'; the last two "written & recorded in our bathroom on 28 June 1995", as stated on the back cover of the CD.

Guiding Star (single – Cast)

Charted: Jun '96; UK Chart Position: 9; Label: Polydor; Album: *Mother Nature Calls*

'Guiding Star' was the second of four singles from Cast's second album *Mother Nature Calls*. It was the band's seventh single and fifth to reach the top ten of the UK chart, where it spent six weeks.

Two versions of the CD single were available to buy. The first included B-sides 'Out of the Blue' and live versions of 'Free Me' and 'Mirror Me', taken from their Manchester Apollo gigs in April '97. The second CD featured 'Keep It Alive', a live recording of Bob Marley's 'Redemption Song' recorded on The World Cafe at WXPN Philadelphia, and an acoustic version of the lead track.

Guigsy (Paul McGuigan) (bass player – Oasis)

"Guigsy liked: weed, Manchester City, cricket and – a very distant fourth – being in Oasis," Noel Gallagher, '16.

Manchester-born Paul McGuigan, better known as 'Guigsy', was one of the founder members of Britpop legends Oasis, playing bass guitar with the band from '91 to '99, when he swapped rock 'n' roll for family life. It wasn't the first time he had left. He wasn't on the video for mega-hit 'Wonderwall' in '95, when he was temporarily replaced by Scott McLeod as he recovered from nervous exhaustion, returning for the band's first appearance at Earl's Court. He was a quiet, reserved character; someone who seemed to prefer to stay in the shadows, rarely speaking in interviews, if at all.

Before Oasis, McGuigan formed The Rain with Chris Hutton and future Oasis members Paul Arthurs and Tony McCarroll. Liam Gallagher later joined, replacing Hutton on vocals and renaming the band Oasis. Once Noel Gallagher joined, he sometimes replaced McGuigan's early bass recordings, despite him being a competent bassist. Staying true to character, McGuigan was the most well-behaved of the band, with very few incidents reported. He met his wife, Ruth Tolhurst, in '94 on a plane to Japan, where the band were about to embark on a tour. They live in London with their son.

H

Haines, Luke (singer/songwriter – The Auteurs)

Most commonly known as the lead singer of The Auteurs, Haines led the band through the decade, releasing several albums and singles and achieving moderate chart success. However, his independent spirirt meant The Auteurs were but a fragment of his musical achievements.

Born in October '67, Haines' debut recording was on singer David Westlake's solo album. He went on to record two albums with The Servants, '90's *Disinterest* and '91's *Small Time*. At the tail end of the nineties, as The Auteurs were winding down, Haines formed indie rock group Black Box Recorder with the Jesus and Mary Chain's John Moore and singer Sarah Nixey. They released several singles and three albums including UK chart top 40 *The Facts Of Life* in '00.

Haines' solo career progressed in various directions, including solo albums *The Oliver Twist Manifesto*, *Das Capital* and *Off My Rocker at the Art School Bop*, and even the soundtrack to British film *Christie Malry's Own Double Entry*. His memoir *Bad Vibes: Britpop and My Part in Its Downfall* was also published in '09, followed by second installment *Post Everything: Outsider Rock and Roll* in '11. He continues to tour, release and write and, among many collaborations, has so far released 13 solo albums, the most recent being '16's *Freqs*.

Hanging Around (single – Me, Me, Me)

Charted: Aug '96; UK Chart Position: 19; Label: Indolent; Album: n/a

'Hanging Around' was the only release by Britpop supergroup Me, Me, Me, finding its way into the top 20 of the UK chart, where it spent a total of four weeks. It was released on Indolent Records and produced by Stephen Street, with Blur's Alex James and Duran Duran's Stephen Duffy on vocals. The song was uplifting, filled with harmonies, interspersed with horns and featured one line sung in French.

The video focussed on an unwanted guest at a birthday party, who, after buying some extra-strong X-ray specs and seeing the guests as skeletons, decided to leave.

The CD single featured B-sides 'Hollywood Wives' and 'Tabitha's Island'. On the cover was a brunette woman wearing a red and white nineties-style vest top with the band's name emblazoned on the front.

Hawley, Richard (guitarist/singer/song-writer – Longpigs/Pulp/solo artist)

Richard Hawley contributed significantly to Britpop, playing guitar with the Longpigs throughout the nineties, playing with Pulp in the noughties and launching his own successful solo career after that.

Born in '67 in Sheffield to a musical family – father Dave played guitar in his own band, Dave Hawley Combo, and The Black Cats, and mother Lyn was a singer on the club circuit – it was almost inevitable that Hawley would embark on a musical career. He toured with Chuck Fowler's rock 'n' roll band as a guitarist while still in his early teens, developing a keen enthusiasm for the music.

Hawley made his name with Britpop band the Longpigs during the nineties and, after they split, played as a session musician for All Saints, Arctic Monkeys, Elbow, Jarvis Cocker and many more.

His incredible solo career began in '01 with a self-titled debut. Since then, he has gone on to release several studio albums, including top 40 hit and Mercury Prize nominee *Coles Corner* in '05, top-ten album

Lady's Bridge in '07, top-20 album *Truelove's Gutter* in '09 and top-ten albums *Standing at the Sky's Edge* in '12, also nominated for the Mercury Prize, and *Hollow Meadows* in '15.

He's on the Phone (single – Saint Étienne)

Charted: Nov '95; UK Chart Position: 11; Label: Heavenly; Album: n/a

Saint Étienne's highest charting single, 'He's on the Phone', was a stand-alone release that didn't feature on any of their albums. It peaked at number 11 in the UK chart when it was released in November '95, and was interestingly re-released two weeks later featuring vocals from French singer and songwriter Étienne Daho, which reached number 22. Together the singles spent a total of ten weeks on the chart.

The original was released as a CD and featured B-sides 'Groveley Road', 'Is it True' and 'The Process'.

Heavy Soul (album – Paul Weller)

Charted: Jul '97; UK Chart Position: 2; Label: Go Discs Island; Singles: 'Peacock Suit' (Jul '96, UKCP 5), 'Brushed' (Aug '97, 14), 'Friday Street' (Oct '97, 21), 'Mermaids' (Dec '97, 30)

Heavy Soul was the fourth solo studio album from Paul Weller, and the much-anticipated follow-up to the highly successful *Stanley Road*. The album narrowly missed out on the UK chart top spot, reaching number two in July '97 and spending 16 weeks on the chart.

It contained the top-ten single 'Peacock Suit', top-20 single 'Brushed' and top-30 singles 'Friday Street' and 'Mermaids', which collectively spent a total of 17 weeks on the chart. The Japanese edition of the album featured bonus track 'Eye of the Storm'.

Weller had found his solo footing with the *Stanley Road* album, and chose to continue the same style on *Heavy Soul*, making the most of the retrospective Britpop sound and going back to his roots, drawing once again on the key sounds that had influenced him. *Heavy Soul* didn't contain the same radio-friendly singles as *Stanley Road*, but it played its part in supporting this stage of his career and provided a suitable influence for the next generation of musicians.

Heavy Stereo (band)

Creation band Heavy Stereo were fronted by Gem Archer, most commonly known for replacing Bonehead in Oasis, bassist Nez, Pete Downing on lead guitar and drummer Nick Jones.

Heavily influenced by seventies glam rock, in particular Gary Glitter and the New York Dolls, they released debut album *Deja Voodoo* in September '96, which resulted in four singles 'Sleep Freak', 'Smiler', 'Chinese Burn', which featured on indie compilation album *Shine 6*, and 'Mouse in a Hole'.

That same year the band supported Oasis at several gigs, but failed to release any further material. In '99 they contributed to compilation album *Fire and Skill: The Songs of the Jam*, covering 'The Gift', and supported Paul Weller on tour. All new material was put on hold, however, when Archer's mother became seriously ill.

During that time, Bonehead left Oasis and Archer got a call from Noel Gallagher. He played with Oasis until the band broke up in '09 and with Liam Gallagher's band Beady Eye until they also disbanded in '14.

Hedonism (single – Skunk Anansie)

Charted: Feb '97; UK Chart Position: 13; Label: One Little Indian; Album: *Stoosh*

'Hedonism' was the third single to be released from Skunk Anansie's second album *Stoosh*, and the band's fourth single to reach the top 20, where it spent six weeks.

Two versions of the CD single were released. CD1 contained B-sides 'So Sublime', 'Let It Go' and 'Strong', and CD2 featured an acoustic version of the lead song, as well as 'Song Recovery', 'Contraband' and 'I Don't Believe'.

Directed by Thomas Krygier, the video, featuring the band performing in a flat, prompted controversy at the time because it showed two women passionately kissing. Perhaps the catchiest of the band's singles, the song became one of their most popular tracks, eagerly anticipated at gigs and featuring a crowd-pleasing chorus, with every word repeated by every audience member.

Helen Love (band)

Welsh indie band Helen Love were named after their Swansea-based lead singer, who formed the band in '92 with Sheena on guitar, bassist Roxy and Mark on keyboards. They released two albums, *Radio Hits* and *Radio Hits 2*, during the Britpop period under label Damaged Goods, though ironically no singles became radio hits.

Despite having no real chart successes, Helen Love became well known in Britpop circles when long-term hero Joey Ramone, from classic punk band The Ramones, asked them to play at a gig in New York after he heard their second single, '(Sheena's in Love with) Joey Ramone'. He later introduced their Radio 1 Evening Session. The band also went on to release another single, 'You Can't Beat a Boy Who Loves the Ramones'.

Though the band were a success on evening radio, they only made limited runs of their singles, which is why they never charted well. Despite releasing 28 singles between '93 and '15 (with no break over the years), just two entered the chart, '97's 'Does Your Heart Go Boom' (number 71) and '98's 'Long Live the UK Music Scene' (number 65). The band have released eight studio albums and are still playing together today.

Help Album, The (charity compilation album)

Charted: Sept '95; UK Compilations Chart Position: 1; Label: Go! Discs; Singles: 'Come Together' (Dec '95, UKCP 19)

The Help Album was a collaborative effort from a number of Britpop giants, including Oasis, Suede and Blur, covering or producing new material for the War Child charity in '95. Much like the concept driving John Lennon's 'Instant Karma' single, in that material should be recorded and released immediately, *The Help Album* was recorded on 4 September and released on 9 September. Highlights included a cover of the Beatles' song 'Come Together' by supergroup the Smokin' Mojo Filters, which included Paul McCartney, Paul Weller, Noel Gallagher, Steve Cradock of Ocean Colour Scene, Paul Weller's drummer Steve White and American soul singer Carleen Anderson.

The Manic Street Preachers recorded a cover of 'Raindrops Keep Fallin' on My Head', which later became a live favourite and was their first recording since the disappearance of guitarist Richey Edwards.

Radiohead debuted a song which would later appear on their third album *OK Computer* called 'Lucky'. The album was initially aimed at the UK Albums Chart on the pretext that all artists were members of a one-off supergroup called War Child, but this was rejected in favour of a 'various artists' album, which could only be released into the UK Albums Compilations Chart.

Help the Aged (single – Pulp)

Charted: Nov '97; UK Chart Position: 8; Label: Island; Album: *This is Hardcore*

'Help the Aged' was the first of four singles from Pulp's sixth studio album *This is Hardcore*, and the band's fifth to reach the top ten of the UK chart, where it spent a total of ten weeks at the tail end of '97. The CD single featured B-sides 'Tomorrow Never Lies' and 'Laughing Boy'.

The song is dressed up as a tongue-in-cheek ditty urging youngsters to respect their elders but, when placed in the wider context of the album, it manages to take on a much deeper resonance. Could it be that songwriter Jarvis Cocker was worried about his own mortality? Perhaps it was a feeling brought on by coming down from the hedonistic years the band's '95 album *Different Class* brought them.

Hey Dude (single – Kula Shaker)

Charted: Sept '96; UK Chart Position: 2; Label: Columbia; Album: *K*

The third of four singles released from Kula Shaker's debut album *K* was the first to have no direct reference to Hinduism or Eastern culture, although its lyrics are still filled with magic realism and poetic metaphor. Narrowly missing out on the top spot of the UK chart (because of the Spice Girls' debut mega-hit single 'Wannabe'), 'Hey Dude' was the band's longest running single on the chart, where it spent ten weeks. Its success was predominantly down to the guttural chant of its anthemic chorus, which drew heaving crowds to every indie-club dancefloor.

Two CD versions of the single were released, the first containing B-sides 'Troubled Mind', debut single 'Grateful When You're Dead', recorded for the BBC, and 'Into The Deep', while the second featured a recording of previous single 'Tattva' for Mark Radcliffe's Radio 1 show in February '96, 'Drop in the Sea' and a recording of lead singer Crispian reading from the *Mahabharata*, also for the BBC.

Hirst, Damien (artist)

The leading figure of the Young British Artists (YBA) movement of the early nineties, Damien Hirst is now widely considered the king of contemporary British art. He is rumoured to be worth upwards of £215m, making him the UK's richest living artist, and broke his own record for the most expensive work of art sold when his whole show, *Beautiful Inside My Head Forever*, sold in one go in '08 for an estimated £111m.

Born in Bristol in September '65, but growing up in Leeds, Hirst began making major waves in the art world at the age of 23, when he curated the first Freeze art exhibition while in his second year of studying for a BA in fine art at Goldsmith's College in London. This was the same course taken by Graham Coxon from Blur, who was a year behind Hirst.

Hirst developed a factory-like way of producing art in the modern world, using scores of assistants to create works from his original ideas. It wasn't new, building instead on the work of the great modernist Marcel Duchamp, who installed a latrine in the middle of a Parisian art gallery in '17 to call into question the very essence of what was and what was not considered art. The artist was at the heart of the equation, not the artwork.

Hirst popularised this concept, using increasingly controversial subject matter, notably the corpses of dead and, in some cases, decomposing animals in formaldehyde-filled glass cases, to push the ideas behind art to the forefront.

Death was a recurring theme in his work. Alongside his iconic *The Physical Impossibility of Death in the Mind of Someone Living*, which featured a shark in a glass tank, he won the prestigious Turner Prize in '95 for his piece *Two Fucking and Two Watching*, which featured the hanging headless corpses of a cow and a bull. The provocative piece was banned in New York because it was feared it would make audiences physically ill.

The continual controversy surrounding Hirst garnered much attention from the media and art dealers, most notably advertising guru and art collector Charles Saatchi, who commissioned the shark in the tank. This attention helped raise the profile of the British art scene, putting it at the centre of the world map, just as Britpop was taking hold. The two worlds met when Hirst directed the over-the-top music video for Blur's 'Country House', the song that saw the band face off against Oasis in the 'Battle of Britpop'. He also partnered with Alex James and actor Keith Allen to create the band Fat Les, who scored a number two hit in '98 with the tongue-in-cheek football world cup anthem 'Vindaloo'.

The band later released a version of the traditional English hymn 'Jerusalem' for the Euro 2000 Championship and, in '12, changed their name to Fit Les to release *The Official Fit Les Olympic Anthem* to coincide with the London Olympics. In addition, just as the world's eyes turned to Britain for the 2012 Games, Tate Modern staged a major retrospective of Hirst's work, featuring all his best-known pieces, co-curated by gallery director and early supporter of his work, Sir Nicholas Serota.

Hirst owns a vast portfolio of properties and land, including a huge artists' compound in Mexico and many townhouses in central London, but spends most of his time on his estate in Devon. He has three sons, Connor, Cassius and Cyrus Joe, with long-term partner Maia Norman, from whom he split in '12 after more than 20 years together. Tracey Emin, a fellow YBA member, has compared Hirst's work in the nineties and beyond to that of Andy Warhol in the sixties.

His 'n' Hers (album – Pulp)

Charted: Apr '94; UK Chart Position: 9; Label: Island; Singles: 'Babies' (Oct '92, UKCP n/a), 'Lip Gloss' (Nov '93, 50), 'Do You Remember the First Time?' (Apr '94, 33), 'The Sisters EP' (Jun '94, 19)

Pulp's fourth studio album *His 'n' Hers* saw the band finally break into the mainstream UK chart, paving the way for the huge commercial success of follow-up *Different Class*. Produced by Ed Buller, who also worked on the album that launched Suede into the Britpop limelight, the album peaked at number nine in the chart, where it spent 55 weeks. The single 'Do You Remember the First Time?' made its way into the top 40, peaking at number 33 in April '94.

The album was recorded at London's Britannia Row and released in April '94, narrowly missing out on that year's Mercury Music Prize to M People's *Elegant Slumming*. The album artwork features Jarvis Cocker before his trademark thick-rimmed glasses, but his innate dry wit and intelligence is there in the lyrics. The album includes some of Pulp and Britpop's much-loved anthems, notably 'Babies' and 'Do You Remember the First Time?'.

HMV (record store)

Now that downloading and streaming music dominate the industry so strongly, it's tough to truly understand the importance of HMV in the story of popular British music. Alongside attending live gigs and listening to the radio, heading to the local record store was a key part of the music scene experience, and the only legal way of getting hold of the latest releases on CD, cassette, vinyl, VHS and, later, DVD.

Named after Francis Barraud's painting *His Master's Voice*, which featured Nipper the dog cocking one ear as he listens to his owner's gramophone recording (the image also became the company's logo), HMV's first store opened on London's Oxford Street in 1921. It came to prominence in the sixties as Britain's leading music retailer and, by the nineties, was a mighty chain of record stores that ran the length and breadth of the country, not unlike Starbucks or McDonalds today. Whether it was the flagship store on Oxford Street (once the world's biggest record store) or a small branch with a handful of staff, most towns boasted their own HMV for music fans to flock to buy and listen to music, or just hang out with like-minded folk.

HMV still stands for something today. It provides a vital face-to-face community where people can interact beyond their computer screen. It's resistance to change and refusal to evolve has proved costly though, almost leading to the company's complete collapse.

A vacuum was caused by HMV's refusal to engage with the changing demands of the public; a vacuum soon filled by iTunes, Amazon and, later, Spotify. When HMV finally decided to try to compete, it was too late and it went into administration in January '13. In January '14, the doors to the world's largest music store were closed for good. However, later that year, HMV started to make something of a recovery and, by the end of '14, was again the UK's biggest seller of physical music, with a new flagship store at the other end of Oxford Street.

During its nineties heyday, bands would play live gigs in HMV's bigger stores, or make appearances and sign records if there was no room for a stage. There was, therefore, a certain amount of kudos associated with working at HMV. It was more than just a job behind the counter in a fetching black fleece bearing the iconic logo; it was a status symbol for any young music fan, someone in a fledgling band, someone keen to join a band or just enthusiastic supporters of the local scene. Many bands were formed in HMV and, although not all of them went on to achieve worldwide super-stardom, the quality of the experience was still important – an experience Amazon could never offer.

Hook, Peter (bassist/singer/songwriter – Joy Division/New Order/Monaco)

Alongside guitarist Bernard Sumner, drummer Stephen Morris and the ill-fated but iconic lead singer Ian Curtis, bassist Peter Hook was one of the founder members of Manchester New Wave band Joy Division, who became New Order after Curtis' death in '80.

One of the most individual bass guitar players in British rock history, 'Hookie' created his own immediately identifiable style of playing. Instead of merely playing the root notes of the chords to provide a rhythmic backdrop to the band's sound, he would often play high up on the fretboard (apparently initiated so he could actually hear what he was playing), creating licks and riffs like a lead guitarist.

Born in Salford the day before Valentine's Day in '56, Hookie met Sumner at school and the pair quickly become friends through a shared love of music, and through learning bass and guitar together as teenagers. They formed Warsaw (later Joy Division) in '76 after seeing the Sex Pistols play in Manchester, and signed to Factory Records in '78.

After the death of Curtis, the band became New Order and slowly created a very different sound, layering drum loops, samples and electronic effects, totally at odds to the Britpop sound. The band unofficially split in '93 just as the Britpop scene was getting underway and, while Sumner focussed on his side project Electronic, Hook founded Monaco in '95. The band released the top-20 album *Music for Pleasure* in '97. A far cry from the rock-tinged electronica of New Order, Monaco were a back-to-basics group that fit perfectly into Britpop.

New Order reformed in '98, releasing new album *Get Ready* in '01, but Hook left the band in '07 after a much-publicised falling out with Sumner. He released part one of his memoirs *Unknown Pleasures* in '13, focussing on his childhood, his time in Joy Division and his recovery from alcoholism and drug addiction during the New Order years. The second instalment, *Substance*, dealing in detail with his

New Order days and his marriage to comedy writer Caroline Aherne, came out in '17.

Apropos of nothing, Hook and drummer Stephen Morris were both questioned by the police in '79 as part of the investigation into the Yorkshire Ripper murders because the Joy Division's touring schedule coincided with some of the attacks.

He continues to play music as Peter Hook and Light, as well as earning his keep as a DJ. He has been married three times and has three children.

Hope Street (single – The Levellers)

Charted: Aug '95; UK Chart Position: 12; Label: China; Album: *Zeitgeist*

'Hope Street' was the opening track on the Levellers' fourth album *Zeitgeist* and the first of four singles released from it. It spent eight weeks on the chart, was the band's fifth single to reach the top 20 and became their longest-running chart single until the release of 'Just the One'.

The CD single featured B-sides 'Miles Away', 'Leave This Town' and 'Busking on Hope St'. The video showed the band playing inside and outside the Hope Tavern on the corner of Hope Street. Singer-songwriter Billy Bragg recorded a new version of the song with the band in '14, which featured on their greatest hits album released the same year.

Continuing the theme of some of their best-known songs, like 'Fantasy' and 'Fifteen Years', 'Hope Street' tells the melancholic story of the many poor and dispossessed souls who spend their time on Hope Street. They drink too much, gamble away their money or root through bins to find food, while singer and lyricist Mark Chadwick asks for the rain to wash the street clean so that they can all start again.

How High (single - The Charlatans)

Charted: Jun '97; UK Chart Position: 6; Label: Beggars Banquet; Album: *Tellin' Stories*

'How High' was the third of four singles released from The Charlatans' fifth album *Tellin' Stories*, and the band's fourth and final top-ten single, spending five weeks on the UK chart. The single, which they performed on TV show *TFI Friday*, was the band's most straightforward rock song with a strong distorted guitar riff. It clocks in at exactly three minutes and stands as the band's most obvious contribution to Britpop, a far cry from their Madchester roots.

The CD single contained B-sides 'Down with the Mook' and 'Title Fight'. The Japanese release featured bonus tracks 'Tellin' Stories' and 'Don't Need a Gun'.

Hundred Mile High City (single - Ocean Colour Scene)

Charted: Jun '97; UK Chart Position: 4; Label: MCA; Album: *Marchin' Already*

The first single to be released from Ocean Colour Scene's third studio album *Marchin' Already* launched the band back into the UK chart with their most foot-stomping, rabble-rousing single to date.

The single reached number four in June '97 and hung around in the charts for nine weeks. It was the band's fourth consecutive single to reach the top ten.

The single appeared as a CD, as well as 7" and 10" promo vinyl. B-sides included 'The Face Smiles Back Easily', 'Falling to the Floor' and 'Hello Monday'. The song also featured as the opening track to Guy Ritchie's UK gangster film *Lock, Stock and Two Smoking Barrels* in '99.

Hurricane #1 (band)

Creation Records band Hurricane #1 were formed by former Ride guitarist and future Oasis bassist Andy Bell in '96. The band line-up was completed by vocalist and guitarist Alex Lowe, bassist Will Peppar and drummer Gareth Farmer, but Bell was the driving force, playing lead guitar, keyboards, singing backing vocals and writing most of the songs. Building on the shoegazing sound of former band Ride, he chose to adapt to the changing times, using the popularity of the back-to-basics approach of Britpop but layering in intricately linked lead guitar lines, taking his influence from John Squire from the Stone Roses.

The band released just two albums during their three years together, their UK top-20 eponymous debut in '97 and follow-up *Only the Strongest Will Survive* in '99, which reached a disappointing number 55, perhaps because the band chose not to include their most successful single (of the same name), which reached number 19. The band hit the singles top 40 on four occasions with the top-20 single 'Step Into My World', 'Just Another Illusion', 'Chain Reaction' and 'Only The Strongest Will Survive'.

After releasing three solo albums, Lowe reformed the band without founder member and key creative driving force Bell in '14. Their third album, *Find What You Love and Let It Kill You*, came out the following year. Fourth album *Melodic Rainbows* was released in '16, though neither album managed to enter the UK chart.

Hurricane #1 (album – Hurricane #1)

Charted: Sept '97; UK Chart Position: 11; Label: Creation; Singles: 'Step Into My World' (May '97, UKCP 19), 'Just Another Illusion' (Jul '97, 35), 'Chain Reaction' (Sep '97, 30), 'Monday Afternoon' (Nov '97, n/a)

Hurricane #1's debut self-titled album was released towards the end of the Britpop era in the summer of '97, narrowly missing out on a top-ten spot in the UK chart. It peaked at number 11 in September '97, and spent a total of three weeks on the chart.

The album resulted in four singles: the top-20 release 'Step Into My World', 'Just Another Illusion', 'Chain Reaction' and 'Monday Afternoon'. Lead guitarist and chief songwriter Andy Bell dedicated the album to his then wife, the Swedish singer Idha Ovelius, who also features on the album's cover.

The album was released worldwide, with the US and Canadian editions featuring bonus tracks 'Touchdown' and 'Smoke Rings'.

Hush (single – Kula Shaker)

Charted: Mar '97; UK Chart Position: 2; Label: Columbia; Album: n/a

Not featured on any album, 'Hush' was a stand-alone single released by Kula Shaker four months after 'Govinda'. It was the band's biggest hit, reaching number two in the UK chart, and is still often played on radio today. The single narrowly missed the top spot, and spent a total of ten weeks on the chart. 'Hush' also featured on the soundtrack to the '97 American film *I Know What You Did Last Summer*.

Written by American singer-songwriter Joe South, the original version of 'Hush' was released by Billy Joe Royal in '67, but was made famous by the UK rock band Deep Purple, who put it out as their debut single in '68, though it was only released in the USA.

There were two versions of the CD single, both featuring B-side 'Raagy One (Waiting for Tomorrow)'. CD1 also contained 'Knight on the Town' (live at the London Astoria) and 'Smart Dogs' (live at Aston Villa Leisure Centre), while CD2 featured B-sides 'Under the Hammer' and 'Govinda' (live at Plymouth Pavilion).

I

I Should Coco (album – Supergrass)

Charted: May '95; UK Chart Position: 1; Label: Parlophone; Singles: 'Caught by the Fuzz' (Oct '94, UKCP 43), 'Mansize Rooster' (Feb '95, 20), 'Lose It' (Mar '95, 75), 'Lenny' (May '95, 10), 'Alright/Time' (Jul '95, 2)

Supergrass' debut album *I Should Coco* propelled the band into the Britpop limelight on its release in May '95, filled as it was with catchy three-minute pop songs that grabbed the attention of the listener and stood out on the radio. Typified by, but not defined by, the band's biggest single 'Alright', which reached number two in the chart two months after the album was released, *I Should Coco* was the feelgood hit of the year in '95. It was Parlophone's biggest selling debut since the Beatles' 'Please, Please Me' in '62, and reached the top spot in the UK chart.

Influenced by seventies punk-pop bands like The Jam and the Buzcocks, the band made *I Should Coco* incredibly quickly in an attempt to capture the excitement and energy of the songs as they performed them live. It was recorded at Sawmills Studio in Cornwall and produced by Sam Williams, who spotted the band playing live in their home town and wanted to express what he had seen at the gig. From the five singles released, 'Lenny' and 'Alright' made the top ten, 'Man-size Rooster' the top 20 and 'Caught by the Fuzz' and 'Lose It' the top ten. The cover featured likenesses of the band, most notably lead singer Gaz Coombes with his mouth wide open.

I'm So Lonely (single – Cast)

Charted: Nov '97; UK Chart Position: 14; Label: Polydor; Album: *Mother Nature Calls*

'I'm So Lonely' was the fourth and final single from Cast's second album *Mother Nature Calls* and, following the success of all eight previous singles released by the band, achieved a top-20 spot in the UK chart, where it spent a total of five weeks.

Two CD versions were released, the first featuring B-sides 'The Things You Make Me Do', a live version of the album's penultimate track 'Never Gonna Tell You What to Do' and a remix of 'History'; the second containing 'Theme From' and another remix of 'History'. The video for the single features several people experiencing lonely moments.

If You Don't Want Me to Destroy You (single – Super Furry Animals)

Charted: Oct '96; UK Chart Position: 18; Label: Creation; Album: *Fuzzy Logic*

'If You Don't Want Me to Destroy You' was the fourth and final single from the Super Furry Animals' debut album *Fuzzy Logic* and the band's second top-20 hit, spending two weeks in the UK chart in October '96. Unlike the speedy pop-punk of the band's previous releases, this showcased a different side to the Welsh band's sound.

The cover featured the band standing on a tank emblazoned with the Welsh phrase "A Oes Heddwch" across the front, meaning, "Is there peace?". B-sides included 'Guacamole' and '(Nid) Hon Yw'r Sy'n Mynd I Achub Yr Iaith'.

If You're Thinking of Me (single – Dodgy)

Charted: Nov '96; UK Chart Position: 11; Label: A&M; Album: *Free Peace Sweet*

'If You're Thinking of Me' was the third of four singles from Dodgy's third album *Free Peace Sweet* and, as a slow, sentimental unrequited love song, was completely different in style to the band's previous releases. The single became their fourth to reach the top 20 in the UK chart, where it spent seven weeks, peaking at number 11 and narrowly missing out on a top-ten spot.

The single, which featured a human eye on the cover, included B-sides 'Pebblemilljam', 'Forever Remain' and a previously unreleased version of the single 'Good Enough'. The video showed the band performing on a platform on an increasingly stormy sea, and ends with a dramatic explosion.

In a Room (single – Dodgy)

Charted: Jun '96; UK Chart Position: 12; Label: A&M; Album: *Free Peace Sweet*

'In a Room' was one of Dodgy's most successful singles, and the first of four released from their third album *Free Peace Sweet*. Narrowly missing out on a top-ten spot in the UK chart, the track was the band's second top-20 hit, after the re-issue of 'Staying out for the Summer '95', and spent six weeks on the chart.

The single, which featured a bird in a cage on the cover, included the tracks 'Self Doubt', an acoustic version of album track 'Long Life' and a remix of the album's penultimate track 'U.K.R.I.P' called 'Jungle UK (No Rest In Peace)'. The video featured the band playing in a living room with the lead singer floating to the ceiling while singing "No one can reach me, no one hears my voice anymore".

In it for the Money (album – Supergrass)

Charted: May '97; UK Chart Position: 2; Label: Parlophone; Singles: 'Going Out' (Mar '96, UKCP 5), 'Richard III' (May '97, 2), 'Sun Hits the Sky' (Jun '97, 10), 'Late in the Day' (Oct '97, 18)

Supergrass were conscious of not repeating the formula of their first album *I Should Coco*, which found them safely installed in the Britpop pantheon in '95, so the follow-up *In it for the Money*, which appeared in record stores exactly two years after the release of their debut, was the much darker and more intense cousin of its predecessor. Gone were the honky-tonk piano lines of hit single 'Alright' and in came the screeching guitars and thundering drums of lead single 'Richard III', and the quiet acoustic introspection of 'Late in the Day'.

The cover saw the three core members of the group busking, purposefully at odds with the tongue-in-cheek cynicism of the title. It also showed they still had some of their cheeky Monkees-style humour, even if they now wanted to be taken more seriously.

Whether it was the new approach, the fact Britpop was at its peak or the simple popularity of the band winning through, the album was an immediate hit, peaking at number two in the UK chart and resulting in three top-ten singles and one that made the top-20. It cemented the band's reputation, proving they were much more than their hit single 'Alright', and set them above many of their contemporaries, resulting in continued success post-Britpop.

In the Name of the Father (single – Black Grape)

Charted: Aug '95; UK Chart Position: 8; Label: Radioactive; Album: *It's Great When You're Straight... Yeah!*

'In the Name of the Father', which takes its name from a traditional Christian blessing, was Black Grape's second of three singles from their debut album *It's Great When You're Straight... Yeah!* and the band's second to use religious imagery in its lyrics.

The single was the band's second to reach the top ten of the UK chart, where it spent four weeks, peaking at number eight in August '95. The opening lyrics, "Come to me, come lie beside me", feature in Scottish novelist Alan Warner's book, *These Demented Lands*, the sequel to his highly successful debut *Morvern Caller*, about the lives of a rough community in the Scottish Highlands, including a DJ who wants to hold a rave to end all raves.

The B-sides included remixes of 'Land of 1000 Karma Sutra Babes' and the lead track. The video, directed by Don Letts and filmed over two days in Jamaica, featured the band as religious missionaries on a remote island.

Inbetweener (single – Sleeper)

Charted: Jan '95; UK Chart Position: 16; Label: Indolent; Album: *Smart*

When Britpop was over and Sleeper had long since disbanded, singer Louise Wener eventually reinvented herself as a novelist, bringing her obsession with the lives of everyday people and their emotional rollercoasters to the page. If you look at Sleeper's breakthrough single 'Inbetweener', it's easy to see how she made the leap.

It tells the story of a romantic liaison between a guy and a girl, in which he wishes for more than she does. In Wener's words, "he's nothing special, he's not too smart; he's just my inbetweener" – subject matter that reflected the changing attitudes toward relationships in the nineties.

Released in January '95, the band's third single from debut album *Smile* peaked at number 16 in the UK chart and set them on the road to mid-level Britpop commercial success. As well as being released on limited edition 7" and 12" vinyl, the CD release featured B-sides 'Little Annie' and 'Disco Duncan'.

Indie (music genre)

All Britpop is indie, but not all indie is Britpop. The term 'indie' was originally attributed to any band who released a record on an independently-owned record label, but over the years it has come to refer more specifically to a musical genre with a style and sound all its own. By the nineties, bands could quite easily be 'indie' while under contract to a major label, like Cast, Supergrass and Pulp, or a smaller label owned by a major name, such as Oasis and Blur.

There have been many independent labels throughout the history of popular music, but the term only really came to prominence in the late seventies once the punk scene was in full flow. Partly because it was so expensive to record and press a record during the fifties and sixties, the majors maintained a monopoly on the musical landscape that was only really possible to counteract once punk gathered momentum. With the advancements in good-quality, affordable sound-recording equipment made during the seventies, it meant almost anyone could release a record as the decade came to an end. Punk was a direct attack not only on the establishment, but also on the pretentious, over-the-top prog-rock bands of the seventies scene. These bands, such as Pink Floyd and Yes, were all signed to major labels.

It soon became pretty uncool to sign to a major and, as the seventies turned into the eighties, some of Britain's best-known independent labels were finding their feet and shaping the sound of the music scene. Rough Trade signed The Smiths, Factory took on Joy Division and Creation Records got the Jesus and Mary Chain and My Bloody Valentine. Although these labels were all from very different parts of the UK, they were drawn together through a shared musical aesthetic. Their guitar sound was often rough and edgy, without being metal or punk.

As the decade wore on, more and more indie labels were founded, most notably: Beggars Banquet (The Charlatans); Heavenly Records (the Manic Street Preachers); Silvertone (the Stone Roses); and Deceptive Records (Elastica). All enjoyed commercial success and were spurred on by the continued development and ease of producing and packaging music releases.

Then, in '92, Alan McGee, facing near-bankruptcy brought on by the spiralling recording costs of My Bloody Valentine's second album, sold nearly half the shares of Creation Records to Sony. Suddenly major labels, perhaps sore about missing out on the most exciting new music, were making the independent labels offers they could not refuse. Some were even happy to take a back seat, allowing – in McGee's case – total creative freedom to release what they wanted, but with the financial backing of a major label behind them. You could argue that this was capitalism in its purest form, with the deep-pocketed bigger boys, with no real passion for the products they were selling, maintaining control of the market place by flashing the cash. Whatever your view, there was no escaping the fact that the majors had bought back control of the music scene.

The term 'indie' survived because it had come to define a genre of music, rather than the labels behind it. Indie bands, then and now, are deemed to have integrity because they often remain underground, sometimes unable to make a living from their music but happy to be doing it for the people who care the most: the fans. They don't sell out, but maintain their art through hard work, dedication and the support of the few who love them. This has led to another sub-group of the movement, the 'indie-er than thou', who come to hate their favourite bands once they achieve any kind of commercial success. This was still some way off in the Britpop era though. It was okay to be indie and sell loads of records. But only for a short while.

Intastella (band)

Manchester band Intastella were singer Stella Grundy, guitarist Martin Wright, bassist Martin Mittler, drummer Spencer Birtwistle and dancer Lil' Anthony, formed from the remnants of The Laugh in '90.

The band were initially signed to MCA Records and released singles 'Dream Some Paradise', 'People' and 'Century', and debut album *Intastella and the Family of People* in the early nineties.

The band then signed to Planet 3 and released EP 'Drifter', which featured Shaun Ryder; their biggest hit 'The Night', which peaked at number 60 in the UK chart; 'Grandmaster', which just made the top ten; and, finally, 'Skyscraper', which peaked at number 81 and featured on indie compilation album *Shine 8*. Second album *What You Gonna Do* was released in '95 and final album *Nuphonia* in '97. None of the albums made the UK chart.

It Doesn't Matter Anymore (album – The Supernaturals)

Charted: May '97; UK Chart Position: 9; Label: Food; Singles: 'Lazy Lover' (Oct '96, UKCP 34), 'The Day Before Yesterday's Man' (Feb '97, 25), 'Smile' (Apr '97, 23), 'Love Has Passed Away' (Jul '97, 38), 'Prepare To Land' (Oct '97, 48)

It Doesn't Matter Anymore was the debut album by Scottish band The Supernaturals. Released in May '97, it went straight into the top ten of the UK chart, where it spent a total of six weeks. The album contained the band's biggest hit 'Smile', as well as the top-40 singles 'Lazy Lover', 'The Day Before Yesterday's Man' and 'Love Has Passed Away'.

The album, with a smiling monkey on the cover, received positive reviews and was the band's most successful long player, with follow-up *A Tune a Day* released one year later, narrowly missing out on the top 20.

Like Travis and Embrace, The Supernaturals came relatively late to the Britpop scene, but managed to secure their place, thanks to their tune-filled catchy choruses and jangly guitar lines, even if they didn't enjoy lasting success once the era came to an end. As the main lyric to their best-known song has it, "Every silver lining has a cloud; you better smile". And, for a couple of years at least, The Supernaturals did just that.

It Girl, The (album – Sleeper)

Charted: May '96; UK Chart Position: 5; Label: Indolent; Singles: 'What Do I Do Now?' (Oct '95, UKCP 14), 'Sale of the Century' (May '96, 10); 'Nice Guy Eddie' (Jul '96, 10); 'Statuesque' (Oct '96, 17)

Sleeper's second album *The It Girl* was released in May '96, not long before Oasis played Knebworth and the Britpop scene reached its peak. In the Battle of Britpop, there was no doubt whose side Louise Wener's band were on (they toured with Blur).

Her songs were always little stories, just like Albarn on the *Parklife* album in '94, nowhere more so that on Sleeper's second – and most successful – album. Just like Blur, the band specialised in creating songs about contemporary English life, of romances lost and won, of nights out at bars and live gigs, of trying to find 'the one' and hanging out with friends, all of which chimed with the record-buying public of the time.

The album peaked at number five in the UK chart, where it spent a total of 42 weeks, supported by the top-20 hit 'What Do I Do Now?' and top-ten entries 'Sale of the Century' and 'Nice Guy Eddie'. The final single, 'Statuesque', which featured on the soundtrack to the film *Trainspotting*, found its way into the top 20 when released in October '96.

It Girls and the Cult of Celebrity

The term 'It Girl' was first used in the UK during the 'Roaring Twenties', at a time when the press was becoming obsessed with the goings-on of the rich and the famous, and 'it' was applied to anything currently in fashion. In the sixties, advancements in photography and videography gave more power to the press and prompted the rise of the fashion model. Now bold pictures could accompany tabloid stories of the rich and attractive, and fame soon came to define the individual.

By the time the sixties-obsessed nineties came around, the idea of the It Girl regained its prominence in society. She was a trendsetter, a style icon, an actor, a singer, a TV presenter or a model. She garnered press attention disproportionate to her achievements. She was famous... for being famous.

It Girls were faces on the scene, written about in lifestyle magazines and photographed in clubs, often with rock star or actor boyfriends. Britpop's most prominent examples were actress Patsy Kensit, who was married to Liam Gallagher; her one-time sister-in-law Meg Matthews, who was with Noel Gallagher, and Elizabeth Hurley, an actress who rapidly rose to fame by wearing a revealing Versace dress (the one with all the safety pins) to the premier of *Four Weddings and a Funeral*, starring her then boyfriend Hugh Grant.

It Girls were judged on what they wore, the company they kept and where they spent their time. Sadie Frost, for example, began her career as an actress and starred in a run of films during the nineties, but was more famous for being married to fellow actor Jude Law. When she graced the pages and covers of British magazines it wasn't her films that were mentioned, but her exploits in Primrose Hill with fellow It Girl Kate Moss.

Tara Palmer-Tomkinson, a socialite from a rich family who sadly died in February '17, was the It Girl to end all nineties It Girls. She wrote articles for lifestyle magazines and presented a few TV shows, but she mainly spent the decade hanging out in clubs and swanky bars, appearing on *TFI Friday* and being written about in the tabloids.

This, of course, was nothing new; people have been famous just for being themselves for as long as there have been people. But the nineties pushed it further, paving the way for the 'cult of celebrity' so prominent in the noughties and beyond. The rise of reality TV programmes like *Big Brother* gave ordinary people unprecedented opportunities to become famous without having any discernible talents.

Soon real actors and musicians began to shy away from the word 'celebrity', fearing its association with *Big Brother* contestants, preferring to be referred to by their actual profession. Celebrity, once a thing to aspire to, became an ugly word, associated with sad individuals, desperate to be noticed by society. It Girls were style icons and trendsetters first and actors or models second. The public was interested in their personal life, not their CV.

It's a Beautiful Thing (single – Ocean Colour Scene)

Charted: Feb '98; UK Chart Position: 12; Label: MCA; Album: *Marchin' Already*

The fourth and final single released from Ocean Colour Scene's third album *Marchin' Already*, 'It's a Beautiful Thing' was the second of two songs on the album to feature sixties Northern Soul singer P P Arnold on vocals.

The single reached number 12 in the UK chart in February '98, just as Britpop was winding down.

It was released on CD only, and featured B-sides 'Mariners Way', 'Going Nowhere for a While' and 'Expensive Chair', and appeared in both a cardboard sleeve and a jewel case.

It's Great When You're Straight... Yeah! (album – Black Grape)

Charted: Aug '95; UK Chart Position: 1; Label: Radioactive; Singles: 'Reverend Black Grape' (Jun '95, UKCP 9), 'In the Name of the Father' (Aug '95, 8), 'Kelly's Heroes' (Dec '95, 17)

It's Great When You're Straight... Yeah! was Black Grape's much-anticipated debut album, the nation eager to see what Bez and Shaun Ryder of the Happy Mondays would do next.

The album was seen as a triumphant comeback for the duo, heading straight to the number one spot in the UK chart, where it spent two weeks (and 48 weeks on the chart in total). The album spawned the top ten singles 'Reverend Black Grape' and 'In the Name of the Father' and the top 20 single 'Kelly's Heroes', which collectively spent 19 weeks in the chart.

The band's decision to mix classic indie-Britpop with a more urban rap focus led to the album being nominated for the '96 Mercury Music Prize alongside Oasis' *(What's The Story) Morning Glory?*, the Manic Street Preachers' *Everything Must Go* and Pulp's *Different Class* (which won). It would remain the band's only really successful album, with the follow-up *Stupid Stupid Stupid* peaking at number 11 in November '97. They split not long afterwards.

J

James (band)

Manchester band James formed in the early eighties and, despite a break between '01 and '07, have been releasing music together for nearly 30 years. They are perhaps best known for their chart successes of the nineties, including the hit singles 'Sit Down' and the Britpop era 'She's a Star', and alongside The Charlatans are one of the few bands to straddle both the Madchester scene of the late eighties and the Britpop scene in the mid-nineties.

The line-up has changed much over the years, but has always consisted of a core of five or six members, who create rather than write their songs, developing them over lengthy jam sessions and sharing both writing credits and royalties. This process meant the band favoured playing live rather than recording, and for the first three years they released no records, even turning down an album deal from Factory Records' Tony Wilson, who saw them play at the now-legendary Hacienda club in Manchester in the mid-eighties. They did record a three-track EP for Wilson though, which caught the attention of the music press and led to a tour with The Smiths, with whom they became firm friends, sharing an ethos and a similar style.

Over the next few years, various albums and singles found their way into the lower reaches of the charts. Then came a re-recorded version of their single 'Sit Down', from third album proper *Gold Mother*, which reached number two in the UK chart in '91. The song was a huge hit for the band, and became an anthem in student unions the country over.

Follow-up albums *Seven* and *Laid* reached numbers two and three respectively, but it wasn't until seventh album *Whiplash* was released in March '97 that the band came close to the same critical and commercial success as their 'Sit Down' period. By this point, Britpop was nearing its peak and the band used the momentum to record an album that left behind the student union and looked outwards. Lead single 'She's a Star' reached number nine in the UK chart, and *Whiplash* peaked at number nine, spending a total of 25 weeks on the chart (*Gold Mother* achieved 34 weeks). Thanks to the quality of the songs and the association with the Britpop scene, the album brought the band back to the mainstream, giving them a second life in a notably fickle industry.

Frontman and spiritual leader of the band Tim Booth left in '01. The band began a lengthy hiatus, returning in '07 to record new music and tour once more. Their 13th studio album *La Petit Mort* was released in June '14 and reached number 11 in the UK chart.

James, Alex (bassist/singer/songwriter/ cheesemaker – Blur/Fat Les)

Sometime columnist, journalist, biographer and, most recently, cheesemaker, Alex James is best known for his years playing bass guitar in Britpop joint chiefs Blur.

Born in Bournemouth on 21 November '68 to a middle-class family, James attended the local grammar school where he first learned to play the bass guitar. He met future Blur guitarist Graham Coxon on the first day of term at Goldsmith's University in London, where James studied French and Coxon studied fine art. Coxon introduced him to Damon Albarn and, together with drummer Dave Rowntree, they formed Seymour, later Blur, in '88. They signed to Food Records in '90 and, after the release of second single 'There's No Other Way' in April '91, the band became a constant fixture in the UK charts.

Taking full advantage of the heady times and the huge success of his band, James embraced the Britpop years wholeheartedly and became a regular decadent face on the London club scene, later claiming to have spent £1 million on champagne and cocaine. Throughout this time, and well into the noughties, he wrote regular columns for *Q* magazine on his latest adventures and, in '07, published his autobiography, the amusingly titled *Bit of a Blur*, about his experiences playing music in the Britpop years.

He married Claire Neate in '03, after Blur went their separate ways, swapping hedonistic adventures for a wife, five children and a farm in rural Oxfordshire, where he launched his cheese-making business and founded The Big Festival, an annual celebration of food and music, with celebrity chef Jamie Oliver. He began a monthly column for *The Sun*, as well as contributing food articles to many British newspapers and magazines. His second book *All Cheeses Great and Small: A Life Less Blurry*, was released in September '11.

In addition to his work with Blur, James co-founded Fat Les with artist Damian Hirst and actor Keith Allen, the tongue-in-cheek novelty act which released the unofficial football world-cup anthem 'Vindaloo' in '98. In more recent years he has worked with many acts, including co-writing and playing bass for Marianne Faithful, Florence and the Machine and Sophie Ellis-Bextor.

Jocasta (band)

Taking their name from the ill-fated mother and wife of the Ancient Greek anti-hero Oedipus, Jocasta were one of the lesser-known Britpop bands. They achieved some mid-level success during the Britpop years, with their first single 'Something to Say', released in November '96, charting at number 80 in the UK chart, and 'Go', released in February '97, becoming Jo Whiley's single of the week on Radio 1, charting at number 50 and featuring on indie compilation album *Shine 8*.

The band's final single to chart was 'Change Me', released in May '97, which became Mark Radcliffe's single of the week on Radio 1 and reached number 60 on the chart. In June '97, the band released their only album, *No Coincidence*, which was recorded with the London Symphony Orchestra. Unfortunately, they split soon after.

Post-Jocasta, lead singer Tim Arnold went on to perform as a solo artist and has released several albums, including debut *Lokutara* in '04, which was written and recorded while he was being treated for drug addiction in Wat Tham Krabok Buddhist monastery in Thailand (later home to The Libertines' Pete Doherty undergoing similar treatment). He is also the founder member of 'Save Soho', a group of performers and politicians interested in preserving Soho as an important landmark for the performing arts.

Jollification (album – The Lightning Seeds)

Charted: Sep '94; UK Chart Position: 12; Label: Epic; Singles: 'Change' (Jan '95, UKCP 13), 'Marvellous' (Apr '95, 24), 'Perfect' (Jul '95, 18), 'Lucky You' (Oct '95, 15)

Jollification was the Lightning Seeds' third album, and their first commercial success. It spent a whopping 75 weeks on the UK chart, ten of which were in the top 20. It was the band's first of three top-20 albums, with *Dizzy Heights* to follow two years later and a 'best of' compilation in November '97, which reached the top ten.

The album contained ten tracks, including the three top-20 singles 'Change', which featured on the soundtrack for nineties teen film *Clueless*, 'Perfect' and 'Lucky You', as well as top-40 single 'Marvellous'. The album cover featured a giant strawberry, with tiny faces superimposed on the seeds.

Joyrider (band)

Irish band Joyrider were frontman Phil Woolsey, guitarist Cliff Mitchell, Simon Haddock on bass and drummer Keith Irwin. The band, from Portadown in Northern Ireland, existed on the periphery of the Britpop scene, and were mostly known for their cover of Jane Wiedlin of The Go Go's 'Rush Hour', which was released as a single in July '96. It featured on indie compilation album Shine 6 and charted at number 22 in the UK chart, where it spent three weeks.

The band released follow-up single 'All Gone Away' a couple of months later, which charted at number 54 and spent two weeks on the chart. As well as several EPs and other non-chart singles, the band released their sole album *Be Special* in '96, one year after supporting Terrorvision on their UK tour. The album didn't chart either, but the band's releases are fondly remembered by their loyal following.

Just the One (single – Levellers)

Charted: Dec '95; UK Chart Position: 12; Label: China; Album: *Zeitgeist*

'Just the One' was the third of four singles released from The Levellers' fourth album *Zeitgeist*, and the band's seventh single to reach the top 20 of the UK chart, where it spent a total of eight weeks. The original recording caught the attention of Joe Strummer from The Clash, and the band re-recorded it for the album with Strummer playing the piano. The quirky lyric, about a day of regrettable hedonism, found its way onto many radio playlists, including the all-important Radio 1, and also saw the band appear on *Top of the Pops*.

B-sides included 'A Promise', 'Your 'Ouse', and 'Drinking For England', the latter recorded and mixed in Brighton at Metway, the derelict factory the band purchased in '94 as their headquarters, rehearsal area and recording studio.

Just When You're Thinkin' Things Over (single – The Charlatans)

Charted: Aug '95; UK Chart Position: 12; Label: Beggars Banquet; Album: *The Charlatans*

'Just When You're Thinkin' Things Over' was the third single from The Charlatans' self-titled fourth album and the band's fifth single to reach the top 20 of the UK chart, where it spent three weeks.

The single, which they performed on *Later... with Jools Holland*, was their first to feature a piano throughout and was a hit, their first top 20 in three years, paving the way for a string of successes to follow. The CD single contained a Chemical Brothers remix, 'Chemical Risk', which also featured on the Japanese edition of the album, and the tracks 'Frinck' and 'Your Skies Are Mine'. The vinyl release included an additional Chemical Brothers remix, 'Nine Acre Dust'.

K

K (album – Kula Shaker)

Charted: Sept '96; UK Chart Position: 1; Label: Columbia; Singles: 'Grateful When You're Dead' (May '96, UKCP 35), 'Tattva' (Jul '96, 4), 'Hey Dude' (Sept '96, 2), 'Govinda' (Nov '96, 7)

Kula Shaker's debut album *K* became the fastest selling debut since Elastica's the year before and headed straight for the number one spot when released in September '96. The album spent two weeks at number one and 51 weeks on the chart in total. It went on to chart worldwide and was the band's most commercially successful album by far.

The album cover art was created by British comic-book artist Dave Gibbons, known for his work on the *Watchmen* series, and featured the faces of people linked to the letter 'K', including Grace Kelly, John F Kennedy, Katharine Hepburn, Karl Marx and Martin Luther King. The album contained a hidden track after final song 'Hollow Man', which featured a recording of the founder of the International Society for Krishna Consciousness, AC Bhaktivedanta Swami Prabhupada.

The album continued the band's much-publicised love affair with Indian culture and music. The album features lyrics sung in Sanskrit, notably singles 'Tattva' and 'Govinda', as well as traditional Indian musical instruments like the sitar, tamboura and tabla. George Harrison had pushed the Beatles in this direction before, but this was the first time Indian music had been mixed with traditionally presented Western rock with such prominence and widespread appeal. The idea chimed with the audience and the album was a big success for the band.

Lead singer and chief songwriter Crispian Mills had wanted a very famous Indian symbol of peace on the album cover. As this was the swastika, a symbol used and abused by the Nazi party, he was dissuaded.

Kelly's Heroes (single – Black Grape)

Charted: Dec '95; UK Chart Position: 17; Label: Radioactive; Album: *It's Great When You're Straight... Yeah!*

'Kelly's Heroes' was the third and final single to be released from Black Grape's huge debut album *It's Great When You're Straight... Yeah!* It spent six weeks on the UK chart, peaking just in the top 20, the band's third single to do so.

The cover art featured an illustration of lead singer Shaun Ryder with eyes of different colours. B-sides on the single included 'The Milky Bar Kid Mix' of the lead track, followed by the original album version, 'The Archibald Mix' and a live version of 'Little Bob' recorded at the Forum, London in October '95.

Kenickie (band)

The female-fronted Sunderland-based band Kenickie formed in '94 and consisted of singer-songwriter (and now DJ and presenter) Lauren Laverne, lead guitarist Marie du Santiago (aka Anne Marie Nixon), bassist Emma-Kate Montrose (aka Emma Jackson) and Laverne's brother Johnny X (aka Pete Gofton) on drums.

Taking their name from the T-birds leader in the seventies classic teen film Grease, the band were one of the few female majority Britpop bands, releasing two studio albums in their few years together. *At the Club* came out in May '97 and charted in the top ten, while *Get In*, released the following year, charted in the top 40.

The band released several singles, including four top-40 hits, 'In

Your Car', 'Nightlife', 'Punka' and 'I Would Fix You', but split towards the end of '98. All the band members have since moved on to various musical projects, most notably Laverne, now a DJ on BBC 6 Music.

Kevin Carter (single – Manic Street Preachers)

Charted: Oct '96; UK Chart Position: 9; Label: Epic; Album: *Everything Must Go*

Lyrically, 'Kevin Carter' was arguably the Manic Street Preachers' most profound single, taking as its subject the '94 Pulitzer Prize-winning photographer famed for his photograph of a starving Sudanese toddler watched by a hungry vulture. The lyrics, "Tribal scars in Technicolor; bang bang club AK 47 hour", refer to the horrific killings Carter witnessed throughout his career, which eventually led to him taking his own life at the age of just 33.

It was the third of four singles released from fourth album *Everything Must Go* and the fourth to reach the top ten of the UK chart, where it spent eight weeks. Two versions of the CD single were released, with CD1 containing B-sides 'Horses Under Starlight', 'Sepia' and 'First Republic' and a quote by dramatist and screenwriter Dennis Potter on the back cover, "Words themselves – the very material of our discourse increasingly take on masks or disguises".

CD2 featured three remixes of the lead track and a quote from playwright Eugene O'Neil, "When I was a kid I used to get fun out of my horrors", while the cassette contained an acoustic version of the lead track. The video featured several scenes of a camera lens repeatedly photographing the band.

King Tut's Wah Wah Hut (music venue)

King Tut's Wah Wah Hut in Glasgow is perhaps most famous for being the spot where Creation Records' founder Alan McGee discovered Britpop legends Oasis in '93, but its reputation for hosting the early gigs of some of Britain's biggest bands began as soon as it opened its doors in '90. In the same fortnight that Oasis played the venue, both The Verve and Radiohead also had their first gigs in Scotland. Today, you're not considered anyone on the Scottish music scene until you've played King Tut's.

DF Concerts began their clubnights not as once a month or once a week engagements, but every single night, with the intention of giving bands somewhere to play at a reasonable hour. This tactic paid off quickly with bands flooding to the venue, where they were guaranteed a good crowd. It wasn't completely random chance that brought Alan McGee to the club that Sunday night. Being a Glaswegian himself, he was aware of the venue's reputation and so, having just missed his train back to London after visiting his sister, thought he might as well pop in to see who was playing. Legend has it that Oasis had arrived to play a gig, having driven up from Manchester, but were denied entry because of a booking mix-up. In what would become classic Oasis style, the band argued their way on to the stage and played a 20-minute set. This was all McGee needed to know that this was the band for him.

In more recent years, King Tut's has branched out into successful monthly comedy nights, and also runs its own stage at Scotland's T in the Park music festival every summer.

Knebworth (concerts 10 & 11 August '96)

When Noel Gallagher declared in his thick Mancunian accent, "This is history! This is history! Right here! Right now! This is history!" to thousands upon thousands of screaming fans on the final night of the Knebworth '96 concerts, every single one of them knew it to be true. Having released two number one albums in a row and a string of top charting singles, Oasis were at the peak of their fame and, "the biggest band in the world... bigger than, dare I say it, fucking God" according to guitarist Noel Gallagher, while brother Liam, complete with signature Lennon-style round glasses, long indie hair and a flowing white shirt could not have looked more 'Rock God' if he tried.

It didn't seem possible that things could get bigger than the Stone Roses' Spike Island gig in May '90 (which Noel Gallagher attended) for British guitar music, but the Knebworth concerts were era-defining and the biggest Britpop had seen. More than a quarter of a million fans attended over two nights on 10 and 11 August, but it could easily have been more as there were more than 2.6 million ticket applications.

Almost exactly a year after the Battle of Britpop, it was the era's second peak, held at a venue synonymous with the greatest acts in rock history, including Led Zeppelin, the Rolling Stones and Queen, with support acts including The Prodigy, Ocean Colour Scene, the Manic Street Preachers, the Chemical Brothers and The Charlatans across the weekend. From 'Cast No Shadow' complete with full orchestra to 'Champagne Supernova' interspersed with strong guitar melodies from the Stone Roses' John Squire, the concerts contained many defining moments that would form a key part of Britpop history. Legend has it that many future successful bands were formed at Spike Island; how many met and formed at Knebworth?

Kula Shaker (band)

Son of Roy Boulting (one half of film directing twins the Boulting brothers, known primarily for '47's *Brighton Rock*), and sixties child star of such classics as *The Parent Trap* Hayley Mills, and grandson of British acting legend Sir John Mills, Kula shaker frontman Crispian Mills was destined for the stage. Although brought up in England, he became interested in Hindu mysticism and Indian culture at an early age, and it was this rather unusual angle to their music – marrying British rock with traditional Indian music – that gave Kula Shaker their original edge.

With various line-ups along the way, the band was formed in '88 by frontman Mills, who met bassist Alonza Bevan at college, Marcus French on drums (later replaced by Paul Winterheart) and rhythm guitarist Leigh Morris, later replaced by Jay Darlington, who added to the band's individual sound with his Hammond organ, drawing comparisons to The Doors.

The band released three studio albums, including number one album *K* in '96, top-ten album *Peasants, Pigs and Astronauts* in '99 and *Strange Folk* in '07. They also released a string of successful singles including five top-ten hits – 'Tattva', 'Hey Dude', 'Govinda', 'Hush' and 'The Sound of Drums' – all released between July '96 and May '98.

L

La's, The (band)

Liverpudlian band The La's were best-known for their hit single 'There She Goes', which was released three times before it successfully charted, peaking at number 13 in the UK chart in late '90. Fronted by Lee Mavers on vocals and guitar and Cast's John Power on backing vocals and bass, the band formed in the early eighties and were active until the early nineties, experiencing several line-up changes along the way.

They released just one eponymous album... twice. It first appeared in October '90, when it peaked at number 30, and again in September '96, when it sat just outside the top 40 at number 41. Despite their perceived lack of commercial success, The La's are considered one of the most influential bands from Liverpool; their jangly guitars influencing key post-Britpop acts like The Coral and The Zutons. Their name is taken from the affectionate Scouse slang for friend, "eh, you alright there la?"

Ladies & Gentlemen We Are Floating In Space (album - Spiritualized)

Charted: Jun '97; UK Chart Position: 4; Label: Dedicated; Singles: 'Electricity' (Aug '97, UKCP 32), 'I Think I'm In Love' (Feb '98, 27), 'The Abbey Road EP' (Jun '98, 39), 'Come Together' (Jul '98, n/a)

Ladies & Gentlemen We Are Floating in Space was Spiritualized's third album and their first to chart in the top ten. It contained the top 40 singles 'Electricity', also featured on indie compilation album *Shine 9*, 'I Think I'm In Love' and the 'Abbey Road EP'. Remixes by Leftfield and Two Lone Swordsmen of the album's standout track 'Come Together' – the lead track on the 'Abbey Road EP' – were also released as a single in July '98, but failed to chart.

Written shortly after frontman Jason Pierce and keyboard player Kate Radley (now married to The Verve's Richard Ashcroft) split up, the dark and emotional album was the band's longest to stay in the

UK chart, where it spent a total of 24 weeks. The album artwork presented itself as medication, with the 'tablets' listed as the songs and the 'ingredients' the band members and contributors to the album, including the London Community Gospel Choir.

The album perfectly represented the sound of a band on the darker side of Britpop, filled with carefully layered, intense soundscapes that built to staggering crescendos, and mixing distorted guitars with gospel vocals. Pierce, who formed the band from the ashes of former space-rock outfit Spaceman 3, found his footing with this album, which stands as a testament to a darker, more atmospheric side of pop music.

Late in the Day (single – Supergrass)

Charted: Oct '97; UK Chart Position: 18; Label: Parlophone; Album: *In it for the Money*

'Late in the Day' was the fourth and final single released from Supergrass' second album *In it for the Money*, and the band's seventh single to reach the top 20 of the UK chart, where it spent four weeks on the chart and peaked at number 18.

The predominantly acoustic CD single was available in two versions. The first included exclusive tracks 'We Still Need More (Than Anyone Can Give)' and a demo of 'It's Not Me', while CD2 contained 'Don't Be Cruel' and 'The Animal'.

The video, nominated for 'Best British Video' at the Brit Awards '98, was shot in black and white and featured the band on pogo sticks crossing London's Albert Bridge to the bandstand in Battersea Park, where the video for previous single 'Going Out' was filmed.

Later... with Jools Holland (music TV show, BBC)

Throughout the history of British popular music, TV has played a vital role, either playing the current releases, such as *Top of the Pops* and *TFI Friday*, or as a showcase for what the powers-that-be think will be popular, such as *The Old Grey Whistle Test* and *The White Room*. *Later... with Jools Holland* managed to straddle both camps, giving exclusive live spots to the cool, young bands of the moment, alongside distinctive world music artists who would not find such a showcase on any other channel. Unfortunately, it is now the last man standing in what has become a diminished marketplace.

Jools Holland began his career as keyboard player with London band Squeeze, who found some success in the late seventies with the hit singles 'Cool for Cats' and 'Up the Junction'. In the early eighties he moved into television, presenting *The Tube*, a late-night magazine show aimed at the youth market, which featured live performances from the bands of the day.

Having tired of the puerile antics favoured by *The Tube* and *The Word*, he began the purely music-based show *Later...* in '92. It has been a fixture on the BBC ever since. The format is simple: half a dozen bands, interspersed with audience members, encircle the studio and play a song or two in turn. Holland wanders around the middle, introducing the bands or interviewing guests at his grand piano, and sometimes even playing along with them.

Much like *Top of the Pops*, *Later...* gained a reputation as being *the* place to play for both up and coming bands and established acts alike, with many noticing a dramatic increase in record sales afterwards. Unlike *Top of the Pops* though, the show is not just about chart music. Holland invites musicians from startlingly different backgrounds the world over to play. It is one of the few places you can see Ladysmith Black Mambazo play after The Libertines.

Laverne, Lauren (singer/guitarist/song-writer/radio presenter – Kenickie)

Lauren Fisher (known professionally as Lauren Laverne) was born in Sunderland on 28 April '78 to a working-class family. She met fellow Kenickie member Marie du Santiago at school, and Emmy-Kate Montrose at college. Drummer Johnny X is her younger brother. Laverne was the band's lead singer and chief songwriter. The band found some mid-level Britpop success with their debut album *At the Club*, which reached number nine in the UK chart in May '97, and its four singles, all of which went top 40.

The band's success was short lived and they split after the release of second album *Get In* in August '98. Laverne was getting noticed for her acerbic wit, notably on music-based panel shows such as *Never Mind the Buzzcocks*, so the move into broadcasting seemed a logical step. Aside from various TV presenting jobs, including the BBC's annual Glastonbury Festival coverage, she has become a fixture on BBC6 Music's team, playing the latest indie music to a whole nation of fans. She published her first novel, *Candypop – Candy and the Broken Biscuits*, in '10, and lives in London with her DJ husband and two children.

Lazy (single – Suede)

Charted: April '97; UK Chart Position: 9; Label: Nude; Album: *Coming Up*

'Lazy' was the fourth of five singles released by Suede from their third album *Coming Up*, and was the band's fourth consecutive single to reach the top ten of the UK chart, where it spent a total of six weeks. The video was directed by Pedro Romhanyi, who had previously worked on 'Animal Nitrate', 'Beautiful Ones' and 'Saturday Night'. The single was performed on TV music shows *TFI Friday* and *Later... with Jools Holland*. Two versions of the CD single were released, the first featuring B-sides 'These are the Sad Songs' and 'Feel', and the second 'Sadie' and 'Digging a Hole', which featured keyboardist Neil Coding on lead vocals.

Leckie, John (record producer)

John Leckie is one of British pop music's finest record producers. He cut his teeth as an engineer at Abbey Road for, among others, John Lennon, George Harrison and Paul McCartney (though not together; he started in '70), Pink Floyd (on *Wish You Were Here*) and Public Image Limited. By the eighties, he was a jobbing producer and an obvious choice to helm Britpop forerunners the Stone Roses debut record in '89. Now considered a classic, the eponymous album is a constant fixture in 'top ten albums of all time' polls.

During the Britpop years, Leckie was the go-to guy, producing, among others, the Stone Roses' long-awaited second album *The Second Coming*, Elastica's debut, Cast's first two albums, Kula Shaker's debut *K*, Radiohead's *The Bends* and The Verve's *A Storm in Heaven*. In '97 he was awarded 'Best Producer' at that year's Brit Awards. Though his output has slowed since his Britpop heyday, he is responsible for Muse's first two albums, as well as The Coral's '10 album *Butterfly House*.

Lenny (single - Supergrass)

Charted: May '95; UK Chart Position: 10; Label: Parlophone; Album: *I Should Coco*

'Lenny' was the fourth of five singles from Supergrass' debut album *I Should Coco* and the band's first to reach the top ten, where it spent a total of four weeks. It was the band's biggest release to date, and so paved the way for the single that would propel the band into the Britpop limelight, 'Alright'.

The B-sides were 'Wait for the Sun' and 'Sex!', and the cover artwork – by the Moody Painters – featured a group of penguins standing before a King penguin called Lenny.

Levellers (band)

The world's most famous hippie or 'crustie' band, Brighton's The Levellers are still touring today after nearly 30 years playing together. It was during the Britpop years though that they enjoyed most success.

Formed in Brighton by frontman and lead songwriter Mark Chadwick, bassist Jeremy Cunningham and drummer Charlie Heather in '88, the band found almost immediate success after their self-funded debut EP was picked up by Radio 2. Their debut album appeared in '90 on French label Musidisc, but they split from them in '91 and signed with China, who brought them to a distinctly more mainstream audience. Their second album *Levelling the Land* appeared that same year and, spurred on by chief single and constant live favourite 'One Way', reached number 14.

The band quickly cemented their reputation as a folk-rock-pop band who sang songs for the underclass and the dispossessed, and over the next few years, as Britpop began to take hold of the country, they experienced their most fruitful time. Supported by the hit single 'This Garden', *The Levellers* album reached number two in the UK chart in September '93 and, after the band's '94 appearance at their spiritual home of Glastonbury, things got even bigger for the underdogs. Success brought them their own Brighton-based headquarters, where they drank, rehearsed, recorded and shared a space with the local anarchist newspaper *ShhNEWS*.

Zeitgeist went straight in at number two in the UK album chart in September '95, and climbed to the top spot the following week. It was packed with some of the band's most loved tunes, including the singles 'Hope Street' and 'Just the One', featuring one of the band's heroes and biggest supporters, The Clash's Joe Strummer, on piano. After more and more extensive touring around the UK and Europe, the band released *Mouth to Mouth* in September '97 but, as the Brit-pop star was beginning to wane, so did The Levellers' commercial success, and it reached number five, despite including the anthemic single, 'What a Beautiful Day'.

The next album the band released was *Hello Pig* in September '00, which reached 24 in the UK chart. Since then, the band have continued to record and release music and have toured extensively. *Letters from the Underground*, their seventh studio album, managed a solid number 24 chart placing in '08, and the second of their two greatest hits collections was released in '14.

Life Less Ordinary, A (single – Ash)

Charted: Oct '97; UK Chart Position: 10; Label: Infectious; Album: n/a

Written specifically for the soundtrack of the '97 Danny Boyle film of the same name, Ash's 'A Life Less Ordinary' was their sole release of '97, and was the first single to feature new guitarist Charlotte Hatherley. It peaked at number 10 in the UK chart, where it spent a total of five weeks.

Two versions of the single were released: the collector's edition on translucent blue 7" vinyl, which featured B-sides 'Where is our Love Going' and 'What Deaner Was Talking About'; and the CD, which also included the extra B-side 'Halloween'.

Lightning Seeds, The (band)

Ian Broudie is at the centre of Liverpool band the Lightning Seeds. He not only sings and plays lead guitar, but also produces and writes all the music. Broudie started the group in '89 when working as a producer. The first single 'Pure' reached number 16 in '90, but its accompanying album *Cloudcuckooland* managed only number 50, and follow-up *Sense* fared even worse, reaching 53 in '93, despite including the catchy singles 'Life of Riley' and 'Sense'.

Broudie finally put his producing on hold in '93, and toured the UK for the first time. This meant that the band's next album *Jollification*, released through new label Epic in September '94, went straight in at number 12. Broudie and the band capitalised on the Britpop years and, like so many of their contemporaries, found much success before the bubble burst. The positively-titled singles 'Lucky You', 'Change' and 'Perfect' all made the top 20, and 'Marvellous' reached number 24.

Then, to mark the British-based Euro '96 football tournament, the band teamed up with comedians David Baddiel and Frank Skinner to release the official English football anthem, 'Three Lions'. Even though England didn't win, the song was a huge success and reached number one in the UK chart, where it stayed for two weeks before spending a further 14 weeks on the chart. It was re-released two years later during the World Cup campaign and returned to the top spot, this time for three weeks.

In November '96, capitalising on the success of 'Three Lions', the band released their third studio album, *Dizzy Heights*. It peaked at number 11 in the UK chart, and remained on the chart for 31 weeks. The band were known for their optimistic, catchy, three-minute bubblegum pop tunes, not unlike the Divine Comedy in that respect, and so it was no surprise that the greatest hits album, *Like You Do*, became their biggest album to date when it was released in November '97. It reached number five in the UK chart, and hung around for 43 weeks.

Post-Britpop, Ian Broudie got back behind his Liverpool mixing desk to produce a wide range of new and emerging artists, including the new breed of Liverpool indie bands such as The Coral and The Zutons. The Lightning Seeds continue to play together, although somewhat sporadically, and released two studio albums between '99 and '09, as well as another greatest hits album.

Line Up (single – Elastica)

Charted: Feb '94; UK Chart Position: 20; Label: Deceptive; Album: *Elastica*

'Line Up' was the second of five singles released from Elastica's debut self-titled album, and their first to dent the top 20 in February '94, peaking at number 20 in the UK chart, where it spent four weeks. The single was the follow-up to their debut (limited edition) single 'Stutter', released in '93.

The CD single included a demo of 'Vaseline' (the original featured on the album), 'Rockunroll' and 'Annie', also on the album. The single was controversial because some said it sounded too similar to Wire's 'I Am The Fly'. This didn't stop it receiving favourable reviews and the matter was settled out of court. The single was performed on TV shows *The White Room* and *The Word* and the official video showed footage of the band hanging out in a cafe and animated scenes of cardboard cut-outs of the individual members.

Live Forever (single - Oasis)

Charted: Aug '94; UK Chart Position: 10; Label: Creation; Album: *Definitely Maybe*

'Live Forever' was the third of four singles from Oasis' debut album *Definitely Maybe*, and the band's first to make the top ten of the UK chart, where it spent a mammoth 66 weeks.

The song was one of the first Noel Gallagher ever wrote, while working at a construction firm in his hometown of Manchester, and the first that made him realise he might be destined for something other than labouring. Throughout the band's touring history, the song was often dedicated to rock legends of the past, against a huge backdrop display. At the Maine Road gig in '95, lead singer Liam Gallagher dropped to his knees as his idol John Lennon appeared at the climax of the song.

The CD single featured an acoustic version of 'Up in the Sky' and a live version of debut single 'Supersonic', as well as the exclusive track 'Cloudburst'. The song title was also used for the '03 Britpop documentary by John Dower.

Live the Dream (single - Cast)

Charted: Sept '96; UK Chart Position: 7; Label: Polydor; Album: *Mother Nature Calls*

'Live the Dream' was the third of four singles released from Cast's second album *Mother Nature Calls* and the band's sixth to reach the top ten, where it spent a total of five weeks, peaking at number seven.

Two CD versions were available: the first featuring B-sides 'Effectomatic Who', 'Hold On' and an acoustic version of the title track; the second 'Flow' and a demo version of 'On the Run', originally the second track on the album.

Loaded (lad mag)

The nineties heralded an unprecedented rise in what became known as 'lad culture' in the UK. Perhaps brought on by a relaxation of alcohol licensing and censorship laws, increased ease of access to recreational drugs, a liberal-minded government and a burgeoning elasticity toward morality, lads were shameless in their hedonism. Lad culture entered the mainstream, and nowhere was it more aptly represented in print than by *Loaded* magazine.

Founded by editor James Brown, Tim Southall and Mick Bunnage in May '94, and aimed directly at a young male audience, *Loaded* was the original 'lad mag', bringing together all things laddish: drinking, eating, partying, clubbing, sex, drugs, music, films and, of course, naked women. Lots of naked women. The first edition featured actress (and acclaimed dress-wearer) Liz Hurley in a see-through negligee and, over the years, an array of young women from TV, film, music and modelling appeared between the covers wearing very little, if anything at all.

The pictures were often accompanied by a perfunctory interview, mainly about the young women's favourite sexual positions. There were also interviews with footballers, actors and musicians, also answering questions on their favourite sexual positions. For the first time, loose morals, base humour and borderline pornography were part of the mainstream media, making *Loaded* a huge hit with its audience, peaking with monthly circulation figures of half a million in the UK alone.

The good times didn't last forever though and, as the years passed, the competition became more intense. Brown left to edit *GQ* in April '97, claiming he wanted nothing more to do with laddism, and the growing backlash against lad culture in the late nineties saw *Loaded*'s main rival *FHM* rise to prominence among a slightly more highbrow but still resolutely male audience.

In the early noughties, *Nuts* and *Zoo* became the first weekly male magazines, both featuring more and more risqué material at a fraction of the cost of the monthly magazines. Far from bringing laddism to an end, these weeklies actually fought *Loaded* at their own game and won.

Loaded reacted by upping the smut, and was soon moved to the top-shelf alongside magazines like *Penthouse*. Circulation dropped, taking a hit from the rise of online publications, and *Loaded* lost its print edition in March '15, launching fully online in November '15.

Local Boy in a Photograph (single – Stereophonics)

Charted: Feb '98; UK Chart Position: 14; Label: V2; Album: *Word Gets Around*

Originally released in March '97, 'Local Boy in a Photograph' was the Stereophonics first proper single. It reached number 51, but was re-released a year later, just after the band won their Brit award for 'Best Newcomer' in February '98. The re-release was their highest charting single to date, reaching number 14 and spending a total of eight weeks on the chart.

Set in the same small town as the rest of the band's songs from debut album *Word Gets Around*, the lyric tells the real-life sad story of a young man killed when hit by a train; his friends "sit on the banks and drink for hours, talk of the way they saw him last". The single is a fast-paced rock 'n' roll song tinged with the melancholia prominent in the band's early work.

The single was released on two CDs. CD1 included B-sides 'Who'll Stop the Rain?' (a Creedance Clearwater Revival cover), 'Check My Eyelids for Holes' (from the band's debut album) and 'Local Boy in the Photograph' (video). CD2 included B-sides 'Not Up to You' (live at XFM), 'The Last Resort' (an Eagles cover) and 'Traffic' (video).

Longpigs (band)

Taking their name from the word that cannibals use to refer to their favourite type of meat, Sheffield's Longpigs were another band of faithful lieutenants to the Britpop cause. They enjoyed limited success with their debut album *The Sun is Often Out* in '96, but failed to replicate it once Britpop was over. The band consisted of lead singer/songwriter and guitarist Crispin Hunt, lead guitarist Richard Hawley, bassist Simon Stratford and drummer Dee Boyle.

Formed in '93, when Britpop was already underway, they initially signed to the American indie label Elektra Records (owned by Warners), who were looking to capitalise on the burgeoning British scene, but were sold to U2's new label Mother Records after Hunt experienced a near-fatal car accident. Their first three singles, 'Happy Again', 'Jesus Christ' and 'She Said', reached only the bottom half of the top ten, but after 'Far' entered the top 40, the band gained some momentum. 'On and On' made the top 20 in March '96, and their debut album went straight in at 26 in the UK album chart in April that year.

The following year was mostly about touring, supporting Supergrass, Echobelly, Radiohead and label heads U2 on their *Popmart* tour. Then, when 'On and On' experienced some success in the States, the band toured America extensively. But by the time they returned to Britain, things had moved on, and their second album *Mobile Home* didn't appear until October '99. Hunt had taken the band in a decidedly more avant-garde direction, which didn't chime with the rest of the band or the public and only reached 33 in the UK chart. The band split after their record label folded in '00.

Interestingly, it is lead guitarist Richard Hawley who has gone on to much post-Longpigs success, initially touring with Pulp, then forming Jarvis Cocker's side-project Relaxed Muscle, before forging a highly successful solo career, releasing seven albums to date and receiving two Mercury Music Prize nominations.

Love is the Law (single – The Seahorses)

Charted: May '97; UK Chart Position: 3; Label: Geffen; Album: *Do It Yourself*

'Love is the Law' was the much-anticipated debut single from former Stone Roses' guitarist and lead songwriter John Squire's new band The Seahorses.

It preceded their sole album *Do It Yourself*, going straight in at number three in the chart, where it spent a total of eight weeks. The single was kept from the top spot by ex-Take That leader Gary Barlow's solo single 'Love Won't Wait' and George Michael's 'Star People '97'.

The single was performed on TV show *TFI Friday* and included B-sides 'Dreamer', written by singer Chris Helme, and 'Sale of the Century', written by Squire, who also produced the cover artwork.

Love me and Leave Me (single – The Seahorses)

Charted: Oct '97; UK Chart Position: 16; Label: Geffen; Album: *Do It Yourself*

'Love me and Leave Me' was the third single from The Seahorses' sole album *Do it Yourself* and the band's third consecutive single to reach the top 20, where it spent six weeks, peaking at number 16.

The lead track was written by John Squire and Liam Gallagher and the single featured B-sides 'Shine', written by Squire, and 'Falling is Easy', written by the band's vocalist Chris Helme. The cover artwork, by Squire, was of a pink Apache helicopter.

Lovelife (album – Lush)

Charted: Mar '96; UK Chart Position: 8; Label: 4AD; Singles: 'Single Girl' (Jan '96, UKCP 21), 'Ladykillers' (Mar '96, 22), '500 (Shake Baby Shake)' (Jul '96, 21)

Lovelife was the third album released by Lush, and was noted for a marked change in sound, moving away from the band's previous shoe-gazing fare towards the energetic, fast-paced indie-rock that placed the band in the Britpop scene. The album was their second to reach the top ten in the UK chart, after their debut album *Spooky* released in early '92. The Japanese version of the album featured a bonus CD containing B-sides from the album and single 'Single Girl'.

Released in early '96, the album contained hit singles 'Single Girl', 'Ladykillers' and '500 (Shake Baby Shake)', all of which narrowly missed the UK top 20, and the track 'Ciao!' which featured Pulp's Jarvis Cocker on vocals.

Lucky Man (single – The Verve)

Charted: Dec '97; UK Chart Position: 7; Label: Hut; Album: *Urban Hymns*

'Lucky Man' was the third of four singles from The Verve's third album *Urban Hymns* and the band's third consecutive single to enter the top ten of the UK chart, where it spent 17 weeks, peaking at number seven in December '97.

The single was released on two CDs, the first containing 'Never

Wanna See You Cry' and 'History', and the second featuring B-sides 'MSG', 'The Longest Day' and a remix of the title track 'Lucky Man (Happiness More Or Less)'.

There were UK and US versions of the video. In the UK, the band played in a building overlooking the River Thames in London, and in the US, they were in an apartment then travelled up a mountain.

Lucky You (single – The Lightning Seeds)

Charted: Oct '95; UK Chart Position: 15; Label: Epic; Album: *Jollification*

'Lucky You' was the first and fifth single from the Lighting Seeds' third album *Jollification*. Initially released in August '94, it peaked at number 43 in the UK chart, where it spent two weeks. It was then re-issued the following year at the height of Britpop, charting in the top 20, where it spent six weeks.

B-sides on the CD single, which featured a golden horseshoe on the cover, included live versions of previous singles 'The Life Of Riley' and 'Pure', and 'Here Today', all taken from their Shepherd's Bush Empire gig in May '95.

Lush (band)

Lush were one of the few female-fronted Britpop bands, exploding onto the scene with their smash hit single 'Ladykillers' in early '96. Fronted by flame-haired lead singer and guitarist Miki Berenyi, the band had actually been around since the late eighties, initially called the Baby Machines before changing their name and signing to independent record label 4AD.

The band released six-track mini-album *Scar* and, soon after, became associated with the shoegazing era. Their first full-length album, *Spooky*, was released in early '92 and charted in the top ten, followed by *Split*, released in '94, which reached the top 20. It was their top ten album *Lovelife*, released in '96, that propelled the band into the Britpop limelight and featured their most successful hits 'Single Girl', 'Ladykillers' and '500 (Shake Baby Shake)', which all narrowly missed the top 20.

The band formed in '87, several years after Berenyi met future bandmate, guitarist and vocalist Emma Anderson at the age of 14.

The line-up changed several times, though mainly included Chris Acland on drums and Phil King on bass. The band played their last performance in late '96, shortly after which Acland tragically took his own life. In '15, the band reunited, with drummer Justin Welch, previously with Elastica and Suede, replacing Acland in the line-up. The band's fast-paced punk-pop songs put them in on a par with Elastica, with whom they shared a similar ethos.

M

M.O.R (single – Blur)

Charted: Sept '97; UK Chart Position: 15; Label: Food; Album: *Blur*

'M.O.R', which stands for 'middle of the road', was the fourth and final single from Blur's self-titled fifth album. The top-20 single spent three weeks on the UK chart and was the band's final release during the Britpop era.

The B-sides included exclusive track 'Swallows in the Heatwave', a William Orbit remix of album track 'Movin' On' and a Moby remix of previous single and album track 'Beetlebum', entitled 'Moby's Minimal House Mix'.

The video, directed by John Hardwick, featured four stuntmen wearing balaclavas representing each band member but using anagrammatic names. Alex James was Lee Jaxsam, Graham Coxon was Morgan C Hoax, Dave Rowntree was Trevor Dewane and Damon Albarn as Dan Abnormal, a name he used previously when playing keyboards for Elastica.

Madan, Sonya (singer/songwriter – Echobelly)

Sonya Aurora Madan was the Delhi-born, pixie-haired lead singer of Echobelly. She formed the band in '93 with Swedish guitarist Glenn Johansson and, as one of the few women to front a Britpop band, made her mark on the scene with enigmatic vocals often compared to Morrissey and lyrics touching on a wide range of themes including sexism, prostitution, homelessness and racism. Despite her family moving to the UK when she was just two, Madan's songwriting influences stemmed from a strict Indian upbringing. Her song 'Father Ruler King Computer' expressed her feelings towards arranged marriage, while 'Give Her a Gun' revealed her thoughts on men having more power than women.

During the band's world tour in the mid-nineties, Madan lost an extreme amount of weight due to a hyperactive thyroid. Although she thankfully managed to get the condition under control, her health issues partly delayed third album *Lustra* and, soon after its release, the band went quiet for a few years. Madan released two more albums with the band in the noughties before forming Calm of Zero in '10 with Johansson, with whom she then produced two mini acoustic session albums. She continues to play with Echobelly and Calm of Zero.

Madchester (aka baggy/psychedelic rock)

The key British music scene immediately before Britpop, Madchester was also known as 'baggy', mainly because of the looseness of the trousers that its key players chose to wear. The name came from the city that dominated the scene – Manchester – and the bands involved were often key influences on the Britpop groups: the Stone Roses, the Happy Mondays, the Inspiral Carpets and The Charlatans, many of whom also recorded in the Britpop years.

Madchester was not just about indie bands with guitars and keyboards though; it centred on a few key record labels such as Factory, who also owned the scene's most famous nightclub, the Hacienda (the Happy Mondays were signed after losing a battle of the bands there). The scene became about the rise of dance music, notably the acid house and rave movements. For the first time, attending a gig became not about the band and the songs they were playing, but who was playing the songs and mixing the records to create something new, something distinct and something different. The success of dance music was bolstered and enhanced by the growing popularity and availability of the illegal drug Ecstasy, which meant that the Hacienda never made any money, because no one was buying drinks from the bar. In fact, it was heavily subsidised by the record sales of New Order and the Happy Mondays.

The pounding beats and crashing piano chords of the music crossed over into the sound of the bands, tying the two together and creating something new, and at odds with what eventually became Britpop. Madchester's two frontrunners, the Stone Roses and the Happy Mondays, were both influenced by dance music, notably the Stone Roses' 'Fools Gold' and the Mondays' 'Step On', which were both created with drum loops and later remixed into actual dance versions.

This became what the Britpop bands rallied against. Noel Gallagher and Damon Albarn, in particular, believed music was becoming too synthesised, with too many drum loops and not enough live instruments. So, back-to-basics became the heart of the Britpop movement. This meant, of course, that Madchester and Britpop had a close but fractious relationship, like feuding siblings. Inevitably, many of the Madchester bands faded in the Britpop years, most notably House of Love and the Inspiral Carpets, while others succeeded by changing their sound and embracing the back-to-basics approach, like James and The Charlatans.

Manic Street Preachers, The (band)

Named after an unfortunate encounter with a passerby during a busking session, Blackwood's Manic Street Preachers are one of Britain's most prolific and immediately identifiable rock bands. Coming of age during the infamous Welsh miners' strike, the four young bandmates were outspoken working-class intellectuals, driven by a passion for left-wing politics married with the nihilism of punk rock.

In '00, they were the first western rock band to be asked to play live in the Cuban capital of Havana, where they were also granted an audience with Fidel Castro. On remarking that their gigs could be rather loud, the Cuban leader asked "Louder than war?" (a quote the band had printed on T-shirts).

Formed in '86 at their South Wales secondary school while Britain was in the throes of Thatcherism, the band comprised singer and guitarist James Dean Bradfield, his cousin and band drummer Sean Moore, their close friend Nicky Wire (formerly Jones) on bass and Richey Edwards, who joined a year or so later, on guitar. The band began writing slogans and creating banners before they could play their instruments, and it was their love of punk, the politics of Karl Marx, the prose of Albert Camus and the glamour of the New York Dolls that gave them their individuality.

Their early singles were little more than a selection of fast and furious punk tracks, but the band quickly established a reputation in the music press for spouting revolutionary rhetoric. The main instigator was Edwards, who shared lyric-writing duty with Wire and appeared live with the band despite not really being able to play guitar.

They signed to Columbia in '91, and their first album *Generation Terrorists* appeared not long after. Much like their early singles, it was a fast-paced, brash piece of work comprised of 18 tracks attacking commercialism and the mainstream. Despite positive reviews, the record failed to sell the 20 million copies the band had predicted, reaching number 13 in the UK chart in January '92. Second album *Gold against the Soul* continued where the band left off a year later, deepening their arguments and showing a clear progression in their sound, but it wasn't until *The Holy Bible* appeared in '94 that fans and critics began to see their true evolution.

Edwards' mental state had slowly worsened over the years, leading to bouts of self-harm, including an infamous episode where, after a gig, he cut the phrase '4 Real' into his arm with a razor blade to prove the band's intentions to a bewildered journalist, future Radio 1 DJ Steve Lamaq. Edwards took over the lyric writing completely on *The Holy Bible*, resulting in a record that dealt with matters ranging from the horrors of the Holocaust to anorexia, from which Edwards himself suffered.

After a string of dates in Japan were abandoned, he disappeared one day and has never been seen since. He left with no money, no passport and his car was found at a known suicide spot by the Severn River, but no body has ever been discovered. His family kept the case open for as long as they could, but he was finally declared legally dead on 23 November '08.

After some extended time away, Nicky Wire began writing what would become 'A Design for Life', the band's first post-Ritchey single, which was eventually released at the height of Britpop. The corresponding album *Everything Must Go* followed in June '96 and, despite missing out on the top spot and peaking at number two, it went on to spend an amazing 102 weeks on the UK chart. The album honoured the band's deep and serious approach to their lyrics, but the music shifted away from the intense punk-rock of their previous work toward a lighter indie-guitar focus, fitting perfectly into the Britpop world.

The band experienced the most commercially successful period of their career. Many festival appearances and UK and worldwide live dates followed and, in September '98, the band achieved their first number one single, 'If You Tolerate This Your Children Will be Next', which was the first single released from number one album *This is*

My Truth, Tell Me Yours, which won the band Best Album and Best Group at the Brit awards in '99. On New Year's Eve that year, the band played live at the Millennium Stadium in Cardiff, seeing in the new year, new decade and new millennium in front of 50,000 fans.

Since then, the band have released a further seven studio albums and three greatest hits collections, all of which have reached either the top ten or just outside of it. The most recent album *Futurology* peaked at number two in July '14.

Mansize Rooster (single – Supergrass)

Charted: Feb '95; UK Chart Position: 20; Label: Parlophone; Album: *I Should Coco*

'Mansize Rooster' was the second of five singles from Supergrass' debut album, *I Should Coco*. It was the first of several top-20 singles in the UK chart, where it spent a total of three weeks, and led to the band's debut live television performance on *The Word* in '95.

The CD single contained the exclusive B-sides 'Sitting Up Straight' and 'Odd?', while the video featured all three members of the band in a bathtub.

Manson, Shirley (singer/songwriter – Garbage)

The smoky-eyed Dusty Springfield of Britpop, Scottish singer, songwriter and actress Shirley Ann Manson was best known as the flame-haired, feisty, no-nonsense frontwoman of Garbage. Born in August '66, she grew up in Edinburgh, where she attended City of Edinburgh Music School, before joining her first major band Goodbye Mr Mackenzie as backing vocalist and keyboardist in the mid-eighties.

The band signed to Capitol records, released one top-40 album, *Good Deeds and Dirty Rags*, which peaked at number 26 in the UK chart, and one single, 'The Rattler', which peaked at number 37. The band subsequently morphed into Angelfish, with Manson as lead vocalist. Future Garbage drummer Butch Vig spotted Manson in the music video for the band's 'Suffocate Me' and asked her to audition in '94. She went on to perform with Garbage throughout the nineties and, on and off, up until the present day, releasing several albums and many singles.

Other notable highlights in Manson's career include co-producing and singing the theme for the James Bond film *The World Is Not Enough* in '99, where the singer appeared alongside a killer android version of herself. Manson also made her acting debut in '08 as Catherine Weaver, a concealed liquid-metal T-1001 Terminator, in *Terminator: The Sarah Connor Chronicles*. She's married to Garbage sound engineer Billy Bush.

Mansun continues to play and record with Garbage, and has released songs with other acts for the soundtracks of *Wet Hot American Summer* in '15 (a duet with Craig Wedren) and *American Gods* in '17 with Brian Reitzell, who was nominated for an Oscar in '03 for his work on the Sophia Coppola film *Lost in Translation*.

Mansun (band)

Rumoured to be named after an abbreviated version of an early Verve B-side, 'A Man Called Sun', Chester's Mansun were best known for their debut album *Attack of the Grey Lantern* and a string of captivating early singles, including the iconic 'Wide Open Space'. The band existed on the edges of the accessible Britpop scene, taking their influence from David Bowie, eighties new wave bands like Joy Division and goth/rock/pop bands like The Cure.

Formed in the north-west city of Chester in the early nineties by lead singer, guitarist and chief songwriter Paul Draper and bassist Stove King, the band didn't have much luck with drummers in their early days and, for quite some time, played along with a drum machine. Dominic Chad, manager of the bar they often drank in, joined later on guitar, providing a foil to Draper's songwriting as well as some deeply sonorous and distinctive guitar lines.

With his inclusion, the band's individual sound was assured. Draper took his time developing their songs in the rehearsal studio and, after two self-financed singles but few live performances, the band eventually signed with Parlophone in '95. It was then that they really started to play live, quickly gaining notoriety for their intense, extravagant gigs, where few could predict what would happen. Military themes were mixed with circus imagery, and they often appeared on stage in orange jump suits, feather boas, gas masks, makeup and glitter, picking up from where Bowie and the New York Dolls had left off.

A loyal following fell quickly in tow, and a string of three EPs appeared between March and September '96, each climbing higher in the charts than the last. 'Egg Shaped Fred' reached number 37, 'Take it Easy Chicken' number 32 and 'Stripper Vicar' number 19, before fourth single 'Wide Open Space' – a mainstay on the radio – launched the band into the mainstream, hitting number 15 in November '96. The band's fifth single 'She Makes My Nose Bleed' gave them their first top-ten single in February '96 (peaking at number nine), paving the way for debut album *Attack of the Grey Lantern* which went straight in at number one in the UK chart two weeks later. Drummer Andy Rathbone finally joined the band full time in August '96, his first gig playing third EP 'Stripper Vicar' live on *TFI Friday*.

It was Draper's individual vision that created the modern masterpiece that is the band's debut album and, although they released their records during the Britpop years and found themselves heavily associated with the movement, ensured they existed only on the periphery of it.

After Britpop, the band's second album *Six* was released in September '98, reaching – somewhat fittingly – number six in the UK chart. Unfortunately, ambition crossed over into indulgence and the album failed to capture the public imagination due to its overproduction and overly complicated song structures, where middle-eights could often be found in the middle of other middle-eights. It gained a reputation, even among the band's fan base, as bordering on pretentious. By the end of '99, the band retreated to the rehearsal room in search of new material.

Their third album *Little Kix* was released in August '00 and, despite a concerted effort by Draper et al to rediscover the band's original simple but effective pop-tinged goth-rock songs, it failed to light up the charts, reaching number 12.

They split during the making of their unreleased fourth album in '03, but the legacy of their first album and those electric first few years remains strong within the British music scene. Singer and band leader Paul Draper returned with a solo album, *Spooky Action*, in August '17, alongside two numerically-named EPs and a single, 'Things People Want'.

Marblehead Johnson (single – The Bluetones)

Charted: Sept '96; UK Chart Position: 7; Label: Superior Quality; Album: n/a

'Marblehead Johnson' was The Bluetones exclusive non-album single, released shortly after debut album *Expecting To Fly* in '96. It was their third top 10 and spent six weeks on the chart.

The single contained B-sides 'The Simple Things', 'Nifkin's Bridge' and 'Are You Blue or Are You Blind?'. The video featured extremely overweight versions of the band members.

Marchin' Already (album – Ocean Colour Scene)

Charted: Sept '97; UK Chart Position: 1; Label: MCA; Singles: 'Hundred Mile High City' (Jun '97, UKCP 4), 'Travellers Tune' (Sept '97, 5), 'Better Day' (Nov '97, 9), 'It's a Beautiful Thing' (Feb '98, 12)

Marchin' Already was the eagerly anticipated follow-up to Ocean Colour Scene's highly successful *Moseley Shoals* and the band's highest charting album, knocking Oasis' *Be Here Now* off the number 1 spot in September '97. The album spent 40 weeks on the chart and contained the top 10 singles: 'Hundred Mile High City', 'Travellers Tune' and 'Better Day', and the top 20 single 'It's a Beautiful Thing'.

For a band who took some time to find success, once they hit their stride, they maintained it, and *Marchin' Already* is the sound of a band aware of exactly what they are doing. Where *Moseley Shoals* is rough around the edges, filled with strong singles but also slightly less accessible songs, its follow-up is the sound of a band aware of who their audience is and filled with a new-found confidence in their deserved success. The four-to-the-floor upbeat tempo of lead single 'Hundred Mile High City' continued where 'The Riverboat Song' had left off; 'Traveller's Tune' and 'It's a Beautiful Thing' saw the band wear their clear cut influences on their paisley sleeves by featuring sixties Northern Soul diva P P Arnold; and the quiet melancholia of 'Big Star' saw singer Simon Fowler bemoan the trappings of his new-found fame. The album remains the band's strongest to date.

In '14, two deluxe editions of the album were available, the first including a bonus CD of B-sides and the second featuring a third CD with live tracks from the band's Manchester Apollo gig in '98.

Marion (band)

Best known for their top-20 hit 'Sleep', Marion's fate was intrinsically linked with lead singer and chief songwriter Jamie Harding's serious drug addiction.

Formed in the Cheshire town of Macclesfield in '93, the band's line-up was completed by guitarists Phil Cunningham and Anthony Grantham, bassist Julian Phillips and drummer Murad Mousa. They were snapped up by Britpop-hungry London Records just one year later. Their debut album *This World and Body* entered the top ten of the UK chart in '96, and resulted in singles 'Sleep', 'Toys for Boys', 'Let's All Go Together' and 'Time'. Success seemingly in the bag, the band gained support slots with several major acts including Morrissey, Echo & The Bunnymen and the Manic Street Preachers, as well as playing several UK festivals including Glastonbury.

The Smiths' guitarist Johnny Marr co-wrote and produced the band's follow up album *The Program*, which was finally released in '98. It failed to chart in the UK due, in part, to Harding's lengthy drug-fuelled absences, which eventually destroyed what could have been a great band. With Marion on hiatus, Cunningham was recruited to play in the live line-up of Marr's band Electronic, before eventually becoming a full-time member of New Order in the early noughties.

Complete with a sober frontman, Marion have so far re-formed three times, in '06, '11 and '15, playing a string of live shows and new material and releasing live album *Alive in Manchester* in '12. Their latest release was 'Rogue Male EP' in May '16.

Marr, Johnny (guitarist/songwriter/producer – The Smiths/Electronic/Johnny Marr and the Healers)

As lead guitarist and joint-songwriter for one of Manchester's most successful and most loved bands, The Smiths, Johnny Marr is something of spiritual leader for the Britpop movement. In particular, he was a major influence on the guitar stylings of Bernard Butler and Noel Gallagher (who he gifted a Les Paul Standard guitar to in the early days of Oasis, which can be seen on the sleeve of *(What's the Story) Morning Glory?*).

Born on 31 October '63 in Manchester to an Irish family, Marr (formerly Maher) formed his first band at the age of 13 with future

Smiths' bassist Andy Rourke, but it wasn't until he met Stephen Patrick Morrissey in '82 at the age of 19 that he found any kind of real success. The Smiths' debut single 'Hand in Glove' was released in May '83 by Rough Trade, but Geoff Travis didn't sign the band to the label officially until 18 months later.

Marr and Morrissey's continued arguments over the band's musical direction meant the young guitarist quit not long after the recording of final album *Strangeways Here We Come* in August '87. By the time it was released in September, the band had split for good. Alongside The Jam, they remain one of the few bands of their ilk not to have re-formed.

In the late eighties, Marr began recording with New Order frontman Bernard Sumner as Electronic, releasing several albums through the nineties. He also co-wrote and produced Britpop band Marion's second album *The Program*. At the same time, he joined Matt Johnson to play with The The, another Manchester-based band, and did extensive session work. In '00, he formed Johnny Marr and the Healers with Ringo Starr's son Zak Starkey and former Kula Shaker bassist Alonza Bevan.

Marr's jangly, clean-toned guitar style is what set him apart, particularly when playing in The Smiths, where his layered licks combined beautifully with Morrissey's deeply melancholic and sometimes bizarre lyrical content to make them a truly original British band.

Marr also produced the band, with his technically intricate work on key Smiths' track 'How Soon is Now?' showcasing his mixing desk talent. Most recently, Noel Gallagher has paid his respects to Marr by inviting him to play live several times with Oasis, and by giving him a featured slot on their album *Heathen Chemistry*. Marr's autobiography *Set the Boy Free* was published in November '16.

Matthews, Donna (guitarist/songwriter – Elastica)

Donna Matthews was the young, photogenic lead guitarist and sometime songwriter of key Britpop group Elastica, who very nearly lost everything to heroin.

Born in South Wales in December '71, she joined Elastica in '92, at the age of 20, after answering an advert in the *Melody Maker*'s 'musicians wanted' pages. Elastica went on to garner much success, even making waves in the American indie music scene, which is where

Matthews' heroin addiction became more prevalent. She struggled on to '99 but then left the band so she could deal with her addiction. After getting clean, she formed several all-female groups and fronted a fictional band in Todd Haynes' '99 film *Velvet Goldmine*, where she played the New York Dolls' 'Personality Crisis'.

With no further musical projects since the turn of the millennium, Matthews has retreated into a quiet life away from the public eye. She appeared on stage with her old band in '00 to play their most well-known song, 'Connection', just a few months before they split for good.

Maximum High, A (album – Shed Seven)

Charted: Apr '96; UK Chart Position: 8; Label: Polydor; Singles: 'Where Have You Been Tonight?' (May '95, UKCP 23), 'Getting Better' (Jan '96, 14), 'Going for Gold' (Mar '96, 8), 'Bully Boy' (May '96, 22), 'On Standby' (Aug '96, 12)

Produced by Chris Sheldon and released via Polydor Records in April '96, *A Maximum High* was the second album from York band Shed Seven and now considered to be their breakthrough long-form release. It was recorded in London at RAK Studios, north of Regents Park, and Master Rock Studios in Kilburn.

Tracks released off the album included lead single 'Where Have You Been Tonight?' in May '95, followed in '96 by a string of singles: 'Getting Better' in January; their most well-known song 'Going for Gold' in March; 'Bully Boy' in May; and 'On Standby' in August. All the singles hit the top 40 of the UK chart, and the album not only cemented the band as key lieutenants in the Britpop cause, but also helped signal the popularity of the movement. It might not be their best record, but the titles of the singles suggested the aspirations of the group and of Britpop as a whole.

Session musicians the Kick Horns and the Phantom Horns also feature on the album, providing an underlying brassy sound. The album received a generally positive response, with comparisons to The Smiths, and peaked at number eight in the UK chart.

McAlmont & Butler (musical duo)

Guitarist and Britpop legend Bernard Butler has lived many musical lives, including this team effort with singer David McAlmont, which produced the indie/soul crossover epic hit 'Yes', released in May '95 at the peak of Britpop. But that's where their association with the Britpop scene begins and ends.

The duo began working together in '94, not long after Butler's departure from Suede during the *Dog Man Star* sessions and, in many ways, the music they produced was a reaction against his former band. McAlmont had released one soul album called *McAlmont* and had few associations with the indie scene. He did have the most startling vocal range though, used to maximum effect by Butler and producer Mike Hedges against the swelling strings of 'Yes'.

After the first single went straight in at number eight in the UK chart – propelled by a key performance on *Later... with Jools Holland* – an album was inevitable. Second single 'You Do' reached number 17 in October '95, followed by the album *Sound of... McAlmont and Butler* in November. But with no tour and few live performances to support the release, it reached a disappointing 33 in the UK chart.

Their momentum gone, the duo worked on separate projects for the next seven years, eventually reuniting for second album *Bring it Back* in May '02. This fared slightly better than its predecessor, peaking at number 18 in the UK chart, where it spent three weeks. To date, most of a third album has been recorded but has not been released, and the duo continue to play live together, including a tour of Britain and Ireland in '15.

McCarroll, Tony (drummer – Oasis)

Tony McCarroll is one of the luckiest and unluckiest drummers in recent rock history. On one hand, he provided the backbeat to one of the UK's most important debut albums, while on the other he left acrimoniously just as the band started recording one of the era's defining records.

McCarroll joined The Rain in early '91, alongside Chris Hutton, Paul 'Bonehead' Arthurs and Paul 'Guigsy' McGuigan. Hutton later left and was replaced by Liam Gallagher, leading to the birth of Oasis. After Noel Gallagher joined the band, they began to be taken seriously by the music scene, quickly finding fame despite allegations of limited musicianship among some band members, McCarroll included.

Despite this, McCarroll's role on *Definitely Maybe* became an important one, with his immediately identifiable opening drum lines key to tracks like 'Live Forever' and 'Supersonic'. The thundering beat of 'Bring it on Down' adds a much needed pace and drive to the song.

The final Oasis track that McCarroll played on was 'Some Might Say', the band's first single from their second album, *(What's the Story) Morning Glory?*, which was also the band's first number one in the UK singles chart. He left the group just before the album was recorded, but was credited in the album sleeve notes, which led to an unfortunate legal dispute over royalties that was later settled in court. He has played in several Manchester-based bands over the years, as well as providing drum lessons.

McGee, Alan (label manager - Creation Records)

Creation Records founder and indie band kingmaker Alan McGee is responsible for signing some of Britain's best-loved indie groups, including: the Jesus and Mary Chain, My Bloody Valentine, Primal Scream, Ride, Teenage Fanclub, the Super Furry Animals and, of course, Oasis. As well as running one of the country's most successful indie labels, he has also managed many of the bands, including The Libertines in '07, when he was charged with controlling Pete Doherty.

Born in Glasgow in September '60, McGee became firm friends with Bobby Gillespie from Primal Scream (and the Jesus and Mary Chain) at school. They played in several punk bands together, before McGee realised his talents lay not in performing music, but in bringing it to an audience. He moved to London in the early eighties and set up Creation Records in '83, while still working full time for British Rail. The label's first successful group were the Jesus and Mary Chain, whose first album *Psychocandy* was a notable indie hit.

Over the next ten years, Creation Records had its ups and downs, always linked with McGee's own, and with his spiralling drugs problem. Not long before he signed Oasis at the now legendary King Tut's show, he quit drugs for good and soon found real success. Oasis quickly became one of the most successful British groups of all time, allowing McGee to focus on developing new talent. He set up the Poptones label in '99, signing, among others, garage rock band The Hives, as well as setting up the DJ club night Death Disco. He continued to DJ live as well as taking over the much-publicised management responsibility of the notorious indie rock group The Libertines, once Creation had finally ended in '99.

In '07, he quit the music business for good, and moved to the countryside to focus on raising his daughter with long-term partner Kate Holmes, who runs the fashion label Client London. He also has a son from his previous marriage. His autobiography, *Creation Stories*, was published in '13, and in '14 he announced that Creation Management had been launched, including as his very first clients, the band with whom he first found success, the Jesus and Mary Chain.

Me and You Versus the World (single – Space)

Charted: Sept '96; UK Chart Position: 9; Label: Gut Records; Album: *Spiders*

'Me and You Versus the World' was released from Space's debut album *Spiders*, and became the band's first single to reach the top ten of the UK chart, where it spent a total of six weeks.

Two versions of the CD single were released, the first containing three remixes of the title track, 'Knickers', 'No Knickers' and 'Crotchless Knickers', and the second featuring exclusive tracks 'Spiders', 'Life of a Miser' and 'Blow Your Cover'.

Me, Me, Me (band)

Short-lived Britpop supergroup Me, Me, Me, formed in '96, featured Blur's Alex James on bass and vocals, Duran Duran's Stephen Duffy on vocals and guitar and Elastica's Justin Welch on drums. James's friend Charlie Bloor also featured as 'musician'.

The band released one single in August '96 on Indolent records, 'Hanging Around', which peaked at number 19. The single featured exclusive tracks 'Hollywood Wives' and 'Tabitha's Island'. No further material was released by the band.

Melody Maker (music magazine)

As famous for its 'musicians wanted' pages, which were responsible for match-making the line-ups of, among others, Suede and Elastica, as its music news, *Melody Maker* was a key music publication alongside the *New Musical Express* or *NME*.

Founded in '26, Melody Maker was one of the world's first musical weekly papers, initially featuring dance hall bands before focusing mainly on jazz in the fifties. It was late to cover rock 'n' roll and, as such, lost much of its possible readership to the *NME*, which began in '53. By the seventies it had started to take a more populist approach, focusing on music in the UK Singles Chart, before taking the near opposite approach throughout the eighties, choosing to focus on the more independent music scenes. Rock and indie became its staple fodder, although articles on dance music and even hip-hop found their way into the pages.

During the Britpop years, *Melody Maker* chose to remain true to its indie roots, despite the mainstreaming of the musical scene, and was more likely to feature smaller independent bands than big bands like Blur and Oasis. The advent of the internet in the late nineties dealt a strong blow to the print media and, after a failed attempt to rebrand as a smaller magazine, *Melody Maker* was forced to merge in '99 with its chief rival, the *NME*, under the latter's name and branding.

Menswear (band)

Menswear were most commonly known for their hit single 'Daydreamer' as well as for being the only band to appear on *Top of the Pops* before releasing a single. Formed in '94, the band consisted of Johnny Dean on vocals, bassist Stuart Black, guitarists Chris Gentry and Simon White, and drummer Matt Everitt.

Signed to Laurel records, the band released their debut single 'I'll Manage Somehow' in April '95, which peaked at number 49 in the UK chart, and which also provided their debut TV performance on *Top of The Pops*, a week before it was actually released. The single featured on their debut album *Nuisance*, which peaked at number 11 in October '95 and contained the top-20 singles 'Daydreamer', 'Stardust' and 'Being Brave' and the top-40 single 'Sleeping In'. The band also released non-album single 'We Love You' in September '96, which peaked at number 22 and signalled a shift in the band's direction.

The band did record a second album, ¡Hay Tiempo!, in '98, but it was only released in Japan.

Post-Britpop, the band went their separate ways, each playing in various bands, though they did re-form in '13 with lead singer Johnny Dean as the only original member. The new line-up played a few live dates to coincide with the 20th anniversary of the release of *Nuisance*, then split for good in August '16. Drummer Matt Everitt is now a radio presenter on BBC Radio 6 Music.

Although never confirmed, the story goes that singer Johnny Dean invented the band so he could blag his way into Glastonbury Festival for free. He apparently came up with the name on the spot and spent the day inventing the band's musical style, only later putting together the actual line-up once back in London. True or not, it perfectly reflects the way Britpop bands – whether they actually existed or not – were being signed by hordes of hungry A&R men.

Metal Mickey (single - Suede)

Charted: Sept '92; UK Chart Position: 17; Label: Nude; Album: *Suede*

'Metal Mickey' was the second single released by Suede in the early days of Britpop, shortly after debut single 'The Drowners'. It was the band's first song to reach the top 20 of the UK chart, where it spent a total of three weeks, peaking at number 17.

The UK single featured exclusive B-sides 'Where The Pigs Don't Fly' and 'He's Dead', while the US version contained only the title track, performed live on America's *Tonight Show With Jay Leno* to coincide with the release.

Milk (single - Garbage)

Charted: Nov '96; UK Chart Position: 10; Label: Mushroom; Album: *Garbage*

'Milk' was the fifth and final single released from Garbage's debut album, coming out several months after 'Stupid Girl' had launched the band into the mainstream. It was the band's second single to reach the top ten of the UK chart. It peaked at number ten and was their longest-running single on the chart, where it spent ten weeks, during the Britpop era.

The song was performed at the '96 MTV Europe Music Awards, where the band also received the award for 'Best New Act'.

Two versions of the CD single were available. The first contained a reworked version of the title track, entitled 'The Wicked Mix', and featuring Massive Attack's Tricky on vocals, followed by a Goldie remix, the original version and a remix of previous single 'Stupid Girl'. The second CD featured 'The Wicked Mix', 'The Classic Remix', 'The Udder Remix' and another remix of 'Stupid Girl'.

Mis-Shapes/Sorted for E's & Whizz (single - Pulp)

Charted: Oct '95; UK Chart Position: 2; Label: Island; Album: *Different Class*

'Mis-Shapes', the rabble-rousing opening track to Pulp's *Different Class* album, was released as a double A-side single with 'Sorted for E's & Whizz'. As with previous single 'Common People', the double A-side narrowly missed out on the top spot, peaking at number two and spending 13 weeks on the UK chart. It was Simply Red's 'Fairground' that stopped Pulp from reaching the number one spot.

Two versions of the single were available. The first featured exclusive track 'P.T.A (Parent Teacher Association)' and a live recording of 'Common People' from Glastonbury '95, while the second contained two further remixes of 'Common People'. The cover artwork on CD1 featured the pattern for a suit jacket above the phrase, "Styling the Pattern for Life (For Misses Petite and Mister Large)", while CD2 contained the instructions for creating a paper 'packet' and the phrase, "Simply Fuss Free".

The songs represented two very different but complimentary sides to Pulp. 'Mis-Shapes' was a call to arms to all those in society who stood out as different, with Jarvis's chief lyric crying out to those at the outer edges that all was not lost, "Brothers, sisters, can't you see? The future's owned by you and me".

'Sorted for E's & Whizz' spoke to the same folk, but the lyric followed the misadventures of Jarvis and his friends as they attended an all-night rave, "Somewhere in a field in Hampshire". The song advocated the use of drugs (if in nothing else but the title) but it was chiefly an anthem about the power of music drawing people together in one fantastic shared experience. They remain two of Pulp's best-loved songs to this day.

Modern Life is Rubbish (album – Blur)

Charted: May '93; UK Chart Position: 15; Label: Food; Singles: 'For Tomorrow' (May '93, UKCP 28), 'Chemical World' (Jul '93, 28), 'Sunday Sunday' (Oct '93, 26)

Britpop's second long-format release, Blur's *Modern Life is Rubbish*, appeared in record stores just a month after Suede's eponymous debut album. Musically very different from their own debut *Leisure*, the album was conceived while the band toured America in '92 by a homesick Damon Albarn.

The intention was to bring the focus back to Britain and, as such, Albarn and the rest of the band began to shift their music away from their previous work, moving closer to classic sixties bands like the Kinks and the Small Faces. Alongside this new style, Albarn's lyrics were less whimsical and more direct and personal, telling of "20th century boys" (on key single 'For Tomorrow') and contemporary life in the early nineties, thus anchoring the songs in a specific place and time while also giving the album a timeless feel.

As in life, there's hope alongside the melancholia and, as much as Albarn is looking forward to tomorrow and what the future might bring, he is also looking at what's going on around him, at young folk unable to make the rent or needing a holiday in the sun, of 'Colin Zeal', sick of his job, of Sunday afternoons reading the paper. In the opening line of 'Advert', a synthesized American voice tells us that, "Food processors are great", reminding us how we are surrounded by commercialism, and how the cultural imperialism of America fell so heavily over Britain in the nineties.

Perhaps because it was too forward-thinking, the album failed to chime with the public and peaked at number 15 in the UK chart in May '93. Singles 'For Tomorrow' and 'Chemical World' both reached number 28 and 'Sunday Sunday' rounded things off by reaching number 26 in October '93. Stand-alone single 'Popscene' was purposefully left off the album because it hadn't fared very well when it was released a year before, only reaching number 32.

The album proved problematic, but the band didn't give up their new direction, heading back into the studio to write and record *Parklife*.

Monaco (band)

Monaco were the side project of New Order bassist Peter Hook and Revenge band member David Potts (aka Pottsy). The band were best known for their hit single 'What Do You Want From Me?', which was released in early '97 and also featured on indie compilation album *Shine 8*. Formed in '95, the band released two albums, *Music for Pleasure* which entered the top 20 in '97 and their self-titled follow-up in '00, as well as several singles including 'Sweet Lips' and 'Shine'.

The band were initially signed to Polydor Records before moving to Papillion in '00. They split shortly after, with Hook reuniting with New Order and Potts pursuing a solo career. In '09, Hook formed new band The Light and, in '13, Potts joined as guitarist.

Moseley Shoals (album – Ocean Colour Scene)

Charted: Apr '96; UK Chart Position: 2; Label: MCA; Singles: 'The Riverboat Song' (Feb '96, 15), 'You've Got It Bad' (Apr '96, 7), 'The Day We Caught The Train' (Jun '96, 4), 'The Circle' (Sep '96, 6)

Moseley Shoals was the highly successful second album from Birmingham's Ocean Colour Scene. Released at the height of Britpop in early '96, the album spent an impressive 92 weeks on the UK chart, narrowly missing out on the number one spot, which was occupied by Take That's *Greatest Hits*. The album included the top-20 single 'The Riverboat Song' and the top ten singles 'You've Got It Bad', 'The Day We Caught the Train' and 'The Circle'.

The album, produced by Brendan Lynch who was known for his work with Primal Scream and Paul Weller, was recorded at the band's studio in Birmingham, named after the album itself. Moseley is the suburb where most of the band grew up. The album cover features the band outside the Jephson Memorial in Leamington Spa.

After the disappointment of their first album, they managed to re-group with *Moseley Shoals* and rediscover their love for all things retro – the Mod scene of the sixties, The Who, The Jam and scooters. This, combined with their strong musicianship and the strength of the album's singles, meant it chimed with its audience and garnered much success.

Mother Nature Calls (album - Cast)

Charted: Apr '97; UK Chart Position: 3; Label: Polydor; Singles: 'Free Me' (Apr '97, UKCP 7), 'Guiding Star' (Jun '97, 9), 'Live the Dream' (Sept '97, 7), 'I'm So Lonely' (Nov '97, 14)

Mother Nature Calls was the eagerly anticipated follow-up to Cast's debut album *All Change* and the band's highest charting album, peaking at number three and spending 46 weeks on the UK chart. It resulted in the top-ten singles 'Free Me', 'Guiding Star' and 'Live the Dream', and top-20 single 'I'm So Lonely'. Stylistically, the album continued what the band had started with *All Change*, taking a slightly more laid-back approach to their sound, exemplified by second single 'Guiding Star'.

Produced by John Leckie, the album sleeve was a microdot creation, designed by Brian Cannon and featuring a rainbow soaring across a blue sky.

In '14, a remastered, deluxe edition of the album was released, featuring exclusive bonus tracks and a DVD containing promo videos and performances from *Top of the Pops*, *Later... With Jools Holland* and *The O Zone*.

Mouth to Mouth (album - Levellers, The)

Charted: Sept '97; UK Chart Position: 5; Label: China; Singles: 'What A Beautiful Day' (Aug '97, UKCP 13), 'Celebrate' (Oct '97, 28), 'Dog Train' (Dec '97, 24), 'Too Real' (Mar '98, 46)

Mouth To Mouth was the fifth album by the Levellers and their third and final album to be released during the Britpop era. Containing the top-20 hit single 'What a Beautiful Day', it was the band's third consecutive album to reach the top ten of the UK chart, where it spent eight weeks, peaking at number five.

The album, regarded in subsequent years as one of the band's finest, signalled the end of their run of commercial success in the charts, with the second and third singles creeping into the top 30, and the fourth not making the top 40. Despite this, the run of chart success the band had previously experienced was impressive.

The album, produced by Jon Kelly, featured brass by London-based horn band the Kick Horns and strings by the London Metropolitan Orchestra. The reissue in '07 included four bonus tracks: 'Bar Room Jury', 'Angels', 'All Your Dreams' and 'Windows'.

Music for Pleasure (album – Monaco)

Charted: Jun '97; UK Chart Position: 11; Label: Polydor; Singles: 'What Do You Want From Me?' (Mar '97, UKCP 11), 'Sweet Lips' (May '97, 18), 'Shine (Someone Who Needs Me)' (Sept '97, 55)

Music for Pleasure was the debut album by Peter Hook's side project Monaco, and the band's sole top-20 album, peaking at number 11 and spending four weeks on the UK chart. Far removed from Hook's other band New Order, Monaco's debut album was filled with fairly straightforward indie-rock songs that fitted perfectly into the Brit-pop landscape.

The album resulted in the top-20 singles 'What Do You Want From Me?', the opening track on the album, and 'Sweet Lips'. A hidden track appeared at the end of the album's final song 'Sedona'.

My Life Story (band)

My Life Story were famed for their unique orchestral pop sound, generated by 12 musicians including both a string and brass section.

Fronted by Jake Shillingford, the band formed in '90 and released their debut single 'Girl A, Girl B, Boy C' (produced by Giles Martin, son of George 'the fifth Beatle' Martin), in '93. Debut album *Mornington Crescent* followed shortly afterwards. It wasn't until the release of their second album *The Golden Mile* that the band enjoyed any kind of real chart success. It peaked at number 37 in the UK chart, with all five of its singles, '12 Reasons Why I Love Her', 'Sparkle', 'The King of Kissingdom', 'Strumpet' and 'Duchess', charting in the top 40.

The band released their third and final album *Joined up Talking* in '00, which included top-40 single 'It's a Girl Thing'. After a six-year hiatus, the band returned with a best of album, *Sex & Videos*, and B-sides and rarities album *Megaphone Theology*. They have since performed a 15th anniversary gig at London's Shepherd's Bush Empire. A new single, '24 Hour Deflowerer', was released in September '16, and the band toured with The Bluetones, Dodgy and Salad in the summer of '17.

N

Naked (single – Reef)

Charted: Jun '95; UK Chart Position: 11; Label: Sony S2; Album: *Replenish*

'Naked' was the second single released by Reef, and the song that moved them into the mainstream after it was featured on a TV advert for the new Sony MiniDisc (the band were signed to Sony's S2 label). Many bands still failed even after one of their songs featured on a TV ad, but this was just the beginning for Reef, and the in-your-face, classic rock 'n' roll single reached number 11 in the UK chart in January '95.

The CD single also featured demo versions of songs 'Choose to Live', which appeared on *Replenish*, and 'Fade'.

Neighbourhood (single – Space)

Charted: Nov '96; UK Chart Position: 11; Label: Gut; Album: *Spiders*

'Neighbourhood' was the debut single release from Liverpool's Space, but it only achieved top 20 status (narrowly missing out on the top ten) on its re-release in November '96, a few months after the success of the band's debut album *Spiders*.

The single was released on two CDs. The first featured B-sides 'Only Half an Angel', 'Crisis' and 'Shut Your Mouth', while CD2 included remixes of 'Welcome to the Neighbourhood', 'Nighthood' and 'Neighbourhood (pissed up stomp remix!)'.

New Generation (single – Suede)

Charted: Feb '95; UK Chart Position: 21; Label: Nude; Album: *Dog Man Star*

Suede's 'New Generation' featured Bernard Butler's guitar on the title track but was notable for largely featuring music by his replacement Richard Oakes. From the band's second album *Dog Man Star*, the single narrowly missed the UK top 20, where it spent four weeks.

Released on two CDs, the first featured exclusive tracks 'Together' and 'Bentswood Boys', and the second live versions of album tracks 'Animal Nitrate', 'The Wild Ones' and 'Pantomime Horse'.

New Musical Express/NME (music magazine)

At the time of Britpop, the *New Musical Express* (or *NME*) was the key musical publication in Britain. More than just a weekly magazine, it had the power to decide who the bands of the moment were, and even demanded that Suede played at the Brit Awards in '93. The paper also had its own stage at Glastonbury between '93 and '95, before it was later renamed 'The Other Stage'.

Founded in '49 by Theodore Ingham, the paper quickly became one of Britain's most widely read music publications, appearing in newspaper broadsheet format once a week. It was one of the first to back rock 'n' roll in the mid-fifties and punk in the late seventies, and so became famous (as its name suggests) for championing new and exciting musical movements including, of course, Britpop. *NME* first put Oasis on the cover in April '94, the week that Kurt Cobain died (shortly after publication), showing yet again how quickly music scenes change.

The paper was reduced in size in '98 and merged with its chief rival *Melody Maker* in '99, but could do nothing to stop the slow demise of print media with the advancement of the internet. An online version was launched in '96, quickly becoming one of the world's most visited music sites, and the print version was relaunched as a free sheet in '15.

Over the years, the *NME* has featured in many song lyrics. Britpop band Denim sang in 'The Great Pub Rock Revival' (from the '96 album *Denim on Ice*): "Everybody believes what they are told to. Everybody believes what they read in the *NME*. Everybody but me." But its most famous reference appears in the Sex Pistols' classic punk anthem 'Anarchy in the UK' when Johnny Rotten roars: "How many ways to get what you want, I use the best, I use the rest, I use the *NME*, I use anarchy!"

Nice Guy Eddie (single – Sleeper)

Charted: Jul '96; UK Chart Position: 10; Label: Indolent; Album: *The It Girl*

Taking its title from one of the only named characters in Quentin Tarantino's '91 debut feature film *Reservoir Dogs*, 'Nice Guy Eddie' was the third single from Sleeper's second album, *The It Girl*. The release marked a short-lived fruitful period for the band and it reached number 10 in July '96 in the UK chart, where it spent five weeks.

The UK release of the CD single featured B-sides 'Pokerface' and 'Blazer Sleeves'. The band also performed the song live on *Top of the Pops* the week of its release.

No More Talk (single – Dubstar)

Charted: Jul '97; UK Chart Position: 20; Label: Food; Album: *Goodbye*

The first single from Dubstar's second album, *Goodbye*, reached number 20 in the UK chart when it was released in July '97. It spent three weeks on the chart.

The single was released on CD, cassette and 7" and 12" vinyl and featured B-sides 'Unchained Monologue', 'La Boheme' and 'Goodbye'.

North Country Boy (single – The Charlatans)

Charted: Apr '97; UK Chart Position: 4; Label: Beggars Banquet; Album: *Tellin' Stories*

'North Country Boy', an ode to those born and raised in the band's native north of England, was the second of four singles released from The Charlatans' key Britpop album *Tellin' Stories*, and one of their best-loved and most successful single releases to date. It reached number four in April '97, paving the way for the album, released a month later, and spent a total of nine weeks in the chart.

The CD single featured B-sides 'Area 51' (an instrumental that also featured on the album) and 'Don't Need a Gun'.

Northern Soul, A (album – The Verve)

Charted: Jul '95; UK Chart Position: 13; Label: Hut/Vernon Yard; Singles: 'This is Music' (May '95, UKCP 35), 'On your Own' (Jun '95, 28), 'History' (Sept '95, 24)

With a title that is both an oblique reference to Britain's Northern Soul movement and a nod to the band's Wigan roots, *A Northern Soul* was The Verve's second studio album. It was released at the height of Britpop in July '95 on Vernon Records, and recorded amid many arguments, fallouts and subsequent make-ups in Loco Studios, Wales, under the production stewardship of Owen 'Oasis' Morris. The album was a change in style for the band as they moved away from the psychedelic rock vibe of first album, *A Storm in Heaven*, towards the indie-rock championed by friends and early touring mates Oasis.

The band had high hopes for the album, but it only achieved moderate success, charting at number 13 in the UK. After Noel Gallagher of Oasis dedicated his song 'Cast No Shadow' to frontman Richard Ashcroft, he returned the favour by dedicating track five of *A Northern Soul* to Noel. Liam Gallagher also provided handclaps on key single 'History', the string-riff of which provided a precursor to the future mega-hit modern classic 'Bittersweet Symphony'.

Ashcroft received a lot of credit for his songwriting, which had moved away from his 'space cadet' early days towards acoustic-heavy personal lyrics. The heartbreak that inspired these mournful odes to lost love was not specified at the time, but is now thought to be based on the early days of his relationship with future wife and former Spiritualized keyboardist Kate Radley.

Tensions between Ashcroft and lead guitarist (and key creative) Nick McCabe, who wanted the band to take a more avant-garde approach, built to an unmanageable level, and the band split not long after the record's release. Luckily for everyone concerned, they eventually made up and, in following the course that this record set, finally realised their full potential.

Northern Uproar (band)

Manchester band Northern Uproar formed at the height of Britpop in '95. They were: frontman Leon Mayer, who also played bass, guitarists Paul Kelly and Jeff Fletcher and drummer Keith Chadwick. The band garnered praise early on after a series of live gigs, which prompted a record label bidding war eventually won by Heavenly Records. Their debut, self-titled album peaked just outside the top 20 of the UK chart in May '96 and contained the top-20 double A-side 'From A Window/This Morning'.

The band's second album, *Yesterday Tomorrow Today*, was released a year later in September '97, peaking at 95 and spending one week on the chart. They toured with several major acts during their career including Black Grape, The Bluetones, Cast, The Charlatans, The Prodigy and Paul Weller. Post-Britpop, the band split in '99, re-forming again in '04. Since '07, they have released three albums, most recently '15's *Hey Samurai!*, and continue to record and tour.

Not So Manic Now (single – Dubstar)

Charted: Jan '96; UK Chart Position: 19; Label: Food; Album: *Disgraceful*

Dubstar's most famous song, if not their most successful (that was 'Stars'), this managed to scrape into the top 20, reaching number 19 in January '96 and spending five weeks in the chart, a full nine months ahead of album *Disgraceful*.

Two CD versions were released. The first featured three different mixes of the A-side, while the second included B-sides 'If It Isn't You', 'Song No. 9' and 'A Certain Sadness'.

Nuisance (album – Menswear)

Charted: Oct '95; UK Chart Position: 11; Label: Island; Singles: 'I'll Manage Somehow' (Apr '95, UKCP 49), 'Daydreamer' (Jul '95, 14), 'Stardust' (Sep '95, 16), 'Sleeping In' (Dec '95, 24), 'Being Brave' (Mar '96, 10)

The sole long-play release from key Britpop band Menswear, *Nuisance* was released in October '95, the week after Oasis released the era-defining album *(What's the Story) Morning Glory?*

Released in September '95, the album reached number 11 and spent a total of nine weeks in the UK chart. It included singles 'I'll Manage Somehow', which peaked at number 49, top-20 singles 'Stardust' and 'Being Brave' and the top-40 single 'Sleeping In'.

The quintessential Britpop 12-track album (from the quintessential Britpop band) was produced by Neill King and released in the UK by Laurel Records. The songs are anthemic and harmonious with gentle but powerful melody lines and lilting guitars often supported by triumphant strings.

O

Oasis (band)

"There's something awe-inspiring about five lads in a band with guitars," said Liam Gallagher in '95. And he wasn't wrong.

Britpop superstars Oasis began their musical career in much the same way as everyone else: rehearsing in the basement of someone's house while hoping to one day become the biggest band in the country. But while most groups fail to get further than playing a handful of gigs on the toilet circuit, something else was in store for these five lads from Burnage and, following in the footsteps of their beloved Beatles, just a few years after forming they had indeed become one of Britain's biggest-ever bands.

The Rain – named after a Beatles' B-side – began playing together in '91, but it was only after original lead singer Chris Hutton was replaced by 19-year-old Liam Gallagher that they started to get serious under their new name, Oasis, which he lifted from a poster on his bedroom wall. With Liam and guitarist Paul 'Bonehead' Arthurs on songwriting duty, the line-up was completed by bassist Paul 'Guigsy' McGuiggan and Tony McCarroll on drums. They began gigging in their native Manchester in '92, a time when the legend of the Stone Roses loomed large over the city.

After he was fired from his job as roadie with the Inspiral Carpets, Liam's older brother Noel came to see Oasis play and offered his services as the lead guitarist the band so clearly needed. He brought along a back catalogue of unrecorded songs he had been storing up with no outlet, which the band began to practice every day. They were soon playing weekly gigs at the Boardwalk and building a following in Manchester. Then came the notorious King Tut's incident, when the band turned up to play only to be told they weren't on the bill. Noel and the others didn't take 'no' for an answer and, after a heated discussion, the promoter allowed them on for 20 minutes. That was all the time they needed. Alan McGee signed them there and then to Creation Records.

He wasn't convinced by their early recordings, so debut album *Definitely Maybe* had to be recorded twice, meaning the band's releasing schedule got off to a somewhat shaky start. When it finally made its way in to music shops, however, it went straight in at the top spot, spending an incredible 231 weeks on the chart. It was accompanied by a string of increasingly successful singles: 'Supersonic', which reached 31; 'Shakermaker', 11; and the band's first top-ten single, the Britpop classic 'Live Forever'. 'Cigarettes and Alcohol' was released in October '94, reaching number seven, and the lads saw out the year by releasing non-album track 'Whatever', which made it to number three in time for Christmas.

Their first year was big, but '95 was something else entirely. They began by releasing 'Some Might Say', their first number one single, and, by August, were making headlines when their next single, 'Roll With It', went head to head with Blur's 'Country House', narrowly missing out on the top spot in the much discussed 'Battle of Britpop'.

Courting headlines quickly became a trademark for the band, who never shied away from offering their opinions to the world or getting photographed falling out of various nightclubs. The Gallagher brothers quickly became constant fixtures in the tabloids, garnering publicity that certainly didn't hurt the band's record sales. Their next single, 'Wonderwall', just missed out on the top spot in November, but went on to become the band's most famous and best-loved song the world over.

Second album *(What's the Story) Morning Glory?* had been released in October and went straight to the top spot, spending a massive 227 weeks on the chart. The album launched the band into the stratosphere and, in '96, they were arguably the country's biggest band. They released one single, 'Don't Look Back in Anger', in February (their second number one) before concentrating on live gigs, playing four huge concerts in Britain, two at Loch Lomond in Scotland and two legendary gigs at Knebworth Park in front of 250,000 people.

Being Britain's biggest band wasn't easy though, with expectations around their third album fuelling the hype to almost unmanageable levels, while everyone in the music industry speculated and judged. The day *Be Here Now* was finally released on 21 August '97, there were snaking queues at the counters of music stores and, unsurprisingly, it went straight in at the top spot, despite being released somewhat unconventionally on a Thursday (a nod to the Beatles, who used the same trick with their album *Sgt. Pepper's Lonely Hearts Club Band* almost exactly 30 years earlier). Where *Morning Glory* had spent ten weeks at the top spot, *Be Here Now* managed five. The backlash was, perhaps, inevitable. It would have been nigh on impossible for them to live up to expectations, and anything less than perfect was never going to be good enough. The end of Britpop was in sight.

With the scene finally over in '98, the band took a step back and re-grouped, taking time off to start families and, in Liam's case, finally move out of his mum's house. Then in '99, with Creation Records now defunct, Oasis began their own label, Big Brother, and, as the old millennium gave way to the new one, they decamped to the south of France to record their fourth album, the grammatically incorrect *Standing on the Shoulder of Giants*. The album reached the top spot in March '00, and resulted in their fifth number one single, 'Go Let it Out'. Where *Be Here Now* was brash and ostentatious, *Giants* (originally known as *Where Did It All Go Wrong?*) was far more introspective, signalling, along with many of their contemporaries, that the party was finally over.

With *Giants* acting as the band's comedown album, it was time for a change. Bonehead and Guigsy left during the recording of the album, soon followed by the band's second drummer in four years, Alan White. They never found a full-time replacement, filling his spot with stand-ins instead (including Ringo Starr's son Zak). Gem Archer joined on guitar in mid-'00 and Andy Bell joined on bass not long after. And so Oasis 2.0 was born, offering the band a new lease of life with each member contributing songs for the first time.

Before their official split in '09, they released a further three studio albums, a live album, a B-sides collection and two best-of albums. They remained incredibly popular to the end, and in the years since each has gone on to highly successful post-Oasis projects.

Ocean Colour Scene (band)

Despite a few member changes over the years, the core of Birmingham's Ocean Colour Scene, and the line-up that achieved the most success, was: Simon Fowler on vocals, Steve Craddock on guitar, Damon Minchella on bass and Oscar Harrison on drums.

The band hit the ground running, signing to Phfftt Records in '90 after being together for just a few months. Their self-titled debut album came out in September that year, but failed to chart because the record company insisted on remixing the album to fit in with the popular Madchester scene. Ocean Colour Scene were firmly retro in their outlook and drew influence from sixties guitar bands like The Kinks and the Small Faces, as well as the hugely popular Northern Soul movement. Unfortunately, this sound didn't fit with the times and they lost their record deal. Then, in '93, Paul Weller invited them to support him on his *Wild Wood* tour, and so began an incredibly close relationship that saw them playing together many times, live as well as on each other's recordings.

The relationship with Weller, which continues to this day, and a support slot with Oasis in '95 gained the band a record deal with MCA. Their second album *Moseley Shoals*, named after the band's Birmingham-based studio in their native Moseley, threw them into the mainstream when it went straight in at number two in the UK chart in April '96. The band's retro sound was finally en vogue and fit perfectly with Britpop, and the catchy singles 'The Day We Caught the Train', 'The Circle' and 'The Riverboat Song', soon became staples of the Britpop canon.

Spurred on by hit single 'Hundred Mile High City', which peaked at number four in the UK chart in June '97, the band's third studio album *Marchin' Already* was released in September '97. Making the most of the band's success and the Britpop scene, it peaked at number one in its first week. Continuing the run of hit singles, 'Travellers Tune' peaked at number five in September '97, 'Better Day' reached number nine and 'It's a Beautiful Thing' which, like 'Traveller's Tune', featured Northern Soul singer P P Arnold on co-lead vocals, peaked at number 12 in February '98. It would be nearly two years until their next album, '99's *One From the Modern*, and as the British music scene had moved on to a very different sound, the band's short but highly successful run in the charts hit a downward spiral.

There have been six studio albums between '01 and '13, as well as two live albums and two best of collections. The band continue to play live together, often with spiritual leader Paul Weller. In '15, the band celebrated their 25th anniversary together and, in '16, toured extensively.

Oh Yeah! (single – Ash)

Charted: July '96; UK Chart Position: 6; Label: Infectious; Album: *1977*

'Oh Yeah!' was a classic 'first love' story set in the summer and, as the fifth and final single released from Ash's debut album *1977*, marked the end of an epic era for the band. It was their second top ten hit and longest-running single on the UK chart, where it spent 11 weeks, peaking at number six.

Backing vocals were provided by Britpop It Girl Lisa Moorish and B-sides included 'T.Rex', 'Everywhere Is All Around' and a cover of Abba's 'Does Your Mother Know'.

Olympian (album – Gene)

Charted: Apr '95; UK Chart Position: 8; Label: Costermonger; Singles: 'Sleep Well Tonight' (Nov '94, UKCP 36), 'Haunted By You' (Mar '95, 32), 'Olympian' (Jul '95, 18)

Gene's debut album *Olympian* was released to much acclaim in April '95. It headed straight into the top ten, peaking at number eight and spending a total of ten weeks on the UK chart, making it their most successful album. Momentum had been building for the band after the album's first single, 'Sleep Well Tonight', peaked at number 36 in November '94. The second single and album opener, 'Haunted by You', peaked at number 32 on its release in March '95, and these two catchy yet epic singles paved the way for the LP that followed.

Influenced more by The Smiths and eighties' indie bands than the Beatles and Stones' sixties sound, *Olympian* helped Gene carve out a niche for themselves at the Britpop table, even though lead singer Martin Rossiter's often existential song lyrics were a far cry from much of the lighter Britpop fare.

The band knew how to write music to suit their melancholic sound, making the most of the slicing guitars and chugging beats that set them alongside Britpop contemporaries like Suede. *Olympian* is incredibly confident and well-rounded for a debut long-form release and remains one of the band's best-loved records.

Olympian (single – Gene)

Charted: Jul '95; UK Chart Position: 18; Label: Costermonger; Album: *Olympian*

The third and final single from Gene's debut album, which shared its name, 'Olympian' was the band's first top-20 single, reaching number 18 in July '95 and cementing them as key additions to the Britpop scene. The song finds the band at their most epic, starting gently and building towards a rousing outro that they often positioned at the end of their live gigs.

Released on limited edition 7" vinyl and CD, it featured B-sides 'I Can't Decide if She Really Loves Me' and 'To See the Lights'. The CD release also featured a cover of the Beatles' 'Don't Let Me Down'.

On (album – Echobelly)

Charted: Sept '95; UK Chart Position: 4; Label: Fauve; Singles: 'Great Things' (Sep '95, UKCP 13), 'King of the Kerb' (Nov '95, 25), 'Dark Therapy' (Mar '96, 20)

On was the successful follow up to Echobelly's debut album *Everyone's Got One* and featured some of the band's most successful singles, including the top-20 hits 'Great Things' and 'Dark Therapy' and the top-40 track 'King of the Kerb'. It was the band's second top ten and both its highest and longest charting album, clocking up 29 weeks and peaking at number four. It also has Britpop's second shortest album title after *K* by Kula Shaker.

The album was re-issued in '14, including bonus tracks of B-sides and rarities as well as a second disc featuring live performances from the band's New York Wetlands gig in '95 and recordings from their Radio 1 *Peel Session* the same year.

On & On (single – The Longpigs)

Charted: Apr '96; UK Chart Position: 16; Label: Mother; Album: *The Sun Is Often Out*

End-of-the-affair love song 'On & On' was the fourth single from the Longpigs' debut album *The Sun Is Often Out* and the band's first top-20 single on the UK chart, where it spent three weeks, peaking at number 16.

The single featured B-sides 'Your Face', album track 'Dozen Wicked Words' and 'Sleep', which also featured as a hidden track at the end of the album. The video saw lead singer Crispin Hunt peering out of a dolls' house at his depressed love interest in her bedroom while singing, "And I wish you would leave me, and I wish you would go".

On Standby (single – Shed Seven)

Charted: Aug '96; UK Chart Position: 12; Label: Polydor; Album: *A Maximum High*

'On Standby' was the fifth and final single released from Shed Seven's second album *A Maximum High* and the band's third top-20 single, spending four weeks on the UK chart and peaking at number 12. The prison-based video saw the band behind bars and having their mugshots taken while singing, "Would you stay on standby, because I need another alibi".

There were two CD versions of the single. CD1 featured a live cover of the Rolling Stones' 'Jumping Jack Flash', taken from the band's *TFI Friday* performance, and album track 'Killing Time', while CD2 included album tracks 'Long Time Dead' and 'Stepping On Hearts'.

On Your Own (single – Blur)

Charted: Jun '97; UK Chart Position: 5; Label: Food; Album: *Blur*

'On Your Own' was the third of four singles released from Blur's self-titled fifth album. Spending eight weeks on the UK chart, it was the band's third consecutive top ten from *Blur* and also featured as a remix on the soundtrack for Danny Boyle's '00 feature film *The Beach*, starring Leonardo DiCaprio. Interestingly, Damon Albarn later said he thought the track was one of the first Gorillaz tunes.

The video, directed by Sophie Muller, was filmed in Barcelona and featured the band hanging out on an industrial estate.

Two CD versions were released, featuring B-sides recorded live at Peel Acres, DJ John Peel's home. The first included non-album track 'Popscene', a treat for fans as it didn't appear on the UK version of *Modern Life Is Rubbish*, album track 'Song 2' and the title track, while the second featured album tracks 'Chinese Bombs', 'Moving On' and 'M.O.R'.

One to Another (single – The Charlatans)

Charted: Sept '96; UK Chart Position: 3; Label: Food; Album: *Tellin' Stories*

'One to Another' was the first of four singles from The Charlatans' fifth album *Tellin' Stories* and marked the start of a new era for the band, which hadn't released any new music for a year after the tragic death of keyboardist Rob Collins.

Spending six weeks on the UK chart, it was the band's highest charting single to date and second of four top tens during their career. With no trace of the band's Madchester roots, the tune was a perfect fit for Britpop (you could easily imagine Liam Gallagher singing along with, "be my Spiderwoman, I'll be your Spiderman").

B-sides included 'Two of Us' and 'Reputation', which both featured on the bonus disc of the album's anniversary edition released in '12.

Our Price (record store)

Our Price, alongside HMV, was the go-to record store to spend your pocket money in. Much later to the game than its chief rival, Our Price was founded in '71 by Gary Nesbitt, Edward Stollins and Mike Isaacs, focusing on the new format of cassette tapes. Over the years, the brand grew until there were hundreds of stores all over the country and a head office on Kensington High Street in London. At its peak in the eighties, the company owned more than 300 stores across the British Isles.

Despite UK record, CD, tape and video sales being among the strongest in the world, competition was stiff, with HMV and Virgin Records gaining a stronger footing in the market place. This meant that by the early noughties, when CD sales were past their peak, Our

Price began selling off its stores. It maintained a strong third place though and, like all of the other music stores at the time, enjoyed long queues when *Be Here Now* was released.

O-Zone, The (TV show)

The O-Zone from the BBC was yet another show dedicated to music in the boom years of the nineties. While *Top of the Pops* and *Later...* were dedicated to live (sort of, in the case of *TOTP*) performances, *The O-Zone* was aimed predominantly at the teen market, often going behind the scenes and focusing on stories about the bands and their music.

The show went through various formats since first airing in '89, finally settling down in '95 with a key BBC2 Friday evening slot, presented by Jayne Middlemiss and Jamie Theakston. The Sunday repeat was a must-watch hangover show for Britpoppers who spent Friday at their local indie night.

The show hosted numerous Britpop artists and, in '96, aired an Oasis special presented by Middlemiss and a Blur special presented by Theakston. A Knebworth special was also aired later that year, including interviews with Ocean Colour Scene, the Manic Street Preachers, Kula Shaker and Cast.

P

Paranoid & Sunburnt (album – Skunk Anansie)

Charted: Sept '95; UK Chart Position: 8; Label: One Little Indian; Singles: 'Selling Jesus' (Mar '95, UKCP 46), 'I Can Dream' (Jun '95, 41), 'Weak' (Jan '96, 20), 'Charity' (Apr '96, 20)

Paranoid & Sunburnt was the debut album from Skunk Anansie and is known, among other things, for its controversial lyrics covering a broad range of subjects from politics to religion and sex. It helped the band achieve their first top ten in the UK chart, where it spent a total of 52 weeks.

The album was recorded at Great Linford Manor Studios, a 17th-century mansion in Milton Keynes, and contained the top-20 singles 'Charity', which reached number 40 when it was originally released in September '96, and 'Weak'. It showcased the band's intense, loud, abrasive, guitar-heavy style, paving the way for their second top-ten album *Stoosh*, released a year later.

Parklife (album - Blur)

Charted: Apr '94; UK Chart Position: 1; Label: Food; Singles: 'Girls and Boys' (Mar '94, UKCP 5), 'To the End' (Jun '94, 16), 'Parklife' (Sept '94, 10), 'End of a Century' (Nov '94, 19)

By '94, the nation was more than ready for Britpop and welcomed Blur's third album *Parklife* with open arms. It was their first album to reach number one, spent an impressive 119 weeks on the chart and resulted in top-ten era-defining singles 'Girls and Boys' and 'Parklife', as well as top-20 songs 'To the End' and 'End of a Century'.

It's often argued that *Parklife* wouldn't be made today. The band's first album, *Leisure*, sold well due to hit single 'There's No Other Way', but their second album, *Modern Life is Rubbish*, hadn't performed as well as the band and their label, Food Records, expected. Today, that may well have been that for Blur, and they could have been out on their ear without a record deal. Luckily for them, however, Food were supportive, and Damon and Co got to finally realise their ambitions.

Though rarely touted as one, *Parklife* is a concept album in that there is a strong theme that links all the songs together. Lyrically, Albarn had only just begun to scratch the surface with *Modern Life* but, with *Parklife*, he wrote songs that were a true reflection of contemporary life the length and breadth of mid-nineties Britain.

The album's 16 tracks range in subject matter from stories of an incredibly personal nature ('Badhead' was about Albarn's struggle with depression) to those about quintessentially British traditions (like 'Bank Holiday'). There was also a sense of looking back, of nostalgia for Britain in the sixties, which gave the album its own style and tone and made it both retrospective and contemporary.

The album was a countrywide success, was nominated for the Mercury Music Prize in '94 and garnered four Brit Award wins, including Best Album. It remains one of British rock music's best-loved albums.

Parklife (single – Blur)

Charted: Sept '94; UK Chart Position: 10; Label: Food; Album: *Parklife*

"It's got nothing to do with your *Vorsprung durch Technik*, you know!"

Recited by actor Phil Daniels, this is a key line in *Parklife*, an era defining song from Blur. The third of four top-20 singles released from their third album of the same name, it won 'Best British Single' and 'Best Video' at the '95 Brits. The chorus was mocked by Liam and Noel Gallagher at the award show the following year, when Oasis collected their 'Best British Album' award.

Daniels, who made his name in the film *Quadrophenia*, has often joined the band on tour over the years to perform the song and also features in the video as a double-glazing salesman. He was chosen to recite the verses partly because of his thick cockney accent and partly because of his appearance in the seminal '78 British film *Quadrophenia*, developed from a concept album by The Who. The film was about identity and the need to fit in, and *Parklife* pushed at the same door, with Albarn telling us that, "we all go hand in hand" as part of the same crowd.

It was the band's third single to reach the UK top ten and featured B-sides 'Supa Shoppa', a French version of album track 'To the End' and 'Beard'.

Peacock Suit (single – Paul Weller)

Charted: Aug '96; UKCP: 5; Label: Go! Discs; Album: *Heavy Soul*

'Peacock Suit' was the first of four singles from Paul Weller's fourth album *Heavy Soul*. Peaking at number five, the track was both his highest-charting and longest-running single, spending nine weeks on the chart.

It featured just one B-side 'Eye of the Storm', which Weller performed with Noel Gallagher, Ocean Colour Scene and Jools Holland at the '96 V Festival. He also performed the single and its B-side on Channel 4's *The White Room*.

Perfect (single – The Lightning Seeds)

Charted: Jul '95; UKCP: 18; Label: Epic; Album: *Jollification*

'Perfect' was the opening track and fourth of five singles from the Lightning Seeds third album *Jollification*. It was the band's third top-20 hit, peaking at number 18 and spending a total of five weeks on the chart.

It featured B-sides 'Howl', an acoustic version of the title track, and an Extended Remix Version of previous album track 'Blowing Bubbles'.

Perseverance (single – Terrorvision)

Charted: Mar '96; UKCP: 5; Label: Total Vegas; Album: *Regular Urban Survivors*

When it was released in early '96, 'Perseverance' became Terrorvision's biggest UK single. With a crashing opening guitar line far removed from the Britpop sound, it nevertheless became caught in the Britpop net.

It was the first of four singles from the band's third album, *Regular Urban Survivors*, and peaked comfortably inside the top ten of the UK chart, where it spent four weeks.

There were two CD versions, the first featuring B-sides 'Wake Up' and 'What Goes Around Comes Around', and the second 'Sick and Tired' and 'Hard To Feel'.

Place Your Hands (single – Reef)

Charted: Nov '96; UKCP: 6; Label: Sony S2; Album: *Glow*

'Place Your Hands' was the first of four singles released from Reef's second album, *Glow*, and their longest-running and highest-charting single, spending 11 weeks on the chart and peaking at number six. To date, it's the song most synonymous with the band, and features on many nineties compilations.

Two CD versions were released. The first featured B-sides 'Uncomfortable', 'The Snob' and 'Weird', and second live recordings of 'Repulsive', 'Speak Lark' and 'Naked', taken from the band's Tokyo gig at Liquid Room in early '96.

Pleased to Meet You (album – Sleeper)

Charted: Oct '97; UK Chart Position: 7; Label: Indolent; Singles: 'She's a Good Girl' (Oct '97, UKCP 28), 'Romeo Me' (Dec '97, 39)

Sleeper's third album *Pleased to Meet You*, the follow-up to the hugely successful *The It Girl*, was the band's last release. Similar in style and tone to its predecessor, the limited success of the album signalled a change of direction in the UK music scene. Lead single 'She's a Good Girl', a catchy three-minute pop song which proved to be a good indication of the direction of the album as a whole, peaked at number 28, while follow-up 'Romeo Me' reached 39 two months later.

The 13-track album was produced by the legendary Stephen Street, known for his work with The Smiths, Blur and The Cranberries, and was released by the band's long-term record company Indolent. They split the following year after touring the album in the UK.

Popscene (single – Blur)

Charted: Apr '92; UKCP: 32; Label: Food; Album: n/a

Interspersed with horns and one of Graham Coxon's most recognisable guitar riffs, 'Popscene' is where it all began for Britpop.

The very first Britpop single, this stand-alone track was released between Blur's first and second albums. Unfortunately, it's now frustratingly difficult to get hold of as it was not on the UK version of *Modern Life is Rubbish* and was released before the digital free-for-all. It did find its way on to the album *Live at The Budokan*, which was released in '96 and also appeared live as a B-side on single 'On Your Own', signalling its semi-legendary status and reputation as a live favourite.

Released in early '92, when the nation was not quite ready for Britpop, the track still managed to break the UK top 40, where it spent two weeks. It featured B-sides 'I'm Fine', 'Mace' and 'Garden Central'.

Popscene is arguably the beginning of Blur's mission to kill grunge and steer music in a new direction. Though understated at the time, the song is now regarded as the birth of Britpop, with its fast pace and catchy brass section accompanied by lyrics celebrating the music scene.

Powder (band)

Often referred to as 'Camden scenesters' by the music press, female-fronted Britpop band Powder were singer Pearl Lowe, guitarist Mark Thomas, bassist Tim McTighe and drummer James Walden. The band were the first to sign to Camden-based label Parkway Records in '94, releasing three singles the following year: '20th Century Gods', 'Afrodisiac' and 'Deep Fried', the latter two charting in the top ten. The band was relatively short-lived and they split in '96, though compilation album *MCMXCV*, featuring all the tracks on the singles, was released in '97.

Lowe was one half of a Britpop power couple with Supergrass drummer Danny Goffey. They married in '05 having been together since '95. Shortly after the demise of Powder, the pair went on to form Lodger, releasing three singles and one album, *Walk in the Park*, on Island Records. The pair have three children together, and Lowe also has a daughter, model Daisy Lowe, with Bush singer Gavin Rossdale.

Power, John (lead singer/guitarist/bass player/songwriter – Cast/The La's/solo artist)

John Power was the lead singer and chief songwriter of Britpop favourites Cast, but it was as the young, understated bass player with Liverpool's The La's that he first found success. He played on many of the band's best-loved songs, including hit single 'There She Goes'.

Born in the Liverpool suburb of Allerton on 14 September '67, Power attended Quarry Bank School, which counts John Winston Lennon among its alumni, where he discovered a love of music at an early age. He joined the ever-evolving line-up of The La's in '86, when he was just 18, and the band found themselves a record deal the following year. His desire to write and perform his own material led to friction with the band's leader, Lee Mavers, and he left the group in '91, forming Cast the following year.

The Cast line-up changed much over the following two years but, with no shortage of eager young musicians in Liverpool, Power finally found the members he thought worked best together. After a support slot with Oasis, the band signed to Polydor in December '94, just as the Britpop scene was gaining momentum. The timing was perfect and the band's first album, *All Change*, became the fastest-selling debut the label had ever had. Cast continued to do well after the Britpop years, only splitting for good in '02. Power continues to write and record music, and has released three solo studio albums, '03's *Happening for Love*, '06's *Willow She Weeps* and '08's *Stormbreaker*. Both The La's and Cast have also re-formed in recent years. Cast released album *Troubled Times* in March '12, followed by *Kicking Up The Dust* in April '17.

Princess Diana and the demise of Britpop

Late in the summer of '97, Oasis' highly anticipated third studio album *Be Here Now* failed to live up to the frankly ridiculous hype that surrounded it. The album was far from perfect, but the hype that surrounded the release meant that anything less than one of the greatest rock records of all time was going to ultimately disappoint. The backlash had begun and it soon became clear that Britpop had passed its peak. The comedown had not quite started, but it was imminent.

Then something happened that stopped the country in its tracks. Diana, Princess of Wales, ex-wife of the heir to the throne, mother to the future king of England and the nation's adored People's Princess, was killed in a car accident in Paris as she was being pursued by paparazzi. Almost overnight, the party finally came to an end. The world was no longer focused on Britain's vibrant culture and Cool Britannia was no more.

The events of Sunday 31 August '97 sent the country into a state of mourning. A sea of flowers was laid outside Buckingham Palace and public pressure forced a state funeral – a ceremony usually reserved only for immediate members of the royal family – to be hastily arranged. Mourners slept overnight on the pavements to secure a space on the funeral procession route, and thousands lined the streets of London on Saturday 6 September as the coffin made its way from St James' Palace to Westminster Abbey, heart-breakingly followed on foot by Diana's two young sons, William and Harry.

Elton John, a close friend of Diana's, performed a rewritten version of his '73 Marilyn Monroe tribute 'Candle in the Wind', which later spent five weeks at number one in the UK chart and became the second biggest selling single of all time (behind Bing Crosby's 'White Christmas').

Pulp (band)

Known chiefly for their hit singles 'Common People' and 'Disco 2000', their Mercury Music Prize winning '95 album *Different Class* and eccentric lead-singer Jarvis Cocker, Sheffield's Pulp were one of Britpop's main players. They were also the band who signalled the end of it, with their '98 album *This is Hardcore*.

Pulp had a changeable line-up (more than 20 people can lay claim to being in the band at some point) but the core members were: Candida Doyle (keyboards), Russell Senior (guitar, violin), Mark Webber (guitar), Steve Mackey (bass) and Nick Banks (drums).

The band got off to a slow start. Their first album, *If*, was released through independent label Red Rhino in '83 but failed to chart, leading to a change in line-up and a rethink of their musical direction by band leader Cocker.

The new and improved band signed to Fire Records in '85, but no album appeared until '87 due to Cocker's near-fatal fall from a window (he was trying to impress a girl). The subsequent album, *Freaks*, and its '92 follow-up *Separations* both failed to chart, but this didn't deter the band and, with a handful of more catchy songs, they signed to major label Island in '92. Their previous single (released via indie label Gift records) 'O.U.' was made single of the week by *Melody Maker*, alongside Suede's Britpop forbear 'The Drowners'. Success, it seemed, was now not far away.

With the Britpop years now in full swing, the band's next album, *His 'n' Hers*, was released in April '94, reaching number nine in the UK chart, spurred on by their first single to reach the top 40, 'Do You Remember the First Time?'. Then, in June '95, the band scored the first of their mega-hits when 'Common People' went straight in at number two, propelling the band on to the Britpop A-list. *Different Class* hit the shelves in November '95 and went straight to number one in the UK chart. It won the band the hotly-contested Mercury Music Prize in '96, and spent a huge 75 weeks on the chart, underlining the band's place at the top table of the Britpop movement.

Mainly through Cocker's quirky and often irony-laden lyrics, Pulp positioned themselves as working-class intellectuals, less provocative than the Manic Street Preachers, but passionate and whip-smart nonetheless. Nowhere is this clearer than on the opening track of *Different Class*. In 'Mis-Shapes', they speak on behalf of an underclass largely ignored by the mainstream, but ready to claim their rightful place in society, not through acts of aggression but by using, "the one thing we've got more of, and that's our minds".

Unfortunately, by the time their next album, *This is Hardcore*, was released in April '98, Britpop was over. The party had finished and the acts were all contemplating their next move. Cocker's success had come at a cost. *This is Hardcore* was a dark and personal album that allowed him to reveal his demons, but it also reflected the end of the scene and the national comedown at the end of '97.

The album was a success and the band regrouped for 01's incredibly positively titled, *We Love Life*, before finally splitting in '02. Each member went on to other musical projects in the following years, and the band reformed in '11 for what was supposed to be a one-off performance at a festival in Hyde Park. The success of this show meant, however, that more touring dates were announced leading well into '13, although Cocker has since confirmed that there will be no new recorded material. In May '15 a music heritage plaque was placed outside the venue that the band played their first gig at, the Leadmill in Sheffield.

Pure Phase (album - Spiritualized)

Charted: Feb '95; UK Chart Position: 20; Label: Dedicated; Singles: 'Medication' (Jul '92, UKCP 55), 'Electric Mainline' (Oct '93, 49)

Spiritualized's second album *Pure Phase* was recorded in Moles Studio, Bath, and became the band's first top-20 album entry on the UK chart, where it spent two weeks and peaked at number 20. There was also a limited edition version with a glow-in-the-dark cover.

Although not as complete or confident as the band's next album, *Ladies and Gentlemen We Are Floating in Space*, the album showcased their sonic soundscapes and set the stage for their genre-defining follow-up.

Pure (album - 3 Colours Red)

Charted: May '97; UK Chart Position: 16; Label: Creation; Singles: 'Nuclear Holiday' (Jan '97, UKCP 22), 'Sixty Mile Smile' (Mar '97, 20), 'Pure' (May '97, 28), 'Copper Girl' (Jul '97, 30), 'This Is My Hollywood' (Nov '97, 48)

More Britrock than Britpop, Creation band 3 Colours Red released debut album *Pure* in early '97 to an abundance of positive reviews.

It achieved a top 20 position in the UK chart, where it spent three weeks, peaking at number 16.

The album cemented the band as a key part of the rock scene in the UK at the time, and showcased their solid guitar licks and pounding drums, combined with melodies that swayed between lilting and gut-wrenching. Produced by the band's manager Terry Thomas at Livingston Recording Studios, the album resulted in four top-40 singles: 'Nuclear Holiday', 'Sixty Mile Smile', 'Pure' and 'Copper Girls', which collectively spent nine weeks on the chart.

Puressence (band)

Manchester band Puressence formed in '92 and were best-known for their single 'This Feeling', which entered the top 40 of the UK chart in May '98. It also featured on indie compilation series *Shine 10* and was performed on *TFI Friday*.

The band was James Mudriczki on vocals, guitarist Neil McDonald, bassist Kevin Matthews and drummer Tony Szuminski, who got together after meeting on a bus to the Stone Roses' '91 Spike Island gig.

Prior to 'This Feeling', the band released one self-titled album and several singles on Island Records, some of which charted in the top ten. Over a career that spanned nearly 20 years, the band released seven studio albums and finally split for good in '11.

Q

Queer (single – Garbage)

Released: Dec '95; UKCP: 13; Label: Mushroom; Album: *Garbage*

'Queer' was the third of five singles from Garbage's debut, self-titled album, giving the band their first top 20 in the UK chart, where it spent six weeks, peaking at number 13.

While most of their other key singles were fast-paced, 'Queer' took a much more melodic approach, with a laidback lo-fi vibe accompanied by a haunting lyric from singer Shirley Manson. The video, shot in black and white and filmed in Los Angeles, was nominated for Breakthrough Video at the '96 MTV Video Music Awards and featured Manson throwing a man to the floor and blindfolding him with tape before stripping and shaving his head.

There were two CD versions of the single. The first featured B-side 'Trip My Wire', and the second a cover of Paul Weller's 'Butterfly Collector'. Both also contained two remixes of the lead song.

R

Radiator (album – Super Furry Animals)

Charted: Sept '97; UK Chart Position: 8; Label: Creation; Singles: 'Hermann Loves Pauline' (May '97, UKCP 26), 'The International Language Of Screaming' (Jul '97, 24), 'Play It Cool' (Oct '97, 27), 'Demons' (Dec '97, 27)

The Super Furry Animals' second album *Radiator* is not what we generally consider Britpop, but because they were signed to Creation and the album made its way to record stores in our timeframe, it finds itself defined by association. The album itself was a major development from the band's debut *Fuzzy Logic*, which was filled with catchy three-minute pop songs, and rather found the band moving into a more experimental space; a bold move for a mainstream pop-rock indie band.

The catchy melodies, layered harmonies and fuzzy guitars were still there, but they were accompanied by a range of keyboard loops and samples that employed a fuller-bodied sound. Chief songwriter Gruff Rhys' lyrics also covered a much broader range of quirky subject matter. Lead single 'Hermann Loves Pauline', for example, was a love song about the parents of scientist Albert Einstein, and its follow up 'The International Language of Screaming' had a chorus that was just... well... screaming.

Each of the four singles made it into the top 30 of the UK chart, and the album peaked at number eight when it was released in September '97. It spent five weeks on the chart, and continued an upward trajectory for the Welsh band that saw them continue to develop their sound in the following years, building a loyal following and a reputation as one of Britain's most interesting and experimental groups.

Radio 1 DJs

In '93, new Radio 1 controller Matthew Bannister caused a major shake-up at Britain's leading radio station by exiling the old guard of 'Smashy 'n' Nicey' type DJs, and replacing them with a bunch of bright young things that included Steve Lamacq, Mark Radcliffe, Sara Cox, Jo Whiley and Chris Evans, who all wanted to play new British music after coming of age under the tutelage of John Peel, widely regarded as the greatest indie DJ of all time. The trickle-down is still being felt on Radios 1 and 2, 6Music, Absolute and Radio X (formerly XFM) today.

The most notable contributions to Britpop were Lamacq and Whiley's *Evening Session* on Radio 1, which launched many bands between '93–'97 and was the first to feature live airplay of Oasis. Lamacq also co-founded Deceptive Records, the label that signed Elastica, while Radcliffe presented live music TV show *The White Room*, another key platform for many bands. Sara Cox helped push ladette culture to the forefront with nineties TV show *The Girlie Show* and Chris Evans brought us *TFI Friday*.

Raise the Pressure (album – Electronic)

Charted: Jul '96; UK Chart Position: 8; Label: Parlophone; Singles: 'Forbidden City' (Jul '96, UKCP 14), 'For You' (Sept '96, 16), 'Second Nature' (Feb '97, 35)

Raise the Pressure was the second album from Manchester supergroup Electronic, and their first long-format release for five years. It was the only album the band released during the Britpop years, and contained some of their best-loved songs including hit single 'Forbidden City', which peaked at number 14 in the UK chart in July '96, and 'For You', which reached number 16 in September.

The album fused electronic dance-orientated sounds and beats with guitar music, particularly in the two main singles. In other parts of the album though the guitars were left aside in favour of a purely electronic approach, notably on the tracks that featured guest collaborator Karl Bartos, famed for his work with the German electronic pioneers Kraftwerk. As side projects go, Electronic was one of the more successful, and the three albums the band have released were both commercially and critically well accepted by the public.

Ready or Not (single – Lightning Seeds)

Charted: Mar '96; UKCP: 20; Label: Epic; Album: *Dizzy Heights*

'Ready or Not' was the first single to be released from the Lightning Seeds' fourth album *Dizzy Heights*, and the last before their mega-hit 'Three Lions' reached the top spot in June '96. It reached number 20 in March '96, and spent six weeks on the chart.

The single was released on two CDs. The first featured B-sides 'Another Girl Another Planet' and 'Whole Wide World'; and the second 'Punch and Judy (Electric '96 Version)' and a cover of Wire's 'Outdoor Miner'.

Ready to Go (single – Republica)

Charted: Mar '97; UKCP: 13; Label: Deconstruction; Album: *Republica*

Britpop anthem 'Ready to Go' was one of two huge singles from Republica's debut album *Republica*. It reached number 13 in the UK chart in March '97, having previously reached 43 when originally released in April '96.

The '97 CD-only release featured the original radio edit of the song as its lead B-side, along with second single 'Bloke' and a remix of 'Holly'. The longevity of the song has been staggering; it still features on adverts to this day.

Reef (band)

They might come from Glastonbury, home of the UK's oldest and most famous music festival, but Reef are less hippie-fest and more straightforward rock. They existed on the periphery of the Britpop scene and had two hit singles 'Naked' and 'Place Your Hands'.

The original line-up was Gary Stringer (vocals), Kenwyn House (guitar), Jack Bessant (bass) and Dominic Greensmith (drums). They hailed from the West Country but formed in London, where they found almost instant success. They were signed in '93 after playing just one gig. They then spent the next year touring incessantly in an attempt to form a fan base. Debut single 'Good Feeling' reached number 24 in April '95, but their next release, 'Naked', featured on a Sony Minidisc player advert and achieved much more commercial success. It went in at number 11 and the album *Replenish* reached number nine in July '96.

Influenced chiefly by seventies rock bands like AC/DC, Reef's approach was at odds with Britpop yet seemed to resonate with its audience. Spurred on by the huge hit 'Place Your Hands', which reached number six in the UK chart in November '96, the band's next album *Glow* made its way to the top spot in February '97. As they were not anchored to the Britpop scene, Reef enjoyed continued success well after the movement was over. Their third album, *Rides*, reached number three in the UK chart in May '99, a full two years after its predecessor.

Continuing the trend for one-word album titles, *Getaway* was released in September '00 and reached number 15. Although the band still play together today, there have been no further albums released other than a 'best of' in '03. In June '16, the band played together again, opening for Coldplay at Wembley.

Regular Urban Survivors (album – Terrorvision)

Charted: Mar '96; UK Chart Position: 8; Label: Total Vegas; Singles: 'Perseverance' (Mar '96, UKCP 5), 'Celebrity Hit List' (May '96, 20), 'Bad Actress' (Jul '97, 10), 'Easy' (Jan '97, 12)

Much like fellow rockers 3 Colours Red and Reef, Terrorvision were not a band immediately identifiable with Britpop. This didn't stop their releases making their way on to the Britpop *Shine* compilations alongside Oasis or Blur. *Regular Urban Survivors* was their third and most successful album, released during the Britpop peak in March '96. The album reached number eight in the UK chart, where it spent a total of 15 weeks.

The album contained some of the band's best-loved songs, including the hit single 'Perseverance', which peaked at number five in the same month the album was released, as well as 'Celebrity Hit List' and 'Bad

Actress'. Stylistically, the album didn't change or develop Terrorvision's sound much, but cemented them as a key chart-worthy band.

Replenish (album – Reef)

Charted: Jul '95; UK Chart Position: 9; Label: Sony S2; Singles: 'Good Feeling' (Apr '95, UKCP 24), 'Naked' (Jun '95, 11)

Reef's debut album *Replenish* peaked at number nine in the UK chart when it was released in July '95. It was filled with guitar riff-dominated songs and pounding four-to-the-floor drum beats and lyrics (often with one-word titles) about growing up in nineties Britain.

Spurred on by hit single 'Naked', the album was generally positively received by the music press and paved the way for their next album, the career-defining *Glow*.

Republica (band)

Somewhat unbelievably, Republica have only released five singles and two albums in a career that spans more than 20 years (and continues even now). Made up of core members Andy Todd (keyboards), David Barbarossa (drums) and current members Tim Dorney (guitar) and Saffron (aka Samantha Sprackling) (vocals), the band formed in '94, when they signed to Deconstruction Records.

Their first single, the non-album track 'Out of This World', was released in '94 but failed to chart. It was quickly followed by 'Bloke', which reached 81 in the UK chart in April '95. With the album recorded, 'Ready to Go' should have been a surefire hit, but it managed only 43 in the charts when originally released in April '96 (exactly a year after 'Bloke'). This meant that plans to release the album were delayed for nearly a year while the band worked hard at building a following. Eventually, the momentum for 'Ready to Go' grew until the song was a staple on the radio, reaching number 13 in March '97. The album finally came out in the same month, slowly working its way up the chart to number four.

Although the band's sound mixed electronica, trip-hop and punk, Saffron's lyrics put the band firmly in the strong, female-centric corner of the Britpop movement alongside Elastica, Sleeper and Lush, even though they shared little in terms of style and tone. This point was highlighted by the tongue-in-cheek follow-up single – and the band's biggest chart success – 'Drop Dead Gorgeous', which features the classic chorus, "I know my ex-boyfriend lies; oh, he does it every time; it's just his permanent disguise; yeah, yeah and he's drop dead gorgeous". The song was a huge hit, prompting a knock-on effect that eventually gave the debut album its own chart success.

Capitalising on their commercial success, the band set about recording their second album. Unfortunately, this was just as Britpop scene came to an end, and *Speed Ballads* met with a muted reception when it was finally released in October '98. The album peaked at number 37 in the UK chart, two weeks after its pre-release single 'From the Rush Hour with Love' reached number 20. With Deconstruction Records dissolving at the end of '98, Republica were forced into a state of hiatus. Their two main singles continue to have a life of their own.

The band officially reformed in '08 and released a live album in '12. In May '15, they finally played new material live, although none has been released to date.

Republica (album – Republica)

Charted: Mar '97; UK Chart Position: 4; Label: Deconstruction; Singles: 'Bloke' (Apr '95, UKCP 81), 'Ready to Go' (Mar '97, 13), 'Drop Dead Gorgeous' (May '97, 7)

Promoted by the success of its two lead singles 'Ready to Go' and 'Drop Dead Gorgeous', Republica's eponymous debut album was a huge hit for the band and their label when it was released in March '97. 'Ready to Go' in particular seemed to be superglued to the radio in the early half of '97, increasing in momentum after its initial release a year earlier in April '96.

This paved the way for the album which, interestingly, performed inversely to many other albums at the time, slowly building its chart success and only reaching its peak position 12 weeks after its release, mainly due to the popularity of the band's fourth single 'Drop Dead Gorgeous', another radio staple that peaked at number seven in May '97.

The rest of the album follows the example set by the two main singles; chiefly, songs with electronic beats and punk-styled guitars, accompanied by shouty female-focused lyrics about broken relationships, nights out and idealised views of the future.

Return to the Last Chance Saloon (album – The Bluetones)

Charted: Mar '98; UK Chart Position: 10; Label: Superior Quality; Singles: 'Solomon Bites the Worm' (Feb '98, UKCP 10), 'If...' (May '98, 13), 'Sleazy Bed Track' (Aug '98, 35), '4-Day Weekend' (Sept '98, UKCP n/a)

The Bluetones' second album, *Return to the Last Chance Saloon*, a spiritually similar follow-up to their debut *Expecting to Fly*, found its way into the top ten of the UK chart when it was released in March '98. Britpop was all but over by this time, and the attention the bands and their releases had enjoyed in the press and the charts was starting to fade. In terms of sound, the album is a great achievement for the band, developing further the jangly, riff-laden songs and quirky lyrics they had become known for.

Lead single 'Solomon Bites the Worm' was a successor in style and sound to 'Bluetonic', but it was on track number seven, second single 'If...', that the band found were at their most epic, with a "nah nah" outro not a million miles away from the Beatles' 'Hey Jude'. The single reached number 13 in the UK chart in May '98.

The album comprised 13 tracks, plus a bonus. Fourth single '4-Day Weekend' was released on 12" vinyl and CD, but didn't chart because it was available through mail order only. The album was recorded in London by producer Hugh Jones, who also recorded the band's debut, and was put out by Superior Quality, the band's long-term record label.

Reverend Black Grape (single – Black Grape)

Charted: June '95; UK Chart Position: 9; Label: Radioactive; Album: *It's Great When You're Straight... Yeah!*

Never one to shy away from controversy, Shaun Ryder took the chorus of 'Reverend Black Grape' directly from one of the Anglican Church's best-loved Christmas carols, 'Oh Come All Ye Faithful'. The controversy – and the catchy chorus – paid off, and the single reached number nine in the UK chart when it was released (nowhere near Christmas) in June '95.

It was released on CD and 12" vinyl, and included B-sides 'Straight out of Trumpton (Basement Tapes)' as well as a remix of the lead track. The 12" vinyl included two separate remixes of the lead track.

Rialto (band)

Known chiefly for their singles 'Monday Morning 5:19' and 'Untouchable', London band Rialto released just one album and four singles during the Britpop years and, like Travis and Embrace, joined the ranks towards the end of the era. Sharing an ethos with Pulp and the Divine Comedy and miles away from the harder rock sound of Skunk Anansie and 3 Colours Red, the band were known for their indie guitars, lilting vocal lines and layered keyboard parts, and the fact that they (for some reason) had two drummers.

Led by singer-songwriter Louis Eliot, the band were: Jonny Bull (guitar), Julian Taylor (bass), Pete Cuthbert (drums), Toby Hounsham (keyboards) and Anthony Christmas (drums). They signed to Warners offshoot East West Records in '96 and debut single 'Monday Morning 5:19' reached number 37 in November that year. 'Untouchable', originally released in early '97 but failing to chart, eventually reached number 20 in January '98. The band were then unexpectedly dropped by their label, despite the fact their debut album had already been recorded. China Records picked them up and put out their eponymous album, which peaked at number 21 in the UK chart in July '98.

A few difficult years followed for the band as they struggled to maintain chart success post-Britpop and both Hounsham and Christmas left in early '00. The band released one more album, *Night on Earth*, in '00, but it failed to make the top ten of the UK chart.

Richard III (single – Supergrass)

Charted: Apr '97; UK Chart Position: 2; Label: Parlophone; Album: *In It for the Money*

Kept from the top spot by R Kelly's 'I Believe I Can Fly', the first release from Supergrass' second album, *In It for the Money*, reached number two in the UK chart in April '97. The interestingly-named 'Richard III' was a thunderingly raucous release, which could not be further away in sound and style from anything the band had done before or since. Its incessant guitar line and catchy melody, combined with the popularity of the band, meant it was a huge success and paved the way for the album.

The single was released on two CDs. The first featured B-sides

'Sometimes I Make You Sad' and 'Sometimes We're Sad', while the second included 'Nothing More's Gonna Get in My Way' and '20ft Halo'.

Ride (band)

As key founders of the experimental shoegazing scene that immediately preceded and helped to create the Britpop movement, Oxford's Ride were not specifically part of the Britpop scene, despite being signed to Creation Records and releasing two successful albums in the timeframe.

They were, however, an important British guitar group, and gave Andy Bell (guitar, vocals) his first of many roles in the musical world. Formed in '88, Ride also included Mark Gardiner (guitar, vocals), Laurence Colbert (bass) and Steve Queralt (drums).

After a gig supporting the Soup Dragons, the band found themselves in a record company bidding war that saw Alan McGee sign them in '89. Debut album *Nowhere* – now considered one of the key releases of the shoegazing era – peaked at number 11 in October '90, and its follow-up *Going Blank Again* reached number five in March '92. The band's success continued when *Carnival of Light* reached number five in July '94. Produced by John Leckie, the album marked an evolution in the band's sound, moving away from shoegazing towards the short-lived psychedelic rock scene, which itself was coming to an end.

Tarantula, released in March '96 (peaking at number 21), appeared just as Bell and Gardiner were breaking up the band. By '96, the two guitarists were pulling in different musical directions, a lack of synergy that led to Bell leaving and forming Hurricane #1 and, later, joining Oasis. Ride re-formed in November '14 to play several live shows. They released their first studio alnum in 21 years, *Weather Diaries*, in June '17, when it reached number 11 in the UK chart.

Riverboat Song, The (single – Ocean Colour Scene)

Charted: Feb '96; UK Chart Position: 15; Label: MCA; Album: *Moseley Shoals*

Remembered not only for its killer guitar riff, but also for being the single that put Ocean Colour Scene on the Britpop map, 'The Riverboat Song' was the entrance music for the guests on *TFI Friday*.

The opening track to the band's breakthrough album *Moseley Shoals* peaked at number 15 in the UK chart when it was released in February '96. The CD single included B-sides 'So Sad' and 'Charlie Brown Says'.

Roll With It (single – Oasis)

Charted: Aug '95; UK Chart Position: 2; Label: Creation; Album: *(What's The Story) Morning Glory?*

One of the most famous number two singles of all time, 'Roll With It' was the second release from Oasis' second album *(What's the Story) Morning Glory?*. It's mostly remembered as the band's contribution to the 'Battle of Britpop' in August '95, which Blur won with 'Country House' and, to rub salt into the wound, also pipped the Manchester boys to the 'Best British Single' gong at the '95 Brit Awards with 'Parklife'.

The B-sides included 'It's Better People', 'Rockin Chair' and a monumental live encore performance of 'Live Forever' from their headline performance at Glastonbury '95. The cover featured the band on the beach at Weston-super-Mare wearing matching duffle coats while sitting side by side in deckchairs each watching their own television. The *Top of Pops* performance of the single saw the Gallagher brothers swapping roles, with Noel pretending to sing Liam's vocals, while Liam mimed playing guitar.

Rowntree, Dave (drummer – Blur)

Sometime Blur drummer and sometime lawyer, Rowntree is rumoured to have said he would rather die than live with any of the other members of Blur. Luckily, he never had to.

He has been the drummer with the band since they began in '89, returning with his sticks in '09 when they re-formed.

Born in Colchester in Essex on 8 April '64, Rowntree took percussion lessons from a young age and began playing in bands with future Blur bandmate Graham Coxon when they were both in their teens. He left his job with the council and moved to London when invited to join what would eventually become Blur in '89. In '06, with Blur on a hiatus, he retrained as a solicitor, and still practices law now. When Blur re-formed in '09, he had to sneak off early after one show because he needed to be at work at 9am the following morning.

A talented computer animator, he created and directed two series of his own animation show, *Empire Square*, which aired on Channel 4 in '05. He has hosted various radio shows, including an occasional evening slot on London's XFM, and is also a keen advocate of the Labour party, attempting to win London-based parliamentary seats in '07, '08 and '10 (he lost out each time to the Tories) and chairing the West End branch. In May '17, Dave finally achieved his goal of gaining public office as county councillor for the University Ward, Norwich, on Norfolk County Council.

Ryder, Shaun (singer/songwriter – Happy Mondays/Black Grape)

Shaun William George Ryder was born in Lancashire on 23 August '62. He formed the Happy Mondays with brother Paul in '80, at the age of 18, and the band signed to Factory Records in '85. Their first album made it to the record stores in '87 and was an immediate hit, leading to four subsequent long-format releases over the following seven years.

Ryder was well-known from the off as a bit of a tearaway with a fondness for drugs, making him an apt frontman for the emergence of Factory Records and the subsequent Acid House scene, which brought together the worlds of drugs and music. Unfortunately, it was also his increasingly problematic relationship with drugs, notably heroin and crack cocaine, that eventually contributed to the Happy Mondays splitting in '92.

With Britpop in full swing, Ryder returned with his next musical project, Black Grape. They were an immediate success and their debut album *It's Great When You're Straight... Yeah!* headed straight to the top of the UK chart in October '95. Rather than follow the route of straightforward indie-rock, Black Grape carried on from where the Happy Mondays had left of, fusing jangly guitar lines with a more hip-hop tinged sound.

It was during this time that Ryder earned himself a lifetime ban from appearing live on Channel 4 after swearing several times on the Chris Evans-fronted magazine show *TFI Friday*.

After the release of second album *Stupid Stupid Stupid* in '98, and with Britpop now well and truly over, Black Grape split amicably. Ryder reunited with his fellow Happy Mondays in '99 for a series of occasional gigs. Ongoing disputes with record companies, management companies and lawyers meant no new music could be recorded until *Uncle Dysfunktional* was released in '07. Five years later, the band got back together again for a major UK and European tour. Black Grape reformed in '15, releasing new album *Pop Voodoo* in August '17, when it reached number 15 in the UK chart.

Ryder and his Happy Mondays bandmates were portrayed in all their technicolour glory in Michael Winterbottom's '02 film about Factory Records and the Hacienda, *Twenty Four Hour Party People*. He has six children and has been married several times, finally settling down with wife Joanna in '10.

S

Saffron (aka Samantha Sprackling) (singer/ songwriter – Republica)

Samantha Sprackling, more commonly known as Saffron, was the red-haired, fiery lead singer of Republica. What's less commonly known is that she was also an actress who performed in the London musical *Starlight Express* for two years from the age of 18.

Born in Lagos, Nigeria in June '68, Saffron is of Chinese, Portuguese and British descent. Her first success in the music world came when she was the female lead in the video for Chesney Hawkes' '91 hit 'The One and Only'. She later joined dance duo, N Joi, as a vocalist and dancer.

She joined Republica in '94 as their lead singer, playing with them until their hiatus in '01, and again for their reunion in '08. During her time with the band, she also provided vocals for The Prodigy's 'Fuel My Fire', one of the key songs from their third album, '97's *The Fat of the Land*. Following Republica's initial hiatus, the singer dyed her hair blonde and collaborated with The Cure on their track 'Just Say Yes'.

Post-Britpop, Sprackling continues to play live with Republica as well as with her solo band. She has also returned to acting, playing a police officer in the '14 *Lock, Stock...* pastiche *Looters, Tooters & Sawn-Off Shooters*.

Saint Etienne (band)

Saint Etienne, named after the French football team AC Saint Etienne, are a London-based indie-dance band who formed in '90 and are still performing together today. Their music existed on the periphery of Britpop, but the fact they were signed to Heavenly Records and released two of their key albums during the key years means they are ripe for inclusion.

Formed by schoolfriends Bob Stanley and Pete Wiggs, the band were completed when singer Sarah Cracknell joined in '90. Taking much of their early influence from the dance music scene that rose to prominence in the early nineties, the band found their own individuality – and created a more accessible sound – by introducing pop lyrics and melodies. First album *Foxbase Alpha* was a fairly faithful house music album and reached number 34 in the UK chart in September '91. Follow-up *So Tough* was released in March '93; its winning combination of dance music and pop making it an immediate hit. It peaked at number seven in the UK chart and was their most successful album to date.

With Britpop in full swing, the band's third album *Tiger Bay* was not an assured success, as the house scene had been driven away from the mainstream in favour of indie-rock music. The band's popularity was growing though, and the album – interestingly enough, inspired predominantly by folk music – peaked at number eight in the UK chart in March '94. With this momentum, the band released the standalone single 'He's on the Phone' in November '95, just missing out on the top ten at number 11.

It was another two years before their next studio album release, a delay that could have killed off another band, but *Good Humour* reached number 18 in May '98. Since then, they have released five further studio albums as well as a best of, and continue to play together. Their most recent album, *Home Counties*, was released in June '17 and reached number 31 in the UK chart.

Salad (band)

Known mainly for their May '95 top-20 album *Drink Me*, Salad were a female-fronted indie band bolstered by the success of the Britpop movement. Formed in '92 by Dutch singer and keyboardist Marijne van der Vlugt and including bassist Peter Brown, drummer Rob Wakeman and guitarist Paul Kennedy, the band signed to Island Records in '93 after their first two self-funded EPs drew attention from the music press.

The first single the band released via Island was 'On a Leash', which reached number 84 in the UK chart in April '94. 'Your Ma' reached number 82 in July '94, and the band's best-known song, the infamous Jonestown Massacre-inspired 'Drink the Elixir', reached number 66 in March '95. Two months later, their debut album *Drink Me* appeared, peaking at number 16 in the UK chart. It was filled with short, sharp pop-punk songs, similar in sound to Lush. Their next single 'Motorbike to Heaven' peaked at number 42 in May '95.

Second album *Ice Cream* was released by Island in '97, but failed to reach the UK top ten, and the band parted ways with their record company shortly after. In '16, Van der Vlugt and Kennedy reunited as Salad Undressed to perform acoustic versions of their nineties songs. They released an album of new songs, *Good Love Bad Love*, in '17 and performed as a full band at the Indie Daze Festival.

Sale of the Century (single – Sleeper)

Charted: May '96; UK Chart Position: 10; Label: Indolent; Album: *The It Girl*

'Sale of the Century' (possibly named after the famously cheesy ITV gameshow) was the second of four singles from Sleeper's second album *The It Girl* and the band's first top-ten single. It spent five weeks in the chart, peaking at number ten.

The CD single featured B-sides 'Package Holiday' and 'Oh Well', while the limited edition vinyl included a cover of Blondie's 'Atomic', a track that appeared on the soundtrack to Danny Boyle's '96 film *Trainspotting*.

Salvation (single – The Cranberries)

Charted: Apr '96; UK Chart Position: 13; Label: Island; Album: *To the Faithful Departed*

'Salvation' was the first single from The Cranberries' third album *To the Faithful Departed*, and the band's highest charting single at the time of its release, peaking at number 13 and spending ten weeks on the UK chart. The song was admired for its directness and visually bold music video, with vocalist Dolores O'Riordan singing, "To all those people doing lines, don't do it," while a clown with needles in his head watches parents grieving the loss of a child.

The CD B-sides included 'I'm Still Remembering' and a live version of 'I Just Shot John Lennon', the originals of which were both on the album.

Sandstorm (single – Cast)

Charted: Jan '96; UK Chart Position: 8; Label: Polydor; Album: *All Change*

'Sandstorm' was the third of four singles released from Cast's debut album *All Change* and the band's first top-ten hit, paving the way for a further two top-ten singles, 'Walk Away' and 'Flying', that same year.

The CD release B-sides included the exclusive track 'Hourglass' and live versions of the album's 'Back Of My Mind' and 'Alright' recorded at Abbey Road Studios. The band performed the single along with 'Alright' on music TV show *The White Room*.

Saturday Night (single - Suede)

Charted: Jan '97; UK Chart Position: 6; Label: Nude; Album: *Coming Up*

'Saturday Night' was the third of five singles from Suede's third album *Coming Up* and, like its predecessors, became yet another top-ten hit, peaking at number six and spending five weeks on the UK chart. In contrast to the album's other singles, 'Trash' and 'Beautiful Ones', 'Saturday Night' is a gentle ballad that shares an identity with previous album's 'The Wild Ones'.

The single was available on two CDs, the first featuring exclusive tracks 'W.S.D' and 'Jumble Sale Mums', and the second 'This Time' and the demo version of the title track. The music video featured English actress Keeley Hawes and was filmed on London Underground at a disused platform.

Seahorses, The (band)

After the the Stone Roses split in '96, everyone wondered what the individual members would do next. Singer Ian Brown enjoyed an extended hiatus in Manchester, as did drummer Reni. Bassist Mani joined Primal Scream and John Squire, the incendiary guitarist and chief songwriter, returned with new band The Seahorses, who released four singles and one album between '97 and '99.

The first member of the band that Squire hired was bassist Stuart Fletcher, who he spotted playing with a local covers band. Singer Chris Helme was spotted while busking on the streets of York, and drummer Andy Watts joined soon afterwards. The band spent much of '96 writing songs – mostly penned by Squire – rehearsing and playing some low-level European dates before releasing their debut single, the late Stone Roses-esque, riff-heavy 'Love is the Law' in May '97. The single was an immediate hit and went straight in at number three in the UK chart, paving the way for the album *Do It Yourself* in June that year. The album reached number two in the UK chart, where it spent a total of 49 weeks.

Helme was a songwriter as well as a singer, and wrote the band's second single, 'Blinded by the Sun', which reached number seven in July '97. 'Love Me and Leave Me', written by Squire with help from Oasis' Liam Gallagher, reached number 16 in October '97.

The band finished the year with another single, the stand-alone, non-album track 'You Can Talk to Me', which reached number 15 in December '97. The band began writing songs for a new album and played many of them live throughout '98, notably during support slots with the Rolling Stones, U2 and Oasis. They went into the studio to record the album in early '99, but the sessions were eventually abandoned due to musical differences and the members each went their separate ways.

Select (music magazine)

Select was the nineties music magazine that gave us the term 'Britpop', when writer Stuart Maconie coined the phrase in relation to Oasis, Suede and Blur.

A key source of music knowledge for avid fans growing up in the pre-internet era, the magazine played a pivotal part in the Britpop movement, with Maconie loudly proclaiming, "Yanks Go Home" on the cover of the April '93 edition, which featured Suede's Brett Anderson adorned in a Union Jack. His full article, entitled "Who Do You Think You Are Kidding Mr Cobain?", paid homage to British bands including Suede, St Etienne, Denim, Pulp and The Auteurs, and successfully set out the country's reaction to America's grunge.

First published in July '90, the magazine was withdrawn in '01, leaving behind a collection of issues that could be described as Britpop history books.

Setting Sun (single – Chemical Brothers)

Charted: Oct '96; UK Chart Position: 1; Label: Virgin; Album: *Dig Your Own Hole*

Featuring Oasis' Noel Gallagher on vocals, the Chemical Brothers' 'Setting Sun' was one of the few singles to marry Britpop with big beats. The single, from the band's second album *Dig Your Own Hole*, was released shortly after their support slot at the August Knebworth gigs and shot straight to number one in the UK chart, where it spent a total of 11 weeks.

The CD single included the full length, radio edit and instrumental versions of the title track as well as exclusive track 'Buzz Tracks'.

Shakermaker (single – Oasis)

Charted: Jul '94; UK Chart Position: 11; Label: Creation; Album: *Definitely Maybe*

Oasis' second single 'Shakermaker' told of Mr Sifter, Mr Clean and Mr Soft, all real-life characters of relevance in Noel Gallagher's world. The first owned the record store in Burnage where the band spent many hours as teenagers.

Gallagher inadvertently used the melody from Roger Cook's 'I'd like to Teach the World to Sing' in the song, which led to them eventually abandoning playing it live because Liam could never resist singing the original lyrics.

The single narrowly missed the top ten of the UK chart, where it spent a total of 60 weeks. It featured B-sides 'D'Yer Wanna Be a Spaceman', 'Alive' and a live version of 'Bring It On Down' (the original featured on the album). The single signalled the band's debut performance on *Top of the Pops*.

She Left Me on Friday (single – Shed Seven)

Charted: Mar '98; UK Chart Position: 11; Label: Polydor; Album: *Let it Ride*

The first single from third album *Let it Ride*, the tongue-in-cheek, guttural anthem 'She Left me on Friday' was Shed Seven's tenth single in a row to make it into the top 40. It peaked just outside the top ten at number 11 in March '98.

There were two CD formats, the first featuring B-sides 'Bottom Upwards' and 'Melpomene', and the second 'My Misspent Youth' and 'You'.

She Makes My Nose Bleed (single – Mansun)

Charted: Feb '97; UK Chart Position: 9; Label: Parlophone; Album: *Attack Of The Grey Lantern*

Released in February '97, Mansun's sixth single was their highest chart-placing, finally breaking into the top ten and peaking at number nine. It spent a total of six weeks on the chart and paved the way for their number one album *Attack of the Grey Lantern*, released in March '97.

The single was released on two CDs. CD1 featured B-sides 'The Most to Gain', 'Flourella' and 'She Makes My Nose Bleed (Acoustic)', while CD2 included B-sides 'The Holy Blood and the Holy Grail', 'Live Open Space' and 'Drastic Sturgeon (Live)'.

She Said (single – Longpigs)

Charted: Jun '96; UK Chart Position: 16; Label: Mother; Album: *The Sun Is Often Out*

Originally released in July '95, the Longpigs' joint highest-charting single, 'She Said', was re-released in June '96, capitalising on the recent success of debut album *The Sun is Often Out*. It peaked at number 16 in the UK chart, where it spent three weeks. It also featured on indie compilation *Shine 5*.

The CD single featured B-sides 'Take It All', 'Devoted' and 'Juicy'.

She's a Star (single – James)

Charted: Feb '97; UK Chart Position: 9; Label: Fontana; Album: *Whiplash*

The lead single from key Britpop album *Whiplash*, 'She's a Star' by Manchester band James was one of their biggest hits, reaching number nine in February '97.

The first release in nearly three years signalled a change in direction for the band normally identified with the Madchester scene, bringing them into line with the guitar-led Britpop bands popular at the time. With its immediately recognisable signature slide guitar riff, the song began a new phase of success for the band.

Three different versions of the CD single were released, with CD1 featuring B-sides 'Stutter (Live)' and 'Johnny Yen (Live)', CD2 'Chunney Chops', 'Fishknives' and 'Van Gogh's Dog' and CD3 'Come Home (Weatherall Remix)', 'She's a Star (Dave Angel's Pat Remix)' and 'She's a Star (Andrea's Biosphere Mix)'.

Shed Seven (band)

Surely the only band named after a trackside railway shed, Shed Seven formed in '90 in York, North Yorkshire, and enjoyed much success during the Britpop years. They split in '03 but re-formed for a greatest hits tour in '07 and continue to play now.

The original line-up comprised Rick Witter (vocals), Tom Gladwin (bass), Alan Leach (drums) and Paul Banks (guitar), who replaced Joe Johnson not long before the band were first signed to Polydor Records in '93. Early comparisons to The Smiths garnered the band some attention in the music press and debut single 'Mark' found its way into the lower reaches of the top ten when it was released in March '93. After a further string of top-40 singles, the band's debut album *Change Giver* found its way into the top 20, peaking at number 16 in the UK chart when released in September '94.

With Britpop entering its peak time in '95, the band rode the wave of commercial success with their second album *A Maximum High*, which appeared in April '95, peaking at number eight in the chart. Two top-40 singles were released from the album, as well as two top-20s and the band's biggest hit, 'Going for Gold', which reached number eight in March '96. They ended their most commercially fruitful year with the top-20 single 'Chasing Rainbows' in November '96 – making them the band who had the most singles in the top 40 in '96.

Taking time off from recording to focus on touring meant the Sheds didn't release any new material at all in '97. By the time the first single from third album *Let it Ride* was released in March '98, Britpop was waning and the scene was winding down. However, the catchy single 'She Left Me on a Friday' ("and ruined my weekend!") still reached number 11. The album managed number nine in June '98, spending 13 weeks on the chart, as opposed to the 37 of its predecessor. The band's label insisted they release a best-of in June '99, leading to disagreements and a parting of ways in late '99. The band carried on, even though Banks left to focus on other musical projects and Joe Johnson rejoined.

The Sheds secured a new record deal with Artful Records and their fourth album, *Truth be Told*, was released in May '01, reaching number 42 in the UK chart. They parted ways with the new label not long afterwards, and split in '03. That wasn't the end of the story though. The original line-up re-formed for a greatest hits tour in '07 and are still playing together today, with a new album out in late '17. They remain one of the key Britpop bands.

Shine (compilation albums)

The *Shine* albums were *the* Britpop compilations and are considered today to be the most accurate collective representation of the music of the time. Beginning in '95, so coinciding with the peak Britpop years, the albums were released by PolyGram TV to capitalise on the indie rock scene. Ten sequentially numbered albums were released between '95 and '98. The first four were single CD releases, with *Shine 5*, released in July '96, the first to stretch to two CDs. There were also two additional releases, *Best of '97* and *Best of Shine*, taking the total number of albums to 12.

The series focused predominantly on British artists and a British audience, although both Greenday and Dinosaur Jr were on the first album, perhaps indicating an intention to widen their appeal to an American audience. As Britpop reached its peak, however, the focus fell squarely on the British Isles and countries heavily influenced by the scene (the Cardigans and the Wannadies were both from Sweden).

The albums were the perfect access point to anyone new to the scene, providing samples of key bands and new names.

Shoegazing (music genre)

Named because of the musicians' habit of staring at the floor and their own shoes rather than the audience, the short-lived shoegazing scene began in Britain in the late eighties and peaked in the early nineties, when many of the associated bands either changed their sound or faded away once Britpop became active.

The scene was all about soundscapes and effects-driven music developed from traditional indie-rock, with vocals often lowered in the mix so the heavily distorted guitars could take centre stage. The key acts were My Bloody Valentine, the Jesus and Mary Chain and, later, Ride, all signed to Creation Records.

My Bloody Valentine were held up as the primary driver, although their lack of releases, other than album *Loveless*, left the scene feeling somewhat bereft. The Verve's first album, *A Storm in Heaven*, is heavily indebted to the scene, and there remained a noticeable focus on soundscapes and effects-driven guitar lines on all of their subsequent releases, most notably *Urban Hymns*.

London was the centre of the movement, but a large proportion of the bands came from predominantly middle-class provinces like

Oxford. This led to a backlash in the music press, which named the movement "the scene that celebrates itself" and dismissed it as self-indulgent music made by the over-privileged.

Grunge did much to dispel the scene before working-class, back-to-basics Britpop bands like Oasis and Pulp took the focus away completely. There was a resurgence in the early noughties from bands such as My Vitriol and Silversun Pickups from the USA as part of another short-lived scene that became known as Nu-gaze.

Shooting Stars (TV show)

Hosted by irreverent comedians Vic Reeves and Bob Mortimer, *Shooting Stars* was (and still occasionally is) a bizarre mix of celebrity panel show and comedy sketch show that started on BBC Two in '95. If there are any rules, no one knows what they are.

The opposing panels – originally led by TV presenter Ulrika Jonsson and comedian and DJ Mark Lamarr – are made up of whichever celebrities are hot that week. Britpop's own Louise Wener from Sleeper was a guest, as was Pulp's Jarvis Cocker, whose sly wit suited the show well. Future *Little Britain* star Matt Lucas got his big break on the show as the giant babygrow-sporting score-keeper George Dawes.

The surreal, anarchic tone and style of the show was a perfect fit for the nineties and it was must-watch TV during the Britpop era.

Short Album About Love, A (album – The Divine Comedy)

Charted: Feb '97; UK Chart Position: 13; Label: Setanta; Singles: 'Everybody Knows (Except You)' (Mar '97; UKCP 14)

The Divine Comedy's fifth studio album is notable for featuring the Brunel Ensemble, who provide brass, wind and string instruments throughout and whose addition creates an altogether more dramatic sound. As the title suggests, *A Short Album About Love* is indeed short, with just seven tracks, although the Austrian version included four bonus tracks, one of which was a cover of Burt Bacharach's 'Make It Easy On Yourself'.

Unlike many of the band's other long-form releases, the album resulted in just one single, 'Everybody Knows (Except You)'. It was, however, their first of five top-20 albums and spent eight weeks on the UK chart. Their third album, *Fin De Siecle*, released a year and a half later, made the top ten.

Silver Sun (band)

Still active today, Silver Sun are an indie-pop band that formed in Camden in '95 and existed on the periphery of the Britpop scene. Famed mainly for their '98 top-20 single 'Too Much, Too Little, Too Late', which was a cover of the Johnny Mathis number one single from '78, the band released two albums through Polydor and a further three through independent label Invisible Hands Music.

The band consisted of James Broad (vocals/guitar), Richard Buckton (guitar), Paul Smith (bass) and Jason Panudy (drums). Heavily influenced by American indie rock bands like Weezer, Silver Sun signed to Polydor in '96 as Britpop was reaching its peak, and their eponymous debut album appeared in May '97, reaching number 30 in the UK chart. It was the first produced by future mixing desk royalty Nigel Godrich, later famed for his work with, among others, Radiohead. Four singles were released from the album, with 'Golden Skin' and the re-release of 'Lava' reaching the top 40.

'Too Much, Too Little, Too Late' was released in June '98 and went straight into the top 20 of the UK chart. Follow-up single 'I'll See You Around' reached number 26 in September '98, but the second album only reached number 74 in the UK chart when it was released in November '98.

The band parted ways with their record company shortly afterwards and returned to Camden. After some time off, their third album was released in '05, with Broad the only musician to play on any of the tracks. The rest of the band joined him when playing live and, despite the fact the album failed to chart, they continued playing together and have subsequently released two further albums.

Sisters EP, The (single – Pulp)

Charted: Jun '94; UK Chart Position: 19; Label: Island; Album: *His 'n' Hers*

Pulp's first single to reach the top 20 of the UK chart featured as its lead track 'Babies', one of the key songs from their breakthrough album *His 'n' Hers*. The single peaked at number 19 in June '94 and spent a total of eight weeks on the chart.

The CD, cassette and limited edition vinyl releases included B-sides 'Your Sister's Clothes', 'Seconds' and 'His 'n' Hers'.

Sixty Mile Smile (single – 3 Colours Red)

Charted: Mar '97; UK Chart Position: 20; Label: Creation; Album: *Pure*

They had little in common with most of the Britpop acts, but 3 Colours Red were signed to Creation Records and the melodic sound of their singles brought with it an association to the scene. 'Sixty Mile Smile' was their second single and the first to reach the top 20, peaking at number 20 in March '97. It spent three weeks on the chart.

The CD release included B-sides 'Zip the Morals' and 'Til I'm Ready'. The single also featured on indie compilation series *Shine 8*.

Skunk Anansie (band)

Formed in '94 and consisting of Skin (vocals), Cass (bass), Ace (guitar) and Mark Richardson (drums), Skunk Anansie were a heavy rock band that found much success during the Britpop years. Taking their name from the Akann folk tales of Anansi the spider-man of Ghana, the band were signed to independent label One Little Indian not long after they were formed in '94. Fourth single 'Weak' peaked at number 20 in the UK chart in January '96 due, in part, to the success of debut album *Paranoid and Sunburnt*, which went in at number eight on the UK chart in September '95.

Second album *Stoosh* peaked at number nine in October '96, propelled on by the band's highest charting single to date, 'All I Want', which peaked at number 14 in September '96. 'Hedonism (Just Because You Feel Good)', a more introspective and tender song, and thus a departure of sorts for the band, found its way to number 13 in the UK chart in February '97, and it's follow-up, 'Brazen Weep', peaked just outside the top ten at number 11 in June '97. It was the band's highest charting single to date.

Parting ways with the independent label that gave them their start, Skunk Anansie signed to major label Virgin in '98. Their third album, *Post Orgasmic Chill*, was released in April '99 and reached number 14 on the UK chart, not quite matching the success of its predecessors. With the Britpop years over, and many of the key bands struggling to find the same type of success they once had, Skunk Anansie split amicably just as the new millennium began.

Skin went on to forge a solo career, releasing two albums, while Richardson joined rock band Feeder, and the other two members collaborated with various bands. The band reformed in '09 to play best of material live, and have since released four studio albums on various labels, including One Little Indian. Their most recent album, *Anarchytecture*, reached number 85 in the UK chart in January '16.

Sleep (single – Marion)

Charted: Mar '96; UK Chart Position: 17; Label: London; Album: *This World and Body*

Propelled by its catchy harmonica riff, Marion's most famous single 'Sleep' was also their highest charting, reaching number 17 in the UK in March '96. It had previously been released as their debut single in February '95, when it reached number 53. The song also featured on the indie compilation album *Shine 5* and was promoted on TV shows *The Word* and *Britpop Now*.

The CD single, released in March '96, featured B-sides 'Waiting for No-One', 'The Collector' and 'Violent Men'.

Sleeper (band)

Named after but bearing no similarity to a '73 Woody Allen sci-fi comedy, Sleeper were an indie-rock guitar band fronted by Louise Wener. They released three top ten albums and eight top-40 singles.

Formed at university in Manchester by Wener and guitarist Jon Stewart, the band was completed via an advert in the now legendary *Melody Maker* 'musicians wanted' pages by bassist Diid Osman and drummer Andy Maclure, who later became Wener's partner after she split with Stewart. The band got a deal with Indolent Records in '93, and their first single, 'Swallow EP', was released in February '94. Another single, 'Delicious', reached number 74 in May '95, then 'Inbetweener', a catchy single about the different expectations two people can have from a relationship, entered the top 20 in January '95. Debut album *Smart* was released a month later and peaked at number five in the UK chart.

The band were often compared to Blur, who they supported on the *Parklife* tour in '94/'95. Wener's style of penning lyrics about everyday life in nineties Britain was similar to Damon Albarn's, meaning their success was pretty much assured. Wener's individuality came from her ability to put across the female point of view, particularly when it came to failed relationships and the inevitable wrestling for control that follows. Her gender led her to be lumped in with other female-fronted groups by the music press, notably Elastica, Lush and Republica, even though the bands shared little in common musically.

Continuing in the same vein as their debut, second album *The It Girl* was a key Britpop long-format release, reaching number five in May '95 and spending 47 weeks on the chart. 'What Do I Do Now?' and 'Statuesque', which appeared on the soundtrack to Danny Boyle's film *Trainspotting*, reached the top 20, while 'Sale of the Century' and 'Nice Guy Eddie' both made it to number ten. The band ended '96, their biggest year, as one of the most successful Britpop bands around.

No new material was released for a year, and when 'She's a Good Girl' came out in October '97, the music scene was starting to change. The single reached number 28 in the UK chart, and its accompanying album *Pleased to Meet You* peaked at number seven a week later, spending just four weeks on the chart. The band split not long after the release of their final single, 'Romeo Me', in December '97. The band re-formed in '17 for a string of live gigs, but have yet to release any new material.

Slight Return (single – Bluetones)

Charted: Feb '96; UK Chart Position: 2; Label: Superior Quality; Album: *Expecting To Fly*

The Bluetones' highest-charting single was their third release, appearing in February '96 and paving the way for their debut album, *Expecting to Fly*. The single surprised everyone by peaking at number two in February '96 in the UK chart, where it spent a total of 11 weeks. It was held off from the top spot by the mega hit 'Spaceman' by Babylon Zoo.

The CD single featured B-sides 'Don't Stand Me Down' and 'Nae Hair On't'.

Smart (album – Sleeper)

Charted: Feb '95; UK Chart Position: 5; Label: Indolent; Singles: 'Swallow EP' (Feb '94, UKCP 76), 'Delicious' (May '94, 75), 'Inbetweener' (Jan '95, 16), 'Vegas' (Apr '95, 33)

Sleeper's debut set the tone for the female-fronted wing of Britpop – sassy, witty and sort of sexy in a wry, ironic way, with Louise's Wener's lyrics telling stories of modern British life. If not quite reaching the artistic flare and inventive lyrical content of second long-format release *The It Girl*, Sleeper's debut certainly paved the way, and 'Inbetweener' in particular is a stand-out track.

Produced by Paul Crockett and Ian Broudie from the Lightning Seeds and mixed by Stephen Street, who produced much of Blur's output, the album was written predominantly by singer Wener, with co-credits going to guitarist Jon Stewart on about half of the 12 tracks. Lyrically, the album covers many of the same subject areas as early Blur, predominantly focusing on stories of urban living, romantic liaisons, watching bands and drinking in pubs. It was released by Indolent in February '95 and peaked in its first week at number five in the UK chart.

Sneakerpimps (band)

More trip-hop than Britpop, the Sneakerpimps were best known for single '6 Underground', which was released from their '96 debut album *Becoming X* at the height of Britpop in October '96. The song featured on indie compilation album *Shine 7*.

The band began with Liam Howe and Chris Corner, who initially produced non-vocal trip-hop beats together under the name F.R.I.S.K. Signed to Clean Up Records, the duo released a couple of EPs before recruiting female vocalist Kelli Dayton, bassist Jo Wilson, drummer Dave Westlake and writer Ian Pickering, who together recorded under the name Sneakerpimps, taken from a man the Beastie Boys hired to track down classic sneakers.

During the Britpop era, the band released one album, *Becoming X*, which resulted in popular singles '6 Underground' and 'Spin Sugar', as well as a remix album *Becoming Remixed*.

Post-Britpop, the band continued without Kelli, releasing albums *Splinter* in '99 and *Bloodsport* in '02. In May '16, Howe announced that the band were re-forming to record their fourth studio album, although nothing has been released to date. As an interesting aside, Noel Fielding, of *The Mighty Boosh* and *Great British Bake Off* fame, once played bass for the band.

So Young (single – Suede)

Charted: May '93; UK Chart Position: 22; Label: Nude; Album: *Suede*

The fourth and final single released from Suede's eponymous debut album, 'So Young' was also the album's opening track, introducing the band to the world at large. It peaked at number 22 in May '93 in the UK chart, where it spent a total of three weeks.

The CD single also featured B-sides 'Dolly' and 'High Rising'.

Solomon Bites the Worm (single – The Bluetones)

Charted: Feb '98; UK Chart Position: 10; Label: Superior Quality; Album: *Return to the Last Chance Saloon*

The first single released from the Bluetones' second album, *Return to the Last Chance Saloon*, 'Solomon Bites the Worm' peaked at number ten in the UK chart when it was released in February '98. Britpop was nearing its end, but the catchy song and quirky title meant that the band still found some success.

The CD single included B-sides 'I Was a Teenage Jesus' and 'I Walked All Night'.

Some Might Say (single - Oasis)

Charted: May '95; UK Chart Position: 1; Label: Creation; Album: *(What's The Story) Morning Glory?*

Oasis' first number one single, 'Some Might Say', was also the first to be released from their second album *(What's The Story) Morning Glory?*. It spent a massive 81 weeks in the UK chart and included exclusive B-sides 'Talk Tonight', 'Acquiesce' and 'Headshrinker' (the first two quickly becoming live favourites). It also has the privilege of being the first Britpop number one single, signalling not only the growing popularity of the band, but also the growth of the scene at large.

The cover sleeve, by Brian Cannon, featured his father holding a wheelbarrow and his mother a mop, while Noel Gallagher holds a watering can and brother Liam looks on from a bridge. The single was the last to feature Tony McCarroll on drums before replacement Alan White stepped in. White's first gig with the band was playing the single on *Top of the Pops*.

Something 4 the Weekend (single - Super Furry Animals)

Charted: Jul '96; UK Chart Position: 18; Label: Creation; Album: *Fuzzy Logic*

The Super Furry Animals' third single was also their first to reach the top 20, peaking at number 18 in July '96, a month after their debut album *Fuzzy Logic* reached number 23 in the UK.

The CD single included B-sides 'Waiting to Happen', 'Arnofio/Glô in the Dark' and the album version of the lead track 'Something 4 the Weekend'.

Something Changed (single - Pulp)

Charted: Apr '96; UK Chart Position: 10; Label: Island; Album: *Different Class*

The fourth single (but fifth song released) from Pulp's mega hit album *Different Class*, 'Something Changed' was also the final release from the band for 18 months. It reached number ten in the UK chart in April '96.

The most gentle and introspective song on the album, it's a ballad that singer Jarvis Cocker penned for his future wife, pondering how easily the chance meeting might never have happened. It remains one of the band's most tender songs.

The CD single was released in two formats; 'boy' and 'girl' copies with different covers. Both featured exclusive B-sides 'Mile End' (from the film Trainspotting) and two versions of 'F.E.E.L.I.N.G.C.A.L.L.E. D.L.O.V.E.' (The Moloko Mix and Live from the Brixton Academy).

Something for the Weekend (single - Divine Comedy)

Charted: Jun '96; UK Chart Position: 14; Label: Setanta; Album: *Casanova*

The Divine Comedy's second single was also their first to chart, reaching number 14 in June '96 and spending five weeks on the chart. The lyrics echo Stella Gibbons' novel *Cold Comfort Farm*, in which a character is said to have seen "something in the wood shed" as a child that scarred her for life. The song was inspired by the '95 BBC adaptation of the book, starring a young Kate Beckinsale.

The single was released on CD, cassette and 7" vinyl and featured B-sides 'Birds Of Paradise Farm', 'Love Is Lighter than Air' and 'Songs of Love (Theme from Father Ted)'.

Song 2 (single - Blur)

Charted: Apr '97; UK Chart Position: 2; Label: Food; Album: *Blur*

Blur's second single from their eponymous '97 album was so named because of its positioning on the album. It somewhat aptly reached number two in the UK chart when released in April '97, begging the question: should the band have made it first on the album?

It's also famous for being the song that brought Blur to the attention of the wider world, with its distinctive "woo-hoos" and fuzz bass line fast becoming a staple of indie club nights the world over.

The single was released on two CDs; CD1 featuring B-sides 'Get Out Of Cities' and 'Polished Stone', and CD2 'Bustin' + Dronin'' and 'Country Sad Ballad Man (Live Acoustic Version)'.

Songs from Northern Britain (album – Teenage Fanclub)

Charted: Aug '97; UK Chart Position: 3; Label: Creation; Singles: 'Ain't That Enough' (Jul '97, UKCP 17), 'I Don't Want Control of You' (Aug '97, 43), 'Start Again' (Nov '97, 54)

Creation Records' band Teenage Fanclub's sixth studio album, *Songs From Northern Britain*, was their highest charting album, peaking at number three in the UK when it was released in August '97.

It spent a total of six weeks on the chart and resulted in three singles: 'Ain't That Enough', 'I Don't Want Control of You' and 'Start Again'.

Spurred on by the success of the band's highest charting single 'Ain't That Enough', which reached number 17 in July '97, the album continues the flow of gentle uplifting melodies and carefully layered harmonies accompanied by jangly indie-style guitars. It remains the band's most commercially accessible album.

Space (band)

One of the more notable success stories to emerge from Paul McCartney's Liverpool Institute for the Performing Arts, Space were a home-grown experimental guitar and keyboard-based indie-rock band. They released two successful albums during the Britpop years and had eight top-40 singles.

The band was formed in '93 by Tommy Scott (vocals/ bass), Jamie Murphy (guitars) and Andy Parle (drums), but it was only when keyboardist Franny Griffiths joined later that same year did that their inimitable sound really started to emerge. They signed with Gut Records not long afterwards and released their first single, 'Money/ Kill-Me', in '95, although it failed to chart. 'Neighbourhood' appeared in April '96, peaking at number 54 (it would later be re-released and reach number 11 in November '96). Their chart success break came when 'Female of the Species' was picked up by the radio and played pretty much non-stop so that it went straight in at number 14. Debut album *Spiders* was released in September '96, peaking at number five in the UK chart.

While many other Britpop bands favoured a retro, back-to-basics approach, Space were a rare exception, combining radio-friendly melodies with an experimental keyboard-led approach, which often included unexpected instruments like a quirky glockenspiel on 'Female of the Species' or layered samples on 'Neighbourhood'.

A tour of the US in '97 was fraught with anguish, leading to the departure of drummer Parle and Scott losing his voice for two months. The band regrouped though, and second album *Tin Planet* appeared in March '98, peaking at number three and spending 27 weeks on the chart. This success was mainly due to the key singles, January '98's 'Avenging Angels' and the band's highest charting single – number four in March '98 – 'The Ballad of Tom Jones', featuring Catatonia's Cerys Matthews on vocals.

Their third album was not released due to difficulties with their label, but the band soldiered on, recording and self-releasing three more albums through their website. The key line-up reformed in '11 to play a one-off gig in Liverpool. The led to them recording new material, releasing their fifth album *Attack of the Mutant 50ft Kebab* in March '14. Another album, *Give Me Your Future*, is set for release in '17.

Speedy (band)

Formed from the ashes of previous band Blammo!, Speedy were a low-level five-piece indie band comprised of Philip Watson (vocals), Bronwen Stone (drums), Moony Wainwright (bass), Paul Turner (keyboards) and Richard Sutcliffe (guitar). The band signed to the Boiler House! label in '94 after a string of successful gigs, and their first single, 'Boy Wonder', was released in November '96, when it reached number 56 in the UK chart.

Two further singles were released in '97, February's 'Anytime Anyplace Nowhere' and June's 'Time for You', both of which reached the lower end of the top ten. Although the band recorded a debut album, the record company didn't release it and, perhaps not surprisingly, they parted ways with the label shortly afterwards.

Following a key lyrical direction of Britpop, Speedy's lyrics focused on issues that affected the young working class in the mid-nineties, including tales of life on the dole, promiscuity, drunken nights out and anything and everything else that the youth of the day were experiencing.

Spiders (album – Space)

Charted: Sept '96; UK Chart Position: 5; Label: Gut; Singles: 'Female of the Species' (Jun '96, UKCP 14), 'Me and You Versus the World' (Sept '96, 9), 'Neighbourhood' (Nov '96, 11), 'Dark Clouds' (Feb '97, 14)

Space's debut album *Spiders* was an incredibly accomplished and ambitious long-form release. Combining melodic indie-pop with quirky lyrical subject matter and keyboard-led, sample-heavy music gave the band their own individual space (pun very much intended) in the music scene of the mid-nineties. The album chimed immediately with audiences, peaking at number five in the UK chart in its first week of release.

Listeners were familiar with lead single 'Female of the Species', which had been a hit in June of the same year and signalled the sound of the rest of the album, and the radio-friendly Bonnie and Clyde-style adventure story that was the follow-up, 'Me and you Versus the World', which was the band's first top ten single in September '96. They proved themselves deft at penning more than one type of song though, as final single 'Dark Clouds' found them at their most introspective. The album helped to put Space on the map, and everyone was keen to see exactly what they would do next.

Spiritualized (band)

Representing the darker side of the Britpop sound, Spiritualized are an atmospheric indie-rock band led by Jason Pierce, the only constant member of the band over their 25-year history. Formed by Pierce after the demise of shoegazing band Spaceman 3, Spiritualized officially began in '90 but didn't release their first album *Lazer Guided Melodies* until April '92, when it reached 27 in the UK chart.

Focusing on the creation of soundscapes rather than typical pop songs, the band could easily have been considered part of the shoegazing movement, were it not for the use of orchestras and backing choirs, which created something more epic in ambition. This also led the band to focus on carefully created albums that often took several years to record rather than shorter pop singles. Their magnum opus coincided with the Britpop years, bringing the band in sync with the scene. *Ladies and Gentlemen we are Floating in Space* peaked at number four when it was released in June '97 and spent a total of 24 weeks on the chart.

Post-Britpop, the band have continued to record and produce the same atmospheric space rock and have so far released seven studio albums, most recently *Sweet Heart Sweet Light*, which reached number 12 in the UK chart in '12. Pierce continues to helm the band that he founded to this day.

Split (album – Lush)

Charted: Jun '94; UK Chart Position: 19; Label: 4AD; Singles: 'Hypocrite' (Jun '94, UKCP 52), 'Desire Lines' (Jun '94, 63)

Female-fronted Britpop outfit Lush's second album, *Split*, appeared mid-career for the band who eventually found their creative feet with album number three. Despite the two singles only reaching the bottom half of the UK chart top ten, the album still reached the top 20, peaking at number 19 in June '94.

The album was a noted departure for a band previously linked to the shoegazing scene, focusing instead on a slower, more melancholic sound, which later transformed into a faster-paced grrl-rock vibe. Of the 12 tracks, four were attributed to vocalist/guitarist Miki Berenyi, while her songwriting partner, Emma Anderson, took credit for the other eight tracks.

Squire, John (guitarist/songwriter/artist – The Stone Roses/The Seahorses/solo artist)

Born in Broadheath in Cheshire on 24 November '62, John Thomas Squire is today considered one of the greatest British guitarists of all time and, alongside Paul Weller, is one of the key spiritual leaders of the Britpop movement, influencing, among many others, Oasis. He is also an incredibly accomplished fine artist, designing the Jackson Pollock-esque covers to the early Stone Roses' singles and holding solo art shows the world over.

Squire met Ian Brown at junior school and, after they both dropped out of secondary school, they formed a songwriting partnership that eventually became the Stone Roses. He had a few lessons, but Squire was predominantly self-taught on the guitar, taking much of his early influence from fellow Mancunian Johnny Marr, who was enjoying much success with The Smiths when Squire was learning to play. The Stone Roses quickly found an audience, with Squire's jangly guitar lines at the heart of the band's sound.

As their success grew, so did Squire's musical ability and, before long, his guitar fluidity and prowess was far outstripping the technical accomplishments of many of his contemporaries. It took the Stone Roses five years to record *The Second Coming*, but their absence from the chart did not mean that their creativity was stemmed. In fact, Squire used the time to develop and express his own growing musicality, resulting in an album filled with carefully layered interlocking guitar lines that showcase his ability.

The fractiousness of the Stone Roses and their frequent legal battles led to their much-publicised break-up in '96, when Squire left the outfit he had begun. He immediately regrouped and formed The Seahorses, who enjoyed two years of chart success before disbanding in '98. By this time the music scene was too much for Squire and he retreated to the world of fine art.

He created a piece of art in '07 that declared there would never be a reunion of "the seminal Manchester band the Stone Roses", but, after releasing two solo albums, Squire eventually made up with Brown when they met again at the funeral of bassist Mani's mother. The band reformed in '11, heading out on a European tour and putting on a mammoth show at Heaton Park in Manchester. The band continue to play together and have so far released two singles, 'All for One' and 'Beautiful Thing', in '16.

Underlining his importance even further, Squire joined Oasis on stage at the legendary Knebworth gig to play guitar on 'Champagne Supernova' and 'I am The Walrus'.

Stand by Me (single – Oasis)

Charted: Oct '97; UK Chart Position: 2; Label: Creation; Album: *Be Here Now*

'Stand by Me' was the second single from Oasis' third album *Be Here Now*. It narrowly missed out on the number one spot due to the reissue of Elton John's 'Candle in the Wind', released in tribute to Princess Diana.

The single spent 22 weeks on the chart and featured exclusive

B-sides '(I Got) The Fever', 'My Sister Lover' and 'Going Nowhere', penned by Noel Gallagher when his train broke down on the way to London to sign a record deal with Creation. It also appeared on the band's '98 B-sides album *The Masterplan*, and remains one of Noel's favourite compositions.

Though rarely played live, an acoustic version of the lead track featured on a BBC documentary aired the night before the release of *Be Here Now*, with Liam, Noel and drummer Alan White sitting by the side of a pool.

Stanley Road (album – Paul Weller)

Charted: May '95; UK Chart Position: 1; Label: Go Discs/ Island; Singles: 'Out of the Sinking' (Nov '94, UKCP 16), 'The Changing Man' (May '95, 7), 'You do Something to Me' (Jul '95, 9), 'Broken Stones' (Sept '95, 20)

Weller's key Britpop album was also the most successful of his solo career, reaching the top spot in the UK chart in May '95. Released just as Britpop was really taking hold of the nation, *Stanley Road* managed to epitomise the third phase of Weller's writing and performing career.

Building on the deeply introspective focus of previous album *Wild Wood*, the then 37-year-old Weller combined this inward focus with the radio-friendly sound of the Britpop movement to present an album of accessible pop songs tinged with the blues. The album was spearheaded by some of his most well-known and well-loved solo songs, including his highest charting single 'The Changing Man' and the thoughtful love song 'You do Something to Me'.

Stardust (single – Menswear)

Charted: Sept '95; UK Chart Position: 16; Label: Laurel; Album: *Nuisance*

Menswear's third single was their second to the reach the top 20 when it was released in September '95. It peaked at number 16 and spent three weeks on the chart.

The CD single featured B-sides 'Back in the Bar', 'Satellite' and a remix of 'Daydreamer-Dubdreamer'.

Stars (single – Dubstar)

Charted: Mar '96; UK Chart Position: 15; Label: Food; Album: *Disgraceful*

One of Dubstar's best-known singles, 'Stars' was originally released by Food Records as their debut single in July '95, when it reached number 40 in the UK chart. After the success of their debut album *Disgraceful* in October '95, the single was re-released and reached number 15 in March '96.

It was released on two CDs, the first featuring several remixes of the lead track and the second including 'Excuse Me Father', 'Starfish' and 'Bow Wow Now'.

Statuesque (single – Sleeper)

Charted: Oct '96; UK Chart Position: 17; Label: Indolent; Album: *The It Girl*

The fourth and final single released from Sleeper's second album *The It Girl* was also the band's fourth top-20 hit in a row. It featured on the soundtrack to *Trainspotting* (in the pub scene when Begbie knocks into a punter, spilling his beers).

The single was released on two CDs. CD1 featured B-sides 'She's a Sweetheart' and 'Spies', while CD2 featured 'Statuesque (The Boxed off Mix)', 'Other End of the Telescope' and 'Atomic (Wubble U Mix)'.

Stay Together (single – Suede)

Charted: Feb '94; UK Chart Position: 3; Label: Nude; Album: n/a

Suede's joint highest charting single managed to make it all the way to number three in the UK chart when it was released in February '94. It was the band's only non-album single.

It was available on 7" and limited edition 12" vinyl, and the CD format included B-sides 'The Living Dead', 'My Dark Star' and 'Stay Together (full length)'.

Staying Out for the Summer '95 (single – Dodgy)

Charted: Jun '95; UK Chart Position: 19; Label: A&M; Album: *Homegrown*

Dodgy's breakthrough single was also their first in a run of five to reach the top 20 of the UK chart, peaking at number 19 on its re-release in June '95. It had previously reached number 38 when released in October the previous year. The song, with its catchy riff reminiscent of The Byrds and its positive, fun-fuelled lyrics, caught the attention of radio DJs the country over and it was a mainstay on the airwaves, quickly positioning itself as the year's summer anthem.

The single was released on limited edition 7" and 12" vinyl. The CD release featured B-sides '(Your Love Keeps Lifting Me) Higher and Higher', 'Crossroads (Live)' and 'Melodies Haunt You (Live)'.

Step into My World (single – Hurricane #1)

Charted: Nov '97; UK Chart Position: 19; Label: Creation; Album: *Hurricane #1*

Hurricane #1's first single, 'Step into My World', originally reached number 29 when released in May '97. On its second release in November of the same year, it fared better, making it into the top 20 of the UK chart, peaking at number 19 a month after the band's eponymous debut album had just missed out on the top ten.

The song underlined band leader Andy Bell's intention with his new project, becoming the group's signature tune and showcasing their post-shoegazing soundscape with lengthy interlocking guitar lines and stargazing lyrics.

The single was released on cassette and CD and included B-sides 'Step into My World (full length version)', 'If You Think it's Easy' and 'Never Mind The Rain'.

Stereolab (band)

London band Stereolab, formed in '90 by couple Tim Gane and Laetitia Sadler, moved into the periphery of Britpop in '94 with the release of album *Mars Audiac Quintet*. They played together until '08.

It was this Britpop-influenced album that shifted the band's musical direction towards indie-pop. It was also the first of two top-20 Stereolab albums to enter the UK chart (followed by *Dots and Loops*), where it spent three weeks.

Recorded in the spring of '94 at Blackwing Studios, London, and mastered at Abbey Road, the album featured the singles 'Ping Pong', 'Wow' and 'Flutter'.

Stereophonics (band)

Influenced by seventies rockers AC/DC, Bad Company and Rod Stewart (whose vocal style is not dissimilar to that of lead singer Kelly Jones) rather than sixties groups, Welsh band Stereophonics were part of the tail end of the Britpop scene, much like their contemporaries Travis. The riff-heavy indie-rock of their first album *Word Gets Around*, combined with lead singer/guitarist Kelly Jones' ability to pen lyrics about the darker side of life in a small Welsh town, clearly evoked the Britpop spirit.

Formed by childhood friends Jones and drummer Stuart Cable in '86 when the former was just 12 years old, the band experienced many line-up and name changes before settling on the power trio format once bassist Richard Jones joined in '92. After playing a handful of gigs in their native Wales and, at the other end of the M4, in London, they found themselves in something of a bidding war when manager John Brand managed to get more than 30 record companies interested in signing them in late '95. They eventually signed to Richard Branson's newly-formed V2 label in May '96, and their first limited edition EP 'Looks like Chaplin' was released in November '96. A string of singles followed, including the band's first top-20 single, 'Traffic', in October '97, and their debut album went top ten when released in September that year, peaking at number six.

Other than the distorted guitar lines and catchy melodies, the band's chief strength lay in Jones's lyrics. An accomplished writer – the BBC was interested in his scriptwriting before the band took off – Jones used his own experiences of growing up in a small, working-class town in south Wales to tell stories of lost innocence: factory workers drinking away their weekends; the dynamics of working on a busy town market stall; and, most prominently, the recurring theme of young lives cut short by teenage suicide, as explored on lead single 'Local Boy in a Photograph', 'Not Up to Me' and album closer 'Billy Davis Daughter'. A Brit Award for 'Best Newcomer' followed in February '98, and the band found their success shifting up a gear just as the Britpop scene was coming to a close. Second album *Performance and Cocktails* went straight in at number one in the UK chart in March '99 and, following the example set by friends Oasis, the band played several big outdoor gigs, including to 50,000 fans at Morfa Stadium in Swansea later in '99. The band's next four albums all hit the top spot and, in March '05, they achieved their first and only number one single, 'Dakota'.

Cable left in '04 after a much-publicised falling out with the rest of the band. He sadly died in '10 after struggling with alcohol addiction. Javier Weyler took over his role in the band, but he also left in '13 and was replaced by Jamie Morrison. The band continue to play together and have released three further albums since '09, as well as a best of and live album. Their most recent album, *Scream Above the Sounds*, is due for release in November '17. They remain one of Wales' most successful rock groups.

Stereotypes (single – Blur)

Charted: Feb '96; UK Chart Position: 7; Label: Food; Album: *The Great Escape*

The third single released from Blur's fourth album *The Great Escape* was also the third to enter the top ten of the UK chart.

Continuing their stories of modern life, it looked at the goings-on behind the net curtains of suburban swingers, with Albarn's lyric announcing, "Wife swapping is your future, you know that it would suit ye!". The single reached number seven in February '96, and spent a total of nine weeks on the chart.

Unusually for Blur's singles, just one CD version was released, including B-sides 'The Man Who Left Himself', 'Tame' and 'Ludwig'.

Stephen Street (music producer)

Stephen Brian Street was born on 29 March '60 in Hackney, East London. He began his career playing bass in various punk bands before moving into production in the early eighties, initially working at Island Records' Fallout Shelter Studio. His first album as engineer was The Smiths' second album *Meat is Murder*, produced by the band's own Johnny Marr.

This began a long working relationship with the band that saw him engineer their next album *The Queen is Dead* and eventually produce their final album *Strangeways Here We Come*, which was released after the band had split up. Street maintained his relationship with Morrissey, and went on to produce the singer's first solo album *Viva Hate*, released in March '88. Street is given co-writing credits on many of Morrissey's solo songs, perhaps indicating that he took Marr's place as the musical lead.

Street first worked with Blur on their second single, the top-ten hit 'There's No Other Way', but he didn't produce the accompanying album. The band remembered him, however, and called on him to produce their next album, the key Britpop record *Modern Life is Rubbish*. Street then helmed *Parklife*, *The Great Escape* and the *Blur* album before taking a break from working with the band as they explored new musical areas. Street also worked with The Cranberries on their first two albums, the worldwide hits *Everybody Else Is Doing It, So Why Can't We?* and *No Need to Argue*.

In more recent years, Street also worked with Blur guitarist Graham Coxon on his third solo album (his first since leaving Blur in '03), the commercially tinged punk-pop crossover record *Happiness in Magazines*. He also worked with and helped to foster a string of young bands in the early noughties, all of whom were heavily influenced by the Britpop bands, including the Ordinary Boys, the Kaiser Chiefs and the Courteeners, and worked with Babyshambles on their second album, *Shotter's Nation*, as well as Pete Doherty's '09 solo album *Grace/Wastelands*, which featured Graham Coxon on guitar.

Street is clearly one of the key Britpop producers, immediately identified with a certain type of indie record leading all the way from The Smiths to the queue of young indie bands still craving his quintessentially British sound. He was, naturally, first choice to produce Blur's '15 comeback album *The Magic Whip*.

Stone Roses, The (band)

Favoured sons of their native Manchester, the Stone Roses are one of British music's most important guitar bands, forerunners to the Madchester indie-dance scene of the early nineties and spiritual leaders of the Britpop movement.

They rose fom the ashes of various other local bands led by childhood friends Ian Brown (vocals) and John Squire (guitar) in a northern city made bleak by the enforced austerity imposed by Thatcher's government. The band originally toyed with a New Wave look before growing their hair long like the bands of the late sixties and mixing jangly guitars with the Northern Soul movement popular at the time.

They tried out several different iterations of a rhythm section before finally settling on Alan 'Reni' Wren on drums and, later, band fan Gary 'Mani' Mounfield on bass. They made an early name for themselves on the local scene by building a buzz, setting up one-off gigs at random locations like obscure abandoned warehouses, often not telling people where they were and not going on until the early hours of the morning.

The band recorded and released a few limited edition singles including 'So Young/Tell Me' before recording 'Elephant Stone', which was paid for by London-based Rough Trade Records in '88. The sound was an incredible development on their early releases and the band were signed by Silvertone not long afterwards. It was around this time that a 16-year-old Liam Gallagher saw them play live and decided to form his own band.

The Stone Roses' eponymous debut album was released in May '89 and eventually peaked at number 19 in the UK chart, where it spent 67 weeks and gained mainly positive reviews. It was around this time that word-of-mouth chatter about the band increased and their popularity began to grow. This was aided by their decision to play large one-off gigs rather than touring in the traditional way. The biggest was at Spike Island nature reserve in Widnes, which was attended by 27,000 people, some of whom went on to launch their own successful indie bands.

Musically, the band's sound was still evolving and *Fools Gold*, released in November '89, clearly showed their decision to take their sound in a more indie-dance direction, combining Squire's quirky guitar lines with drum loops and samples. 'One Love' was their highest charting single, reaching number four in July '90. Unfortunately, the band didn't build on this success by heading into the studio to record their next album straight away, falling out with their record label instead, which meant that they were prevented from releasing any new music for five years.

While the band were away the music scene changed and Britpop – itself heavily influenced by the Stone Roses – was taking hold of the nation. *The Second Coming* eventually reached record stores in December '94 and peaked at number four in the UK chart, signalling a new birth for the band. It wasn't to last, however, and Squire finally left the band in '96 to be replaced by Aziz Ibrahim (who would go on to produce Ian Brown's solo work). Reni also left and, after the band's final gig at Reading Festival in August '96, they officially split.

Each of the members went on to other projects, Squire founding The Seahorses and, later making two solo albums, Mani joining Primal Scream and Ian Brown enjoying a highly successful solo career.

Then, in October '11, the seemingly impossible happened: the band announced they were getting back together for a series of worldwide gigs, culminating in two huge outdoor concerts at Manchester's Heaton Park. Tickets sold out in 14 minutes, and the rehearsal and subsequent tour were captured by British director Shane Meadows in his documentary *The Stone Roses: Made of Stone*. The band released two new singles in '16, 'All for One' and 'Beautiful Thing', and are still considered one of Britain's most influential guitar bands of all time.

Stoosh (album – Skunk Anansie)

Charted: Oct '96; UK Chart Position: 9; Label: One Little Indian; Singles: 'All I Want' (Sept '96, UKCP 14), 'Twisted (Everyday Hurts)' (Nov '96, 26), 'Hedonism (Just Because You Feel Good)' (Feb '97, 13), 'Brazen (Weep)' (Jun '97, 11)

Skunk Anansie's second album followed hard on the heels of their debut release, continuing to showcase their brand of intense, heavy, guitar-led indie-rock accompanied by political lyrics and personal stories about lost love penned by singer Skin.

Released in October '96, it was spurred on by hit single 'All I Want' to peak at number nine in the UK chart, one place lower than their previous album, although it remained on the chart for a massive 69 weeks. In all, four of the 11 tracks were released as singles, each making the top 20 in the UK chart.

The album was recorded in London and produced by veteran Canadian hard-rock producer Garth Richardson. It was well received by the music industry and cemented the band as key players on the UK music scene. It was their last record released in the Britpop years.

Strangelove (band)

Bristol band Strangelove released their debut album *Time for the Rest of Your Life* in August '94, sending their popularity immediately soaring. It quickly caught the attention of Suede, who invited the band to support them on their *Dog Man Star* tour, thus upping their Britpop exposure even further.

Formed in '91, Strangelove were frontman Patrick Duffy, who was spotted by drummer David Francolini while busking, guitarists Alex Lee and Julian Poole and bassist Joe Allen.

Being labelmates of Blur and Dubstar at Food Records and their close bond with Suede meant the band were destined for Britpop success. They quickly developed a strong following, despite their chart successes remaining moderate. Second album *Love and Other Demons* charted much higher than the first at number 44 and resulted in the top-40 single 'Beautiful Alone'.

The band released their self-titled third album in October '97, resulting in another top-40 single, 'The Greatest Show on Earth'. They split not long afterwards.

Stupid Girl (single – Garbage)

Charted: Mar '96; UK Chart Position: 4; Label: Mushroom; Album: *Garbage*

Garbage's breakthrough single 'Stupid Girl' was their first to reach the top ten, peaking at number four in the UK chart in March '96 and strongly supporting their debut album, which was released in October '95. It announced them as an intense, guitar-led, electro-tinged, female-fronted band; new contenders on the scene.

The single was released on CD and included B-sides 'Stupid Girl (Tee's Radio Edit)' and 'Driving Lesson'. The video featured Shirley Mansun brooding in a sixties-inspired outfit and was nominated for 'Best New Artist in a Video' at the '96 MTV Video Music Awards.

Stupid, Stupid, Stupid (album – Black Grape)

Charted: Nov '97; UK Chart Position: 11; Label: Radioactive; Singles: 'Get Higher' (Nov '97, UKCP 24), 'Marbles' (Mar '98, 46)

Shaun Ryder's second band Black Grape's second album *Stupid, Stupid, Stupid* was released in November '97. Unlike its predecessor, it failed to reach the top spot, only getting to 11 in the UK chart.

The ten tracks are in a similar vein to the band's previous work and the album was produced by Danny Saber, who also worked on their previous release. As it didn't achieve the same success as their first album, the band decided to call it a day and moved on to other projects.

The album included single 'Get Higher', which made the top 30, and 'Marbles', which reached number 46 in March '98.

Suede (band)

One of Britpop's big five bands, London's Suede are also one of modern British music's most significant and well-loved bands. Considered co-founders of the Britpop scene, they released their first single, 'The Drowners', in May '92 just a month after Blur's 'Popscene' signalled the beginning of a new movement.

The first line-up appeared in '89, when singer Brett Anderson, his then girlfriend Justine Frischmann (who played guitar) and childhood friend Mat Osman on bass got together while they were all studying at University College London. Nineteen-year-old Bernard Butler answered an advert in the 'musicians wanted' pages of *Melody Maker* and the band started gigging around Camden not long afterwards, accompanied by a drum machine.

Comedian Ricky Gervais, who worked at UCL's students' union, was their manager and, after they signed to indie label RML, he signed up Simon Gilbert on drums. To the surprise of the band themselves, Mike Joyce, formerly of The Smiths, played drums for a few weeks after answering an advert. He soon left, however, fearing they would not be able to find their own identity while playing with a member of the band that was their biggest influence.

Frischmann left when she and Anderson split, and the new four-piece signed to indie label Nude Records in early '92. The band didn't fit into the grunge-heavy scene dominant at the time, making it tough for them to find their place. Consequently, their first single, 'The

Drowners' reached number 49 in the UK chart in May '92.

Many didn't know how to deal with a band who were influenced by both the anarchism of punk and the sexual androgyny of David Bowie but, as Anderson and Butler's songwriting partnership strengthened, their next release, 'Metal Mickey', went to number 17 in September '92. It also earned them the music press moniker of 'best new band in Britain'.

After the *NME*-sponsored campaign to get the band to play the Brit Awards in February '93, their next single, 'Animal Nitrate', went all the way to number seven in the UK chart. The subsequent eponymous album went straight in at number one in April '93 and went on to win the Mercury Music prize in September, confirming them as one of the biggest new groups in the country. Suede had arrived.

The creative relationship at the heart of the band was a fraught one, with Anderson's extrovert qualities opposite in almost every way to Butler's careful introspection, leading to spiralling arguing and Butler's eventual departure before the release of second album *Dog Man Star* in October '94. The band carried on, replacing Butler with 17-year-old Richard Oakes and adding Gilbert's cousin Neil Codling on keyboards.

The band enjoyed their most commercially successful time from '96–'97, with the release of their third album, the radio-friendly, hit-machine *Coming Up*, which peaked at number one in the UK chart, where it spent 59 weeks. Frischmann even joined the band at some of their bigger gigs in '97, singing on the early songs.

The band continued to record and release music after Britpop, but their success waned, although fourth album *Head Music* hit the top spot in '99. The band split in '03 after the commercial disappointment of fifth album *A New Morning*, which failed to reach the top 20. Unlike fellow Britpop founders Blur, they failed to move with the changing times and their music remained too rooted in the Britpop sound to gel with modern audiences.

Anderson and Butler eventually made up and have played music together as The Tears but, when Suede reformed in '10, it was with Oakes playing guitar. The band continue to play together and, together with various best of collections, they have released two further studio albums: '13's *Bloodsports* (which made number ten) and '16's *Night Thoughts* (number six).

Suede (album – Suede)

Charted: Mar '93; UK Chart Position: 1; Label: Nude; Singles: 'The Drowners/To the Birds' (May '92, UKCP 49), 'Metal Mickey' (Sept '92, 17), 'Animal Nitrate' (Mar '93, 7), 'So Young' (May '93, 22)

Suede's eponymous debut album is one of Britpop's defining records and helped launch the band and the scene into the mainstream. Unlike Blur's *Modern Life is Rubbish*, *Suede* was not misunderstood by the press or the fans, and its blend of Smiths-inspired lyrics and Bowie-infused vocals helped it become the fasting-selling album for ten years. It went straight to the top spot in March '93, two months before *Modern Life is Rubbish* was released.

At the core of the album lies the songwriting power of guitarist Bernard Butler and singer Brett Anderson. Together they managed to meld slick and instantly memorable guitar lines, melancholic melodies and dark, troubled lyrics. Anderson explored his public image in his lyrics, notably on lead single 'Animal Nitrate', which references a sexual stimulant, to talk about promiscuity and recreational drugs, both undoubtedly popular with bands at the time but rarely sung about. It was this illicit content that so excited fans, while at the same time creating a carefully constructed image.

The album was recorded at Master Rock Studios in London and produced by Ed Buller who, unlike contemporary Stephen Street, brought a sparseness to the sound that laid bare both the band and their music. The record chimed with fans and critics alike and it went on to win the Mercury Music Prize for British Album of the Year in '93.

Sugar Coated Iceberg (single – Lightning Seeds)

Charted: Jan '97; UK Chart Position: 12; Label: Epic; Album: *Dizzy Heights*

The second single released from the Lightning Seeds' fifth and highest charting album, the aptly-named *Dizzy Heights*, 'Sugar Coated Iceberg' reached number 12 in the UK chart in January '97.

The single was released on two CDs. CD1 featured B-sides 'This Power', 'S.F. Sorrow Is Born' and 'Porpoise Song', while CD2 featured 'Why Why Why (Group Version '97)' and 'Telling Tales (Group Version '97)'.

Sun Hits the Sky (single – Supergrass)

Charted: Jun '97; UK Chart Position: 10; Label: Parlophone; Album: *In it for the Money*

The second single from Supergrass' second album *In it for the Money*, 'Sun Hits the Sky' replaced the band's squeaky clean pop image with a more raucous guitar-driven one. It reached number ten in the UK chart in June '97, where it spent four weeks.

The single was released on CD and included B-sides 'Some Girls Are Bigger Than Others' and 'Sun Hits the Sky (Radio 1 *Evening Session*)'.

Sunday Sunday (single – Blur)

Charted: Oct '93; UK Chart Position: 26; Label: Food; Album: *Modern Life Is Rubbish*

The third and final single from Blur's second album *Modern Life is Rubbish*, 'Sunday Sunday' continued the band's new style of penning tracks about life in contemporary Britain, this time telling the story of a simple Sunday afternoon and its various quaint activities. It peaked at number 26 in the UK chart when released in October '93.

The single was released on 7" and 12" vinyl, and the CD release included B-sides 'Long Legged' and 'Mixed Up'.

Super Furry Animals (band)

When Alan McGee signed the Super Furry Animals in '95, he thought they were singing in Welsh. They were singing in English, but it's easy to see how he could have been confused. The band were formed in Cardiff in '93, their first language is Welsh and many of their early recordings were in Welsh. They soon realised, however, that they needed to at least accommodate English if they wanted to make a mainstream impact. McGee, who later claimed the group were the last great Creation Records band, signed them after seeing them play at the Monarch in Camden in '95, only their second gig outside Wales.

Formed from the ashes of several techno and indie bands, the line-up has always been Gruff Rhys (lead vocals, guitar), Huw Bunford (lead guitar, vocals), Guto Pryce (bass guitar), Cian Ciaran (keyboards, synthesisers) and Dafydd Ieuan (drums, vocals). Actor Rhys Ifans was once a part-time member.

The incredibly inventive band first found fame via their relatively straightforward pop-indie crossover debut album *Fuzzy Logic*, which was filled with idiosyncratic two and three-minute bubblegum pop songs with indecipherable lyrics, catchy choruses, distorted guitars and 'boo-woop' backing vocals. It reached number 23 in the UK chart in June '96 and set in motion a career spanning nine top 30 albums and 21 singles.

Incidentally, the band has the dubious honour of releasing the song with the largest number of uses of a swear word in December '96's 'The Man Don't Give a Fuck'. That same year, they also bought a former military tank from the American band the Eagles and converted it into a moving techno DJ desk, driving it around the summer music festivals and refusing to turn the music off.

With their second album, *Radiator*, the band's sound began to develop into the psychedelic-indie-techno they became known for. The album contains some of the band's best-loved songs, including 'The International Language of Screaming', 'Play it Cool' and 'Hermann Loves Pauline'.

Despite being signed to one of the key Britpop record labels, the Super Furries managed to distance themselves from the scene, and so found that their critical and commercial success didn't diminish when Britpop came to an end in '98. In fact, their next three albums, released between '99 and '03, are regarded as some of their best. The band carved out their own niche and guaranteed future success by fusing experimental techno with dance music and traditional pop songs, influenced predominantly by the Beach Boys and ELO.

Alongside the Manic Street Preachers, Catatonia and, later, the Stereophonics, they are key members of the renaissance of Welsh music that came in the late nineties. Their song 'Bad Behaviour' was played over the credits of cult '97 Welsh film *Twin Town*, starring a young Rhys Ifans. The band went on an extended hiatus between '10 and '14, during which lead singer Gruff Rhys released several solo albums, but re-formed to play again in late '14. A new single, 'Bing Bong', was released in May '16, and the band have played both their albums, *Fuzzy Logic* and *Radiator*, live in full. So far, however, no new album has been announced.

Supergrass (band)

Formed from the ashes of The Jennifers, who released one single on Nude Records in the early nineties, Supergrass were an indie-rock band from Oxford. They were formed in '93 by singer Gaz Coombes, drummer Danny Goffey and bassist Mick Quinn. Gaz's older brother Rob played keyboards for the band throughout their career, but decided to remain in the background until officially joining in '02. Coombes Snr was actually responsible for some of the band's most identifiable riffs, including the piano intro to mega-hit 'Alright'.

After early championing from legendary Radio 1 DJ John Peel, the band signed to Parlophone Records in '94 and put out their first single 'Caught by the Fuzz' in October '94, when it reached number 43 in the UK chart. 'Mansize Rooster' reached number 20 in February '95, and the band's debut album *I Should Coco* was released in May '95, hitting the top spot.

The band were on a roll and their next single, 'Alright', became the feelgood hit of the summer, superglued to the radio and making it all the way to number two in the UK chart, where it spent ten weeks.

Fully aware that their success had come from writing the kind of catchy bubblegum pop not seen in the indie scene since the sixties, the band wanted to reinvent themselves as serious scene contenders without alienating their existing fan base. Their second album managed to do just that; the guitars became more distorted and dominant, the subject matter became darker and more serious and the band's success was assured. *In it for the Money*, aptly represented by the hit single 'Richard III', peaked at number two in the UK chart in May '97, held from the top spot by The Charlatans' *Tellin' Stories*.

It was nearly two years before the band released any new material and, like so many of their contemporaries, when they finally did the scene had changed around them. 'Pumpin' on the Stereo', a return to the tongue-in-cheek quirkiness of their debut album, was the first single released from third album *Supergrass*. It peaked at number 11 in June '99 and the subsequent album reached number three in October '99.

The band continued to play and record together in the post-Britpop years, and their subsequent three albums all made the top 20. In '10, having recently signed to new label Cooking Vinyl, the band split citing musical differences during the recording of what would have been their seventh studio album. The record remains unreleased.

Supernaturals, The (band)

Attempting to ape the success they found with Supergrass, Parlophone signed the quirky, happy-go-lucky Glasgow band The Supernaturals in May '96, releasing their debut album *It Doesn't Matter Anymore* to critical and commercial success in May '97, when it reached number nine in the UK chart. The line-up consisted of singer/ guitarist James McColl, lead guitarist Derek McManus, bassist Mark Guthrie, drummer Gavin Crawford and keyboardist Ken McAlpine.

Known predominantly for their catchy single 'Smile', which missed out on the Ivor Novello Award for songwriting in '98 to The Verve's 'The Drugs Don't Work', as well as a run of top-40 singles that included 'Lazy Lover', 'The Day Before Yesterday's Man' and 'Prepare to Land', the band didn't quite match the commercial success of their contemporaries, but managed to release three albums and eight singles during a career that spanned five years. Then, in '12, the orginal founding members re-formed to release new album *360* in April '15.

Supersonic (single – Oasis)

Charted: Apr '94; UK Chart Position: 31; Label: Creation; Album: *Definitely Maybe*

Oasis' debut single 'Supersonic' was released in early '94, several months before their debut album *Definitely Maybe*, when the nation hadn't quite figured out who the soon-to-be Kings of Britpop were. The release was their lowest charting single, peaking at number 31 in the UK chart, where it spent a total of 60 weeks.

The B-sides included acoustic number 'Take Me Away', featuring Noel Gallagher on his first lead vocal, 'I Will Believe' and a demo version of album track 'Columbia'. The band made their debut TV performance playing the single live on *The Word*, followed by appearances on *Jools Holland* and *MTV Most Wanted*.

Sussed (band)

Cheshire band Sussed formed in Northwich in the mid-nineties and were best known for the single 'One in a Million', which was released in late '96 and featured on indie compilation *Shine 6*. The single was released on two CDs, the first featuring the tracks 'I Know' and

'Heaven Scent', and the second 'Promises' and 'LA Nites'.

Signed to The Charlatans' Dead Dead Good label and managed by Stephen Harrison, the band recorded one album, *All Hail the Young Assassins*, and released a few singles, of which 'One in a Million' and 'Time's Up' made the UK top ten in October '96 and May '97 respectively. The latter featured brass by the Kick Horns.

The band were short-lived and lead singer Richard Nancollis went on to form the Rain Band in '00.

Sweet Lips (single – Monaco)

Charted: May '97; UK Chart Position: 18; Label: Polydor; Album: *Music for Pleasure*

The second of three singles by Peter Hook's side project Monaco, 'Sweet Lips' was on the band's debut album *Music for Pleasure*. It reached number 18 in the UK chart in May '97, spending four weeks on the chart.

The single was released on two CDs. CD1 included B-sides 'Sweet Lips (Joey Negro Main Slice)', 'Sweet Lips (Farley & Heller's Ambient Mix)' and 'Sweet Lips (Instrumental)', while CD2 featured 'Shattered', 'Sweet Lips (Fire Island Vocal)' and 'Sweet Lips (Tony De Vit Trade Mix)'.

Symposium (band)

Formed in London's Shepherd's Bush in '94 while the band were still at school, Symposium (taking their name from an Ancient Greek drinking party) were made up of: Ross Cummins (vocals), Hagop Tchaparian (guitar), Joe Birch (drums), William McGonagle (guitar) and Wojtek Godzisz (bass).

Famed for their live gigs, the band found little difficulty in getting a record deal, signing to Infectious Records – home to Ash – in '95. Their debut single, 'Drink the Sunshine', made it into the top 100, peaking at number 89 in November '96, but it was the catchy single 'Farewell to Twilight' that launched the band into the top 30 of the UK chart in March '97. The band's debut mini-album, *One Day at a Time*, reached number 29 in November '97.

Less an indie band and more a pop-punk outfit influenced by American bands like Greenday and Weezer, their sound developed over the few years they were together, focusing on the more intense harder rock sound that made up debut album proper *On the Outside*, which reached number 32 in May '98.

The band split not long after the release of final single 'Killing Position' in '99, citing musical differences. Several members went on to form Hell is for Heroes, and chief songwriter Godzisz is still penning songs for various artists.

T

Tattva (single – Kula Shaker)

Charted: Jul '96; UK Chart Position: 4; Label: Columbia; Album: *K*

Kula Shaker's 'Tattva' was the second of four singles from their debut album *K*, and the first of five top-ten singles released by the band over their career. It spent eight weeks on the UK chart and peaked at number 4. Tattva is a Hindu concept meaning 'thatness' and the song featured lyrics written in Sanskrit, setting in motion the band's Indian-inspired theme.

The single was available on two CDs, with CD1 featuring B-sides 'Dance In Your Shadow', 'Moonshine' and the Lucky 13 mix of the title track, and CD2 opening with the mix 'Tattva On St George's Day' followed by 'Moonshine' and 'Red Balloon (Vishnu's Eyes)'.

Taxloss (single – Mansun)

Charted: May '97; UK Chart Position: 15; Label: Parlophone; Album: *Attack of the Grey Lantern*

'Taxloss' was the final single from Mansun's debut album *Attack of the Grey Lantern*, and the band's fourth to reach the top 20 of the UK chart, where it spent four weeks, peaking at number 15.

In the video, director Roman Coppola threw £25,000 of five pound notes over an unsuspecting crowd at London's busy Liverpool Street Station. The ensuing mayhem aptly showcased the song's themes of corruption and the all-powerful force of money on modern society.

The single was released on two CDs. CD1 featured exclusive track 'Grey Lantern' and a Lisa Marie Experience Remix of the title track, while CD2 included 'The Impending Collapse of it All', a live version of 'Ski Jump Nose' and an acoustic version of the album's 'Wide Open Space'.

Teenage Fanclub (band)

Glaswegian band Teenage Fanclub came to prominence in the Britpop era after the release of their fifth album *Grand Prix* in '95, followed by *Songs from Northern Britain* in '97. Both albums achieved top-ten positions in the UK chart, the latter resulting in their biggest single, 'Ain't That Enough'. Formed in '89 and signed to Creation Records by Alan McGee in '90, the band's jangly guitars and layered harmonies were reminiscent of sixties American bands like The Byrds and Crosby, Stills and Nash.

The line-up consisted of Norman Blake on vocals and guitar, Raymond McGinley on vocals and lead guitar, bassist Gerard Love and drummer Francis MacDonald. Though their time at Creation was the band's most commercially successful, they went on to record several more albums after the demise of the label as well as pursuing personal projects.

In total, the band have released 19 singles and 11 albums that have reached the top ten of the UK chart. Their most recent release, *Here*, reached number ten in the UK chart in '16.

Tellin' Stories (album – The Charlatans)

Charted: May '97; UK Chart Position: 1; Label: Beggars Banquet; Singles: 'One to Another' (Sept '96, UKCP 3), 'North Country Boy' (Apr '97, 4), 'How High' (Jun '97, 6), 'Tellin' Stories' (Nov '97, 16)

Tellin' Stories was The Charlatans' fifth studio album, and the band's third to reach the top spot of the UK chart, after their debut *Some Friendly* and their self-titled '95 LP. Spending a total of 40 weeks on the chart, with two weeks at number one, it became their most successful album and resulted in three top-ten singles: 'One to Another', 'North Country Boy' and 'How High'. The title would also eventually be used by lead singer Tim Burgess for his autobiography, the more formally titled *Telling Stories*.

The album marked a notable development in musical style for the Madchester band, a development begun with their previous LP. They proved they were malleable enough to update their sound to fit with the changing times while remaining true to their original ethos. Understandably, the tragic death of their keyboardist Rob Collins two years earlier had meant the band's trademark Hammond organ was stripped back in favour of a more guitar-led sound, courtesy of Rob's brother Mark.

Rob Collins did feature on the album though, and Primal Scream's Duffy filled in where needed, including playing live, notably at the Oasis Knebworth gig three months after the release of the album. Fittingly, the final track on the album was called 'Rob's Theme'.

In '13, the band released the DVD *Mountain Picnic Blues*, a documentary on the making of the album.

Tellin' Stories (single – The Charlatans)

Charted: Nov '97; UK Chart Position: 16; Label: Beggars Banquet; Album: *Tellin' Stories*

'Tellin' Stories' was the fourth and final single from The Charlatans' fifth album of the same name. It spent three weeks on the UK chart, peaking at number 16.

The cover of the single used the infamous naked portrait of Christine Keeler, the former call-girl who caused a scandal in the sixties when, at the height of the Cold War, she slept with both British and Russian government officials. The photo was taken by Lewis Morley and, in '89, the affair was turned into a film, *Scandal*, starring Joanne Whalley, Sir John Hurt and Sir Ian McKellen.

The CD single featured B-sides 'Keep It to Yourself', 'Clean Up Kid' and a live version of 'Thank You' taken from their Phoenix Festival performance in July '97 (the original featured on their previous self-titled album).

Ten Storey Love Song (single - The Stone Roses)

Charted: Mar '95; UK Chart Position: 11; Label: Geffen; Album: *The Second Coming*

'Ten Storey Love Song' was the second of three singles from the Stone Roses' highly anticipated second album *The Second Coming*.

Written by lead guitarist John Squire, the single spent six weeks on the UK chart and peaked at number 11, becoming the band's seventh top-20 release to date. It featured exclusive tracks 'Moses' and 'Ride On', with cover artwork by John Squire.

Terrorvision (band)

More likely to feature in the pages of *Kerrang* than *Melody Maker* or the *NME*, Terrorvision were more of a rock band than a Britpop band, and so are only tenuously linked to the scene by association and timing. This puts them in the company of other acts like Skunk Anansie and Reef, representing the harder rock edge of the Britpop world.

Hailing from the Yorkshire city of Bradford, the band originally formed in '87, changing their name to Terrorvision in '91. It was around this time that they signed to the major label EMI, although all their recordings were put out on their own label Total Vegas. The key line-up was Tony Wright (vocals), Mark Yates (guitars), Leigh Marklew (bass) and David Ian 'Shutty' Shuttleworth (drums).

Their first album *Formaldehyde* was released in May '93 and made it to number 75 in the UK chart. After the success of the catchy pop-rock single 'Oblivion' in April '94, when it reached number 21, their second album *How to Make Friends and Influence People* cracked the top 20, peaking at number 18 in April '94. This began a run of chart success for the band, peaking with the release of the remixed version of their song 'Tequila' in January '99, which was kept from the top spot by Offspring's mega hit 'Pretty Fly (for a White Guy)'. Despite this success, the band were dropped by EMI and split in '01 after their fifth album *Good to Go* reached number 48 in the charts.

The band's fan base was loyal though, and they re-formed in '05 for several UK tours, continuing to play through various changes in membership. They toured again in '16, supporting rock band Thunder.

TFI Friday (TV show)

Presented by Chris Evans, Channel 4's entertainment show *TFI Friday* was one of the key platforms for Britpop bands in the nineties. With its early Friday night slot at 6pm followed by a later repeat, the show gathered a large following during its initial run from January '96 to December '00.

The first episode kicked off with Chris announcing the death of *Top of the Pops* then introducing Ocean Colour Scene, who played 'The Riverboat Song', which was then used throughout the series to introduce each guest. The show's main theme music was taken from the British sixties TV series *Man in a Suitcase*, composed by Ron Grainer, who also wrote the theme music for *Doctor Who*.

The show became renowned for its quirky features including 'Fat Lookalikes', which featured overweight guests with an uncanny resemblance to a thinner celebrity, and 'Freak or Unique', where guests would reveal their weird and wonderful party tricks.

Britpop highlights included Shed Seven's 'Going for Gold'; Blur's 'Stereotypes'; Jarvis Cocker's interview following his infamous '96 Brit Awards incident; Echobelly's 'Great Things'; Supergrass' 'Going Out'; Menswear's 'Being Brave'; Cast's 'Walk Away'; Suede's 'Beautiful Ones'; and the Noel Gallagher interview filmed at Chris Evans' house. Playing this show was a key stepping stone for any Britpop band, and almost always guaranteed chart success for whichever single they were promoting.

Chris Evans left the show after series five, leaving series six to be hosted by various guest presenters including the Spice Girls, Sara Cox and Davina McCall. The show returned with Chris Evans hosting for a 20th anniversary special in June '15, featuring Blur's 'Coffee & TV' and Liam Gallagher joining Roger Daltrey, Bonehead, Zak Starkey and Ian Broudie for a supergroup performance of 'My Generation'. The special was later followed by a ten-episode run of the series.

These Animal Men (band)

Brighton band These Animal Men were initially classed by the music press as part of the short-lived 'New Wave of New Wave' genre, a term coined by journalists to describe a sub-genre of nineties British rock influenced predominantly by the New Wave bands of the seventies and eighties such as Joy Division. The band's initial line-up was

Alexander Boag on vocals and guitar, Julian Hewings (aka Hooligan) on backing vocals and guitar, bassist Patrick Murray and drummer Stevie Hussey.

During their brief time together, the band released two albums, *(Come On, Join) The High Society* in '94 and *Taxi For These Animal Men* in '95. They resulted in several singles including debut 'Speed King', which controversially featured a plate of white powder and four rolled-up banknotes on the cover. Perhaps not surprisingly, the band were accused of glamorising drug use and were banned from playing a tour of school youth clubs.

The band often played live with S.M.A.S.H, also part of the NWONW scene, and both feature in *Flawed is Beautiful*, a documentary on the short-lived era. Post-Britpop, the band went on to pursue other musical projects including bands Mo Solid Gold and The Orphans.

This Life (TV series)

Complete with seasickness-inducing camera angles, gratuitous arse shots and more white wine than your average booze cruise, *This Life* was 'Britpop the television series'. The show centred on a Southwark house occupied by five 20-something lawyers and followed their misadventures as they shagged around, snorted drugs and drank enough wine to make the viewers pray they never found themselves represented by one of them in court.

Commissioned by British television production legend Tony Garnett (responsible for much of Ken Loach's early output) and heralded for its now much-copied gritty realism, the docu-drama style made the show feel almost like real life, especially in its unprecedented depiction of gay sex and recreational drug use. The characters were never villainised or victimised for their antics; instead the show depicted life as it was with all its uncontrollable ups and downs and controllable right and wrong choices. The audience was never patronised, but rather left to make up their own minds about the morality of the situations at hand. In other words, this was a house we all wanted to live in, if we didn't already.

Running for just two seasons on BBC2 from '96 and '97 (and returning for a somewhat misjudged tenth anniversary episode in '07), the show launched the careers of Andrew Lincoln, Jack Davenport and Daniela Nardini, as well as giving a young Ricky Gervais one of his early television jobs as music supervisor. The realism didn't allow for non-diegetic music, so Ricky had to pick the best Britpop tracks of the day for the characters to listen to on their stereos and radios while sitting around in their converted Victorian terraced house or in their offices happily puffing away on Silk Cut cigarettes. A bit like having your song played in Kath's caff in *Eastenders*, Britpop bands knew they had made it if Egg, Millie, Miles, Anna and Warren tuned in to their song during their daily grind.

This World and Body (album – Marion)

Charted: Feb '96; UK Chart Position: 10; Label: London; Singles: 'Toys and Boys (May '95, UKCP 57), 'Let's All Go Together' (Oct '95, 37), 'Time' (Feb '96, 29), 'Sleep' (Mar '96, 17)

Marion's debut album *This World and Body* was released on London Records in early '96, heading straight to number ten on the UK chart, where it spent a total of four weeks. The album resulted in the band's best-known top-20 single 'Sleep', plus 'Toys and Boys', 'Let's All Go Together' and 'Time', and gained the band a reputation as, according to *Q Magazine*, "stadium rock Gods in waiting – the new Joy Division".

The band promoted the album with a relentless period of gigging, touring with the likes of Echo & The Bunnymen, the Manic Street Preachers, Morrissey, Menswear and Radiohead as well as short tours of Japan and America and appearances at Glastonbury Festival.

Three EP (single – Mansun)

Charted: Sept '96; UK Chart Position: 19; Label: Parlophone; Album: *Attack of the Grey Lantern*

Before the release of debut album *Attack of the Grey Lantern*, Mansun released a string of EPs in '96, aptly named 'One', 'Two' and 'Three' EP. 'One' had the title track 'Egg Shaped Fred' (which also featured on their debut album); while 'Two' was led by 'Take it Easy Chicken' (not on the first album). They both charted in the top 40 in the UK.

Led by 'Stripper Vicar' (on the album), 'Three' was the band's first top-20 single. It spent three weeks on the chart, peaking at number 19. It also featured 'The Edge', 'The Duchess', 'An Open Letter to a Lyrical Trainspotter', 'No One Knows Us' and 'Things Keep Falling off Buildings'.

Three Lions (single – The Lightning Seeds ft. Baddiel and Skinner)

Charted: Jun '96; UK Chart Position: 1; Label: Epic; Album: n/a

"It's coming home, it's coming home, it's coming, football's coming home!"

'Three Lions' was England's official football anthem for Euro '96. Written by Ian Broudie, the song was a collaboration between the Lightning Seeds and comedians Frank Skinner and David Baddiel, who also appeared in the music video alongside many of the England Euro championship team.

The song gave the band their first number one in the UK chart, where it spent a whopping 39 weeks (two at the top spot), and featured an extended mix and karaoke version of the lead track as B-sides.

Chanted at football stadiums throughout the world, the single was re-released in the summer of '98 with new lyrics for the World Cup, when it again hit the number one spot in the UK, this time spending 17 weeks on the chart (three at number one).

Thurman (band)

Oxfordshire band Thurman were one of the many underrated bands of Britpop. The sheer number of bands the scene created meant that there was no way all of them could share the spotlight.

Similar in sound to Blur, the band were vocalist brothers Nicholas and Simon Kenny on guitar and bass respectively, with Paul Disley on drums. They released one album, *Lux*, which featured several lipsticks on the cover and resulted in singles 'English Tea', 'Talk to Myself', 'Famous' and 'She's a Man', the third of which charted in the top ten in the UK.

And that was pretty much it. The band were together from '94–'96 and, following their demise, the Kenny brothers went on to form the Four Storeys with new drummer Dan Goddard, formerly of The Nubiles. After releasing one album, the trio went on to form the Long Insiders with Sarah Dodd on vocals.

Tiger (band)

Formed in '96, Tiger released their first single in the same year on the independent label Fierce Panda (later home – briefly – to among others Embrace and Coldplay).

They went on to release several singles on the Trade 2 label, five of which reached the top ten of the UK chart. But it was only after they were invited to play on the notorious *NME* Brat Bus tour in '97 that their popularity and reputation for playing incendiary live shows took a marked rise.

The band were on the periphery of the Britpop scene, favouring keyboard samples over the straightforward guitar sound popular at the time. Hailing from London, the band's initial line-up was Dan Laidler and Julie Sims on vocals and guitar, keyboardists Tina Whitlow and Dido Hallett and drummer Seamus Feeney.

Their debut album *We Are the Puppets* resulted in the singles 'Race', 'My Puppet Pal' and 'On the Rose'. It failed to reach the top ten in the UK when released in November '96. 'Race' was the band's sole release to chart in the top 40. Second album *Rosaria*, released in '99 and produced by Stephen Street, failed to chart so the band split.

Tin Planet (album – Space)

Charted: Mar '98; UK Chart Position: 3; Label: GUT; Singles: 'Avenging Angels' (Jan '98, UKCP 6), 'The Ballad Of Tom Jones' (Mar '98, 4), 'Begin Again' (Jul '98, 21), 'The Bad Days EP' (Dec '98, 20)

Tin Planet was the second album from Space and the band's highest charting release, spending 27 weeks on the UK chart and peaking at number three. It was kept from the top spot by Madonna's *Ray of Light* album and the official soundtrack to the film *Titanic*. Stylistically, the album was not a huge leap forward for the band, whose debut showcased an impressive approach for a first long-format release with its samples and drum loops set against quirky lyrics of imagined scenarios. *Tin Planet* followed the same blueprint, developing the band's musical style a little further while cementing them as one of Britpop's most imaginative bands.

The album resulted in their two biggest singles, 'Avenging Angels', which reached number six in January '98, and 'The Ballad of Tom Jones', which reached number four in March '98 and featured Catatonia's Cerys Matthews on vocals. The other single releases were 'Begin Again', which peaked at number 21, and the top-20 single 'The Bad Days EP', which featured seven tracks, including a cover of The Animals' 'We Gotta Get Out Of This Place' from a live performance on *TFI Friday*.

The album's artwork was produced by The La's founding member Mike Badger and showed how to build a robot. A limited edition of the album was also available in a tin case.

To the End (single – Blur)

Charted: Jun '94; UK Chart Position: 16; Label: Food; Album: *Parklife*

'To the End' was the second of five singles from Blur's third album *Parklife* and the band's third top-20 single, spending seven weeks on the chart and peaking at number 16. Usually opting for upbeat pop-style single releases, it was the band's first ballad and featured a full orchestra.

Lyrically, the song detailed a couple's relationship difficulties, although the tone was generally upbeat, with the main line of the chorus running, "So it looks like we might have made it; it looks like we made it to the end". The song was one of singer and chief songwriter Damon Albarn's favourite Blur songs.

Stereolab's Laetitia Sadier featured on vocals, singing some verse lines in French. A full French version of the single was recorded in '95 with French singer Françoise Hardy taking the lead vocal. It was called 'To the End (La Comedie)'.

The single was available on two CDs. CD1 featured exclusive tracks 'Threadneedle Street' and 'Got Yer!', while CD2 included two remixes of 'Girls and Boys' by the Pet Shop Boys.

To the Faithful Departed (album – The Cranberries)

Charted: May '96; UK Chart Position: 2; Label: Island; Singles: 'Salvation' (Apr '96, UKCP 13), 'Free to Decide' (Jul '96, 33), 'When You're Gone' (Nov '96, N/A), 'Hollywood' (May '97, N/A)

To the Faithful Departed was the third album by The Cranberries, and was dedicated by lead singer Dolores O'Riordan to "all those who have gone before us". This was in honour of her own grandfather and Denny Cordell, who signed the band to Island Records, who had both died that year. Tonally, the album maintained the band's musical direction and style, continuing the heavy guitars and more intense and speculative lyrics of the previous album *No Need to Argue*.

The album narrowly missed the number one spot and went on to spend 20 weeks on the UK chart. It gave us the top-20 hit 'Salvation' and top-40 single 'Free To Decide'. In '02, the album was re-released as *To the Faithful Departed (The Complete Sessions 1996–1997)*, featuring B-sides and bonus tracks.

Tomorrow (single – James)

Charted: May '97; UK Chart Position: 12; Label: Fontana; Album: *Whiplash*

'Tomorrow' was the second single from James' seventh album *Whiplash* and the band's seventh top-20 single, spending four weeks on the UK chart and peaking at number 12. It continued the band's newly reclaimed success and became one of their best-loved songs, building to an intense climax over its three-and-a-half minute running length.

The single was available on three CDs. CD1 featured 'Gone Too Far', 'Honest Pleasure' and 'All One To Me'; CD2 live versions of 'Lost A Friend', 'Come Home' and 'Greenpeace' from Radio 1's Mark Radcliffe Session; and CD3 three remixes of the lead track.

Top of the Pops (TV show)

Just as tuning in to the Sunday evening Radio 1 chart show was essential listening for every British music fan, so *Top of the Pops* was the crucial watching experience of the week. Screened for more than

30 years on the BBC, it initially started life on Thursday evenings on BBC1 at 7.30pm, later moving to Fridays, before finally moving to BBC2 in '05 and ending its regular transmission altogether in '06 after the steep rise of MTV and, later, iTunes and Spotify. The show is now relegated to one-off Christmas specials.

The setup was pretty simple (and changed very little since its first transmission on New Year's Day in '64): a small studio audience surrounded half a dozen tiny stages where bands and solo artists would perform whatever songs were causing a ruckus in the chart that week. Compère duties would fall to whichever TV or radio presenter was currently in vogue, giving them the chance to stand in the middle of a throng of eager youngsters all vying for screen time and to see their favourite bands play (sort of) live.

No one could ever be sure who would play live, who would sing live against a backing track and who would just move their lips and hope for the best. Kurt Cobain of Nirvana famously sang hit single 'Smells Like Teen Spirit' an octave lower and refused to re-record. And, after the much-publicised 'Battle for Britpop', the Gallagher brothers swapped roles for their number two single 'Roll With It', with Noel pretending to sing while Liam mimed on the guitar.

If bands couldn't be in the studio, their music videos would be shown instead or, pre-Queen's 'Bohemian Rhapsody' and the invention of vidoes, house dancers Pan's People would perform a blindingly obvious routine (probably as an incentive for the band to turn up).

The intensity of all those huge egos and hot tempers in a confined space meant the show was never far from controversy. In fact, its very first episode ended in a punch-up in the BBC canteen between the Rolling Stones and the Swinging Blue Jeans, after someone made a quip about Mick Jagger's hair.

Traffic (single – Stereophonics)

Charted: Oct '97, UK Chart Position: 20; Label: V2; Album: *Word Gets Around*

Stereophonics' fourth single was their first to reach the top 20 in the UK, peaking at number 20 in October '97 a month after the release of their debut album *Word Gets Around*. The single was the band's first to move away from the fast-paced pop-rock of their earlier releases, and was their first attempt at a rock epic, beginning with a gentle acoustic guitar before building to a tumultuous climax.

Lyrically, the song continued lead singer Kelly Jones' style of telling stories of small town life in Wales, this time from behind the wheel in a traffic jam. The idle protagonist looks around at his fellow commuters and wonders, "She got a body in the boot, or just bags full of food? Those are model's legs, but are they women's or are they men's?". It was an inventive way for him to tell his stories and remains one of his most lyrically ambitious songs.

The single was released on two CDs. CD1 featured B-sides 'Tie Me Up Tie Me Down', 'Chris Chambers' and 'Traffic' (album version), while CD2 consisted of live recordings and featured B-sides 'More Life in a Tramp's Vest', 'A Thousand Trees' and 'Local Boy in the Photograph', all taken from the band's debut album.

Trainspotting (film/book)

"Choose life. Choose a job. Choose a career. Choose a family. Choose a fucking big television."

BAFTA-winning and Oscar-nominated, Danny Boyle's second feature film was based on the '93 novel by Scottish writer Irvine Welsh, who described his Booker Prize-longlisted debut as nothing more than a collection of short stories with a heist scam tagged on the end.

John Hodge's screenplay lingered in development for so long it nearly didn't make it to the screen at all. But when it did, it vividly told the story of Mark Renton (Ewan McGregor) and his gang of hopeless, drug-addled friends as they struggle to stay on and off the 'skag' in working-class, mid-nineties Edinburgh. Noted for its harrowing depictions of drug abuse, the film was accused by some of glamourising the use of heroin. But anyone who watched Renton going cold-turkey with only a dead baby for company or searching for his next fix down the most disgusting toilet in the world might beg to differ.

Famed for its Britpop-packed soundtrack that included Pulp, Sleeper, Elastica and Primal Scream alongside old stalwarts Iggy Pop and Lou Reed, the film was intrinsically linked with the music world and the album was a must-have for Britpop fans. The sequence that shows Renton, Spud and Sick-Boy hurtling down Princes Street as 'Lust for Life' thunders over the soundtrack has become an iconic moment in nineties' British film, cementing Danny Boyle's reputation as the director of his generation.

In the same way, the poster featuring the main characters against a white backdrop with an orange and black banner has become so iconic that it has been parodied many times over. In '17, sequel *T2 Trainspotting* was released, featuring the original cast.

Trash (single – Suede)

Charted: Aug '96; UK Chart Position: 3; Label: Nude; Album: *Coming Up*

'Trash' was the first of five singles from Suede's third album *Coming Up* and the band's third to reach the top ten of the UK chart, where it peaked at number three. The single was the band's highest-charting alongside 'Stay Together' and their longest-running on the chart, where it spent ten weeks.

It was the first single released with Richard Oakes on guitar, and signified a major change in musical direction for the band, from the darker, melancholic sound of their previous work towards a cleaner, anthemic, more radio-friendly tone.

The single was available on two CDs. The first featured B-sides 'Europe Is Our Playground' and 'Every Monday Morning Comes', and the second 'Have You Ever Been This Low?' and 'Another No-One'.

Travellers Tune (single – Ocean Colour Scene)

Charted: Sept '97; UK Chart Position: 5; Label: MCA; Album: *Marchin' Already*

'Traveller's Tune' was the second of four singles from Ocean Colour Scene's third album *Marchin' Already*, and the band's fifth consecutive top ten single in the UK chart, where it spent eight weeks and peaked at number five. The song was the first of two collaborations with sixties' Northern Soul singer P P Arnold, who features on backing vocals during the chorus.

Available on CD, cassette and 7" vinyl, the CD featured B-sides 'Song for the Front Row', a cover of Neil Young's 'On the Way Home' and 'All God's Children Need Travelling Shoes'.

Travis (band)

Named after Robert De Niro's character Travis Bickle in the '76 Martin Scorsese film *Taxi Driver*, Scottish band Travis are generally considered to be part of the post-Britpop second wave alongside the likes of Embrace and, later, Coldplay and Keane. However, as their debut album *Good Feeling* (which reached number nine in the UK chart) was released at the tail-end of Britpop in September '97, they remain a key part of the movement.

Formed in Glasgow in '90, the band experienced several membership changes before settling on the key line-up of Fran Healy on lead vocals and rhythm guitar, Dougie Payne on backing vocals and bass, lead guitarist and backing vocalist Andy Dunlop and drummer Neil Primrose.

Despite the success of *Good Feeling*, the band only really took off post-Britpop, when their second album *The Man Who* found its way to the top spot of the chart some 13 weeks after its initial release in June '99. This late success was mainly due to the single 'Why Does it Always Rain on Me?', a radio slow-burner that eventually peaked at number ten in September '99.

The success of *The Man Who* was partly due to its more stripped-back approach, which tapped into an emotional lyrical depth not heard on their debut. This was mirrored in the music, which took a much sparser approach, with acoustic guitars and lilting lead lines taking the place of the harder indie-rock of their first album.

The band were heavily influenced by Britpop (lead single 'Writing to Reach You' uses the same opening chords as Oasis' 'Wonderwall') but they developed a sound all of their own and their own fragile individuality.

Their success continued with '01's *The Invisible Band* – a reference to Healy's feeling that his bandmates often went unnoticed – which also peaked at number one in the UK chart, this time in its first week. There have been five top-20 albums since, as well as one best of collection. The band continue to record and tour together, and *Everything At Once* reached number five in the UK album chart in June '16.

U

Ugly Beautiful (album – Babybird)

Charted: Nov '96; UK Chart Position: 9; Label: Echo; Singles: 'Goodnight' (Aug '96, UKCP 28), 'You're Gorgeous' (Oct '96, 3), 'Candy Girl' (Feb '97, 14), 'Cornershop' (May '97, 37)

Ugly Beautiful was the debut album by Babybird and included their hit single 'You're Gorgeous', both written entirely by singer Stephen Jones. Spending 18 weeks on the UK chart, the album peaked inside the top ten and also resulted in top-40 singles 'Goodnight', 'Candy Girl' and 'Cornershop'.

Stylistically, Babybird's modus operandi was more in line with Pulp and Edwyn Collins than any of the other bands. It was guitar-led indie-rock, fitting perfectly into the Britpop style, and the lyrics were often tongue-in-cheek puns on sexual liaisons with spoken verses accompanied by anthemic choruses. The album artwork was designed by Stephen Jones and featured a pair of dirty feet with a tag attached to the right big toe reading, "Love Me".

Universal, The (single – Blur)

Charted: Nov '95; UK Chart Position: 5; Label: Food; Album: *The Great Escape*

Complete with orchestra and a huge anthemic chorus, 'The Universal' was the second of four singles from Blur's fourth album *The Great Escape*. It has been the band's final song at live gigs since they reformed in '09.

The video paid tribute to Stanley Kubrick's film *A Clockwork Orange* and featured the band dressed as 'droogs', with Albarn wearing eyeliner, while the cover artwork was designed to imitate the film's poster. The film was withdrawn in the UK at the request of the director after it was linked in the courts to cases of real-life violence, so it's unlikely that many of Blur's audience actually saw the movie in full until Kubrick's death in '99 when it was officially re-released.

The single was available on two CDs, the first featuring B-sides 'Ultranol', 'No Monsters in Me' and a remix of 'Entertain Me', and the second, named 'The Universal II – Live at the Beeb', with live versions of the lead song, 'Mr Robinson's Quango', 'It Could Be You' and 'Stereotypes'.

Urban Hymns (album – The Verve)

Charted: Oct '97; UK Chart Position: 1; Label: Hut; Singles: 'Bittersweet Symphony' (Jun '97, UKCP 2), 'The Drugs Don't Work' (Sept '97, 1), 'Lucky Man' (Dec '97, 7), 'Sonnet' (limited edition, May '98, 74)

Urban Hymns was the third album from The Verve and their most successful by far, spending 161 weeks on the UK chart, with 12 weeks at number one. It also took home the '98 Brit Award for 'Best British Album'.

The album contained the top ten singles 'Bittersweet Symphony', 'The Drugs Don't Work' (the band's only number one single) and 'Lucky Man'. Only a limited number of copies of 'Sonnet' were later made available. A hidden track, 'Deep Freeze', appears at the end of the album and the cover artwork features the band sitting in London's Richmond Park.

Like its predecessor *A Northern Soul*, but unlike the band's shoe-gazing debut *A Storm in Heaven*, the album found lead singer Richard Ashcroft writing many of the songs on his acoustic guitar before bringing them to the band, who then layered them with their own musical lines. This was a typical approach to songwriting by Britpop bands but, in this case, the tracks sat alongside the likes of 'The Rolling People' and the album's epic closer 'Come On', which were created from lengthy jam sessions (an approach the band started out with, and one favoured by their lead guitarist Nick McCabe).

This was the band's most eclectic album, bringing them a whole new audience, but also sparking musical differences between McCabe and Ashcroft, who were trying to pull the band in different directions. It remains one of British indie-rock's best-loved albums, cementing the band as one of our most important groups.

V

Verve, The (band)

Originally called Verve, but forced to change their name because it belonged to an American record label, Wigan band The Verve were formed in '90 by college friends Richard Ashcroft (vocals/ guitar), Nick McCabe (lead guitar), Simon Jones (bass) and Peter Salisbury (drums). Simon Tong joined on guitar/keyboards for the recording and live touring of their third album, the iconic *Urban Hymns*.

Playing locally, the group quickly became known for their incredibly intense live gigs that were dominated by McCabe's blistering guitar work and Ashcroft's emotionally driven vocal performances. After just a handful of sold-out live shows, they signed in '91 to Hut Records, where their style of psychedelic rock fitted perfectly into the shortlived shoegazing-obsessed scene.

Although their early singles, 'All in the Mind' and live favourite 'Gravity Grave', were critically acclaimed, they failed to find their way into the UK chart. 'She's a Superstar' reached number 66 in July '92, the same year the band played the first of their iconic shows at Glastonbury. Debut album *A Storm in Heaven* – a record made up of songs created from lengthy jam sessions – was released in July '93 and peaked at number 27 in the UK chart, where it spent two weeks.

The band continued to do what they did best – play live gigs – and lengthy tours in '93 and '94 brought them into contact with a fledgling Oasis, who supported them many times as they found their own footing.

The two bands shared a cause – shaking up the early nineties music scene – and even shared song titles, with Noel Gallagher naming his song 'Slide Away' after The Verve's fifth single. The influence worked both ways and soon Ashcroft was following Noel's example of writing songs on his own before bringing them to the band for their additions. *A Northern Soul* combined these with the band's original formula of developing songs together in the rehearsal room to create an album that fitted well with the peak Britpop scene, filling a spot on the darker, more introspective side of the movement. The album peaked at number 13 in July '95, almost exactly two years after its predecessor.

Growing musical differences between the band's creative leads,

Ashcroft and McCabe, soon led to infighting, and this, combined with Ashcroft's failing health, meant that the band split not long after the release of the album.

Two years later they were back with their strongest material to date. Despite lengthy legal wrangling, *Bittersweet Symphony* launched the band back onto the UK musical scene, carving a new and entirely individual place for themselves as they entered their most commercially successful period. 'The Drugs Don't Work' reached number one in the UK chart in September '97, as did their third album *Urban Hymns* when it appeared a month later. The album launched the band into the top tier of legendary UK indie bands and even became a success in the USA, where the band toured heavily in '98.

The band made a triumphant return to Wigan in May '98 to play to 33,000 fans at Haigh Hall, their biggest live gig to date. Despite this enormous success, the infighting soon returned and McCabe left the band after he and Ashcroft literally came to blows after a gig in Germany. The band continued on for quite some time – considering they had no guitarist – before officially splitting in April '99. Each member went on to their own musical projects: Ashcroft had a highly successful solo career; Salisbury continued to play drums for him; Jones and Tong formed several new bands, including The Shining; and McCabe continued to create the psychedelic avant-garde music he was so fond of.

Fast forward to '07 and, once again, the band put aside their differences to play together, including an incredible headline slot at Glastonbury in '08, 16 years after their festival debut. The band even premiered a new song, 'Love is Noise', which was released as a single in August '08, reaching number four.

Forth followed in September '08 (11 years after *Urban Hymns*), entering the UK chart at the top spot and spending 13 weeks on the chart. In '16, the band released box-set versions of their first two albums *A Storm in Heaven* and *A Northern Soul*.

VHS (media format)

The Video Home System (VHS) was the predecessor of the Digital Video Disc (DVD) and the standard medium during the eighties and nineties for live gig documentaries and, most importantly, recording *Top of the Pops*, *Later... with Jools Holland*, *The White Room* and *The Girlie Show*.

The first VCR (Videocassette Recorder) to use VHS was developed in the late seventies in the USA and started appearing in most households in the mid-eighties, when MTV was in development and The Buggles were already claiming that "video killed the radio star". Radio didn't die though, and nor did television; video just offered another medium to keep people consuming.

Although the format was revolutionary when it first arrived in the eighties, allowing viewers to watch recorded footage whenever they wanted, the quality was not very good. And so, just as tapes were replaced by CDs, videos were replaced by DVDs in the noughties. Although you couldn't record Oasis playing live on *Top of the Pops* on a DVD.

Wake Up Boo! (single – The Boo Radleys)

Charted: Mar '95; UK Chart Position: 9; Label: Creation; Album: *Wake Up!*

'Wake Up Boo!' was the first major hit for Merseyside band the Boo Radleys. It entered the charts at number nine in March '95 and stayed for 11 weeks. A snippet of the song was later used by Chris Evans on his BBC Radio 1 *Breakfast Show*.

The anthemic brass section and layered vocals telling us to "wake up, it's a beautiful morning" were at odds with the band's darker indie roots, but the song's positivity was so infectious it became one of the summer anthems of '95.

The single was available on two CDs. CD1 featured B-sides 'Janus', 'Blues for George Michael' and 'Friendship Song', while CD2 contained '...And Tomorrow The World' and 'The History Of Creation Parts 17 & 36'.

Wake Up! (album – The Boo Radleys)

Charted: Apr '95; UK Chart Position: 1; Label: Creation; Singles: 'Wake Up Boo!' (Mar '95, UKCP 9), 'Find the Answer Within' (May '95, 37), 'It's Lulu' (Jul '95, 25)

Wake Up! was the fourth studio album from the Boo Radleys and their first and only album to reach the number one spot on the UK chart, released at the height of Britpop and driven by its key top-ten single 'Wake Up Boo!'.

The album was recorded at Rockfield Studios in Wales and spent 23 weeks on the chart, resulting in the top-40 singles 'Find the Answer Within' and 'It's Lulu'. It was reissued in '10 with two bonus discs containing all the B-sides from the album's singles.

Waking Up (single – Elastica)

Charted: Feb '95; UK Chart Position: 13; Label: Deceptive; Album: *Elastica*

'Waking Up' was the fourth of five singles from Elastica's debut self-titled album and their highest charting single, peaking at number 13 in February '95. It spent five weeks on the chart and featured Blur's Damon Albarn on keyboards.

The CD single included B-sides 'Gloria', 'Car Wash' and 'Brighton Rock', and the accompanying music video featured the band surrounded by naked men.

Walkaway (single – Cast)

Charted: Mar '96; UK Chart Position: 9; Label: Polydor; Album: *All Change*

'Walkaway' was the fourth and final single from Cast's debut album *All Change*. The tender acoustic ballad was released in March '96 and was their second single to reach the top ten of the UK chart, where it spent seven weeks, peaking at number nine.

The CD single featured exclusive B-sides 'Fulfill' and 'Mother', while the 7" vinyl edition replaced 'Mother' with an acoustic version of debut single 'Finetime'. They performed the single on *TFI Friday*, *Later... with Jools Holland* and *Top of the Pops*.

Warm Jets (band)

Warm Jets, who took their name from Brian Eno's '73 album *Here Come the Warm Jets*, were best-known for their '98 single 'Hurricane', which reached number 34 in April '98.

The band formed in London in '95 and consisted of founding members Louis Jones (vocals), Paul Noble (guitar) and Ed Grimshaw (bass). In '96, they signed to This Way Up Records and bass player Colleen Browne joined (later replaced by Aki Shibahara). Following the release of debut EP 'Autopia', the band supported Blur on tour in '97 and played numerous festivals. Their sole album *Future Signs* peaked in the top 40 of the UK chart in March '98, resulting in top-40 singles 'Never Never' and 'Hurricane'. Shortly after, the band split up.

Long before she married Norman Cook (aka Fatboy Slim), Radio 1 DJ and Britpop It Girl Zoe Ball briefly dated the band's lead singer Louis Jones, gaining the band some additional low-level media attention.

We Are the Pigs (single – Suede)

Charted: Sept '94; UK Chart Position: 18; Label: Nude; Album: *Dog Man Star*

'We Are the Pigs' was the first of three singles from Suede's second album *Dog Man Star* and the band's fourth to reach the top 20 of the UK chart, where it spent six weeks, peaking at number 18.

The epic, intense music perfectly supports the anthemic melody and the lyrical claims that lead singer Brett Anderson, Suede and their fans sit on the darker, more debauched side of the movement. The track featured brass by the Kick Horns and a photograph on the cover artwork taken from Ulrike Ottinger's German comedy *Freak Orlando*. Available on vinyl, cassette and CD, the latter featured B-sides 'Killing of a Flash Boy' and 'Whipsnade'.

We Could Be Kings (single – Gene)

Charted: Feb '97; UK Chart Position: 17; Label: Polydor; Album: *Drawn To The Deep End*

Tragic love song 'We Could Be Kings' was one of Gene's most popular singles, and the second of four released from second album *Drawn To The Deep End*. It was their third top-20 hit, and spent two weeks on the chart, peaking at number 17.

B-sides included 'Dolce & Gabbana or Nowt' and 'Wasteland', and the video featured the band performing in a bowling alley.

Weak (single – Skunk Anansie)

Charted: Jan '96; UK Chart Position: 20; Label: One Little Indian; Album: *Paranoid and Sunburnt*

'Weak' was the fourth and final single released from Skunk Anansie's debut album *Paranoid and Sunburnt* and arguably the band's most popular song. It was their first to reach the top 20 and spent five weeks on the chart. The release manages to epitomise the band's style of writing rock anthems with melancholic lyrics.

Released on two CDs, the first featured B-sides 'Selling Jesus' and their debut single 'Tour Hymn', while the second contained remixes of the lead track, 'Charity', '100 Ways to be a Good Girl' and 'Rise Up'.

Weird (single – Reef)

Charted: Aug '95; UK Chart Position: 19; Label: S2; Album: n/a

'Weird' was the third single from Somerset band Reef, a non-album track released between their first two albums.

It featured B-sides 'Sunrise Shakers', 'Together' and a live version of 'End', originally featured as the final track on debut album *Replenish*, recorded for the Clyde 1 FM *Rock Show*.

Weller, Paul (singer/songwriter/guitarist – The Jam/The Style Council/solo artist)

Long before he adopted the moniker of the 'Modfather', John William 'Paul' Weller formed a band called The Jam at the age of just 17. This was London in '75, and the band couldn't help but find themselves lumped in with the punk scene that overtook the capital in '76. The three-piece joined The Clash on their *White Riot* tour in '77 and released a string of intense yet melodious guitar-led singles, such as 'In the City' and 'All Around the World', before going on to create classics like 'Going Underground' and 'Town Called Malice'. The band went on to release six albums over the course of five years, all before Weller turned 25.

He quickly made a name for himself not only as an incredibly talented guitarist and singer, but also as a songwriter whose ascerbic lyrics covered aspects of modern life in the bleak austerity of Margaret Thatcher's Britain in the late seventies and early eighties. This style, most notable on the single 'That's Entertainment', was an early precursor for what would become a key aspect of Britpop.

Having had four singles all reach the top spot, and clearly at the top of their game, Weller surprised everyone by disbanding The Jam in '82, moving quickly on to a new musical project, the Style Council, a much more experimental group with a flexible line-up influenced by musical genres as wildly diverse as folk and electronica.

They released six critically and commercially successful albums between '83 and '89, including '85's number one album *Our Favourite Shop*, and several top-ten singles, including '84's Northern Soul-influenced 'Shout to the Top'. By '90 though the changing man was ready to move on to pastures new once more and, reclaiming his trusty Epiphone guitar, he began a highly successful solo career that saw him returning in style and tone to his musical roots, notably the blues and soul bands from the sixties and seventies. His '92 eponymous solo debut and '93's follow up, *Wild Wood*, set the tone for his solo career and produced some of his most iconic songs to date, but it was with '95's *Stanley Road* that his commercial success went stratospheric. It was his most successful album ever, peaking at number one in the UK chart, where it spent an enormous 105 weeks.

By this point, Weller was being widely touted as one of the greatest British artists of all time, alongside his own heroes John Lennon and Mick Jagger, and was, in turn, becoming an icon for the next generation. He gave Ocean Colour Scene their big break by asking them to play live with him in '95, and provided lead guitar to Oasis' album closer 'Champagne Supernova' that same year. He went on to play with both acts as well as a host of others in the following years.

To date, he has released ten solo albums since *Stanley Road* (13 in total) and, in '10, was awarded the Ivor Novello Lifetime Achievement Award for his songwriting. He continues to play live and record new work. His latest album, *A Kind Revolution*, was released in May '17.

Wener, Louise (singer/guitarist/songwriter – Sleeper)

Frontwomen like Sleeper's Louise Jane Wener, born in London on 30 July '66, often found it challenging to stamp their identity on a heavily male-dominated music scene, but she managed to success-fully carve out a place for herself as a talented songsmith, astute when it came to lyrics about complex modern stories of love and loss in the nineties.

Always the spiritual leader of the band, Wener founded Sleeper in '87 while still at university in Manchester with guitarist Jon Stewart and, by '93, had signed a record deal with Indolent Records. In '95, their debut album *Smart* arrived, just as Britpop was peaking, and its success led to a period of commercial success that was topped by follow-up album *The It Girl* in '96, the title of which is a tongue-in-cheek reference to the type of girl that Wener wasn't. The album was a notable success for the band and their place in the Britpop canon was assured.

Post-Sleeper, Wener transferred her skills to novels: *Goodnight Steve McQueen*, *The Big Blind (aka The Perfect Play)*, *The Half Life of Stars* and *Worldwide Adventures in Love*. In June '10, her auto-biography, *Different for Girls: My True-life Adventures in Pop (aka Just for One Day: Adventures in Britpop)*, was published. She lives with husband (and ex-Sleeper drummer) Andy MacLure and their two children in Brighton. Sleeper re-formed for a string of live gigs in '17, but no new material is currently in the pipeline.

What a Beautiful Day (single – The Levellers)

Charted: Aug '97; UK Chart Position: 13; Label: China; Album: *Mouth To Mouth*

If not the Levellers' most commercially successful single, 'What a Beautiful Day' is definitely their best-known, even though it signalled the end of a hugely successful run of top-20 singles for the Brighton band. The optimistic summer anthem reached number 13 in the UK chart, where it spent five weeks after its release in August '97.

The single was released on two CDs. CD1 featured B-sides 'Bar Room Jury' and 'All Your Dreams', while CD2 included 'Price Of Love', 'Hang On To Your Ego' and 'Germ Free Adolescence'. It was also released on cassette with the same track-listing as CD1.

What Do I Do Now? (single – Sleeper)

Charted: Oct '95; UK Chart Position: 14; Label: Indolent; Album: *The It Girl*

The first single from Sleeper's second album *The It Girl*, 'What Do I Do Now?' was their highest charting single to date, peaking at number 14 in October '95 and signalling the beginning of a run of commercial success for the band. Lyrically, it highlighted a personal story for the band's chief songwriter Louise Wener.

The single was released on two CDs. CD1 featured B-sides 'Paint Me' and 'Room at the Top', and CD2 'Disco Duncan (Live)', 'Vegas (Live)' and 'Amuse (Live)'.

What Do You Want From Me? (single – Monaco)

Charted: Mar '97; UK Chart Position: 11; Label: Polydor; Album: *Music for Pleasure*

The first of just three singles released by former New Order bassist Peter Hook's side project Monaco, 'What Do you Want From Me?' was also the band's most successful, peaking at number 11 in March '97 on the UK chart, where it spent six weeks.

It was released on CD and featured B-sides 'Bicycle Thief', 'Ultra' and 'What Do You Want From Me? (Instrumental)'.

What If (single – Lightning Seeds)

Charted: Nov '96; UK Chart Position: 14; Label: Epic; Album: *Dizzy Heights*

'What If' was the second of four singles from the Lightning Seeds' fourth album *Dizzy Heights*. Released shortly after the success of 'Three Lions', it spent seven weeks on the UK chart and peaked at number 14.

The single featured B-sides 'Lightning Seeds Mix 'N' Match' and a remix of the lead track entitled 'Leuroj's Easy Disco Dub Mix'. A limited edition version contained exclusive tracks 'Never' and 'The Crunch'.

Whatever (single – Oasis)

Charted: Dec '94; UK Chart Position: 3; Label: Creation; Album: n/a

Released in Christmas week '94, Oasis' fifth single, 'Whatever', was the band's highest-charting single to date, peaking at number three. It marked the end of an incredible first year in the charts for one of Britain's biggest bands and underlined their growing popularity.

The suitably epic 'Whatever' wasn't actually written as a Christmas song and, in a year that the race to number one was incredibly fierce, the Manchester band were kept from the top spot by Mariah Carey's 'All I Want for Christmas' and East 17's 'Stay Another Day'.

The CD single continued the trend of mini-album releases for the band. The B-sides included '(It's Good) To Be Free', 'Half the World Away' and 'Slide Away', taken from their debut album *Defintely Maybe*.

(What's the Story) Morning Glory? (album – Oasis)

Charted: Oct '95; UK Chart Position: 1; Label: Creation; Singles: 'Some Might Say' (May '95, UKCP 1), 'Roll With It' (Aug '95, 2), 'Wonderwall' (Nov '95, 2), 'Don't Look Back In Anger' (Mar '96, 1)

Recorded in just six weeks in a session as famous for its punch-ups as its music, Oasis' second album is one of Britpop's – and, indeed, Britain's – most memorable, successful and important records. Chief songwriter and co-producer Noel Gallagher found his stride in terms of the anthemic choruses he wanted to write, the band's distinct layered sound and, vocals and drums aside, it's rumoured he played nearly all the music himself.

From the ground-stomping, rabble-rousing opener 'Hello', all the way through to the delicate yet anthemic closer 'Champagne Supernova', Noel managed to hit just the right tone, seeming to tap directly into the public consciousness. As a consequence, there were very few mid-late nineties' British households that didn't have a copy.

Released in October '95, it came five months after the band earned their first number one single with 'Some Might Say' and also after the infamous 'Battle for Britpop' with Blur. The album went straight to the top spot, returning there a further three times over its mammoth 227-week run in the UK chart. It was back in the top ten as recently as '12, 17 years after its initial release.

Alongside 'Some Might Say' and 'Roll With It', the other singles released from the album were instant classics. 'Wonderwall' and 'Don't Look Back in Anger' were massive, the latter reaching the top spot in March '97. In addition, the album also features some of the band's best-loved songs, like acoustic classic 'Cast No Shadow', dedicated to The Verve's Richard Ashcroft, and 'Morning Glory', the band's most intense rock 'n' roll song.

Despite the changing tone and pace of the songs, the album feels like one long piece of music, flowing from track to track, linked by sonorous quirks that give it its edge (like Noel's cough just before the opening chords of 'Wonderwall'. It remains not only one of the most important albums of Britpop and of the nineties, but one of the most important in British musical history.

When I Was Born For the 7th Time (album – Cornershop)

Charted: Sept '97; UK Chart Position: 17; Label: Willja; Singles: 'Good Ships/Funky Days Are Back Again' (Jun '97, UKCP 92), 'Brimful of Asha' (Feb '98, 1), 'Sleep On The Left Side' (May '98, 23)

Cornershop's breakthrough third album was released near the end of Britpop and contains the band's hit single 'Brimful of Asha', which reached number one when remixed by DJ Norman Cook, aka Fatboy Slim. The single had originally reached the lower half of the top ten when released in August '97 but, when the remix gained traction on the radio, it was re-released in February '98 and went all the way to the top.

The album was recorded at 657 Holloway Road, London; Eastcote Studios, London; Sun Plantation, San Francisco; and West Organge Studios, Preston, Lancashire. It was produced by the band's own Tjinder Singh, plus legendary American hip-hop producer Dan the Automator and Daddy Rappaport. The album has a massive 15 tracks, the last of which is a cover of the Beatles' 'Norwegian Wood (This Bird Has Flown)', famous for its use of the sitar, an Indian string instrument.

Whiplash (album – James)

Charted: Mar '97; UK Chart Position: 9; Label: Fontana; Singles: 'She's a Star' (Feb '97, UKCP 9), 'Tomorrow' (May '97, 12), 'Waltzing Along' (Jul '97, 23)

Whiplash was the seventh studio album from Manchester band James, and the band's fourth to reach the top ten in the UK chart, where it spent 25 weeks and peaked at number nine in March '97. It was their first album in two and a half years and, with its radio-friendly nature, was a noted departure for a band used to allying themselves with the Madchester/baggy scene. The album contained some of the band's best-known and best-loved songs, including hit single 'She's a Star' and the epic 'Tomorrow', which (for those of you interested in such things) speeds up a sixth of a beat every six bars.

The 11-track album was produced by Stephen Hague and took nearly two years to complete at various studios around the world. The title referred to the injury lead singer Tim Booth sustained in a car crash that very nearly killed him.

Whipping Boy (band)

Irish band Whipping Boy were another low-key group caught up in Britpop. They released four singles that reached the top ten in the UK chart between July '95 and May '96, and two albums which failed to chart. Formed in Dublin in '88, the band comprised Fearghal McKee (vocals), Paul Page (guitar), Myles McDonnell (bass, vocals) and Colm Hassett (drums).

After releasing a handful of self-funded EPs, they signed to Liquid Records and released their debut album *Submarine* in '92. The band then signed to the major label Columbia, which released their second album *Heartworm* in '95. A single from the album *Twinkle* featured on the indie compilation *Shine 5*.

Disappointing sales meant the band were dropped by Columbia in '98, and their third album was unreleased. They continued on alone and released their own eponymous album in '00. They split not long afterwards, but re-formed in '05 for a string of live shows in their native Ireland.

White Room, The (music TV show)

Channel 4's *The White Room*, presented by Mark Radcliffe, was an acclaimed music show that championed the best in live music. It was a chance to see bands perform B-sides, rarities and special collaborations in an actual white room, offering an edgier version of BBC rival *Later... with Jools Holland*.

Paying little attention to chart trends and avoiding interviews, the show was all about raw live performances with a real plug-in-and-play feel. It ran for three series during Britpop's peak years ('94 to '96) and highlights included Oasis' B-sides 'Acquiesce', '(It's Good) To Be Free' and 'Round Are Way'; Blur's Damon Albarn collaborating with The Kinks' Ray Davies on 'Waterloo Sunset'; and Pulp performing 'Little Girl With Blue Eyes' and 'Monday Morning'.

Q magazine's February '96 edition with Noel Gallagher and the question "The greatest songwriter of the 90s?" on the cover, came with the free cassette of *The White Room Album*, featuring seven exclusive tracks from the show including a collaborative performance of Oasis' 'Talk Tonight' with Paul Weller and Noel Gallagher; 'A Girl Like You' with Edwyn Collins and Bernard Butler; and Sleeper's 'Inbetweener'.

White, Alan (drummer - Oasis)

Younger brother of Steve White, long-term drummer for Paul Weller's solo work, and not to be confused with the Alan White who drummed on John Lennon's solo album *Imagine* in '70, this Alan White was the drummer for Oasis during their peak years of '95–'04. He joined the band after Tony McCarroll left, just as they were heading into the studio to record their second album *(What's the Story) Morning Glory?*. His famous drum-fill on 'Don't Look Back in Anger' is one of the band's most identifiable moments.

Born in Lewisham in south London on 26 May '72, White played drums from a young age, even auditioning for future Oasis' member Gem Archer's band Whirpool when he was just 15. He played with Starclub from '91 to '94, although the band never released any material.

He first came to Noel Gallagher's attention while drumming in a recording studio where his brother was working with Weller. The next day he played with Oasis for the first time at their *Top of the Pops* recording of their first number one single, 'Some Might Say'. His first gig with the band was at Glastonbury in June '95, when his drumming on instrumental B-side 'The Swamp Song' was recorded live.

After *Morning Glory*, White played on the band's next three albums: '97's *Be Here Now*, '00's *Standing on the Shoulder of Giants* and '02's *Heathen Chemistry*. He left in '04 citing musical differences, apparently not happy with how some of his drum parts were being replaced by drum loops. He has not played with any other bands since leaving Oasis and lives in the country with his family. Legend has it that he was the only member of Oasis who could match Liam Gallagher's drinking.

Whiteout (band)

Although Scottish band Whiteout were officially active between '91 and '99, it was for their four singles and one album released during '94 and '95 that they are best known.

Their best-known line-up was Andrew Caldwell (vocals), who co-founded the band in Glasgow in '91, Paul Carroll (bass), Eric Lindsay (guitar) and Stuart Smith (drums). As well as supporting Pulp and The Charlatans, the band also co-headlined a tour with a young Oasis, who had yet to release any material at the time.

In '91, they were the first band to sign to Manchester-based label Silvertone, who went on to enjoy much success with the Stone Roses, although it wasn't until '94 that their first proper single was released. 'No Time' peaked at 79 in the UK singles chart in February '94, signalling a run of three further single releases, all of which made the top ten. The most well-known was 'Jackie's Racing', which reached 72 in February '95. Their debut album, *Bite It*, was released in July '95 and reached number 71 in the UK. Follow-up *Big Wow* was finally released in '98, but failed to chart. The band split not long afterwards.

Wibbling Rivalry (single – Oasis)

Charted: Nov '95; UK Chart Position: 52; Label: Fierce Panda; Album: n/a

Released under the name OAS*S by indie label Fierce Panda in November '95 when Oasis were at the height of their fame, 'Wibbling Rivalry' was not a music single in the classic sense, but rather '14 minutes of verbal mayhem'. It was basically just an argument between brothers Liam and Noel Gallagher.

A must-have for any mega fan, it was released on CD and 7" vinyl with a track list comprised of 'Noel's Track... A Lot of Swearing and Cussing' and 'Liam's Track... Even More Swearing and Cussing'. The cover featured two other famous brothers, London-based sixties gangsters the Kray twins.

Wide Open Space (single – Mansun)

Charted: Dec '96; UK Chart Position: 15; Label: Parlophone; Album: *Attack Of The Grey Lantern*

Mansun's epic fourth official single 'Wide Open Space' is perhaps the band's most iconic song, and was the first to break from their tradition of naming their songs by release number. It was also their highest-charting single to date, peaking at number 15 in the UK in December '96.

The single was released on two CDs, the first featuring B-sides 'Rebel Without a Quilt', 'Vision Impaired' and 'Skin Up Pin Up', and the second 'The Gods of Not Very Much', 'Moronica (Acoustic Version)' and 'Lemonade Secret Drinker (Acoustic Version)'.

Wild Ones, The (single – Suede)

Charted: Nov '94; UK Chart Position: 18; Label: Nude; Album: *Dog Man Star*

'The Wild Ones' was the second of three singles from Suede's second album *Dog Man Star*, alongside 'We Are the Pigs' and 'New Generation'. Spending seven weeks on the chart and peaking at number 18, it was the band's fifth top-20 song on the UK chart.

In much the same way that previous release 'We Are the Pigs' showcased a raw, impassioned side to Brett Anderson and Bernard Butler's songwriting, 'The Wild Ones' offered another more delicate and introspective side to their musical personalities. The careful acoustic build-up to the anthemic chorus delivers a classic song, and had many of the band's most ardent fans bemoaning the fact that Butler had left.

The single was available on cassette, vinyl and two CDs, the first featuring 'Modern Boys' and 'This World Needs a Father', and the second a Brian Eno Remix called 'Eno's Introducing the Band' and 'Asda Town'.

Wonderwall (single – Oasis)

Charted: Nov '95; UK Chart Position: 2; Label: Creation; Album: *(What's The Story) Morning Glory?*

It is hard to believe that Oasis' best-known song and key Britpop anthem 'Wonderwall' didn't make the top spot, peaking instead at number two in November '95. The single that beat it was the Simon Cowell-produced housewives' favourite Robson and Jerome with 'I Believe/Up on the Roof', perhaps echoing the time the Beatles' 'Penny Lane/Strawberry Fields Forever' was beaten to the top spot by Englebert Humperdink's 'Please Release Me' in March '67.

Despite not reaching number one, the single was a huge success and spent a mammoth 77 weeks on the chart, returning as recently as August '12, when it peaked again at 38.

It was Oasis' first ballad and the story goes that Noel presented it, along with 'Don't Look Back in Anger', to brother Liam, saying that he was going to sing one of the songs. Liam, thinking it was written for Noel's then partner Meg Matthews, insisted on singing 'Wonderwall' himself to annoy his sibling. It was the right move though, as

Liam's guttural vocal delivery meant the song steered clear of being overly sentimental.

Noel later claimed the song was actually about an imagined situation, its title taken from Beatle George Harrison's '68 solo album *Wonderwall Music* (the soundtrack to a psychedelic film of the same name).

The single became an instant classic, with the opening chord sequence fast-becoming a favourite with aspiring guitarists learning their craft and recording artists looking for something to cover. Alt-country star Ryan Adams covered the song in a hauntingly delicate style on his '04 album *Love is Hell*, while the most famous alternative version came from Mike Flowers Pop, who released a fifties-style novelty version just a month later in December '95. It also peaked at number two, meaning the two versions were competing in the chart at the same time. Many radio DJs joked that Flowers' version was the original, leading to much confusion.

The CD single featured three other Oasis classics as B-sides: 'Round Are Way', 'The Swamp Song' and 'The Masterplan', which gave its name to the band's '98 B-sides album.

Word, The (music TV show)

Channel 4's *The Word* was the often controversial show that hosted both Oasis' debut live TV performance in March '94 and Nirvana's volcanic performance of 'Smells Like Teen Spirit' in '91, when Kurt Cobain let the world know that future wife Courtney Love was "the best fuck in the world".

Notorious for 'The Hopefuls' feature, where people would do literally anything to get on television, from licking the sweat off fat people and eating the contents of a full ash tray to kissing an OAP and drinking their own puke, the show ran for five series from the early to mid-nineties. It was hosted by, among others, Amanda de Cadenet, Dani Behr, Mark Lamarr and Terry Christian.

A risqué show, it was one of the forerunners in youth TV, paving the way for programmes like *The Girlie Show* while defying boundaries, dripping attitude and daring to go that little bit too far. Perhaps not surprisingly, this meant it was moved from its initial 6pm slot to an 11pm one.

Word Gets Around (album - Stereophonics)

Charted: Sept '97; UK Chart Position: 6; Label: V2; Singles: 'Looks like Chaplin' (Nov '96, UKCP N/A), 'More Life in a Tramps Vest' (May '97, 33), 'A Thousand Trees' (Aug '97, 22), 'Traffic' (Oct '97, 20), 'Local Boy in a Photograph' (Feb '98, 14)

Each of the tracks on the debut album by Stereophonics links directly with the title of the record, which is itself also the chief theme, making this one of the most lyrically ambitious of the Britpop albums. The subject matter covered is perhaps best summed-up in the track 'Goldfish Bowl', as in "life in a goldfish bowl". Each of the 12 tracks tells an individual story of life in a small working-class British town, examining how judgemental gossip and hearsay can impact upon the life of the individual. Though inspired by Jones' own youth in Cwmaman, the town in the album could actually be anywhere in the UK any time in the last 50 years, although there is a melancholy in the tracks reminiscent of other Welsh bands, most notably the Manic Street Preachers.

The songs cover the heartbreak of lost relationships ('Same Size Feet'); young factory workers masking their misery with alcohol ('Last of the Big Time Drinkers'); and, in album opener 'A Thousand Trees', how gossip can quickly solidify into fact when a local teacher is accused of inappropriate activity with a young female student. 'More Life in a Tramps Vest' is a little more lighthearted, with Jones talking about his own experiences working on a market stall, while 'Too Many Sandwiches' is the story of a typical working-class wedding from the point of view of a casual observer. Teenage suicide is a recurring theme, with at least two of the album's key tracks dealing directly and indirectly with it. Although it's not explicit that it was suicide that ended the life of the young man in 'Local Boy in a Photograph', it tells of youngsters drinking to their friend who will "always be 23", while the album's mournful acoustic closer talks of "Billy Davey's second daughter [who] threw herself into dirty water". Jones' lyrics, alongside those of Richey Edwards of the Manic Street Preachers, support the reputation the Welsh had at the time for ingrained melancholia.

But these are not poems but pop songs and, as such, the music is just as important. Like Oasis and many Britpop bands, Stereophonics kept the music simple and the melodies strong and catchy. There are flourishes here and there, such as the intense build toward the climax of 'Too Many Sandwiches', but the album is mainly filled with four-to-the-floor rock 'n' roll songs that played well at live gigs. It's easy to see why The Who asked them to play live with them, and why the album caught the attention of the late Britpop crowd, looking for an intelligent and exciting debut album.

X, Y, Z

XFM/Radio X (radio station)

London's XFM station has been the home of indie music in the capital since it was founded by Sammy Jacob and Chris Parry in '93. Throughout the Britpop years, XFM was only a part-time, independently-run enterprise that broadcast from Charlotte Street in Soho but, by '97, the popularity of the genre meant they could go full-time. It was around this time that future creators of *The Office* Ricky Gervais and Stephen Merchant were presenters on the station, something they continue to do intermittently to this day.

In '98, the station was bought by Capital Radio Group and moved to Leicester Square. XFM's attitude to music has always been in line with the indie scene, and protests were held in Leicester Square after the Capital buyout meant the station became commercial and started to play adverts. The temporary move to soft rock rather than traditional indie didn't go down too well either.

As well as breaking new acts, the station has always supported up-and-coming groups, holding an annual unsigned competition by playing bands' demo tapes and asking listeners to vote for their favourite in the hope that one will get a deal. They have also sponsored and put on many live events over the years in London and around the country.

In '05, XFM began to broadcast in Manchester. In '06, its reach extended to Scotland and, in '07, Wales was finally added to the line-up. The advent of digital radio also means, of course, that anyone in the world can get access through the internet. The station was rebranded as Radio X in September '15, but to its loyal listeners it'll always be XFM, the home of indie music.

As well as Gervais and Merchant, many other former XFM DJs

have found fame, including Karl Pilkington, Jimmy Carr, Simon Pegg, Christian O'Connell, Russell Brand, Justin Lee Collins, Adam and Joe, Alex Zane, Tim Lovejoy, Dermot O'Leary and Josh Widdicombe. Even Blur's Dave Rowntree presented an infrequent evening slot until September '15.

Yes (single – McAlmont & Butler)

Charted: May '95; UK Chart Position: 8; Label: Hut; Album: *The Sound of... McAlmont & Butler*

'Yes' was the epic, highly-anticipated debut single by McAlmont & Butler from their debut album *The Sound of... McAlmont & Butler*. It was their most successful single and their only release to reach the top ten, where it spent eight weeks, peaking at number eight.

Some might argue that it's not necessarily immediately identifiable as a Britpop record as it relies less on guitars and more on strings and brass, with McAlmont's vocals more gospel than indie, but Butler's own credentials make it a shoe-in.

Two versions of the CD were available, the first featuring B-sides 'What's The Excuse This Time?' and 'Disappointment', and the second 'Don't Call It Soul' and 'How About You?'.

You Can Talk to Me (single – Seahorses)

Charted: Dec '97; UK Chart Position: 15; Label: Geffen; Album: n/a

'You Can Talk to Me' was The Seahorses' only non-album single and their fourth consecutive release to reach the top 20, spending eight weeks on the UK chart and peaking at number 15. It was the first single released with writing credits for both guitarist John Squire and singer Chris Helme.

It featured B-sides 'Don't Try', written by Chris Helme, and '3 Wide' by John Squire.

You Do (single - McAlmont & Butler)

Charted: Nov '95; UK Chart Position: 17; Label: Hut; Album: *The Sound of... McAlmont & Butler*

'You Do' was the second single from McAlmont & Butler's debut album *The Sound of... McAlmont & Butler*. It peaked at number 17 and spent a total of four weeks on the chart. If not quite as epic or memorable as its predecessor 'Yes', 'You Do' still managed to convey the band's inimitable style and tone.

Two versions of the CD were available, the first featuring B-sides 'Although' and 'The Debitor', and the second 'Tonight' and 'You'll Lose a Good Thing'.

You Do Something to Me (single - Paul Weller)

Charted: Jul '95; UK Chart Position: 9; Label: Go! Discs; Album: *Stanley Road*

His most tender release to date, Paul Weller's piano-infused, emotionally-driven ballad 'You Do Something to Me' was the third of four singles from his third solo album *Stanley Road*, and his second to reach the top ten, where it spent seven weeks, peaking at number nine.

It featured B-sides 'My Whole World Is Falling Down', 'A Year Late' and 'Woodcutters Son', taken from BBC Radio 1's live Evening Session in May '95.

You Showed Me (single - Lightning Seeds)

Charted: Apr '97; UK Chart Position: 8; Label: Epic; Album: *Dizzy Heights*

'You Showed Me' was the fourth and final single from the Lightning Seeds' fourth album *Dizzy Heights*. Written by Jim McGuinn and Gene Clark of sixties band The Byrds and released by The Turtles in '69, the Lightning Seeds' version peaked at number eight and spent seven weeks on the UK chart (their second top ten after 'Three Lions').

There were two CD versions, each featuring several remixes of the lead track. The song also featured on the soundtrack of the film comedy *Austin Powers: International Man of Mystery*.

You're Gorgeous (single - Babybird)

Charted: Oct '96; UK Chart Position: 3; Label: Echo; Album: *Ugly Beautiful*

Babybird's breakthrough single 'You're Gorgeous', released from their debut studio album *Ugly Beautiful*, was their biggest hit.

With its Jarvis Cocker-esque vocals and saucy lyrics that everyone knew the words to, the single was the band's sole top-ten hit, spending 19 weeks on the UK chart and peaking at number three.

It featured on *Now That's What I Call Music 35* and was available on two CD singles. The first contained B-sides 'You're Gorgeous Too', 'Hong Kong Blues' and 'KW Jesus TV Roof Appeal', and the second 'Bébé Limonade', 'Ooh Yeah' and 'Carcrash'.

You've Got It Bad (single - Ocean Colour Scene)

Charted: Apr '96; UK Chart Position: 7; Label: MCA; Album: *Moseley Shoals*

Ocean Colour Scene's 'You've Got It Bad' was the follow-up single to 'The Riverboat Song', also released from their second album *Moseley Shoals*. Peaking at number seven in the UK chart, it remained on the chart for eight weeks and was the band's first top-ten single, paving the way for a further five consecutive top-ten releases.

The single, which they performed on *TFI Friday*, was available on two CDs, the first featuring B-sides 'Robin Hood', 'I Wanna Stay Alive With You' and 'Huckleberry Grove', and the second a demo of the title track, 'Here In My Heart', 'Men Of Such Opinion' and 'Beautiful Losers'.

Zeitgeist (album - Levellers)

Charted: Sept '95; UK Chart Position: 1; Label: China; Singles: 'Hope St' (Aug '95, UKCP 12), 'Fantasy' (Oct '95, 16), 'Just the One' (Dec '95, 12), 'Exodus (live)' (Jul '96, 24)

The Levellers' fourth album *Zeitgeist* managed to knock The Charlatans' self-titled album off the top of the UK chart in '95. It spent a total of 18 weeks on the chart and produced three of the band's best-loved songs, the top 20 singles 'Hope St', 'Fantasy' and 'Just the One' and the top-40 track 'Exodus (live)', marking a fruitful time for the band and earning its somewhat apt name.

A special deluxe 2CD edition was released in '12; the second CD featuring B-sides of the singles and tracks from the *Zeitgeist* outtakes fan club CD.

100 club (music venue)

Made famous by the infamous punk scene of the late seventies, when the Sex Pistols, The Clash, The Damned and The Cult all screamed to be heard, London's 100 Club has been the home of indie-rock music for nearly five decades, and has been hosting live bands for nearly eight. Situated at 100 Oxford Street, from which it took its name, its first live gig was at the end of October '42 when the Second World War was still raging. Originally named the Feldman Swing Club, it eventually became the 100 Club during the swinging sixties, when a new manager took over from his father.

Glen Miller, Ronnie Scott (who had his own eponymous Soho jazz club) and even Louis Armstrong graced the stage in the early days, when it was patronised by upper-class Etonian types, known at the time as 'Hooray Henrys'. By the early seventies, things were changing, and it became home to the RnB spin-off, the shortlived UK Beat scene, in '71. In September '76, the venue hosted the first international punk festival, headlined by the Sex Pistols and The Clash, and the scene that had up until that point been underground came into the mainstream. With a guttural roar, punk was born. The venue continued to host burgeoning punk bands over the years, before the Northern Soul movement arrived in the eighties.

The venue was under serious threat in '10 because of spiralling rents, but Paul McCartney joined a local campaign that immediately went national and resulted in clothing label Converse coming to the rescue. Blur played a (not so) secret warm-up gig for their '12 live shows at the 350-capacity venue. Many Britpop fans who couldn't get a ticket queued up outside the doors, listening in.

12 Reasons Why I Love Her (single – My Life Story)

Charted: Aug '96; UK Chart Position: 32; Label: Parlophone; Album: *The Golden Mile*

My Life Story's debut chart entry '12 Reasons Why I Love Her' was the opening track on second album *The Golden Mile* and the first of a string of consecutive top-40 hits for the band, spending two weeks on the UK chart and peaking at number 32.

The CD single featured a pink love heart on the cover imprinted with the words "12 Reasons Why" and included B-sides 'Lady Somerset', 'Silently Screaming' and Heaven Suitcase'.

1977 (album – Ash)

Charted: May '96; UK Chart Position: 1; Label: Creation; Singles: 'Kung Fu' (Apr '95, UKCP 57), 'Girl from Mars' (Aug '95, 11), 'Angel Interceptor' (Oct '95, 14), 'Goldfinger' (Apr '96, 5), 'Oh Yeah!' (Jul '96, 6)

Perhaps more punk rock than Britpop, Ash's debut album was released in May '96 at the height of the era. Its quirky songs about life for young Britons in the nineties helped ally it with the Britpop movement.

Named after the year two of the band members were born (and perhaps more importantly when *Star Wars* was released), the album begins with the sound of a TIE-fighter storming through a galaxy "far far away" and ends with the track 'Darkside Lightside'.

The album was the first of the band's two number one albums, spending a total of 32 weeks on the UK chart. It led to a string of hit singles, including top-20 releases 'Girl from Mars' and 'Angel Interceptor', and the top-ten singles 'Goldfinger' and 'Oh Yeah!'. It remains the band's best-loved album.

3 Colours Red (band)

Creation band 3 Colours Red were best known for their hit single 'Beautiful Day' and, although they're not officially a Britpop band, their close association with the scene, combined with the fact it was music legend Alan McGee who signed them, means they're included in the canon.

Named after the final instalment in the classic Polish/French film trilogy by Krzysztof Kieślowski (after *Three Colours Blue* and *White*), it later transpired the band had chosen their name by sticking a pin in the cinema listings of the local newspaper.

Formed through a shared love of classic hard rock, the band's driving force was the melding of Chris McCormack's dense guitar lines and vocalist and bassist Pete Vuckovic's melodic vocal lines. Together, they created a sound somewhere between the hard rock of their roots and the indie music so popular at the time. McCormack and Vuckovic put the band together in '95 along with Ben Harding on guitar (later replaced by Paul Grant) and Keith Baxter on drums. The band, who were individually well-known on the UK music rock scene, put out the single 'This is my Hollywood' on indie label Fierce Panda in '96.

Alan McGee saw them play and signed them to Creation after just one gig, comparing them to the Sex Pistols, and their first proper single, 'Nuclear Holiday', went straight in at number 22 in January '97. Debut album *Pure* reached number 16 in May '97.

By this time, it seemed the band had found their audience and quickly slipped into a routine of intense energetic live gigs and hard rock releases until 'Beautiful Day' appeared in January '99. The first single from second album *Revolt* saw the band taking a more tender emotional approach to their music, surprising much of their original audience while drawing in a more mainstream one. The single peaked at number 11 and opened the band up to some limited popular success, which culminated with Revolt peaking at number 17 in February.

'Beautiful Day', written predominantly by chief lyricist Vuckovic, took the band in a new direction and, perhaps inevitably, led to musical differences between the co-leads. The band eventually split in '00 after parting ways with Creation, re-forming in '03 after McCormack and Vuckovic put aside their musical differences. After much touring, they released their third album, Union of Souls, in '04 on Mighty Atom Records, but after it failed to make the top ten of the UK chart, they split again in '05.

500 (Shake Baby Shake) (single – Lush)

Charted: Jul '96; UK Chart Position: 21; Label: 4AD; Album: *Lovelife*

'500 (Shake Baby Shake)' was the final single released by Lush in the nineties, and was their third consecutive single – after 'Single Girl' and 'Ladykillers' – to narrowly miss the top 20 of the UK chart.

It was available on two CDs, the first featuring B-sides 'I Have The Moon', 'Piledriver' and an acoustic version of album track 'Olympia', and the second 'I'd Like To Walk Around In Your Mind', an acoustic version of 'Kiss Chase' and a remix of album track 'Last Night' entitled 'Hexadecimal Dub Mix'.

6 Underground (single – Sneakerpimps)

Charted: Jun '97; UK Chart Position: 9; Label: Clean Up; Album: *Becoming X*

More trip-hop than Britpop, '6 Underground' was the powerfully evocative debut single by the Sneakerpimps. Initially released in October '96, it reached number 15 on the UK chart, where it spent four weeks. The single went on to appear in American film *The Saint* and was re-released shortly after, this time reaching number nine in June '97 and spending a further four weeks on the chart.

Due to the popularity of the album version, which featured a sample of the harp in the James Bond song 'Golden Girl' (taken from the film *Goldfinger*), the band went on to release several remixes, including 'Nellee Hoopers Edit', still frequently played today in clubs. The video featured lead singer Kelli Dayton spinning around in a dentist's chair, while the cover artwork included a Lego moonscape.

60ft Dolls (band)

Welsh trio Richard Parfitt, Michael Cole and Carl Bevan were the 60ft Dolls, one of a string of bands to come out of the south Wales rock music scene alongside Catatonia, Gorky's Zygotic Mynci, the Manic Street Preachers, Stereophonics and Super Furry Animals. Formed in Newport in '92, the Dolls were part of the first NME Brat Bus tour in '95, playing alongside Marion and Skunk Anansie. Their first single, 'Happy Shopper', was released via Townhill in '94, but after their second release, 'White Knuckle Ride', was released on Rough Trade Records in May '95 and scraped into the top ten, the band were signed by Indolent Records.

They released their next single, 'Pig Valentine', in November that same year, and went on to release their debut album *The Big 3* in June '96. It peaked at number 36 in the UK chart and resulted in top-40 singles 'Talk to Me' and the re-release of 'Happy Shopper'.

An intensive touring schedule and a host of personal issues took their toll on the band and, when their second album *Joya Magica* was eventually released in '98, it failed to chart. They parted ways with Indolent not long afterwards before disbanding altogether.

Each member has gone on to other musical projects, whether producing, teaching or recording solo work. Parfitt, who discovered Welsh diva Duffy and put her on the road to success, is now a senior lecturer in popular and commercial music at the University of South Wales.

Anecdotally, bassist Cole was apparently asked to fill in on bass for Oasis after Guigsy dropped out of a US tour, but declined because he wanted to stay with the Dolls.

Tier system: defining the era

Tier 1 - Big 5

Blur
Elastica
Oasis
Pulp
Suede

Tier 2 - ex Big 5

60ft dolls
Ash
Bawl
Bennett
Bis
Bluetones
Cast
Divine Comedy
Dodgy
Echobelly
Eggman
Elcka
Gene
Geneva
Jocasta
Kenickie
Kula Shaker
Lightning Seeds
Longpigs
Lush
Mansun
Marion
McAlmont & Butler

Me, Me, Me
Menswear
My Life Story
Northern Uproar
Ocean Colour Scene
Powder
Rialto
Republica
Salad
Seahorses
Shed Seven
Sleeper
Space
Speedy
Strangelove
Supergrass
Supernaturals
Sussed
Thurman
Verve
Whipping Boy
Whiteout

Tier 3 - Peripheral

3 Colours Red
Audioweb
Auteurs
Babybird
Belle & Sebastian
Black Grape
Boo Radleys
Candyskins
Catatonia
Charlatans
Chemical Brothers
Cornershop
Cranberries
Denim
Dubstar
Edwyn Collins
Electronic
Embrace
Garbage
Gorky's Zygotic Mynci
Heavy Stereo
Helen Love
Hurricane #1
Intastella
James
Joyrider

La's
Levellers
Manic Street Preachers
Monaco
Paul Weller
Puressence
Reef
Ride
Saint Etienne
Silver Sun
Skunk Anansie
Smiths
Sneakerpimps
Spiritualized
Stereolab
Stereophonics
Stone Roses
Super Furry Animals
Symposium
Teenage Fanclub
Terrorvision
These Animal Men
Tiger
Travis
Wannadies
Warm Jets

Key:

Tier 1: all Official Charts singles/albums '92-'98
Tier 2: top 20 '92-'98
Tier 3: top 20 peak years '95-'97

NUMBER 1 SINGLES

SINGLE NAME, BAND NAME
INITIAL CHART ENTRY DATE, CONSECUTIVE WEEKS ON THE CHART

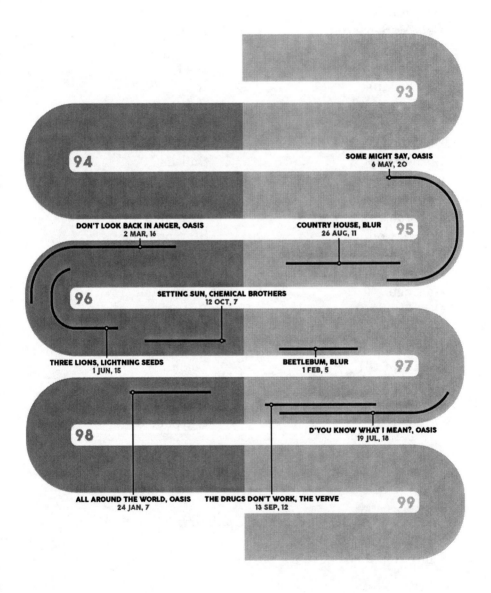

93

94

SOME MIGHT SAY, OASIS
6 MAY, 20

DON'T LOOK BACK IN ANGER, OASIS
2 MAR, 16

COUNTRY HOUSE, BLUR
26 AUG, 11

95

96

SETTING SUN, CHEMICAL BROTHERS
12 OCT, 7

THREE LIONS, LIGHTNING SEEDS
1 JUN, 15

BEETLEBUM, BLUR
1 FEB, 5

97

98

D'YOU KNOW WHAT I MEAN?, OASIS
19 JUL, 18

ALL AROUND THE WORLD, OASIS
24 JAN, 7

THE DRUGS DON'T WORK, THE VERVE
13 SEP, 12

99

NUMBER 1 ALBUMS

ALBUM NAME, BAND NAME
INITIAL CHART ENTRY DATE, CONSECUTIVE WEEKS ON THE CHART

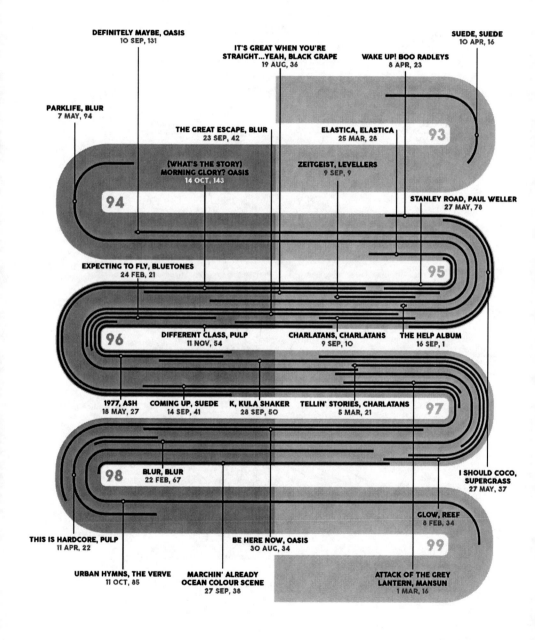

DEFINITELY MAYBE, OASIS
10 SEP, 131

SUEDE, SUEDE
10 APR, 16

IT'S GREAT WHEN YOU'RE STRAIGHT...YEAH, BLACK GRAPE
19 AUG, 36

WAKE UP! BOO RADLEYS
8 APR, 23

PARKLIFE, BLUR
7 MAY, 94

THE GREAT ESCAPE, BLUR
23 SEP, 42

ELASTICA, ELASTICA
25 MAR, 28

93

(WHAT'S THE STORY) MORNING GLORY? OASIS
14 OCT, 143

ZEITGEIST, LEVELLERS
9 SEP, 9

STANLEY ROAD, PAUL WELLER
27 MAY, 78

94

EXPECTING TO FLY, BLUETONES
24 FEB, 21

95

DIFFERENT CLASS, PULP
11 NOV, 54

CHARLATANS, CHARLATANS
9 SEP, 10

THE HELP ALBUM
16 SEP, 1

96

1977, ASH
18 MAY, 27

COMING UP, SUEDE
14 SEP, 41

K, KULA SHAKER
28 SEP, 50

TELLIN' STORIES, CHARLATANS
5 MAR, 21

97

BLUR, BLUR
22 FEB, 67

I SHOULD COCO, SUPERGRASS
27 MAY, 37

98

GLOW, REEF
8 FEB, 34

THIS IS HARDCORE, PULP
11 APR, 22

BE HERE NOW, OASIS
30 AUG, 34

99

URBAN HYMNS, THE VERVE
11 OCT, 85

MARCHIN' ALREADY OCEAN COLOUR SCENE
27 SEP, 38

ATTACK OF THE GREY LANTERN, MANSUN
1 MAR, 16

BAND ORIGIN

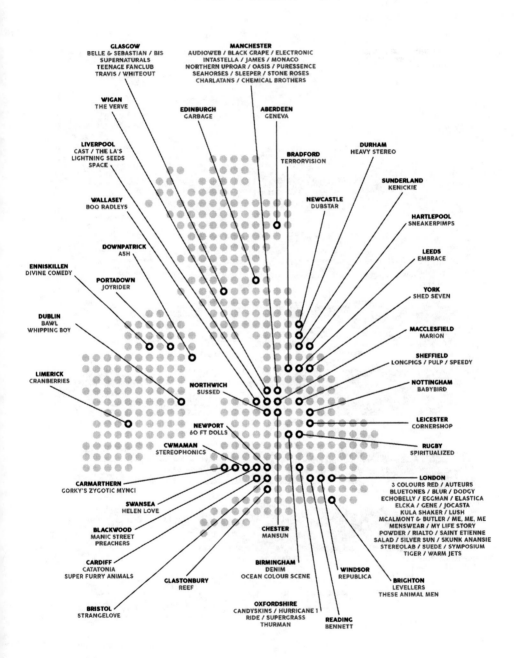

GLASGOW
BELLE & SEBASTIAN / BIS
SUPERNATURALS
TEENAGE FANCLUB
TRAVIS / WHITEOUT

MANCHESTER
AUDIOWEB / BLACK GRAPE / ELECTRONIC
INTASTELLA / JAMES / MONACO
NORTHERN UPROAR / OASIS / PURESSENCE
SEAHORSES / SLEEPER / STONE ROSES
CHARLATANS / CHEMICAL BROTHERS

WIGAN
THE VERVE

EDINBURGH
GARBAGE

ABERDEEN
GENEVA

LIVERPOOL
CAST / THE LA'S
LIGHTNING SEEDS
SPACE

BRADFORD
TERRORVISION

DURHAM
HEAVY STEREO

SUNDERLAND
KENICKIE

WALLASEY
BOO RADLEYS

NEWCASTLE
DUBSTAR

HARTLEPOOL
SNEAKERPIMPS

DOWNPATRICK
ASH

LEEDS
EMBRACE

ENNISKILLEN
DIVINE COMEDY

PORTADOWN
JOYRIDER

YORK
SHED SEVEN

DUBLIN
BAWL
WHIPPING BOY

MACCLESFIELD
MARION

SHEFFIELD
LONGPIGS / PULP / SPEEDY

LIMERICK
CRANBERRIES

NORTHWICH
SUSSED

NOTTINGHAM
BABYBIRD

NEWPORT
60 FT DOLLS

LEICESTER
CORNERSHOP

CWMAMAN
STEREOPHONICS

RUGBY
SPIRITUALIZED

CARMARTHERN
GORKY'S ZYGOTIC MYNCI

LONDON
3 COLOURS RED / AUTEURS
BLUETONES / BLUR / DODGY
ECHOBELLY / EGGMAN / ELASTICA
ELCKA / GENE / JOCASTA
KULA SHAKER / LUSH
MCALMONT & BUTLER / ME, ME, ME
MENSWEAR / MY LIFE STORY
POWDER / RIALTO / SAINT ETIENNE
SALAD / SILVER SUN / SKUNK ANANSIE
STEREOLAB / SUEDE / SYMPOSIUM
TIGER / WARM JETS

SWANSEA
HELEN LOVE

BLACKWOOD
MANIC STREET
PREACHERS

CHESTER
MANSUN

CARDIFF
CATATONIA
SUPER FURRY ANIMALS

WINDSOR
REPUBLICA

BRIGHTON
LEVELLERS
THESE ANIMAL MEN

BRISTOL
STRANGELOVE

GLASTONBURY
REEF

BIRMINGHAM
DENIM
OCEAN COLOUR SCENE

OXFORDSHIRE
CANDYSKINS / HURRICANE 1
RIDE / SUPERGRASS
THURMAN

READING
BENNETT

Index

CPSIA information can be obtained
at www.ICGtesting.com
Printed in the USA
LVOW10s0224100418
572906LV00007B/192/P